This is a new, thoroughly revised edition of the acclaimed *Using French*, first published as *A Guide to Contemporary French Usage* in 1982. It provides guidance for those who have already acquired the basics of French and wish to extend their fluency and confidence. Unlike conventional grammars, it gives special attention to those areas of vocabulary and grammar which cause most difficulty to English-speakers, and incorporates the concept of register differences throughout. This third edition takes account of the expanding vocabulary and changing grammatical usage of contemporary French.

- designed to promote fluency and accuracy vital to effective communication

- tailored to the needs of the English-speaking user

- clear format for ease of reference

- full treatment of key grammatical areas

- important section on vocabulary extension, with index for efficient access

- invaluable to all advanced learners, and to anyone requiring up-to-date guidance on points of grammar and vocabulary

R. E. BATCHELOR is an experienced teacher of French and author of numerous books in this and related fields, including *Using French Synonyms* (1993), *Using Spanish* (1992), *Using Spanish Synonyms* (1994), *French for Marketing* (1997) and *Usage pratique et courant des synonymes anglais*. He has also published many articles on literary, philosophical and historical aspects of European thought.

M. H. OFFORD is Reader in French at the University of Nottingham, and the author of books including *Varieties of Contemporary French* (1990), *Using French Synonyms* (1993), *A Reader in French Sociolinguistics* (1996) and of many articles on lexicology, syntax, sociolinguistics and stylistics.

Companion titles to *Using French*

Using French Synonyms
R. E. BATCHELOR and M. H. OFFORD
ISBN 0 521 37277 1 hardback
ISBN 0 521 37878 8 paperback

Using French Vocabulary
JEAN H. DUFFY
ISBN 0 521 57040 9 hardback
ISBN 0 521 57851 5 paperback

French for Marketing
Using French in Media and Communications
R. E. BATCHELOR and M. CHEBLI-SAADI
ISBN 0 521 58500 7 hardback
ISBN 0 521 58535 X paperback

Using Spanish
A Guide to Contemporary Usage
R. E. BATCHELOR and C. J. POUNTAIN
ISBN 0 521 42123 3 hardback
ISBN 0 521 26987 3 paperback

Using Spanish Synonyms
R. E. BATCHELOR
ISBN 0 521 44160 9 hardback
ISBN 0 521 44694 5 paperback

Using German
A Guide to Contemporary Usage
M. DURRELL
ISBN 0 521 42077 6 hardback
ISBN 0 521 31556 5 paperback

Using Russian
A Guide to Contemporary Usage
DEREK OFFORD
ISBN 0 521 45130 2 hardback
ISBN 0 521 45760 2 paperback

Using German Synonyms
MARTIN DURRELL
[forthcoming]

Using Italian Synonyms
HOWARD MOSS and GIOVANNA MOTTA
[forthcoming]

Using Italian
A Guide to Contemporary Usage
JOHN KINDER
[forthcoming]

Using Japanese
A Guide to Contemporary Usage
WILLIAM MCCLURE
[forthcoming]

Further titles in preparation

Using French

A guide to contemporary usage

R. E. BATCHELOR
Formerly of the University of Nottingham

M. H. OFFORD
Reader in French Language, University of Nottingham

CAMBRIDGE
UNIVERSITY PRESS

CAMBRIDGE UNIVERSITY PRESS
Cambridge, New York, Melbourne, Madrid, Cape Town,
Singapore, São Paulo, Delhi, Tokyo, Mexico City

Cambridge University Press
The Edinburgh Building, Cambridge CB2 8RU, UK

Published in the United States of America by Cambridge University Press, New York

www.cambridge.org
Information on this title: www.cambridge.org/9780521645935

First published 1982
Fifth printing 1991
Second edition 1993
Fourth printing 1998
Third edition 2000
Fourth printing 2008

A catalogue record for this publication is available from the British Library

ISBN 978-0-521-64177-7 Hardback
ISBN 978-0-521-64593-5 Paperback

Contents

Contents

Foreword

This book provides the student with an essentially practical guide to the contemporary French language. It is practical first because it attempts to deal with many of the major aspects of the language by defining and illustrating them through everyday examples. Second, its practical nature may be seen in the attention paid to the levels of register in French, a feature of this book which breaks new ground. It not only clarifies points of usage and grammar, but shows the circumstances in which words, expressions, grammatical constructions, and so on, are most appropriate. Third, a serious and systematic attempt has been made to help the English student work his/her way through the complex web of *faux amis*, paronyms, prepositions, etc, where English language patterns can easily provoke error. It will be understood once and for all that a French person says 'La clef est *sur* la porte' and 'Le boxeur est *sur* le ring', that *lier* and *relier* are not the same, and that *sous*, *au-dessous de*, *en dessous de*, and *à travers*, *en travers de*, *au travers de* are more complicated than may first appear.

The book is unusual in that it combines a survey of both vocabulary and grammar. Traditional French grammar books for English students are naturally largely confined to matters of grammar; books on vocabulary, *faux amis* and other aspects of lexis are not concerned with grammar. The inextricable association of grammar and vocabulary in language is implicit in the conception of this book.

The authors do not claim to provide a comprehensive guide to all aspects of the French language. For example, no section on adverbs is included, partly because it is felt that adverbs do not present the same problems as, for instance, prepositions. Neither is space given to the definite and indefinite articles. Adjectives are not given a section to themselves, but are found in the chapter on word order, for instance. The whole point of the book is that it is less concerned with the prescriptive rules of grammar than with the way the language is actually used. It has been conceived on the basic assumption that the student has already acquired a certain expertise in the French language. Indeed some readers may well be acquainted with many, if not all, of the concepts presented in the section on register. In that section we have deliberately avoided discussion and criticism of previous work on the subject and have attempted to provide as simple and straightforward a model of register as possible, in keeping with the aims of this book.

Much of the material in the book has been set out in tabular form for the sake of clarity. It is hoped that the student will be able to seize and memorise the essential points more easily through the visual impact.

Authors' acknowledgements
We are immeasurably indebted to the following:

Philippe Lanoë, Malliga Chebli-Saadi and Hadj Saadi

We should also like to thank all our students whose generous mistakes over the years have provided us with the raw material for this book.

Foreword to second edition

In the ten years since the first edition of the *Guide*, much has changed in the world, technically, socially, geographically even, with new countries coming into being as old power blocs are dismembered. This seems therefore an appropriate moment to ask ourselves whether the French language has also changed, whether it reflects in any way the changes occurring in the outside world and more specifically whether the *Guide* should be revised in the light of these developments. There is no doubt that much new vocabulary has come into being to describe many new phenomena and attitudes, but because of the nature of the *Guide*, not being a conventional dictionary, many such innovations will have to be ignored. However, a few additions have been made to various divisions of the Vocabulary section, and certain names of countries and organisations have been altered to correspond to the current international and national scene. On the other hand, the basic structures of the language, one of the major preoccupations of the book, have by and large remained stable. Consequently not many changes have been introduced in that section of the book. Revision is mainly limited to incorporating recommendations made to us over the years by kindly readers, correcting a few errors and supplying additional information and examples as appropriate. Our hope is that this new edition will prove a useful resource to advanced students of French.

Foreword to third edition

The French language continues to evolve – the vocabulary is forever expanding and even grammatical usage changes, although nowhere near at the same rate as the vocabulary. This new edition of *Using French* attempts to keep abreast of such developments as well as refining previous editions. The whole text has been radically reviewed, and extensive modifications have taken place – there is scarcely a page which has not been revised in some way. In addition to revision of previous editions, new sections have been added, some providing more idiomatic expressions (involving colour and numbers in particular), use of which marks a comfortable confidence in the language, and others relating to what we call semi-technical vocabulary, the sort of vocabulary every educated person ought to be familiar with and which is used in various circumstances. Social changes have meant that new attitudes prevail in some areas of French national life, and this impacts upon vocabulary – consequently the section on gender has been largely rewritten to reflect the accession of more and more women to high-status positions in society. We have maintained our philosophy not to include the basics of French grammar (conjugation of verbs, the different articles and so on) but to concentrate upon aspects of French usage which concern advanced students and to incorporate the concept of register differences throughout. As before, we hope that this book will continue to serve advanced students of French effectively – and to provide an accurate and stimulating account of contemporary French.

R. E. Batchelor
M. H. Offord

Abbreviations

adj	adjective	qch	*quelque chose*
F (f)	feminine	qn	*quelqu'un*
fig	figurative	R1	see **1.4**
gen	generally	R1★	see **1.4**
impers	impersonal	R2	see **1.4**
infin	infinitive	R3	see **1.4**
intr	intransitive	sb	somebody
lit	literal	sg	singular
M (m)	masculine	st	sometimes
occ	occasionally	sth	something
pej	pejorative	subj	subjunctive
pft	perfect	trans/tr	transitive
ph	past historic	usu	usually
pl	plural	/	or
pp	past participle	(. . .)	non-use of preposition
pres	present		(see **3.4.1.1**)

1 Register

In order to appreciate fully what is meant by the term 'register' and how vital it is in the advanced study of a foreign language, it is necessary first of all to consider it against the general background of what are known as varieties of language.

1.1 Varieties of language

Students talking among themselves would use a different type of vocabulary and even different grammatical structures from those they would use when addressing their teacher, or when being interviewed for a job, or when talking to a young child – or a dog. They would use different vocabulary and structures when writing an essay on 20th–century French literature, when talking about pop music or feminism with friends in a pub, or when visiting grandparents. A person can speak formally or informally, or can use an appropriate shade of formality. The intention can be to persuade, to encourage, to inform, to amuse. One can express oneself in writing, in conversation, in a speech. A person can speak in a professional role, for instance as a teacher, a lawyer or a doctor. It is clear that people have at their command many different ways of expressing themselves depending upon circumstances. Language is used for a variety of purposes, in a variety of situations and is expressed by a variety of means. A language should not therefore be seen as a homogeneous whole, but as a collection of varieties. There exist varieties of English; there are also varieties of French, German, Spanish, and so on.

At the same time as children acquire the grammar, vocabulary and pronunciation systems of their own language, they acquire in addition an increasing intuitive awareness of the varieties available in their language and of when to use them appropriately. However, for the foreign-language learner, acquiring the capacity to operate within an appropriate variety of language is a more conscious matter, although even here, with increasing competence, selection of the appropriate variety becomes increasingly automatic.

A variety of language is determined by a number of factors; some are peripheral, others central in importance. In this book we are not concerned with varieties themselves, but with one of the essential factors which constitute them, register.

1.2   Peripheral factors

The way French speakers use their language is affected by such matters as their sex (a woman may have different general speech characteristics from a man), their age (for example whether they are adolescents or octogenarians), where they come from (for example a Parisian, a Marseillais and a Martiniquan will all have idiosyncrasies of speech which are due to their places of origin), and their socio-economic standing (that is to say the degree of education they have received and their social and professional status). These are factors over which the speaker has little, if any, control, as they are deeprooted ingredients of his/her individuality. They are, therefore, of secondary importance in an analysis of varieties of language.

1.3   Central factors

Of much greater immediate importance in determining the composition of varieties are the following factors: subject matter, purpose, medium and register.

1.3.1   Field

What one is talking about affects the way one expresses oneself. For example, when the French discuss politics they will draw upon a certain vocabulary which would be quite inappropriate in a discussion on zoology, although, of course, there are certain 'common core' features which are used whatever the topic under discussion. The term 'field' is used to denote the subject matter of a conversation, speech, etc. It means a collection of words and expressions relating specifically to a certain topic, for example politics, and covers the many types of situations in which politics may be discussed. It may be politics as practised by a politician, or as reported by a political correspondent in the press, or as debated over a glass of wine between friends in a bar. The field includes, therefore, not only the technical vocabulary of the professional but also the less technical vocabulary used by the non-specialist talking about the same subject.

1.3.2   Purpose

Whatever the status of the speaker – whether he/she is a politician, or the political correspondent of a daily newspaper, or simply a layperson talking politics with a friend – language is used with a purpose. The politician will attempt to persuade; the political journalist to inform, comment and/or evaluate; the layman may simply chat, or may adopt the stance of the politician or journalist depending upon knowledge, inclination or intention.

1.3.3   Medium

The medium of communication also needs to be taken into account. By medium is meant the vehicle through which the subject matter is conveyed to a listener or an audience. In politics it may be a speech made in parliament or at the hustings, it may be a written report of a debate or a manifesto, a piece of propaganda used in an election campaign, or simply a conversation. The spontaneous expression of a conversation will contrast with the carefully prepared wording of a speech: the medium therefore places constraints on the way one expresses oneself.

1.3.4   Register

The final factor to consider in this analysis of varieties of language is register. Register is concerned with the relationship that exists between a speaker and the person he/she is speaking to. In other words it is the degree of formality or informality which a speaker accords the listener. This degree of formality/informality depends in turn upon four variable factors, in increasing order of importance: sex, age, status and intimacy. The sex of the speaker or listener, the least important of the variables, may not even be relevant in certain situations. However, sometimes it is: exclusively male or female gatherings often have their own peculiar speech habits which are a direct result of the company present; a young man talking to his girl-friend may use a different standard of language from that which he will use when he is chatting to his male friends; it may involve only a slight adjustment – does he swear in the presence of women? However, even this question is not so straightforward as it may seem – that men should consider moderating or changing their language in the company of women would be ill received by certain women. Conversely, certain young and not-so-young women now take pride in adopting as free a manner to express themselves as they feel men already have. Differences between the language used by the two sexes are tending to disappear among some groups. The age of a speaker has already been mentioned in **1.2** as having a bearing upon the way he/she speaks – elderly speakers have different speech habits from younger ones – but in this section it is the possibility of varying the way one speaks, according to the age of the person spoken to, that is relevant. Parents talking to young children will use a different, simpler, vocabulary and grammar from that which they would use when talking to colleagues or contemporaries. In the same way, a teacher will use a different level of language in classroom and common room. Status also plays an important role in determining register. When discussed in **1.2**, status was used to refer to the degree of education and the social and professional standing of the speaker. In this section it refers to the ability of a person to adjust his/her speech according to the status of the person addressed: an employee in a factory talking to a director, the director in turn talking to an employee, a shop assistant serving a customer, will use different registers because of their respective positions in the social or professional hierarchy. Finally and most important, intimacy, the degree to which speakers know and trust each other, affects the way they speak to each other. A first encounter between two persons requires a different register from that required by a conversation between a husband and wife celebrating their fourth wedding anniversary. These four factors, sex, age, status and intimacy, combine to produce register, the relationship of formality/informality existing between speakers.

The relationship between these factors, particularly those of age and status, and the peripheral factors mentioned briefly in **1.2**, needs to be considered briefly. There is, of necessity, some interaction between the two types of factor. To examine first the relationship between the age of the speaker (peripheral) and the age of the person addressed (central), it is clear that in certain cases the age of the speaker will override his/her ability to adjust to the level of the person addressed: for example, a child will not have the necessary linguistic sophistication to adjust its speech in order to address an adult in an adult way; at the other end of the age range, an elderly person may lose the expertise he/she once possessed to adjust his/her speech to become comprehensible to a child, or such a person may never have had sufficient experience of children's language to realise what adjustments should be made. Similarly for status: it is well known that, for certain people, the linguistic patterns peculiar to their class or profession are so indelibly ingrained that they are unable or would consider it demeaning to vary their speech: it is unlikely that a poorly-educated person will be in a position to produce the appropriate level of language when conversing with a person of higher social standing; conversely a person of aristocratic stock may find it extremely difficult to eliminate from his/her speech those linguistic elements which are all but innate, when addressing someone of lower social rank. There are circumstances, therefore, when a certain neutralisation of the effects of the various factors occurs.

A corollary of register concerns the character of the language actually produced, more precisely the degree of explicitness which is necessary for communication within a given situation. In particular, the more intimately one knows someone, the more similar the socio-economic status and to a lesser degree the ages involved, the more information that can be taken for granted in conversation and the less need for formal structuring of language (**1.6.1**): there is no need to be explicit about family matters within the family or about business affairs with close colleagues, because in these cases so much is common knowledge and may be left unspecified. On the other hand, strangers meeting for the first time or students attending an induction course require detailed explanations of every aspect of this new experience or undertaking and an elaborate, grammatically correct structuring of what is said (**1.6.4** and **1.6.5**).

It is now possible to show in diagrammatic form how all these factors combine to constitute a variety of language.

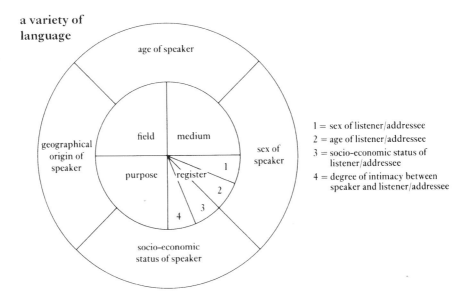

a variety of language

age of speaker

geographical origin of speaker

field

medium

purpose

register

sex of speaker

socio–economic status of speaker

1 = sex of listener/addressee
2 = age of listener/addressee
3 = socio-economic status of listener/addressee
4 = degree of intimacy between speaker and listener/addressee

1.4   Register as used in this book

According to the definition of the previous section (**1.3.4**), register involves the relationship of formality/informality existing between the two participants in a conversation or any other situation in which language is used. The most accurate way of representing register would be to envisage it as a scale extending from extreme informality at one end to extreme formality at the other, with a multitude of different shades of formality in between. However, for ease of reference and use in this book, the scale will be divided into three distinct sections, each of which will cover a third of the scale of formality. These three sections will be known as R1, R2 and R3 and their major characteristics may be summarised in the following way:

extreme
informality

extreme
formality

←——→

R1
very informal, casual,
colloquial, familiar,
careless, admitting new
terms almost
indiscriminately, certain
terms short-lived, at times
truncated, elliptical,
incorrect grammatically,
prone to redundant
expressions, includes slang
expressions and
vulgarisms, likely to
include regional variations

R2
standard, polite, educated,
equivalent of 'BBC
English', compromise
between the two extremes

R3
formal, literary, official,
with archaic ring, language
of scholars and purists,
meticulously correct,
reluctant to admit new
terms

It must be stressed once more that these sections are the result of an artificial division and that the reality behind them consists of subtle, imperceptible shifts, not of rigidly defined categories. (We have confined these register divisions to three, as being more practicable to handle, although scholars in the field often distinguish five.)

A few comments on the above schematisation of register are called for. Because the divisions are arbitrary, some examples (**2.10.1**) do not fit exactly into one of the sections: in such circumstances the notation R1/R2 or R2/R3 is used. When a usage occurs in two registers the notation R1 and R2 or R2 and R3 is used. Whereas R2 and R3 appear more homogeneous as divisions of register, R1 covers a rich range of informal language, stretching, for example, from obscene interjections to unobjectionable ones (**2.10.1**); the notation R1★ is used to encompass vulgar language (eg **foutre**, **merde**, **putain**). At times language included in R1 is in fact grammatically incorrect and frequently swings from elliptical usage to an extensive use of unnecessary repetition.

Looking towards the future, it is possible that some of what at present are deemed incorrect usages contained in R1 will become socially acceptable language. It is interesting to observe that the *tolérances* – lists of grammatical and orthographical usages previously condemned but now accepted – issued by the French government for the benefit of examiners quite frequently concern matters of register (although this is not explicitly acknowledged by the authorities). What was considered typically R1 usage, and therefore shunned by the users of 'correct' R2/R3 French, is raised by decree to at least R2 status:
eg   an examiner may now accept:
c'est là de beaux résultats
as well as the traditionally only acceptable
ce sont là de beaux résultats

similarly, in the matter of sequence of tenses with the subjunctive
(**3.7.1**),

j'avais souhaité qu'il vienne sans tarder

is now tolerated as well as

j'avais souhaité qu'il vînt sans tarder

Although the *tolérances* have official backing, they do not always find
universal acceptance outside such circles:

eg   **la fillette, obéissante à sa mère, alla se coucher**

j'ai recueilli cette chienne errante dans le quartier

étant données les circonstances (3.6.3.2)

Another characteristic of R1 usage which should be stressed is the
fact that many items of its vocabulary are ephemeral in nature. In slang
and popular speech there are noticeable preferences for certain types
of words, namely those which are striking by their sound or by the
manner in which they are created (usually as a result of a metaphorical
extension of meaning). Such words are frequently victims of the
ravages of fashion and within a relatively short period of time tend to
become overworked, thus losing their impact and appeal, and need to
be replaced. A rapid turnover in vocabulary is the result: words that
are on everyone's lips one year, or even for part of a year, seem
terribly dated the following year, and using an out-of-date term may
well mark a speaker as being 'past it' or at least old-fashioned. (For this
reason a number of the terms included in **2.10.1** will have a limited
life-span.)

The phenomenon of register switch should also be illustrated. It is
likely that uneducated speakers will use only R1 whatever social
situation they find themselves in, whereas an educated speaker will be
able to command all three with equal ease, passing from one end of
the scale to the other without great difficulty. To go further than was
possible in section **1.3.4** and to give a specific example drawn from
higher education, a formal lecture would normally be delivered in R3,
whereas a seminar would normally be conducted in R2, and,
depending upon the degree of friendliness existing between lecturer
and student, it is conceivable that a one-to-one tutorial might be
carried on in R1: linguistic distinctions based upon differences of sex,
age and status disappear with deepening intimacy. It is not, of course,
only lecturers who have the ability to switch register! A native
speaker's ability to adjust his/her register in various circumstances is
the key to avoiding offence and to gaining acceptance in any given
situation. The degree to which a foreign learner can achieve that
ability to adjust his/her register is a mark of competence in, and
mastery of, the foreign language.

1.5   Illustration of register

Register affects all aspects of language: pronunciation, vocabulary and
grammar. Although vocabulary and grammar are the major

preoccupations of this book, it is worthwhile considering briefly some of the effects of register upon the pronunciation of French.

1.5.1 Pronunciation and liaison

The making of valid general comments upon the issues raised by pronunciation is fraught with risks. Pronunciation is the least stable, most variable aspect of a person's speech habits, and it is well known that a single individual will not necessarily always pronounce the same word in the same way. Consequently the observations that follow must be appreciated in the light of such a reservation. Another problem is that certain tendencies of pronunciation are restricted to a particular region; in such cases disentangling accent from register is very difficult.

On the whole, as might be expected, an R1 speaker tends to be less careful about pronunciation than an R2 and particularly an R3 speaker. In what follows, R1 usage is contrasted with R2 and R3 usages, and regionalisms will be kept as far as possible to a minimum.

The most obvious general characteristic of R1 pronunciation is a relative laziness of articulation, resulting in, amongst other things, the loss of certain sounds or the introduction or change of others. This is illustrated in the following ways. It should be noted that it is not always a matter of, for example, the clear-cut presence or absence of /r/ (ie /kat/ versus /katr/), but of a gradual movement from precise articulation to more indistinct articulation of the sound.

Register marked in treatment of	R1 and example		R2+R3	written form
consonants:				
reduction of groups of consonants	/gʒ/ → /ʒ/	/syʒɛsjɔ̃/	/sygʒɛstjɔ̃/	*suggestion*
	/ks/ → /s/	/ɛskyz/	/ɛkskyz/	*excuse*
		/ɛspedisjɔ̃/	/ɛkspedisjɔ̃/	*expédition*
		/ɛsplwa/	/ɛksplwa/	*exploit*
	/lk/ → /k/	/kɛkʃoz/	/kɛlkəʃoz/	*quelque chose*
	/st/ → /s/	/ʒɛsjɔ̃/	/ʒɛstjɔ̃/	*gestion*
	/tr/ → /t/	/ptɛt/	/pøtetr/	*peut-être*
		/kat/	/katr/	*quatre*
		/vɔt/	/vɔtr/	*votre*
dropping of consonants	/l/	/i fɛ bo/	/il fɛ bo/	*il fait beau*
		/i vjɛ̃/	/il vjɛ̃/	*il vient*
	/r/	/rəgade/	/rəgarde/	*regarder*
	/t/	/vɛ̃dø/ to	/vɛ̃tdø/ to	*vingt-deux* to
	(all numbers from 22 to 29)	/vɛ̃nœf/	/vɛ̃tnœf/	*vingt-neuf*
change of consonant	/s/ → /z/	/ãtuzjazm/	/ãtuzjasm/	*enthousiasme*
		/idealizm/	/idealism/	*idéalisme*
		/sɔsjalizm/	/sɔsjalism/	*socialisme*

Register marked in treatment of	R1 and example		R2+R3	written form
vowels:				
confusion of *e*-sounds	/ə/ → /e/	/rekɔ̃stitɥe/	/rəkɔ̃stitɥe/	*reconstituer*
		/reose/	/rəose/	*rehausser*
	/e/ → /ə/	/rəbɛljɔ̃/	/rebɛljɔ̃/	*rébellion*
	/e/ → /ɛ/	/ʒ pø vu lasyrɛ/	/ʒə pø vu lasyrɛ/	*je peux vous l'assurer*
		/dəgrɛ/ (Parisian)	/dəgrɛ/	*degré*
	/ɛ/ → /e/	/me/	/mɛ/	*mais*
		/frãse/	/frãsɛ/	*français*
		/rezɔ̃/	/rɛzɔ̃/	*raison*
treatment of mute *e*	pronounced where normally silent	/apəle/	/aple/	*appeler*
		/ãsɛɲəmã/	/ãsɛɲmã/	*enseignement*
		/evenəmã/	/evɛnmã/	*événement*
		/mɛ̃tənã/	/mɛ̃tnã/	*maintenant*
	silent where normally pronounced	/fra/	/fəra/	*fera*
		/frɔ̃/	/fərɔ̃/	*feront*
		/fzɛ/	/fəzɛ/	*faisait*
	introduction of /ə/	/arkə də trijɔ̃f/	/ark də trijɔ̃f/	*Arc de Triomphe*
		/avɛkə/	/avɛk/	*avec*
		/lɔrsəkə/	/lɔrskə/	*lorsque*
lengthening of /a/	/a/ → /aː/	/gaːto/	/gato/	*gâteau*
confusion of *o*-sounds	/o/ → /ɔ/	/ɔt/	/otr/	*autre*
		/o ʃɔd/ } Southern	/o ʃod/	*eau chaude*
		/sɔte/	/sote/	*sauter*
		/voʒ/	/voʒ/	*Vosges*

Liaison – the phenomenon which, in closely linked groups of words, causes the normally silent final consonant of a word to be sounded before the initial vowel of the next word – may also be affected by considerations of register. However, first of all it should be stressed that in certain circumstances liaison is compulsorily applied and in others it is prohibited; in other words all speakers, regardless of their normal register of speech, are obliged to observe these rules of liaison, as briefly illustrated in the following table:

	circumstance	examples	
liaison compulsory	between qualifier + noun	*ses amis*	/sez ami/
		deux ans	/døz ã/
		de grands arbres	/də grãz arbr/
		NOTE: an adjective ending in a nasal vowel is denasalised in liaison and is	

	circumstance	examples	
liaison compulsory (*cont.*)		pronounced like the corresponding F form: *le prochain arrêt*: /lə prɔʃɛn arɛ/	
	between pronoun + verb/ verb + pronoun	*elles ont* *nous avons* *allez-y*	/ɛlz ɔ̃/ /nuz avɔ̃/ /alez i/
	between monosyllabic adverb or preposition + article, noun, pronoun adjective or adverb	*sous une chaise* *moins utile* *plus important*	/suz yn ʃɛz/ /mwɑ̃z ytil/ /plyz ɛ̃ pɔrtɑ̃/
	after the conjunction (not interrogative) *quand*	*quand il vient*	/kɑ̃t il vjɛ̃ /
	after the following words ending in a nasal vowel: *en, on, un, mon, ton, son, bien, rien*	NOTE: partial denasalisation occurs with *en, on, un, mon, ton, son*, the degree of denasalisation depending upon a variety of factors (eg register, place of origin): *mon ami* /mɔ̃n ami/ or /mɔn ami/ This does not apply to *bien* and *rien*: *bien indisposé* is always /bjɛ̃ n ɛ̃ dispose/.	
liaison prohibited	before numeral beginning with a vowel	*les onze* *cent un crayons*	/le ɔ̃z/ /sɑ̃ œ̃ krɛjɔ̃/
	after *et*	*et alors*	/e alɔr/
	before *oui*	*mais oui*	/mɛ wi/
	between singular subject + verb	*le soldat est parti*	/lə sɔlda ɛ parti/
	after words ending in a nasal vowel not specified above	*selon eux* *bon à rien*	/səlɔ̃ ø/ /bɔ̃ a rjɛ̃/
		NOTE: however, when *bon à rien* is a noun, liaison occurs	
	before words with aspirate *h*	*un héros* *le hibou*	/œ̃ero/ /lə ibu/
		NOTE: R1 speakers tend to disregard the aspirate *h* in: *les handicapés* *les haricots* *les Hollandais*	

There are on the other hand, circumstances where liaison is optional. Practice may be summed up in the following simple formula: the more formal the language, the more liaisons are made; the more informal, the fewer liaisons. The dividing line may normally be situated within R2: a slightly higher register is struck when liaison is made. Use of liaison is often accompanied by an element of emphasis.

	circumstances	examples	R1 + R2	R2 + R3
liaison optional	between plural noun + verb, adjective or adverb	*des mots impossibles à comprendre*	/mo ɛ̃pɔsibl/	/moz ɛ̃pɔsibl/
		les trains arrivent	/trɛ̃ ariv/	/trɛ̃z ariv/
	between verb + past participle, infinitive, adjective, adverb or prepositional expression	*je suis en retard*	/sɥi ɑ̃ rətar/	/sɥiz ɑ̃ rətar/
		je suis heureux	/sɥi œrø/	sɥiz œrø/
		je suis assez content	/sɥi ase kɔ̃tɑ̃/	/sɥiz ase kɔ̃tɑ̃/
	after polysyllabic adverbs and prepositions and monosyllabic conjunctions (except *et* and *quand*)	*extrêmement assidu*	/ɛkstrɛməmɑ̃ asidy/	/ɛkstrɛməmɑ̃t asidy/
		pendant une semaine	/pɑ̃dɑ̃ yn səmɛn/	/pɑ̃dɑ̃t yn səmɛn/
		mais il riait	/mɛ il riɛ/	/mɛz il riɛ/

1.5.2   Vocabulary and grammar

As already stated, it is with vocabulary and grammar that this book is primarily concerned. The following tables give a preliminary picture of the repercussions of considerations of register upon French vocabulary and grammar.

In the interpretation of the tables it is important to draw a distinction between those concerning vocabulary and those concerning grammar. In the former, terms that are designated R2 are not necessarily confined exclusively to R2 usage and may also occur in R1 and R3 usages, without disconcerting an addressee. On the other hand, R1 and R3 terms are normally (that is, with the reservations mentioned earlier) restricted to the relevant register. For example, *boue*, recorded in the table as R2, is a neutral term as far as register is concerned, and may be used not only in R2 but also in R1 and R3 usages, whereas *gadoue*, recorded as R1, immediately evokes an R1 context and *fange*, recorded as R3, evokes an R3 context, both terms being rarely used outside those register-divisions. In other words, an R1 speaker may choose between a distinctive R1 term, *gadoue*, and a neutral, 'common core' term *boue*; similarly an R3 user may opt for a term redolent of R3 usage, *fange*, or the neutral term *boue*.

It will be noticed that there are not in all cases terms for each of the three register-divisions: no vocabulary of any language is characterised by perfect regularity. The occasional gaps in the tables, therefore, under R1 and R3 (eg *bruit* and *faire (du) mal à/vexer*) may be accounted for by the fact that there is no distinctive R1 and R3 term in those cases, and that the term recorded as R2 should be understood as being appropriate there as well.

However, the same flexibility is not applicable in the case of the tables concerning grammar. In some cases, there are three distinct forms (eg R1: *fermez la porte*; R2: *(vous) fermez la porte, s'il vous plaît*; R3: *je vous prie de fermer la porte*). In such cases the R2 form is characteristic of the middle register-division, as opposed to the two outer divisions, and R1 and R3 speakers would not have recourse to it, except as a deliberate attempt to improve, in the case of an R1 speaker, or downgrade, in the case of an R3 speaker, their normal speech habits. On the other hand it sometimes happens that a particular form is perfectly appropriate for two or even all three divisions. This is indicated by arrows across the columns in the tables. Thus *au début de janvier* may occur quite normally in both R2 and R3 usages, and no particular effect would be produced; if it were used in R1 speech it would immediately imply a desire on the part of the speaker to converse in a higher register.

There are also gaps in the grammar tables. These should be interpreted as implying that in such cases there is no closely corresponding version available or that in that particular register-division speakers are unlikely to express that idea at all.

There is, of course, nothing exclusive about these divisions. R3 speakers are perfectly at liberty to use an R1 form in their speech; the effect will be arresting, probably humorous, evoking momentarily a situation which is quite foreign to the speakers. Similarly if R1 speakers suddenly use an isolated R3 form, the result is that their speech will briefly acquire a pedantic tone.

All the foregoing remarks hold good for the two major parts of the book. In **Part 2: Vocabulary**, sections **2.1** to **2.5**, R2 terms may generally be used in R1 and R3 usages as well; in later sections concerning the vocabulary, restricting comments are sometimes made. In **Part 3: Grammar**, the tables and comments specify how usages are to be applied.

Register marked in treatment of vocabulary	R1	R2	R3
		accorder/donner/remettre	conférer décerner
	donner un coup de main	aider	assister/seconder
	sympa	aimable/gentil/plaisant/sympathique	affable/amène
	crevant/marrant/rigolo/tordant	amusant/drôle	cocasse
	gadoue	boue	fange
	j'en ai marre/j'en ai ras-le-bol j'en ai ralbol	j'en ai assez	j'en suis saturé
		bâtir/construire	édifier/ériger
	boucan/chahut	bruit	
	d'acc/OK	d'accord	entendu/soit
		dire au revoir/saluer	faire ses adieux/prendre congé
	énerver/emmerder **R1**★/enquiquiner	ennuyer	importuner
		enterrement	obsèques
		faire (du) mal à/vexer	blesser/offusquer
	bonne femme	femme = *lady*	dame
		femme = *wife*	épouse
	gueule/trogne/bouille/binette/tronche	figure/visage	face
	fille/nana/souris	jeune fille	demoiselle
	gars	garçon/jeune homme	
		honnête	intègre/probe
		il y a des romanciers qui	il est des romanciers qui
	balancer/bazarder/flanquer/foutre en l'air	jeter	
	dégueulasse/crado	malpropre/sale	ordurier
	louper/rater	manquer	
	homme (*as in*: mon homme)	mari	époux

13

Register marked in treatment of vocabulary	R1	R2	R3
	bon homme/mec/type	monsieur/homme	
	se foutre de **R1★**/ mettre en boîte	se moquer de	se gausser de
		mort	décès/trépas
		obscurité	ténèbres
		pour	afin de
		raconter/rapporter	narrer/relater
		remplir	emplir
	réaliser	se rendre compte de	prendre conscience de
	paie	salaire/traitement	rémunération
	je me rappelle de	je me souviens de/ je me rappelle	j'ai souvenance de/ il me souvient de
	se casser la figure	tomber	

Register marked in treatment of grammar	R1	R2	R3
ellipsis	malade, lui? impossible	il n'est pas malade, ce n'est pas possible	
		il est impossible/ ←———— n'est pas possible ————→ qu'il soit malade	
	(à la) fin mai	←——— à la fin (du mois) de mai ———→	
	(au) début janvier	←——— au début de janvier ———→	
redundancy of expression	comme par exemple	←——— par exemple ———→	
	mais ils ont cependant	←——— mais/cependant ils ont ———→	
	et puis après	←——— et puis/et après ———→	
	descendre en bas	←——— descendre ———→	
	monter en haut	←——— monter ———→	
	prévoir à l'avance	←——— prévoir ———→	
	entrer dedans	←——— entrer ———→	
	sortir dehors	←——— sortir ———→	

Register marked in treatment of grammar	R1	R2	R3
imperative	fermez la porte	(vous) fermez la porte, s'il vous plaît	je vous prie de fermer la porte
	fermez pas la porte	ne fermez pas la porte, s'il vous plaît	je vous prie de ne pas fermer la porte
exclamation	ça alors, il est déjà là	quelle surprise, il est déjà là	cela m'étonne/ surprend qu'il soit déjà là/je m'étonne qu'il soit déjà là
	ce qu'il a grandi/ qu'est-ce qu'il a grandi	←———— comme/qu'il a grandi ————→	
highlighting	l'objectif, c'est de	←————— l'objectif est de —————→	
	le whisky, ça j'aime pas	←———— je n'aime pas le whisky ————→	
	je la casse, la vitre	←———— je casse la vitre ————→	
inversion	←———————— il est à peine arrivé ————————→		
	←———————— à peine est-il arrivé ————————→		
	←———— elle est du moins la meilleure de la classe ————→		
	←———— du moins est-elle la meilleure de la classe ————→		
	←———— on peut dire tout au plus ————→		
	←———— tout au plus peut-on dire ————→		
	←———— j'ai vu une voiture qu'un vieillard conduisait ————→		
	←———— j'ai vu une voiture que conduisait un vieillard ————→		
subjunctive	←——— après qu'il soit venu ———→		après qu'il est venu
	←——— le seul/dernier/premier homme que je connais ———→		
	←——— le seul/dernier/premier homme que je connaisse ———→		
	aucun pays ne permet ça	il n'y a aucun pays qui permet cela	il n'y a aucun pays qui permette cela
	c'est pas vrai qu'elle est arrivée	il n'est pas vrai qu'elle est arrivée	il n'est pas exact qu'elle soit arrivée
tense of subjunctive		le fait qu'il soit (= *was*) le premier à partir	(le fait) qu'il fût le premier à partir

Register marked in treatment of grammar	R1	R2	R3
past tenses	c'était qui le premier ministre?	qui était le premier ministre?	qui fut le premier ministre?
	Louis XIV, il était roi de France quand?	quand est-ce que Louis XIV a été roi de France?	quand Louis XIV fut-il roi de France?
agreement with *c'est*	c'est eux	←——————— ce sont eux ———————→	
	c'est les meilleures voitures	←——— ce sont les meilleures voitures ———→	
interrogatives	vous dites quoi?	qu'est-ce que vous dites?	
		←——— que dites-vous? ———→	
	hein?/quoi?	comment?/pardon?	plaît-il?
	elle vient?	est-ce qu'elle vient?	vient-elle?
	vous venez d'où/ d'où vous venez?	d'où est-ce que vous venez?	d'où êtes-vous originaire?
	pourquoi (qu')il vient?	pourquoi est-ce qu'il vient?	
		←——— pourquoi vient-il? ———→	
	elle vient quand?	quand est-ce qu'elle vient?	
		←——— quand vient-elle? ———→	
	il le fait comment?	comment est-ce qu'il le fait?	
		←——— comment le fait-il? ———→	
	c'était qui le premier ministre?	qui était le premier ministre?	qui fut le premier ministre?
***que* versus inversion**	peut-être qu'il viendra		
	←——————— il viendra peut-être ———————→		
	←——— peut-être viendra-t-il ———→		
	sans doute qu'elle a raison		
	←——————— elle a sans doute raison ———————→		
			sans doute a-t-elle raison

Register marked in treatment of grammar	R1	R2	R3
pronouns	ça	←——— cela (celui-ci/celui-là) ———→	
	on est content, les gens nous aident	on est content d'être aidé par les gens	nous sommes heureux que les gens nous viennent en aide
	c'est difficile de	←——— il est difficile de ———→	
	je vois la maison – c'est grand	←——— je vois la maison – elle est grande ———→	
pronouns and possessive adjectives with parts of the body	une pierre est tombée sur ma tête	←——— une pierre m'est tombée sur la tête ———→	
prepositions	le chapeau à Marc	←——— le chapeau de Marc ———→	
	il va en vélo	←——— il va à vélo/bicyclette ———→	
	←——— dans l'église ———→		en l'église
negation	j'ose pas le faire	je n'ose pas le faire	je n'ose le faire
		il n'a pas cessé de pleuvoir	il n'a cessé de pleuvoir
	(je) sais pas (moi)/j'en sais rien	je ne sais pas	je ne sais
	ça vaut pas le coup de le faire/	ce n'est pas la peine de le faire	
	c'est pas la peine (de le faire)	←——— il n'est pas nécessaire de le faire ———→	
partitive article with adjective before plural noun	je vois des grands arbres, des grosses carottes		
		←——— je vois de grands arbres, de grosses carottes ———→	
infinitive versus *que*-clause	←——— demande à ton père de venir ———→		demandez au ministre qu'il vienne
	←——— dis à ta sœur de venir ———→		dites au ministre qu'il vienne
euphony	←——— si on constate que ———→		si l'on constate que

As has already been implied in the preceding tables, R1 speech is occasionally (sometimes frequently) characterised by a certain grammatical or lexical carelessness, which may in fact involve significant departure from the grammatical rules accepted in R2 and R3 usage. The following table illustrates a few of the most widespread examples; the standard forms in R2 and R3 are also given.

R1 characterised by grammatical carelessness	R2 + R3
je m'en rappelle	je me le rappelle
du point de vue littérature	du point de vue littéraire
un espèce de fou	une espèce de fou
neuf francs chaque	neuf francs chacun
se fâcher après	se fâcher contre
aller au dentiste/docteur	aller chez le dentiste/docteur
nous avons convenu de (= *we agreed to*)	nous sommes convenus de NOTE: *this is being replaced by* nous avons convenu de
ce n'est pas de sa faute	ce n'est pas sa faute
il fait pareil que vous	il fait comme vous
partir à Lyon/en Italie/à la campagne	partir pour Lyon/l'Italie/la campagne NOTE: *the distinction between* à/en *and* pour *is blurred here. Many R2 speakers would readily use* à/en.
ce que j'ai besoin, c'est . . .	ce dont j'ai besoin, c'est . . .
ce que j'ai peur, c'est . . .	ce dont j'ai peur, c'est . . .
lire sur le journal	lire dans le journal
la lettre dans laquelle je vous annonce	la lettre par laquelle je vous annonce
une avion	un avion
une élastique	un élastique
un autoroute	une autoroute
la mode d'emploi	le mode d'emploi
revenant de voyage, notre père est venu nous chercher à la gare	notre père est venu nous chercher à la gare à notre retour

R1 characterised by lexical carelessness	R2 + R3
on oppose son véto	on met son véto
cette nouvelle s'est avérée fausse	cette nouvelle s'est révélée fausse
messieursdames	mesdames et messieurs
il risque de gagner	il a des chances de gagner
de l'argent plein les poches	les poches pleines d'argent
j'ai très faim	R3: j'ai grand-faim
	NOTE: *although* très *is frowned upon by purists, it is widely used in such circumstances in R2 speech*

In the body of this book unless it is specifically stated otherwise, the word or expression or grammatical construction under discussion will belong to R2.

1.6   Passages illustrating levels of register

NOTE: *From passage 1.6.1 to 1.6.5 there is a gradual movement from R1 to R3.*

1.6.1   A la sortie du cinéma

awesome / tough / huge [handwritten annotation]

Martine: Ah, c'était trop bien.

Julien: Ah bon?

Martine: Je vois pas ce que t'as trouvé de si dément dans ce film. Ben, j'sais pas c'qu'i te font, les cascades et tout . . . Géant. Il est trop <u>balèze</u>, le mec.

Julien: OK, il est p'tet balèze, mais c'est du déjà-vu. Moi, j'en ai ras-le-bol de ce genre de film.

Martine: J'suis pas du tout d'accord.

Julien: Oh allez, l'aventure, les cascades, les nanas . . . c'est bien mignon tout ça, mais moi, ça m'emballe pas des masses.

Martine: Pourquoi tu vas au ciné, toi?

Julien: Chais pas. En tout cas, c'est pas mon genre de film. Je m'attendais à aut'chose un petit peu, euh, quequ'chose d'un petit peu plus sérieux, mais enfin, oh, c'est Belmondo. J'aurais dû m'y attendre.

Martine: Oh, pourtant, c'est aut'chose à côté de Delon.

Julien: Belmondo, Belmondo, vous ne jurez que par lui.

Martine: Et à raison.

Julien: Ouais ben, c'est un peu limite, je trouve.

Martine: Ben, moi, j'ai trouvé ça vraiment super.

Julien: OK pour les cascades et les poursuites en bagnoles!

Martine: Ouais, et puis le paysage, c'est génial le Mexique. Et la musique.

Julien: Ben, à ce moment-là, t'as qu'à aller voir un documentaire.

Martine: Ça va pas, non? Un documentaire! T'es ouf!
Julien: Au point de vue docu, j'trouve ça pas terrible.
Martine: Bon ben, moi, j'ai aimé – alors la ferme!
Julien: Enfin, j'aurais mieux fait d'dépenser mes quarante balles dans un café.
Martine: C'est clair que c'est plutòt ça ton truc.

Vocabulary	**trop**	= very (marks emphasis)
	dément	= fantastic
	géant	= great
	balèze	= brill
	le mec	= guy, bloke
	j'en ai ras-le-bol	= I'm fed up with it
	les nanas	= birds
	emballer	= to send
	des masses	= a lot, much
	le ciné	= pictures
	chais pas	= *je ne sais pas*
	limite	= limited
	super	= great
	la bagnole	= car
	génial	= fantastic
	un docu	= documentary
	ouf	= mad (verlan for *fou*)
	la ferme	= belt up
	une balle	= new franc (in this passage, also = *centime* for older people)
	clair	= certain
	ton truc	= what you like
Form of address	**t'(u)**	
Verbs	restricted range of tenses	only present, perfect, 1 conditional perfect; complete absence of subjunctive mood
Elision/ellipsis	**t'as trouvé**	**aut'chose**
	j'sais pas	**quequ'**
	c'qu'	**t'es ouf**
	p'têt	**au point de vue docu**
	j'suis	**j'trouve**
	chais pas	**la ferme!** (= belt up!)
Highlighting	**il est trop balèze, le mec**	
	moi, j'en ai ras-le-bol	
	moi, ça m'emballe pas	
	moi, j'ai trouvé ça vraiment super	

Interjections	ah	euh
	ah bon	ouais ben
	ben	bon ben
	oh allez	

Manner of speech	short, sharp sentences reflecting immediate personal reactions

1.6.2   Une agence de voyages

Monsieur:	Bonjour, mademoiselle.
Mademoiselle:	Monsieur, vous désirez?
Monsieur:	Je ne suis pas très sûr encore, vous voyez.
Mademoiselle:	Eh bien, nous avons trois formules à votre disposition. Soit vous partez seul, selon des conditions que vous avez fixées au préalable. A ce moment-là, ça risque d'être assez cher, parce que nous n'avons pas tous les avantages et toutes les réductions que peut apporter un voyage en groupe.
Monsieur:	Oui, très bien.
Mademoiselle:	Ou, alors, vous participez à un voyage de groupe, soit un circuit . . .
Monsieur:	Oui.
Mademoiselle:	Vous visitez des villes suivant un itinéraire établi d'avance, ou bien vous séjournez dans un hôtel près de la mer et vous restez le temps que vous voulez avec possibilité, bien sûr, de faire des excursions, mais à ce moment-là, c'est à votre charge, en plus du séjour.
Monsieur:	Ah, je vois, non. En fait, le problème est très simple. Bon, je voudrais passer quinze jours en Israël, euh, à un prix tout à fait raisonnable, tout en faisant le maximum de choses et en profitant à fond.
Mademoiselle:	Dans ce cas, nous pouvons vous proposer le grand tour d'Israël . . . vous aurez l'occasion, bien sûr, de visiter de nombreux monuments et puis vous traverserez Jérusalem. Vous pourrez également vous rendre compte par vous-même de l'atmosphère des kibboutz.
Monsieur:	Bien.
Mademoiselle:	Le long du parcours, vous visiterez les kibboutz au bord de la Mer Morte.
Monsieur:	Euh, on bénéficie d'un guide?
Mademoiselle:	Oui, bien sûr, vous voyagerez en autocar climatisé. Chaque soir, vous vous arrêterez dans un hôtel de bon standing avec nourriture continentale. Vous aurez, bien sûr, la possibilité de goûter de la nourriture plus typique. Vous aurez aussi l'occasion d'assister à des spectacles de danse folklorique. En ce moment, le prix est de 9000F pour quinze jours.
Monsieur:	D'accord, et vous m'avez dit que le voyage se faisait en car.
Mademoiselle:	Oui, c'est cela, en car.
Monsieur:	Ça doit être assez fatigant, je suppose.
Mademoiselle:	Non, rassurez-vous – pas du tout.
Monsieur:	Bien, nous sommes le combien aujourd'hui? Le quinze juin, euh, bien, je voudrais partir début août, mais j'aimerais réfléchir avant de

donner une réponse. Sera–t–il trop tard pour la réservation, si je reviens la semaine prochaine?

Mademoiselle: Oui, à ce moment-là, si vous voulez partir un peu plus tard parce que ça nous laisse à peine trois semaines, un mois, pour faire la réservation.

Monsieur: Oui. Il faudrait que je vous donne la réponse, disons, euh . . .

Mademoiselle: Le plus tôt possible. Et, à ce moment-là, je vous demanderais de verser dix pour cent de la somme.

Monsieur: Hmmm.

Mademoiselle: Et ensuite, le reste environ une semaine avant de partir.

Monsieur: Bien, euh, vous avez quelques prospectus?

Mademoiselle: Ah, oui, tout ce qu'il vous faut. Tenez.

Monsieur: Je vous remercie. Bon, très bien, merci. Au revoir, mademoiselle.

Mademoiselle: Au revoir, Monsieur.

Vocabulary	Business–like: the customer is enquiring about a holiday. The vocabulary is quite formal, but colourful.	**désirez** **proposer** **trois formules** **à votre disposition** **des conditions** **au préalable** **un itinéraire** **vous séjournerez** **soit** **réductions** **établi d'avance** **à votre charge** **raisonnable** **maximum**	**parcours** **Mer Morte** **bénéficie** **autocar** **monuments** **kibboutz** **climatisé** **également** **danse** **folklorique** **réservation** **verser** **dix pour cent** **prospectus**
Grammar	The agent speaks with more confidence than the customer, and with more fluent, slightly more sophisticated grammatical structures.		
Form of address	**vous**		
Interjections	**euh**, **oui**, **alors**, **ah**, **en fait**, **bon**, **hein**, **d'accord**, **enfin**, **hmmm**, **bien**		
Ellipsis	R2 usage does not allow ellipsis. The situation is quite formal.		
Verbs	Variety of tenses corresponds to quite sophisticated atmosphere, present, conditional (**voudrais**, **aimerais**, **demanderais**, **faudrait**) which tones down feelings, and future. Inversion is also used: **que peut apporter**.		
Manner	Formal, quite elegant. The travel agent tends to speak like the brochure. **avec possibilité**, **avec nourriture continentale**, **verser dix pour cent de la somme**.		

1.6.3   Part of a debate between Michèle-Laure Rassat and Georges Kiejman organised by *L'Express*

L'Express: Il n'y avait plus un seul condamné à mort dans les prisons françaises. Et puis, le 14 juin, le jour même où la Commission des lois votait en faveur de l'abolition de la peine capitale, la cour d'assises du Tarn prononçait une condamnation à mort. On pouvait penser que la France allait vers une abolition de facto, comme en Belgique et en Grèce. Ce verdict relance le débat de fond: faut-il aller jusqu'à l'abolition, dans la loi, de la peine de mort?

Mme Michèle-Laure Rassat: Il ne faut pas confondre l'existence de la peine de mort et son utilisation effrénée. Le problème est de savoir s'il n'y a pas des cas où il faut exécuter. C'est une question de principe. Le système du maintien a sur le système purement abolitionniste l'avantage de ne pas éliminer tout recours possible à la peine de mort en présence de personnalités criminelles exceptionnelles. Dans la perspective qui est la mienne, il pourrait s'agir d'une exécution tous les cinq ou six ans, ou peut-être moins.

Maître Georges Kiejman: Ceux qui croient à l'utilité de la peine de mort ne cessent de faire des concessions défensives: à les entendre, ce qui importe, c'est qu'elle existe, quitte à ne l'appliquer que très rarement. Comment la justifier sans croire à son caractère dissuasif, exemplaire? Or, elle ne peut avoir un effet dissuasif que si elle est appliquée assez largement . . .

M.-L. Rassat: Non, si elle est simplement applicable.

Maître Kiejman: La peine de mort simplement virtuelle ne peut avoir d'effet dissuasif, c'est évident. Or, les partisans de son maintien admettent qu'elle ne doit être prononcée que pour un nombre de crimes de plus en plus réduit. C'est la position du garde des Sceaux, qui propose de faire la toilette du Code pénal. C'est un fait, aussi, qu'on souhaite l'appliquer le moins souvent possible, puisque le ministère public la requiert beaucoup moins qu'autrefois. Si bien que, finalement, la peine de mort n'est plus qu'un symbole – un symbole politique, j'en suis persuadé – bien plus qu'elle n'est nécessaire à la répression criminelle.

L'Express: Selon la théorie traditionnelle, la peine de mort aurait quatre fonctions: l'amendement du criminel, l'expiation, l'intimidation, l'élimination. Que valent ces justifications?

Peine de mort: que faire?
L'Express, 30 juin, 1979, p.76

Vocabulary	much legal vocabulary	**Commission des lois**
		cour d'assises = Assize Court
		prononçait
		condamnation à mort
		abolition

Vocabulary (*cont.*)		verdict	
		peine capitale/de mort	
		personnalités criminelles	
		exécution	
		garde des Sceaux = Lord Chancellor	
		Code pénal	
		requiert (a form often used by lawyers, but not by average French speakers; past participle requis is the only form of requérir generally used)	
Grammar	very formal	inversion	faut-il aller?
			que valent ces justifications?
		loss of pas in negation	ne cessent de faire
		expletive ne	bien plus qu'elle n'est nécessaire
Form of address	no direct form	il ne faut pas	
	the impersonal viewpoint gives rise to impartial language	dans la perspective qui est la mienne	
		on	
		comment la justifier? à les entendre	
Manner	the tone is highly rhetorical and impersonal	the 2 elements of the exceptive expression ne . . . que are widely separated, creating a sense of balance	elle ne peut avoir un effet dissuasif que si . . .
			elle ne doit être prononcée que . . .
		repeated use of or marks passage from one idea to another in a formal way	
		logical thought processes are apparent in use of abstract nouns	l'amendement du criminel l'élimination
	Sentences here are invariably longer than in the previous passages. However there is still some spontaneity associated with ordinary speech.	et puis, le 14 juin	
		à les entendre, ce qui importe, c'est	
		c'est un fait, aussi, qu'on . . .	

1.6.4 Passage from de Gaulle's *Mémoires*

Ce fut fait le 23 mars. M. Peake vint me rendre visite. Il me remit une note m'annonçant que son gouvernement n'insistait pas pour que Muselier restât commandant en chef et veillerait à ce que, pendant un mois, l'amiral ne pût prendre contact avec aucun élément des forces navales françaises. Le Gouvernement britannique le recommandait, toutefois, à ma bienveillance pour une affectation conforme à ses services. Sur ces entrefaites, Auboyneau, arrivé du Pacifique, prit en main l'administration et le commandement de la marine. Au mois de mai, voulant offrir à l'amiral Muselier une chance de servir encore, je l'invitai à venir me voir pour régler avec lui les conditions d'une mission d'inspection que je comptais lui confier. Il ne vint pas. Quelques jours plus tard, cet officier général, qui avait beaucoup fait pour notre marine, me notifia que sa collaboration à la France Libre était terminée. Je l'ai regretté pour lui.

C. de Gaulle, *Mémoires de Guerre*, vol. 1, Plon, Paris, 1959, p. 233

Vocabulary	strong diplomatic and military associations	**remettre une note** **annonçant** **commandant en chef** **amiral** **forces navales françaises** **affectation** **notifia**	
Grammar	stringently precise	slightly ponderous constructions involving imperfect subjunctive; 3rd person sg forms only are used omission of **pas** in negation	**n'insistait pas pour que** **veiller à ce que** **l'amiral ne pût prendre**
Verbs	This is a narrative passage, hence the pervasive use of the past historic, which also suits the impartial viewpoint, creating a distance between the writer and the events he describes. The sudden change to the perfect tense links the narrative to the present moment.	**ce fut fait** **vint** **remit** **prit** **invitai** **notifia**	
Manner	an elegantly written, lofty passage, characteristic of de Gaulle's refined style; at the same time, a personal touch recurs with **me**, **ma**, **je**, etc.		

1.6.5   Passage from Albert Camus' *La Peste*

L'intention du narrateur n'est cependant pas de donner à ces formations sanitaires plus d'importance qu'elles n'en eurent. À sa place, il est vrai que beaucoup de nos concitoyens céderaient aujourd'hui à la tentation d'en exagérer le rôle. Mais le narrateur est plutôt tenté de croire qu'en donnant trop d'importance aux belles actions, on rend finalement un hommage indirect et puissant au mal. Car on laisse supposer alors que ces belles actions n'ont tant de prix que parce qu'elles sont rares et que la méchanceté et l'indifférence sont des moteurs bien plus fréquents dans les actions des hommes. C'est là une idée que le narrateur ne partage pas. Le mal qui est dans le monde vient presque toujours de l'ignorance, et la bonne volonté peut faire autant de dégâts que la méchanceté, si elle n'est pas éclairée. Les hommes sont plutôt bons que mauvais, et en vérité ce n'est pas la question. Mais ils ignorent plus ou moins, et c'est ce qu'on appelle vertu ou vice, le vice le plus désespérant étant celui de l'ignorance qui croit tout savoir et qui s'autorise alors à tuer. L'âme du meurtrier est aveugle et il n'y a pas de vraie bonté ni de bel amour sans toute la clairvoyance possible.

La Peste, Gallimard, Paris, 1947
p. 106

Vocabulary	very abstract, dealing with moral preoccupations	**belles actions**	**bons**
		mal	**mauvais**
		ignorance	**vertu**
		bonne volonté	**vice**
Grammar	few or no unusual expressions, even more lofty than the previous passage, an excellent example of clear French prose	expletive **ne**	**n'en eurent**
		balancing of the idea with the exceptive negative	**n'ont tant de prix que**
		repetition of **parce que** by **que**	
		use of **ni**	**il n'y a pas . . . ni**
Verbs	The present tense is usually used. The conditional tense **céderaient** increases the impersonal tone; the past historic **eurent** fixes the idea in time. The impartial viewpoint is underlined by the past participles of semi-auxiliary verbs, **tenté** and **laissé**, and is given more general stress by the infinitives **donner**, **exagérer**, **croire** and **supposer**.		
Manner	Camus adopts an elevated and impartial tone to convey the validity of his argument.		

1.6.6   Passages from *Le Monde* and *Libération*

The following two articles, from *Le Monde* and *Libération*, report on a weekend of accidents in France. They are compared in detail to discover similarities and differences, and to highlight the various stylistic techniques used by journalists.

**Accidents de la route: une quinzaine
de morts au cours du week-end**

UNE SÉRIE d'accidents de la route a fait une quinzaine de morts et plusieurs dizaines de blessés, dont de nombreux jeunes gens ou enfants, au cours du week-end. Dimanche 12 juillet, tôt le matin, une collision entre un car et une voiture a fait deux morts, cinq blessés

5   graves et vingt-cinq blessés légers, à Châteauroux (Indre). A Sury-près-Léré (Cher), quatre personnes ont été tuées et trois autres légèrement blessées dans la nuit de samedi à dimanche au cours d'une autre collision.

En Meurthe-et-Moselle, un adolescent de quatorze ans est décédé

10   et sept autres personnes ont été blessées dimanche dans un accident près de Longuyon. Deux voitures se sont heurtées de plein fouet sur une route nationale, rendue glissante par la pluie. Par ailleurs, trois jeunes gens ont été placés en garde à vue après une course poursuite entre quatre voitures sur l'autoroute A1, qui a provoqué vendredi 10 juillet

15   au soir, à hauteur de Stains (Seine-Saint-Denis), un accident dans lequel une mère et ses trois enfants ont trouvé la mort.

Le Monde 14 juillet 1998 p. 8

Week-end sanglant sur les routes

Les embouteillages étaient prévus, les accidents aussi. Ce week-end pré-14 Juillet n'a pas dérogé à la règle. Il a commencé par de très imposants bouchons, en particulier autour de Paris, vendredi soir et toute la journée de samedi. Mais surtout, il a été marqué par de graves

5   accidents.

Dès vendredi soir, dans la banlieue parisienne. Une jeune mère de 37 ans et ses trois enfants, âgés de 16 mois, 4 ans et 16 ans, rentrent chez eux en Seine-Saint-Denis. Mais ils se retrouvent pris dans une course-poursuite entre plusieurs véhicules. L'une des quatre voitures, qui

10   roulent à une vitesse largement excessive en direction de la province, percute alors le véhicule de la famille. Elle prend immédiatement feu. La mère et ses trois enfants meurent carbonisés. Trois jeunes gens ont été placés en garde à vue et devaient être déférés au parquet de Bobigny dimanche soir.

15   Autre lieu, autre hécatombe. Cela se déroule dans la nuit de samedi à dimanche près de Sury-près-Léré (Cher). C'est l'histoire bête et classique de la Clio d'un jeune homme regagnant seul son domicile. Il se déporte sur la gauche. Et percute alors une Rover arrivant en sens inverse; à l'intérieur, six membres d'une famille revenant d'un

20   mariage.

Le conducteur de la Clio est tué sur le coup, de même que celui de la Rover, et deux de ses passagers arrière, son fils de 2 ans et sa belle-mère. Une enquête est en cours, mais la découverte du moteur de la Clio à 10 mètres de la voiture accrédite l'hypothèse d'une vitesse excessive.

25

A Châteauroux, un accident entre un bus et une voiture a fait deux morts, cinq blessés graves et vingt-cinq blessés légers, dimanche. Et la liste pourrait s'allonger . . .

Libération 13 juillet 1998 p. 20

	Le Monde	*Libération*
Structure	title: neutral summary	title: graphic but enigmatic
	opening statement: general, matter of fact	opening statement: brief, dramatic, elliptical, organised symmetrically
	remainder of text: list of places where accidents occurred; few details provided Châteauroux Sury-près-Léré Meurthe-et-Moselle Longuyon Seine-Saint-Denis	remainder of text: detailed descriptions of accidents, the victims and the consequences; finishes with note of suspense (l.27)
Tone	that of a detached observer, recording, enumerating events	that of someone personally involved, judging others' behaviour (ll.10, 16, 24)
Focus	on events, places and number of victims, the extent of the injuries	on victims themselves, giving personal details and circumstances of accidents

Grammar	*Le Monde*	*Libération*
	number of words: 173 number of sentences: 6 words/sentence: 29	number of words: 295 number of sentences: 20 words/sentence: 15
	verbless sentences: 0	verbless sentences: 2 (ll.6, 15)
	sentences with subordinate clauses: 1 (ll.14, 15)	sentences with subordinate clauses: 1 (l.9)
	present participles: 0	present participles: 3 (ll.17, 18, 19)

	Le Monde	*Libération*
tenses	perfect only	para 1: imperfect (l.1), perfect (ll.2, 2, 4); para 2: present (ll.7, 8, 10, 11, 11, 12), perfect (l.12), imperfect (l.13); para 3: present (ll.15, 16, 18); para 4: present (ll.21, 23, 24); para 5: perfect (l.26), conditional (l.28)
passive/active voice	3/9 verbs (ll.6, 10, 13)	3/21 verbs (ll.13, 13, 21)
first element of sentences	subject (ll.1, 11), adverbial expression (ll.3, 5, 9, 12)	subject (ll.1, 1, 2, 6, 8, 9, 11, 12, 12, 15, 16, 17, 21, 23, 27), adverbial expression (ll.4, 6, 26)

Vocabulary	*Le Monde*	*Libération*
verbs	faire (ll.1, 4), tuer (l.6), blesser (ll.7, 10), décéder (l.9), se heurter (l.11), placer en garde à vue (l.13), provoquer (l.14), trouver la mort (l.16): alternation of cause and death/injury; two repeated	prévoir (l.1), déroger à la règle (l.2), commencer (l.2), marquer (l.4), rentrer (l.7), se retrouver pris (l.8), rouler (l.10), percuter (ll.11, 18), prendre feu (l.11), mourir (l.12), placer en garde à vue (l.13), déférer (l.13), se dérouler (l.15), être (ll.16, 23) regagner (l.17), se déporter (l.18), arriver (l.18), revenir (l.19), tuer (l.21), accréditer (l.24), faire (l.26), s'allonger (l.28): mixture of abstract and highly concrete verb, but the majority denote actions
words for incidents	accident (ll.1, 10, 15) collision (ll.4, 8), course poursuite (l.13)	embouteillage (l.1), bouchons (l.3), accident (ll.15, 26), course-poursuite (l.8), hécatombe (l.15)
adjectives	glissante (l.12)	imposants (l.3), graves (ll.4, 27), parisienne (l.6), excessive (ll.10, 25), carbonisés (l.12), bête (l.16), classique (l.16), légers (l.27)
description of victims	jeunes gens (ll.2, 12), enfants (ll.3, 16), adolescent (l.9), mère (l.16)	jeune mère (ll.6, 12), enfants (ll.7, 12), famille (ll.11, 19), jeunes gens (l.12), jeune homme (l.17), conducteur (l.21), passagers (l.22), fils (l.22), belle-mère (l.22)
R3 vocabulary	décéder	déroger à la règle, accrédite l'hypothèse, déférer au parquet

Stylistic features:

Le Monde:
    generally perfectly neutral, precise as to dates and basic details;
    sentences more carefully constructed, with abundant use of
    adverbial expressions;
    one colourful expression: *se heurter de plein fouet*;
    delay of object: l.14ff.

Libération:
    a generally lively account, full of small (personal) details, more
    expansive on dates;
    sentences tend to be brief, and two-thirds begin with subject;
    personification of weekend: l.1;
    new vocabulary: l.2 *ce week-end pré-14 Juillet*;
    picture and imagery: l.2 *déroger à la règle*;
    adjectives preceding noun: l.2 *de très imposants bouchons*, l.4 *de graves
    accidents*;
    verbless sentences (see above): l.6 beginning with *Dès* is especially
    dramatic and evokes immediacy;
    dramatic division of sentences: l.18 *Il se déporte sur la gauche. Et
    percute alors . . .*

2 Vocabulary

2.1 Misleading similarities: deceptive cognates

Apparent similarities between words in the English and French languages are a constant source of confusion. Words which look the same or very similar in the two languages, but which have different meanings, are called 'deceptive cognates' or more commonly *'faux amis'*. Deceptive cognates may be divided into two types: 1. deceptive cognates proper, in which the meanings are completely unconnected, and 2. partial deceptive cognates, in which only part of the meanings of the words coincides. Partial deceptive cognates will be discussed and illustrated in **2.1.2**.

2.1.1 Deceptive cognates proper

'Faux ami'	English translation	English	French translation
achèvement (m)	*completion*	achievement	*accomplissement* (m), *exploit* (m)
achever	*to complete*	to achieve	*accomplir*
actuel	*present*	actual	*véritable*
agenda (m)	*diary (for future events)*	agenda	*ordre* (m) *du jour*
agonie (f)	*death pangs*	agony	*angoisse* (f)
agoniser	*to be suffering death pangs*	to agonise	*être au supplice*
agréer	*to suit (impers), accept with approval*	to agree	*être d'accord, convenir* (**2.4** *agreeing*)
agrément (m)	*pleasure*	agreement	*accord* (m), *traité* (m)
allée (f)	*path (as in garden)*	alley	*ruelle* (f)
s'altérer	*to change for the worse*	to alter	*changer*
avertissement (m)	*warning*	advertisement	*annonce* (f), *publicité* (f)
axe (m)	*axle, axis, major trunk road*	axe	*hache* (f)
balancer	*to sway, to rock; R1 to chuck*	to balance	*se tenir en équilibre*

'Faux ami'	English translation	English	French translation
barrage (m)	*dam, roadblock, barricade*	barrage (of questions)	*déluge* (m)
blouse (f) (2.3)	*smock (usually extending to the knees), overall*	blouse	*chemisier* (m)
box (m)	*lock-up garage, stall (for horses), dock (in court)*	box	*boîte* (f)
car (m)	*coach*	car	*auto* (f), *voiture* (f)
cargo (m)	*cargo-boat*	cargo	*cargaison* (f)
casserole (f)	*saucepan*	casserole	*ragoût en cocotte* (m)
caution (f)	*security, guarantee*	caution	*précaution* (f)
cave (f)	*cellar*	cave	*caverne* (f), *grotte* (f)
change (m)	*exchange*	change	*changement* (m),
échange (m)		small change, coins	*monnaie* (f)
charade (f)	*riddle (exclusively of type: mon premier est un petit animal qui boit du lait; mon second est le contraire de tard; mon tout est une grande maison – chat + tôt = château)*	charade	*charade mimée* (f), *comédie* (f) (with an idea of pretence)
chips (mpl)	*potato crisps*	chips	*pommes frites* (fpl)
comédien (m)	*actor*	comedian	*comique* (m)
commando (m)	*commando platoon or terrorist gang (occ = commando, but restricted to newspapers influenced by English)*	commando	*membre* (m) *d'un commando*
commercialiser	*to market (no pej connotation in French, unlike English)*	to commercialise	*profiter de*
complainte (f)	*lament (song)*	complaint	*plainte* (f), **grief** (m)
complexion (f)	*constitution* (**2.2.5.2**), *temperament*	complexion	*teint* (m)
conducteur (m)	*driver*	conductor	*receveur* (m) (on bus), *chef* (m) *d'orchestre*
conférence (f)	*special lecture*	conference	*congrès* (m)
conforter R3	*to strengthen, to confirm*	to comfort	*réconforter*
conséquent	*rational, consistent*	consequent	*résultant*
conservatoire (m)	*academy (of music)*	conservatory (at side of building)	*verrière* (f)

'Faux ami'	English translation	English	French translation
content	*happy*	content	*satisfait*
convenance (f)	*convention, agreement*	convenience	*avantage* (m), *commodité* (f) (*but inconvenience = inconvénient* (m))
convenances (fpl)	*conventions*	public conveniences	*toilettes* (fpl)
course (f)	*race*	course	*série* (f) *de cours* (m), *stage* (m)
courtier (m)	*broker (in commerce)*	courtier	*courtisan* (m)
débonnaire	*easy-going, good-natured*	debonair	*jovial, insouciant*
déception (f)	*disappointment*	deception	*tromperie* (f)
se dégrader	*to deteriorate (of weather, health, situation)*	to degrade	*avilir, humilier*
délai (m)	*time allowed (but* **sans délai** *= without delay)*	delay	*retard* (m)
demande (f)	*request*	demand	*exigence* (f)
demander	*to ask for*	to demand	*exiger*
député (m)	*Member of Parliament*	deputy	*adjoint* (m), *remplaçant* (m)
désaffecté	*disused (of building, school, church)*	disaffected	*mécontent*
destituer	*to dismiss*	destitute	*indigent*
destitution (f)	*dismissal*	destitution	*dénûment* (m)
dilapider	*to waste (money, a fortune)*	dilapidated	*délabré* (house), *dépenaillé* (person)
disgracieux	*ungainly*	disgraceful	*honteux, infâme*
disposer de	*to have at one's disposal*	to dispose of	*se débarrasser de, expédier* (of work, meal)
donjon (m)	*castle keep*	dungeon	*cachot* (m)
drôle	*funny*	droll	*falot, saugrenu*
éducateur (m)	*youth worker, social worker (with children)*	educator	*pédagogue* (m)
effectif (m) (usually pl)	*equipment, personnel*	effective	*efficace*
effectivement	*in reality, sure enough*	effectively	*efficacement*
énerver	*to annoy*	to enervate	*affaiblir*
engin (m)	*device*	engine	*moteur* (m)
entretenir	*to maintain in good condition*	to entertain	*amuser, divertir*

'Faux ami'	English translation	English	French translation
étable (f)	*cowshed*	stable (**2.2.5.2**)	*écurie* (f)
éventuel	*possible*	eventual	*final*
éventuellement	*possibly*	eventually	*à la longue, en fin de compte*
évidence (f)	*obviousness, fact*	evidence	*témoignage* (m), *preuve* (f)
évincer R3	*to remove (sb from office)*	to evince	*exprimer, manifester*
expertise (f)	*(written) valuation, assessment*	expertise	*compétence* (f)
exténuer	*to exhaust*	to extenuate	*atténuer*
facile	*easy*	facile	*complaisant*
fastidieux	*boring, wearisome*	fastidious	*délicat, difficile à satisfaire*
forfait (m)	*fixed rate, package deal, heinous crime*	forfeit	*amende* (f), *confiscation* (R3) (f), *gage* (m)
fou	*mad*	fool	*idiot, sot*
gag (m)	*funny incident (organised by sb), trick*	gag	*bâillon* (m), *blague* (f)
gala (m)	*variety show, spectacle*	gala	*fête* (f), *compétition* (f) *de natation*
génial	*inspired, full of genius*	genial	*bienveillant, doux*
goal (m)	*goalkeeper*	goal	*but* (m)
grief (m)	*grievance, complaint*	grief	*douleur* (f)
groin (m)	*snout (of animal)*	groin	*aine* (f)
grosse tête (f)	*very intelligent person*	big head	*crâneux, prétentieux*
habileté (f)	*skill*	ability	*capacité* (f)
hagard	*wild-eyed*	haggard	*les traits tirés*
halle (f)	*covered market*	hall	*vestibule* (m)
harasser	*to exhaust*	to harass	*harceler*
hardi	*bold*	hardy	*dur, robuste*
hurler	*to howl (of animal), to roar or yell*	to hurl	*jeter, lancer*
impotent	*physically disabled, infirm*	impotent	*impuissant (sexually and fig)*
incessamment	*immediately*	incessantly	*sans cesse*
incidence (f)	*repercussion*	incidence	*récurrence* (f), *taux* (m)
ingénu	*ingenuous*	ingenious	*ingénieux*
ingénuité (f)	*ingenuousness*	ingenuity	*ingéniosité* (f)

'Faux ami'	English translation	English	French translation
injure (f)	*insult*	injury	**blessure** (f)
instances (fpl)	*authorities*	instances	**cas** (mpl), **exemples** (mpl)
intoxiquer	*to poison (food, etc)*	to intoxicate	**enivrer, soûler**
issue (f)	*outcome, end*	issue	**cas** (m), **question** (f)
large	*wide*	large	**grand**
lecture (f)	*reading (a book, etc)*	lecture	**cours** (m)
libraire (m, f)	*bookseller*	librarian	**bibliothécaire** (m, f)
librairie (f)	*bookshop*	library	**bibliothèque** (f)
licence (f)	*(university) degree; licentiousness*	licence	**permis** (m)
lift (m)/**lifter**	*topspin/to put topspin (in tennis)*	to lift	**soulever**
logeur (m) (**logeuse** more common)	*landlord (landlady)*	lodger	**locataire** (m, f)
luxure (f)	*lust*	luxury	**luxe** (m)
luxurieux	*lustful*	luxurious	**luxueux**
machiniste (m)	*props man, scene shifter (in theatre)*	machinist	**mécanicien** (m)
malice (f)	*mischievousness*	malice	**malveillance** (f), **méchanceté** (f)
maniaque	*finicky*	maniac	**dément**
marron	*brown*	maroon	**carmin**
misère (f)	*poverty, destitution*	misery	**tristesse** (f)
molester	*to manhandle, to knock about*	to molest	**importuner**
monnaie (f)	*change (money)*	money	**argent** (m)
motoriste (m)	*car manufacturer*	motorist	**automobiliste** (m), **conducteur** (m)
notoire	*well-known*	notorious	**mal famé, mal réputé**
nurse (f)	*nanny*	nurse	**infirmier/infirmière** (m/f)
ombrelle (f)	*parasol, sunshade*	umbrella	**parapluie** (m)
palace (m)	*sumptuous building/hotel*	palace	**palais** (m)
pantomime (m)	*mime show*	pantomime	**spectacle** (m) *de Noël*
parking (m)	*car-park*	parking	**stationnement** (m)
parloir (m)	*reception room (in school, etc)*	parlour	**salon** (m)
passer (**un examen**)	*to sit (an exam)*	to pass (an exam)	**être reçu** (*à un examen*)

'Faux ami'	English translation	English	French translation
pédestre	**randonnée pédestre** = *ramble*	pedestrian	*piéton* (noun), *médiocre* (adj)
performant (of high-performing machine/technique)	*highly efficient*	performing	*qui accomplit/ remplit (un devoir)*
pétulant	*lively, frisky*	petulant	*irritable*
physicien (m)	*physicist*	physician	*médecin* (m)
pièce (f)	*room; special item (as in* **pièce d'identité, pièce à conviction**)	piece	*morceau* (m)
pondre	*to lay (an egg)*	to ponder	*méditer*
pope (m)	*Greek/Russian Orthodox priest*	pope	*pape* (m)
portier (m)	*doorman*	porter	*porteur* (m), *concierge* (m)
précipice (m)	*a chasm, abyss (eg* **on tombe dans un précipice**, *but* = *Eng precipice in such expressions as* **il était au bord du précipice**)	precipice	*paroi* (f) *abrupte*
préjudice (m)	*detriment*	prejudice	*préjugé* (m), *prévention* (f)
présentement	*at present*	presently	*tout à l'heure*
préservatif (m)	*male contraceptive, condom*	preservative	*agent de conservation* (m)
prétendre	*to claim, to assert*	to pretend	*faire semblant, feindre*
prévariquer (R3)	*to be guilty of corrupt practices*	to prevaricate	*tergiverser*
procès (m)	*trial*	process	*processus* (m) (**2.3**)
râper	*to grate (food)*	to rape	*violer*
remarquer	*to notice*	to remark	*faire remarquer*
rente (f)	*(unearned) income, pension*	rent	*loyer* (m)
replacer	*to put back (again)*	to replace	*remplacer*
reporter	*to postpone, to delay*	to report	*rapporter*
ressentir	*to feel (an emotion, not sth tangible like a table)*	to resent	*être irrité, offensé* NOTE: but **ressentiment** = *resentment*
résumer	*to summarise*	to resume	*reprendre*
rétribution (f)	*remuneration, reward*	retribution	*châtiment* (m)
rude	*rough*	rude	*impoli*
sanguin	*blood (of product, analysis)*	sanguine	*optimiste*

'Faux ami'	English translation	English	French translation
schéma (m)	*outline, sketch*	scheme	***projet*** (m), ***magouille*** (f)
sensible	*sensitive, perceptible*	sensible	***sensé, raisonnable, sage***
socquette (f)	*ankle sock*	socket	***prise*** (f) (***de courant***)
square (m)	*public garden (often in a square)*	square	***place*** (f)
stage (m)	*training period*	stage	***scène*** (f), ***estrade*** (f), ***étape*** (f)
starter (m)	*choke (for car)*	starter	***démarreur*** (m)
studio (m)	*small flat (but* **studio d'émission** = *broadcasting studio)*	studio	***atelier*** (m), ***studio*** (m)
susceptible	*touchy, impressionable* (**être susceptible de faire/recevoir**, *etc* = *to be capable of doing/receiving, etc)*	susceptible	***sensible, prédisposé à***
sympathiser avec	*to get on well with*	to sympathise with	***témoigner de la sympathie pour, être solidaire de, présenter ses condoléances à***
trivial	*commonplace, vulgar*	trivial	***insignifiant***
trouble (m)	*agitation, confusion*	trouble	***peine*** (f), ***difficulté*** (f)
truculent R3	*highly-coloured (of speech, face, etc)*	truculent	***agressif, brutal, féroce***
user	*to use up, to wear out; R3 to use*	to use	***employer, se servir de***
valable	*valid*	valuable	***précieux, de valeur***
venue (f)	*arrival*	venue	***rendez-vous*** (m)
verbaliser	*to book (of police)*	to verbalise	***traduire en paroles***
vers (m)	*line of verse*	verse	***strophe*** (f), ***verset*** (m)
vicaire (m)	*curate*	vicar	*no exact equivalent:* ***pasteur*** (m) (***de l'église anglicane***)

2.1.2   Partial deceptive cognates

Partial deceptive cognates arise because of an ambiguity in a French or English word: for example the meaning of a French word may be included amongst the meanings of a similar-sounding English word, with the result that the two words have the same meaning in some but not all circumstances. In some respects this is a more troublesome and problematic area than that involving deceptive cognates proper, since, because in these cases there is overlap between the meanings of the French and English words, it is not possible to dismiss categorically the '*faux ami*', as on occasions it may be a true equivalent. The asymmetry of the meanings of certain French and English words may be illustrated by the following examples. The English word in the upper right quarter section of the diagrams provides the normal equivalent of the French word in the upper left section. It is in the lower part that the problem posed by partial deceptive cognates is highlighted. In the lower left section, the word in parenthesis implies occasional equivalence with the English word in the lower right quarter, while beneath it is given the more usual equivalent of the English word.

French	English
assistance (f)	audience (**2.2.5.2**)
(assistance (f) R3) aide (f)	aid
corps (m) (corps (m)) cadavre (m)	body corpse
emphase (f) (emphase (f)) force (f)	bombast emphasis
emphatique (emphatique) énergique	bombastic emphatic
fameux (fameux) célèbre, distingué, bien connu	notorious famous

Many other examples of deceptive cognates proper and partial deceptive cognates are to be found in **2.2** Homonyms and ambiguity, **2.3** Paronyms and **2.4** Synonyms, where they are indicated by an ★.

2.2   Homonyms and ambiguity

Pairs and occasionally groups of words which are identical in sound but which are different in meaning are called homonyms, and are an obvious cause of ambiguity in a language. French in fact seems to be particularly affected by homonymy. However, various means of overcoming such ambiguity exist, the principal ones being context, gender and spelling. Because context is infinitely variable and is therefore not easily classified, the following sections show how gender and spelling, both singly and in combination, help distinguish between homonyms.

2.2.1 Homonyms differentiated by gender but with identical spelling

aide	M	assistant
	F	help; female assistant
aigle	M	male eagle (also general); insignia bearing an eagle (eg **l'aigle blanc de Pologne**)
	F	female eagle; heraldic sign; standard surmounted by eagle (eg **les aigles romaines**)
aspirine	M	an aspirin (tablet)
	F	aspirin (the medicament)
champagne	M	champagne
Champagne	F	Champagne region
chef	M	boss
	F	R1 (female) boss (eg où est la chef?)
chose	M	R1 = thingummybob
	F	thing
crêpe	M	crepe (material)
	F	pancake
critique	M	critic
	F	criticism
diesel	M	diesel (fuel)
	F	diesel (car, etc)
dramatique	M	drama (ie what is dramatic)
	F	short play on TV
finale	M	finale (in music)
	F	final (in football, etc)
garde	M	guard, warden
	F	protection; guards; private nurse
geste	M	gesture
	F	courageous exploit (eg une chanson de geste = medieval epic poem)

gîte	M	resting place, lodging (used largely in **Les Gîtes de France**)
	F	list of ship
greffe	M	record office
	F	graft, transplant
guide	M	guide (person or book)
	F	rein; girl guide
hymne (national)	M	national anthem
	F	hymn
livre	M	book
	F	pound (weight or money)
manche	M	handle (of broom, etc)
	F	sleeve; **la Manche** = English Channel
manœuvre	M	labourer
	F	manoeuvre
martyre	M	martyrdom
	F	female martyr
mémoire	M	long dissertation, report; pl = memoirs
	F	memory
merci	M	thank you (**un grand merci** = a big thank you)
	F	mercy (**à la merci de qn** = at sb's mercy)
mode	M	method, mood (linguistic)
	F	fashion
mort	M	dead person (male)
	F	death
moule	M	mould (for making sth)
	F	mussel
mousse	M	ship's boy
	F	moss; froth (on beer etc); rubber foam
office	M	function (**2.2.5.1**), role, bureau,
	F	butler's pantry
œuvre	M	R3 = collected works
	F	(individual) work; R1, R2 = collected works
ombre	M	grayling (fish)
	F	shade, shadow

| page | M | page-boy |
| | F | page of book or newspaper |

| pendule | M | pendulum |
| | F | clock |

| physique | M | physique |
| | F | physics |

| poêle | M | stove |
| | F | frying pan |

| politique | M | politician |
| | F | politics, policy (see **2.3**) |

| poste | M | job, station; set (radio, TV) |
| | F | postal services |

| pub | M | (English) public house/pub |
| | F | R1 (=**publicité**) advertising, advertisement |

| pupille | M | ward (as in **les pupilles de la nation**) |
| | F | pupil of the eye |

| radio | M | wireless operator |
| | F | X ray, radio |

| somme | M | snooze |
| | F | amount, sum |

| tour | M | trick; turn |
| | F | tower; rook (chess) |

| vague | M | vagueness |
| | F | wave |

| vapeur | M | steamer |
| | F | steam |

| vase | M | vase |
| | F | slime |

| vigile | M | night watchman, security guard |
| | F | vigil (on the day before a feast day, eg **la vigile de Noël** = Christmas Eve) |

| visa | M | visa (permission to enter a country) |
| | F | Visa (credit card) |

| voile | M | veil |
| | F | sail |

2.2.2 Homonyms differentiated by both gender and spelling

air	M	air
ère	F	era
aire	F	playing area; threshing floor; eyrie
bal	M	ball (dance)
balle	F	ball (spherical), shot; bale; bullet; R1 franc
bar	M	bar (for serving drinks)
barre	F	bar (of wood, metal, etc); tiller
but	M	aim, goal
butte	F	hillock
capital	M	capital, assets
capitale	F	capital city; capital letter
central (téléphonique)	M	telephone exchange
centrale (électrique, nucléaire)	F	(generating) station
chêne	M	oak tree
chaîne	F	chain
col	M	collar; pass (in mountain)
colle	F	paste, glue
coq	M	cock
coque	F	shell, hull
cours	M	course; waterway; class
cour	F	court, yard
court (de tennis, de squash, etc)	M	court
fait	M	fact
faîte	M	apex of roof
fête	F	festival
foie	M	liver
foi	F	faith
fois	F	time, occasion
gène	M	gene
gêne	F	discomfort
hall	M	entrance, vestibule, hall
halle	F	(often pl) covered market

maire	M	mayor
mer	F	sea
mère	F	mother

pair	M	peer
paire	F	pair
père	M	father

parti	M	party (political, etc); decision
partie	F	part
surprise-partie R3	F	social party

pois	M	pea
poids	M	weight
poix	F	pitch

pot	M	pot
peau	F	skin

sel	M	salt
selle	F	saddle

2.2.3   Homonyms differentiated by spelling only

In these cases and also in those in **2.2.4** where no external distinction exists either by gender or spelling, the danger of ambiguity arises only if the words belong to the same word-class (part of speech) or closely related word-classes. In other words, it is unlikely for *vers* the preposition to be confused with *vert* the adjective, or for *tends* the imperative to be confused with *taon* the noun, whereas the identical pronunciation of *dessein* and *dessin,* and *tache* and *tâche* could well cause difficulty in understanding. In this section and the next, only those examples of homonyms involving words belonging to the same word-class or closely related word-classes (eg noun and adjective) are given.

censé		supposed
sensé		sensible

chair	F	flesh
chaire	F	throne, pulpit
cher/chère		dear

compte	M	account
comte	M	count, earl
conte	M	story

cou	M	neck
coup	M	blow
coût	M	cost

dégoûter		to disgust
dégoutter R3		to drip
dessein	M	plan
dessin	M	drawing; art (school subject)
être	M	being
hêtre	M	beech tree
faim	F	hunger
fin	F	end
haler		to tow, haul
hâler		to tan (of sun)
hâlé		sunburnt
jeune	M	youth
jeûne	F	fast(ing)
martyr	M	martyr
martyre	M	martyrdom
pain	M	bread
pin	M	pine tree
roder		to run in (of an engine)
rôder		to prowl around
saut	M	jump
sceau	M	seal (wax)
seau	M	bucket
sot	M	fool
sain		healthy
saint	M	saint, holy (adj)
sein	M	breast, bosom (also fig, eg **le sein de la terre**)
seing R3	M	signature
tache	F	spot, stain
tâche	F	task
vair	M	squirrel fur
ver	M	worm
verre	M	glass
vers	M	line of verse
vert		green

2.2.4   Homonyms with no external distinction either of gender or spelling

balle	F	ball (spherical)
balle	F	bale

goûter (noun)		snack
goûter (verb)		to taste
limon	M	fertile alluvium, silt
limon	M	lime(fruit)
louer		to hire
louer		to praise
ressortir		to go out again
ressortir		to be under the jurisdiction of
conjugated like **finir**		
(but this is often not		
respected and the verb		
is used like **sortir**)		
son	M	bran
also **taches** (f) **de**		
son	M	freckles
son	M	sound
timbre	M	stamp
timbre	M	bell
vol	M	flight
vol	M	theft
voler		to fly
voler		to steal

2.2.5   Words with more than one meaning: incommensurability of French and English

Similar problems arise when a single word in one language has two distinct meanings, or denotes two shades of meaning, each of which is expressed by a different word, in the other language. When the words in the two languages sound alike, this frequently produces partial deceptive cognates (**2.1.2**): such cases are indicated by an asterisk. The important point to grasp is that the words in the two languages do not cover precisely the same areas of meaning, and confusion can arise.

2.2.5.1   *French examples*

acteur★ (m)	actor
	(important) player/participant
allumer	to light (fire)
	to switch on (TV, etc)
amusant★	amusing
	enjoyable

French examples

appréhender	to arrest R3 = to fear
arrêter	to stop to decide, to fix (decree, rules)
assassinat★ (m)	(often political) assassination murder
assister★	to attend R3 = to help, to assist
balancer	to swing R1 = to chuck
bandit★ (m)	bandit (as in a western) crook, ruffian
bâtiment (m)	building boat (as in **bâtiment de guerre**)
chasser★	to go hunting to chase away
cité★	old historical part of a town housing estate
complaisance★ (f)	complacency willingness
confronter★	to compare to confront (legally)
conscience★ (f)	conscience consciousness
contrôler★	to control to verify, to check
conventionnel★	conventional according to decorum
cynique★	R3 = entirely scornful of social convention (as in black humour) cynical (with regard to human goodness)
découper	to cut out (from newspaper, etc) to cut up (meat)
découvrir★	to discover R3 = to uncover (only used reflexively = to take one's hat off)
délivrer★	to free from captivity to deliver (letter, message)
dénoncer★	R3 = to reveal to denounce
dossier★ (m)	dossier, file back (of chair)

French examples

émotion★ (f)	emotion agitation, excitement
enveloppe★ (f)	envelope bribe
équipement★ (msg)	equipment, material
équipements (mpl)	facilities (as in **équipements** **portuaires/sportifs/scolaires**)
évoluer★	to develop, evolve to move around, along (fish in pool, cars on track, dancers in hall)
excéder★	to exceed R3 = to tire out
expérience★ (f)	experience experiment
fermer	to shut to switch off (TV, etc)
figure (f)	face shape
formation★ (f)	formation training
hôte★ (m)	host guest
ignorer★	not to know (of things) to ignore (a person)
important★	important, outstanding serious (eg damage)
incliner★	to bow (**s'incliner**) to be inclined to (**incliner à, être enclin à**)
instruction★ (f)	instruction judicial investigation (likewise **instruire**)
intelligence★ (f)	intelligence R3 = understanding (with sb)
intervention★ (f)	intervention, speech, lecture operation (as in **intervention chirurgicale**)
intolérance★ (f)	intolerance excessive sensitivity, allergy
livrer	to place in custody to deliver (parcel, furniture), to yield (a secret)
loyal ★	frank faithful

French examples

métropole★ (f)	metropolis, large city (Metropolitan) France
moral★ (m)	moral (adj) morale, state of mind
morale★ (f)	morals moral of story
office★ (m)	function, office (**2.2.5.2**) agency, bureau (eg **l'Office National du Tourisme**)
opportunité★ (f)	opportuneness R1 = opportunity
orphelin★ (m)	orphan lacking one parent (eg **il est orphelin de père**)
parents★ (m pl)	members of a family mother and father
partition★ (f)	partition (of a country) (music) score
percevoir★	to perceive to receive money (official)
place (f)	(market) square, position seat, room (space)
placement (m)	investment placing of a child in a foster home
ponctuel★	punctual relevant, precise, localised, selective
populaire★	popular working-class (eg a district in a town)
prétendre	to claim, to be a candidate to assert
primitif★	primitive original (eg **le sens primitif d'un mot**)
publicité/ pub (f) R1	advertising advertisement
(se) relaxer★	to relax
relaxer	to free, discharge (a prisoner)
retransmettre★	to broadcast (often live) to retransmit (message or information)
sanctionner	to approve, validate (less used with this meaning than to penalise) to penalise

French examples

sensible★	sensitive perceptible
spécial★	special odd, strange, peculiar
spectacle★ (m)	spectacle show, play
supporter★	to bear, put up with to support (eg a football team) (condemned by purists, but very common)
susceptible	touchy, sensitive capable (of), able (to)
terrible★	frightening, terrible extraordinary R1 = great, fantastic
trafic★ (m)	trading (eg drugs) traffic (**2.2.5.2**)
tronc★ (m)	trunk (of body, tree) collecting box in church
vain★	R3 = vain empty, sham
vicieux★	vicious faulty (eg reasoning, expression)
voix (f)★	voice an individual's vote

2.2.5.2   English examples

to abuse★	to insult to take advantage of	**insulter, injurier** **abuser de**
accomplishment★	completion artistic attainment	**accomplissement** (m) **talent** (m)
application★	diligence for a job	**application** (f) **demande** (f)
audience★	with an important personage in cinema, etc	**audience** (f) **assistance** (f), **spectateurs** (mpl)
to balance	to keep in equilibrium of accounts, etc	**maintenir en équilibre, équilibrer** **dresser le bilan**
ball★	spherical dance	**boule** (f), **balle** (f) (**2.4** *balle*) **bal** (m)

English examples

bank★	of river	**rive** (f)
	for money	**banque** (f)
bar★	for serving drinks	**bar** (m)
	of metal, wood	**barre** (f)
change★	transformation	**changement** (m)
	money	**monnaie** (f)
character★	distinctive nature	**caractère** (m), **caractéristique** (f)
	person (in book, etc)	**personnage** (m)
comfortable★	of person	**bien à l'aise**
	of thing	**confortable**
competition★	rivalry	**concurrence** (f)
	contest in sport	**compétition** (f)
	academic	**concours** (m)
consistent★	in reasoning	**conséquent**, **logique**
	in food	**consistant**
constitution★	political	**constitution** (f)
	of body	**composition** (f)
to cry★	to shout	**crier**
	to weep	**pleurer**
cure★	restoration to health	**guérison** (f)
	course of treatment	**cure** (f)
decent★	of wage, film, etc	**correct**, **décent**, **honnête**
	of moral quality	**honnête**
editor★	of book	**éditeur** (m)
	of newspaper	**rédacteur** (m)
epic★	noun	**épopée** (f)
	adj	**épique**
figure★	of body	**taille** (f)
	number	**chiffre** (m)
invalid★	unwell	**invalide**, **infirme**, **alité**
	not valid	**non–valable** (eg of train ticket)
to marry	to get married (**2.4** *se marier*)	**épouser**, **se marier à/avec**
	to give in marriage	**marier**
modest★	humble	**modeste**, **humble**
	chaste	**pudique** (**2.3**)
office★	place of work	**bureau** (m)
	function	**office** (m) (**2.2.5.1**)
to order★	in commerce, restaurant	**commander**
	to command	**ordonner**, **commander**

English examples

organ★	of the body	**organe** (m)
	musical	**orgue** (m)
pathetic★	moving	**attendrissant, émouvant, pathétique**
	pitiful	**pitoyable**
place★	location	**endroit** (m), **lieu** (m)
	room, space	**place** (f) (**2.2.5.1**)
to preserve★	to keep in good condition, to maintain	**conserver**
	to protect	**préserver**
to realise★	to understand	**réaliser, se rendre compte**
	to fulfil	**réaliser, créer**
to recover★	to get better	**guérir**
	to retrieve	**récupérer**
	to cover again, to cover over	**recouvrir**
relations★	connections, relationships	**relations** (fpl), **rapports** (mpl)
	members of family	**parents** (mpl)
to save★	to rescue	**sauver**
	money	**épargner, économiser,** R3 = **thésauriser**
sensible	aware	**conscient**
	well-behaved	**sage, bien élevé**
sentence★	in language	**phrase** (f)
	legal	**sentence** (f), **jugement** (m), **verdict** (m)
square★	market square, large square	**place** (f)
	square with garden in centre	**square** (m)
	geometrical	**carré** (m)
stable★	noun	**écurie** (f)
	adj	**stable, ferme**
study	intellectual	**étude** (f)
	room	**cabinet** (m) **d'étude, bureau** (in a private house)
to succeed★	to be successful	**réussir**
	to follow	**succéder à, suivre**
traffic★	on roads	**circulation** (f)
	air, sea, road usage	**trafic** (m)
trunk★	of body	**torse** (m), **tronc** (m)
	of tree	**tronc** (m)
	of car	**coffre** (m)
	for packing	**coffre** (m), **malle** (f)
	of elephant	**trompe** (f)

2.3   Paronyms

It quite frequently happens that certain pairs or groups of words are
easily confused in French because, although they are not homonyms,
they nevertheless sound very similar to one another. Such sets of
words are called paronyms. The problem of confusion is further
compounded when the meanings of the words are related to some
extent. Such is often the case in the examples that follow. However, in
a number of cases, a set of paronyms, linked by form and meaning is
also related to other words, but by meaning only. Such cases are
treated in section **2.4** Synonyms, and are indicated by an asterisk.
They may be located by reference to the Vocabulary List.

abaisser to reduce height of, also fig (eg un mur, ses critères, ses ambitions)	**baisser** to lower (general, eg la tête, le store, le volet roulant)	**rabaisser** to lower (eg un prix; R1 le store)
absorber to absorb (eg un liquide, des idées)	**résorber** to absorb (an excess, eg de la circulation)	
accroissement (m) increase (in number, amount)	**croissance** (f) growth (organic, eg d'une plante, d'un enfant, de l'économie)	
accroître★ (eg son salaire, la production, le patrimoine, ses forces)	**s'accroître** R3 (often reflex when fig, eg la tension/la population s'accroît de jour en jour)	**croître** (eg ses connaissances croissent)
achever to finish (eg un livre, ses études), to kill (d'une balle dans la tête)	**parachever** to finish (more effort implied R3), to put the finishing touches to (eg parachever un livre)	
affaiblir trans, to weaken (eg l'opération l'a beaucoup affaibli)	**s'affaiblir** same as faiblir, to weaken (eg il s'est affaibli à la suite de l'opération)	**faiblir** tr and intrans, to weaken, to get older, to lose one's strength (eg elle faiblit; l'opération l'a beaucoup faibli)
affronter to face sb, sth (eg un danger)	**confronter** to place face to face (eg confronter l'accusé avec la victime), to compare	

agrandir★	**grandir**
to make bigger, to extend (eg on va agrandir la maison)	to get bigger, to grow bigger (eg qu'est-ce qu'il a grandi; les ténèbres grandissaient; le bruit grandit)

alpin	**alpestre**
alpine (eg le ski, le paysage, un club, une station, une fleur, un relief)	R3 (eg le paysage)

amener★	**ramener**
R2 to bring (a person) (eg amène ton père, si tu veux); R1 to bring (an object) (eg tu peux amener ton vélo)	R2 to bring (a person) back (eg ramène ton fils vers 19h); R1 to bring (an object) back (eg si tu empruntes mes livres, ne manque pas de les ramener)

an (m)	**année** (f)
year (general and specific) (eg elle a six ans, en l'an deux mille, l'an dernier, le nouvel an, bon an mal an)	year (emphasis on duration) (eg au cours des années soixante, dans la sixième année, les premières années de sa vie, l'année dernière, l'année nouvelle)

anoblir	**ennoblir** R3
to confer nobility upon (eg la reine a anobli Elton John)	to exalt (suggests moral stature) (eg ce qui ennoblit l'homme, c'est sa capacité créatrice)

apercevoir	**s'apercevoir**	**percevoir**
to perceive (visually) (eg je l'ai aperçu dans le parc)	to become aware (eg je me suis aperçu qu'elle était kleptomane)	to perceive with senses (of a higher level than the other two verbs) (eg elle a perçu l'originalité de la phrase/de la nuance tout de suite), to receive (money) (eg percevoir de l'argent, il est toujours agréable de percevoir des droits d'auteur)

aplanir R3	**aplatir**
to level (eg le terrain); to smooth away (fig, eg les difficultés)	to flatten (eg la pâte)

apparition★ (f)	**parution** (f) (see **2.4**)

apporter★
to bring (eg je t'ai apporté des bonbons)

rapporter
to bring back (NB if the speaker is in the presence of the person addressed, the former would use **rapporter**, eg tu vas à la gare? rapporte-moi le journal, s'il te plaît; otherwise **apporter** would be used)

---

apposer
to affix (eg une plaque au mur)

déposer
to put down, to leave, to drop off, to deposit, to register (eg déposer sa candidature, une gerbe sur une tombe, une personne à la gare; une marque déposée)

disposer
to dispose (eg l'homme propose mais Dieu dispose)

poser
to place (eg un objet), to pose (d'un modèle)

(se)reposer
to rest (eg je ne sors pas ce soir, je me repose); but not reflexive when fig (eg ce principe/cette idée repose sur la proposition suivante) and when the subject is dead (eg le corps reposait dans la chambre mortuaire; see **3.6.5**)

---

approcher★
to approach, to bring nearer (lit and fig, eg approche la chaise, elle approche la quarantaine)

s'approcher
to approach (usu lit and with intention) (eg elle s'est approchée de la porte pour l'ouvrir)

rapprocher
to bring nearer still (lit and fig, eg rapproche la chaise, rapprocher deux idées – NB **approcher** not possible here)

---

apurer
to solve, to discharge (eg une crise, une dette)

épurer
to purge, to purify (eg un parti politique, les eaux d'une rivière)

purger
to purge, to serve (eg les intestins, une peine en prison)

purifier
to purify (eg ô mon Dieu, comment purifier mon âme?; Malherbe purifia la langue française au dix-septième siècle)

---

arc (m)
arc; style, shape of arch, bow (eg l'arc de Robin des Bois)

arche (f)
arch (d'un pont, etc), ark (eg l'arche de Noé)

---

argenté
silver-plated, silvery (couleur)

argentin
silvery (de qualité, son)

---

argument (m) argument supporting idea, fact	**argumentation** (f) line of reasoning, way of arguing (l'argumentation se compose de plusieurs arguments)	
arrivage (m) arrival of goods (often in pl, at the back of warehouses)	**arrivée** (f) arrival of person	
assembler★ to put together (suggesting order and construction) (eg l'auteur a assemblé ses poèmes dans un seul ouvrage; l'enfant a assemblé toutes les pièces de son puzzle)	**rassembler** to collect, to bring together (in a less organised way than **assembler**) (eg je vais rassembler les enfants dans la cour; il faut rassembler tous ces bouquins)	
asservir R3 to enslave, to subjugate (eg une personne, un peuple)	**desservir** to serve town, etc (as with bus, train); to clear away	**servir** to serve person, country
attacher to tie (eg attache le chien avec la laisse)	**rattacher** to connect (eg je ne peux pas rattacher ces deux tuyaux, appelle le plombier)	
attentif paying attention to what is said (eg un enfant attentif)	**attentionné** full of consideration (eg un homme attentionné)	
attractif★ which attracts (eg un prix attractif)	**attrayant** attractive (eg une femme, une maison attrayante; un prix attrayant)	
auprès de near in space (suggests *with*, eg il travaillait auprès de l'ambassade de France; R3 auprès de ma blonde qu'il fait bon dormir), fig (eg j'ai appris la nouvelle auprès de sa sœur))	**près de** near in space (**3.4.4.1**)	
avance (f) military advance; financial advance; **faire des avances** = to make (amorous) advances	**avancée** (f) advance (eg l'avancée des découvertes technologiques); projecting part (eg d'un toit, d'un rocher)	**avancement** (m) career advance; advance of salary

baiser
R3 = to kiss; R1 = to have
intercourse with (indecent)
R1★ = to fuck

baisser
to lower, see above
abaisser

---

balance (f)
balance (eg des
paiements), scales (for
weighing fruit,
vegetables); R1 =
supergrass

balancier (m)
pendulum (eg d'une
pendule)

balançoire (f)
swing (eg au parc)

bascule (f)
platform (for
weighing lorries),
seesaw

---

balle★ (f)
ball (smaller than
ballon, but R1
balle de foot is
common) (**2.2.4**)

ballon (m)
ball; balloon (eg
souffler dans le
ballon = *to take
the breath test*)

boule (f)
ball (eg une
boule de neige,
de pétanque;
jouer aux boules)

boulet (m)
ball (eg un
boulet de canon;
le boulet des
prisonniers =
*prisoners' ball and
chain*)

boulette (f)
small ball (eg
une boulette de
viande, de pain,
de papier)

---

balle (f)
bale (of cotton, merchandise,
etc)

ballot (m)
packet, bundle; R1 = fool

---

banc (m)
bench (often outside,
suggesting a roughness of
style) (eg on va casser la croûte
sur le banc) (except for **le
banc des accusés** = *the dock*,
which is both inside and a
smooth surface)

banquette (f)
bench (usu made of leather
or cloth) (eg on s'est assis sur
une banquette dans le café;
la banquette arrière d'une
voiture)

bans (mpl)
marriage banns (eg afficher
les bans; mettre au ban de la
société = *to ostracise*)

---

baril (m)
small barrel (for wine, oil,
powder)

barrique (f)
barrel (size variable, according
to province, for wine)

barillet (m)
pistol barrel

---

barre (f)
bigger and stronger than
barreau (eg barres parallèles;
une barre de chocolat) (**2.2.2**)

barreau (m)
bar filling a specific space (eg
d'une chaise, d'une fenêtre,
d'une prison, d'une cellule)

---

battre★
to beat (eg Bordeaux
a battu Nantes trois à
zéro)

se battre
(eg les deux garçons
se sont battus dans la
cour; also fig, eg elle
s'est longuement
battue contre la
maladie)

abattre
to cut down, to
knock down, to
shoot down, to put
down (eg abattre un
arbre, abattre à coups
de pistolet, abattre un
chien)

combattre
to fight (eg
combattre au front,
pour la liberté,
contre les inégalités,
la faim, une maladie)

beugler to moo (R1 of a person = to bawl)	**meugler** as beugler	
blockhaus (m) (military) pillbox	**blocus** (m) (economic) blockade	
blouse (f) smock (usu to knees; suggests protection)	**blouson** (m) short jacket (suggests embellishment, eg un blouson d'aviateur = *bomber jacket*, un blouson noir = *rocker*)	
bord (m) edge (eg au bord de la route)	**bordure** (f) edge (eg en bordure de route, de pelouse, d'une robe)	
box (m) lock-up garage (in large community garage), stall (for horses), dock (in court, eg le box des accusés)	**boxe** (f) boxing	
cabane (f) hut (of wood)	**cabanon** (m) habitable cabin (in S of France), garden shed (but this word is slowly disappearing from use)	**cabine** (f) cabin (of ship); call-box (telephone)
calculette (f) calculator	**calculatrice** (f) calculator (small, for pocket) (has more functions than **calculette**)	
camp (m) group of tents (eg un camp itinérant, un camp de colonie de vacances) (but a **camp militaire** does not necessarily consist of tents) (**un camp** is more temporary than **un campement**)	**campement** (m) encampment, suggesting family group (eg gypsies, bedouin)	**camping** (m) camp-site
cantatrice (f) opera singer, etc (no M form)	**chanteur** (m) singer (general)	**chantre** (m) R3 bard (eg **chantre de la Révolution**)
capot (m) bonnet of car	**capote** (f) military great-coat, hooded coat; hood (of car); R1 capote anglaise = *condom*	

capter	**capturer**	**captiver**
to intercept, to receive (as on radio)	to capture	to captivate

capuche (f)	**capuchon** (m)	
hood (of anorak)	monk's hood, hood, top (eg d'une plume)	

caractère (m)	**caractéristique** (f)	
person's character, main feature, character in printing (eg en gros caractères; en caractères gras = in bold)	particular feature	

carnassier	**carnivore**	
flesh-eating (animals, characterised by ferocity)	flesh-eating	

carré (m)	**carreau** (m)	
geometrical square	window pane, tile (eg chemise à carreaux = *check shirt*)	

cavalier	**chevalier**	
horse-rider; also = partner, escort (for dance)	knight; chevalier servant = *escort* (for dance) (NB there is no F form, except chevalière = *signet ring*)	

cave (f)	**caverne** (f)	**caveau** (m)
cellar (eg il a une bonne cave); une cave à vin = *wine store* (this may be above ground, whereas **cave** by itself is below ground)	large, natural cave	sepulchre (eg un caveau de famille (common in French cemeteries))

cerveau (m)	**cervelas** (m)	**cervelle** (f)
intellectual capacity	saveloy	brain (organic)

chaire (f)	**chaise** (f)	
pulpit (eg le prédicateur est monté en chaire), professor's chair	chair (general)	

change (m)	**changement** (m)	
currency exchange (**2.1**)	passing from one state to another	

char (d'assaut) (m)	**chariot** (m)	**charrette** (f)
tank	wagon (in Western films); fork-lift truck; supermarket trolley	farmer's cart

charge (f) load, burden (lit and fig) (eg la charge maximale (for a lorry); j'avais la charge de trois enfants = *charge*)	**chargement** (m) load, cargo, contents (eg le chargement du camion déborde)	
chasser to go hunting, to chase away **(2.2.5.1)**	**pourchasser** to pursue, to chase in order to catch	
se chauffer to warm oneself (eg near the fire) (not necessarily from cold) (eg se chauffer au soleil; on se chauffe au gaz/gazoil)	**s'échauffer** to warm up, to prepare oneself (eg athlete)	**se réchauffer** to warm oneself up (when cold)
chercher to look for (general) (eg je cherche mes lunettes)	**rechercher** to look for (more effort, more formal than **chercher**) (eg la compagnie recherche deux secrétaires; un repris de justice recherché par la police)	
cheveux (mpl) hair (general)	**chevelure** (f) hair (a professional term)	**cheveu** (m) a single hair; R3 = hair (in hairdressing profession)
chute (f) fall (general)	**rechute** (f) relapse (as in illness); error	
cisailles (fpl) shears (for cutting hedge, metal, etc)	**ciseaux** (mpl) scissors	
civil civil (eg un mariage civil)	**civique** civic, civil (eg les droits civiques)	
classement (m) classification (gen) (eg le classement d'hôtels par étoiles; le classement général du Tour de France)	**classification** (f) classification (scientific, suggesting more rigour) (eg la classification d'insectes/ d'oiseaux) (both **le classement/la classification des langues** are found)	
classer to classify (gen)	**classifier** to classify (scientific)	
cloche★ (f) bell; R1 imbecile	**clocher** (m) steeple	**clochette** (f) small bell

coasser (**coassement** (m)) to croak (of frog)	**croasser** (**croassement** (m)) to caw (of crow)	
coffre (m) chest (box), boot of car	**coffret** (m) small, ornate chest, presentation box	
col (m) collar, pass (in mountains)	**collet** (m) trap for small animals	**collier** (m) necklace
combine (f) wangle, wheeze	**combiné** (m) handset (eg un combiné téléphonique), equipment made up of more than one item combined (eg un combiné électroménager = *combined fridge and freezer*)	
composant (m) component, constituent (scientific) (eg un des composants de cet élément est le souffre; les composants de l'eau)	**composante** (f) component, part (eg les composantes d'un parti, d'un raisonnement)	
compréhensible understandable	**compréhensif** inclusive; understanding	
compromis (m) compromise	**compromission** (f) abandonment, compromise (of a principle)	
compter to count (eg tu sais compter jusqu'à dix maintenant?)	**conter** R3 to relate (eg conter un récit)	**raconter** to tell, to relate (eg raconter des histoires = *to tell stories, to tell a load of lies*)
concilier to reconcile (ideas, etc)	**réconcilier** to reconcile (people)	
confiance (f) confidence	**confidence** (f) secret, item of confidence	
congeler to freeze (food) (eg je vais congeler ce poisson)	**geler** to freeze (general, of weather, etc) (eg j'ai les pieds gelés)	**surgeler** to deep freeze (eg le rayon des (produits) surgelés)
conserver to keep in good condition (eg conserver du beurre, des aliments)	**préserver** to protect (eg il faut préserver la nature/les espèces en voie de disparition)	

consommer	**consumer**	
to consume (food and drink), to consummate (a marriage))	to burn, to consume (with passion)	
coquillage★ (m)	**coquille** (f)	
shell (outer part and inside, edible) (eg ramasser des coquillages pour le repas)	shell (outer part), error in typing, shell-shape (eg une coquille de beurre; qu'est-ce qu'il y a comme coquilles dans ces épreuves!)	
cordage (m)	**corde** (f)	**cordée** (f)
ropes, rigging	rope	party of climbers roped together
couler	**s'écouler**	
to flow (water)	to flow, to elapse (time), to flow away (water)	
cour (f)	**cours** (m)	**course** (f)
court, yard (NB faire la cour à qn = *to court sb*)	class (eg in school), school (eg un cours privé, le Cours Dauzat); course of river, course of time (eg l'année en cours)	race (eg une course à pied)
créateur adj	**créatif**	
creative (used only in l'esprit créateur); noun = creator (used only in le Créateur)	creative; inventive (eg enfant/ l'esprit créatif)	
décade (f)	**décennie** (f) R3	
R3 period of 10 days (often = *decade* also)	decade	
dédicace (f)	**dédication** (f)	
handwritten dedication	dedication (of book, monument, etc, general)	
dédicacer★	**dédier**	
to make hand-written dedication in book	to dedicate (book, monument, etc, general)	
défaut (m)	**faute** (f)	
blemish, defect (in machine, etc, failing (in character)	error, misdeed, offence (in sport)	
défectueux	**défectif**	
defective (general)	defective (grammatical term eg un verbe défectif)	

dégagement (m)
clearance (of a ball, in sport),
release (from promise)

désengagement (m)
disengagement (military)

---

dégoûter
to disgust, to sicken (eg cette
puanteur me dégoûte)

dégoutter R3
to drip (of liquid)

s'égoutter
to drip (of crockery, etc)

---

délivrer
(2.2.5.1) to free (eg un
otage), to deliver (eg un
message, une lettre, un
paquet)

livrer
to deliver (eg un colis, un
secret, un meuble)

---

demi-finale (f)
semi-final (in sport)

demi-seconde (f)
half a second

semi-remorque (m)
articulated lorry

semi-remorque (f)
semitrailer

---

dentaire
relating to teeth (eg les études
dentaires, un appareil
(dentaire) = *brace*)

dental
dental (phonetic term)

---

dépasser
to overtake (eg une
voiture); to surpass
(eg les espoirs, les
compétences de qn)

outrepasser
R3 as **surpasser** but
stronger

surpasser
to go beyond (in
most senses)

se surpasser
to go beyond one's
limits (eg se surpasser
en endurance
physique pour un
examen)

---

désert
deserted, uninhabited

désertique
with desert conditions

---

désespérance (f)
R3 despair (literary) (vivre
dans la désespérance = *to live
without faith* (not necessarily
despair))

désespoir (m)
despair (general)
(eg être au désespoir)

---

désintérêt (m)
lack of interest

désintéressement (m)
unselfishness

---

destin (m)
destiny (usu of an individual),
(eg son destin a fait qu'il soit
médecin; le destin d'une
civilisation, de l'humanité,
d'un ouvrage littéraire)

destinée (f)
destiny (more gen than **destin**,
usu of a people rather than
an individual) (eg la destinée
d'une civilisation, de
l'humanité, d'un ouvrage
littéraire)

---

devis (m)
estimate, quotation (for a job
to be done)

devise (f)
foreign currency, slogan,
watchword

dévotion (f)	**dévouement** (m)
devotion (usu religious)	devotion (general)

différence (f)	**différend** (m)
difference	dispute

difforme	**informe**
deformed	shapeless

dormir	**endormir**	**s'endormir**	**se rendormir**
to sleep (general)	to put to sleep	to fall asleep	to go back to sleep

double adj	**double** (m)	**doublé** (m)	**doublet** (m)	**doublette** (f)
double (eg un double avantage, un agent double)	copy (of a page, etc), double (of a person), doubles (in tennis)	double (in sport, eg winning the league and the cup)	doublet (in a language)	pair (of players) (eg en pétanque on joue à deux doublettes)

durcir	**(s')endurcir**
to harden (trans and intrans; more concrete than **endurcir**, suggests hardening of materials (eg soil) and attitudes) (eg la terre, la colle durcit; ils ont durci leur point de vue)	to harden (used largely in abstract sense) (eg elle endurcit sa position; son attitude s'endurcit; l'homme s'est endurci = *the man won't budge*)

éboulement (m)	**éboulis** (m)
landslide in motion	result of landslide

échapper à	**s'échapper de**
to avoid (eg échapper à un danger)	to get out of (eg s'échapper de la maison)

éclairer	**(s')éclaircir**
to give light (lit and fig) (eg éclairer le chemin, une pièce; le critique a éclairé un côté obscur du romancier)	to explain (eg vous pouvez m'éclaircir sur ce point?), to thin (out) (eg éclaircir une sauce; la foule s'éclaircit; elle s'est éclairci la voix = *she cleared her throat*)

économe	**économique**
thrifty (of persons) (m) vegetable/fruit peeler	relating to economics, economical (eg un vol, un voyage, l'essence)

effarant	**effrayant**
bewildering; scary	frightful; terrifying

embûche (f)
ambush (lit and fig), trap
(when fig) (eg un sujet plein
d'embûches)

embuscade (f)
ambush (lit only)

---

emmêler
to mix up, to muddle
(suggesting confusion)
(eg les cheveux
emmêlés)

mêler
to mix up, to muddle
(eg mêler l'eau et le
vin; une personne se
mêle à une affaire)

mélanger
to mix (suggesting
confusion or
homogeneity) (eg
elle mélange ses idées,
tous ses papiers;
mélanger used of a
liquid does not
necessarily imply
confusion)

démêler
to unravel (lit and fig)
(eg démêler ses
cheveux, les fils
d'une intrigue)

---

emplir
R3 to fill

remplir
to fill (general)

---

s'empresser
R3 to hasten

se presser
to hasten

---

enchérir
R3 to go one better (less
common)

renchérir
to go one better

surenchérir
to offer a higher sum

énergique
energetic

énergétique
pertaining to energy (eg la
crise énergétique)

---

enfantin
childlike (with positive or
negative connotations) (eg
mes expériences enfantines;
un langage enfantin; même à
vingt ans il avait un
comportement enfantin)

infantil
relating to childhood (with
positive or negative
connotations) (eg une
maladie infantile; le stade
infantil du développement;
un comportement/un ton
infantil) (**enfantin** and
infantil are often
interchangeable with a
negative connotation)

---

enfermer
R3/2 to shut in

renfermer
to shut in (more effort +
intention), stronger than
enfermer

fermer
to close, to shut (eg tu fermes
la porte, s'il te plaît?)

(s')enfler
to swell (often involuntarily,
eg une jambe, un bras)

(se) gonfler
to swell (often voluntarily,
eg les poumons)

---

entretenir	maintenir	soutenir
to maintain, keep in good condition (eg une voiture; entretenir son corps = *to keep in good condition*)	to maintain, to keep in a fixed position (eg maintenir un point de vue, un niveau, des mesures, une institution; se maintenir en bonne forme = *to keep in good shape*)	to support sth which might fall (lit and fig) (eg une poutre, un argument, une idée) (more effort is required than with **maintenir**)
entretien★ (m)	entrevue (f)	interview (f)
interview (for a job)	R3/2 interview (suggesting sth serious in politics or business) (eg le premier ministre a eu une entrevue avec le Président de la République)	interview (in media, with film star, etc)
envahissement (m)	invasion (f)	
progressive occupation, encroachment (eg l'envahissement du pouvoir central)	brutal, rapid occupation (eg l'invasion de la France en 1940)	
épreuve (f)	preuve (f)	
trial; in pl proofs (d'un livre)	proof (general)	
éruption (f)	irruption (f)	
eruption (eg une éruption de violence, d'un volcan), rash (on skin)	sudden entry or exit (eg elle a fait irruption dans la pièce)	
escadre (f)	escadrille (f)	escadron (m)
squadron in navy	squadron in airforce; flotilla of small ships	squadron in army
espérance (f)	espoir (m)	
hope (more permanent, and philosophical) (eg l'espérance est une grande consolation; l'espérance en Dieu)	hope (more precise) (eg il est très malade, il n'y a plus d'espoir; l'espoir en Dieu)	
éveiller	réveiller	
R3/2 to rouse from sleep	to wake up fully	
exciter★	surexciter	
R3/2 to excite (eg ça les excite, rien qu'à penser à Noël)	to excite (stronger than **exciter**; mainly used in passive) (eg les enfants sont surexcités)	

exhibition (f)
spectacle (of animals or
people)

exposition (f)
exhibition (often suggesting
an artistic event (of objects))
(eg une exposition de
peintures, de voitures)

---

expérience (f)
experience (eg l'expérience
de la vie), experiment

expérimentation (f)
experimentation

---

exploitant
sb who exploits (eg
exploitant agricole)

exploiteur
sb who exploits illegally (eg
un exploiteur d'enfants)

---

facilité (f)
ease

faculté (f)
amenity; university faculty
(**fac** R1)

---

finlandais
m/adj, Finn, Finnish; also =
Finnish (language) (but not
accepted by purists although
more common than **finnois**)

finnois
R3 m/adj, Finn, Finnish
(language)

---

fondation (f)
foundation (lit and fig) (eg les
fondations d'une maison; la
fondation Rockefeller)

fondement (m)
basis, foundation (usu fig) (eg
le fondement de sa pensée)

---

fosse (f)
pit, grave (eg la fosse
commune)

fossé (m)
ditch (eg la voiture est
tombée dans le fossé)

---

fourche (f)
fork (in road, for gardening,
for bicycle front wheel)

fourchette (f)
fork (for eating); range or
margin (statistics)

---

fourgon (m)
large van

fourgonnette (f)
small van

---

froid (m)
cold (general)

froideur (f)
cold temperament (of person)

froidure (f)
R3 coldness of air

---

garde (m)
guard (single person, eg un
garde militaire, un garde
champêtre)

garde (f)
group of guards

gardien (m)
warden, keeper (of prison,
building)

---

gel★ (m)
frost (the natural
phenomenon) (eg les vignes
ont été endommagées par le
gel)

gelée (f)
frost (specific) (eg on a eu
cette nuit une forte gelée)

---

gentilhomme (m) R3 man of noble descent	**gentleman** (m) affected term for *gentleman*	
glacé frozen (lit and fig) (eg la terre, une boisson, la nourriture, la crème glacée; un accueil glacé)	**glacial** icy (usu of wind and weather)	
glisse (f) gliding along (on the ground), skiing (R1) (eg les fanas de la glisse)	**glissade** (f) slide (on ice, etc)	**glissière** (f) as in **porte à glissières** (= *sliding door*)
grain (m) grain; squall (eg un grain de café; NB un grain de beauté = *beauty spot (on face)*)	**graine** (f) seed; bean (eg monter en graine = *to go to seed*)	
grogner to grumble	**grommeler** to mumble, to speak gruffly, inarticulately	
grosseur (f) size; swelling	**grossesse** (f) pregnancy	
groupe (m) group (general) (eg son groupe sanguin)	**groupement** (m) grouping (eg groupement politique)	**groupuscule** (m) R3/2 small political party
guérilla (f) guerrilla war	**guérillero** (m) guerrilla	
hache (f) axe (general)	**hachette** (f) small axe	
histoire (f) story, history (eg un drôle d'histoire; elle étudie l'histoire)	**historique** (m) recounting (eg elle a fait l'historique de l'incident)	**historique** adj historic, historical (eg un record historique)
humeur (f) mood	**humour** (m) humour	
idiome (m) dialect; language; idiom	**idiotisme** (m) idiom	
immeuble (m)	**immobilier**	
real, fixed, of property; each restricted to certain fixed expressions		
(eg biens immeubles/ immobiliers)	(eg sociéte de crédit immobilier = *building society*, agence immobilière = *housing agency*)	

immigrant (m)
immigrant (suggesting in the process of arriving)

immigré (m)
immigrant (more common than **immigrant** as adj, eg les travailleurs immigrés)

---

immobilier
(biens immobiliers = *real estate*, agence immobilière = *estate agent*)

mobilier
(biens mobiliers = *movable / personal effects*; le mobilier = *furniture*)

---

inclination (f)
(fig) action of will

inclinaison (f)
(lit) incline, slope

---

infecter
to infect

infester
to infest

---

influencer
to influence (general)

influer sur
R3 to influence (technical)

---

ingénieux★
ingenious

ingénu
ingenuous

---

ingéniosité (f)
ingenuity

ingénuité (f)
R3 ingenuousness

---

intérêt (m)
interest (general)
(in pl = financial interest from an investment)

intéressement (m)
industrial involvement (eg l'intéressement des travailleurs = *worker participation*)

---

interrogation (f)
question; short written or oral test

interrogatoire (m)
interrogation (by police, etc)

---

isolation (f)
insulation

isolement (m)
isolation

Israélien (m)
Israeli

Israélite (m)
Israelite (biblical)

---

joindre★
to join together, to get (on phone) (eg joindre les mains, les deux bouts = *to make ends meet*; je n'arrivais pas à la joindre au téléphone)

se joindre
to join, to meet up with (eg on se joint ce soir?; il s'est joint au groupe le lendemain matin)

rejoindre
to join, to meet up with (eg je te rejoins dans la matinée; rejoins-moi à 17h) (NB **se joindre** and **rejoindre** both = *to meet people*, but not always in the same context, cf the examples)

---

jour (m)	**journée** (f)	
day (general) (eg ce jour-là on est parti de bonne heure)	day (emphasis on duration) (eg je suis là pour la journée; journée portes ouvertes = *open house*)	

judiciaire	**juridique**
judicial	legal (NB very often the two words are interchangeable: la police, une procédure, une bataille, une enquête, un texte, un système judiciaire; sous contrôle judiciaire :: un avis, un cadre, un problème, une querelle, une décision, une bataille, une interprétation juridique)

labeur (m)	**labour** (m)
R3 labour	ploughing

langage (m)	**langue** (f)
language as means of communication, variety of **langue** (eg le langage des enfants, des mathématiques, de la chimie, de la psychologie)	language of a country, tongue (eg elle parle plusieurs langues; je l'ai sur le bout de la langue; nous avons mangé la langue de bœuf; elle a un cheveu sur la langue = *she lisps*)

lécher	**pourlécher**
to lick (general)	usu restricted to **se pourlécher les babines** (= *to lick one's chops*)

lézard (m)	**lézarde** (f)
lizard (faire le lézard = *to bask in the sun*)	R3/2 crack (in a wall)

lier	**délier**	**relier**
to tie up (eg a parcel)	to untie (lit and fig) (eg le geôlier délia les mains du prisonnier; délier les fils d'une intrigue)	to connect (eg 2 roads)

livre (m)	**livre** (f)	**livret** (m)
book (general)	pound (currency and weight)	small book (eg un livret scolaire, le livret = *bank book*)

| **logement** (m) | **logis** (m) | |
| accommodation | R3 dwelling, R2 les Logis de France = *group of small, family-run hotels* | |

| **luire**★ | **reluire** | |
| to gleam | to shine (suggesting reflection and intensity) (eg on cire une table pour qu'elle reluise/ pour la faire reluire; le soleil/ la lune reluit sur l'eau) | |

| **luxueux** | **luxurieux** | **luxuriant** |
| luxurious (likewise **luxe** (m)) | lecherous (likewise **luxure** (f) = *lust*) | lush (of vegetation) |

| **main d'œuvre** (f) | **manœuvre** (m/f) | |
| manpower, work force | manoeuvre (eg faire une manœuvre en voiture); labourer (**2.2.1**) | |

| **manier** | **manipuler** | |
| to handle deftly (R2 lit eg manier un couteau); (R3 fig eg elle manie bien la langue de Racine, les chiffres) | to handle, using broader movements (R2 lit and fig, eg manipuler un couteau; manipuler une personne = *to manipulate*) | |

| **manque** (m) | **manquement** (m) | |
| lack (eg être en manque de drogue = *to need drugs*; être en manque de vitesse = *to be losing speed*) | failure, weakness | |

| **marais** (m) | **marécage** (m) | |
| marsh | swamp | |

| **matériau**★ (m) | **matériel** (m) | **matière** (f) |
| something one works on | something one works with | matter, substance |

| **maternelle** (f) | **maternité** (f) | |
| nursery school | maternity unit, ward | |

| **matin** (m) | **matinée** (f) | |
| morning (eg j'y irai ce matin) | R2/3 morning (emphasis on duration) (eg j'y irai dans la matinée) | |

| **mentor** (m) | **menteur** (m) | |
| mentor (eg Socrate fut le mentor de Platon) | liar | |

mess (m) officers' mess	**messe** (f) mass (religious)
meuble (m) item of furniture	**mobilier** (m) suite of furniture, furniture in general
mitraillette (f) sub–machine gun	**mitrailleuse** (f) machine gun
moral (m) moral (adj), morale (eg ça va, le moral? = *how're you feeling?*) morals (**2.2.5.1**)	**morale** (f) morality, moral (eg morale de de l'histoire – ne pas bousculer le travail) (**2.2.5.1**)
musée (m) museum (general)	**museum** (m) natural history museum
natif★ native, coming from (eg je suis natif de Marseille)	**natal** native (eg ma ville, ma langue, ma maison natale; mon pays natal)
négatif (m) photo negative	**négative** (f) negative (eg répondre à la négative)
nettoiement (m) cleaning (eg le service du nettoiment, le nettoiement des rues, d'un plancher)	**nettoyage** (m) cleansing, dry cleaning, washing (eg le nettoyage ethnique, le nettoyage par le vide, à sec, du linge)
nommer to nominate, to appoint	**nominer** to nominate (for an award) (eg nominer pour un Oscar, un César (French equivalent of an Oscar))
nounou (f) nanny	**nounours** (m) teddy bear

nuage (m) cloud (general), touch (eg un nuage de lait)	**nuée** (f) R3 large cloud (suggesting a content, eg hail, locusts)	**nues** (fpl) R3 clouds (limited to certain expressions) (eg porter qn aux nues = *to praise sb to the skies*, tomber des nues = *to arrive out of the blue*)
offensant offensive (of a remark)	**offensif** (adj) offensive (military)	**offensive** (f) offensive (eg offensive militaire)

offenser R3 to offend (personally)	**offusquer** R3 to offend (personally)

officiel (m) official (representing authority)	**officier** (m) (military, etc) officer

officiel official (eg de source officielle)	**officieux** semi-official, officious (eg de source officieuse)

offrande (f) offering, with religious connotation	**offre** (f) offer (general) (eg l'offre et la demande = *supply and demand*)

oppresser R3 to upset (lit and fig) (eg l'asthme l'oppresse, une angoisse l'oppressait)	**opprimer** to oppress with violence (eg un régime qui opprime ses citoyens)

originaire★ coming from (a place) (eg elle est originaire de Besançon)	**original** peculiar, unusual (but **original** seems to be extending its meaning to cover that of **originel**, eg le sens original, le texte original)	**originel** going back to the origins (eg le péché originel, le sens originel, le texte originel)	**d'origine** original (used of anything mechanical) (eg la pièce d'origine)

os (m) bone of man, animal	**ossature** (f) frame (eg l'ossature du corps), framework (lit and fig) (eg l'ossature d'un cours, d'un programme, d'un ouvrage)	**ossements** (mpl) bones of dead person

paie★ (f) pay (monthly)	**paiement** (m) a single payment (for a specific purpose)

palace (m) luxury hotel	**palais** (m) palace

paraître to seem (eg il paraît que = *it seems*)	**apparaître** to appear physically (but il apparaît = *it seems*)	**comparaître** to appear (in court of law)

part (f) share, portion	**parti** (m) party (political, etc) (NB parti pris = *bias, prejudice*)	**partie** (f) part of a whole (**2.2.2**)

partial biassed	**partiel** partial, incomplete

pénalité (f) penalty (in rugby) (eg transformer une pénalité = *to* *convert a penalty*)	**penalty** (m) penalty (in football) (NB *penalty shootout* = tirs au but)
peser to weigh with machine	**soupeser** to estimate weight
pétrolier related to oil (adj), oil-tanker (noun)	**pétrolifère** oil-bearing (strata, etc)
photographe (m) photographer	**photographie** (f) photo
plier to bend (general)	**ployer** R3 to bend (more formal)
plongée (f) dive below surface (eg une plongée sous–marine)	**plongeon** (m) dive from a height (eg in diving competition)
point (m) dot, speck (eg un point à l'horizon)	**pointe** (f) sharp point (lit and fig) (eg une pointe d'ironie)
poitrail (m) breast or chest of animal	**poitrine** (f) female breast (bosom), chest (of human being)

politicien (m) politician (st pejorative, but this value is disappearing)	**politique** (m) politician (**2.2.1**)	**politique** (f) politics, policy	**politologue** (m/f) political commentator

porteur (m) porter, investor (eg un petit porteur = *small investor*)	**portier** (m) doorman, gatekeeper
poule (f) hen (eg ça me donne la chair de poule = *that makes my flesh* *creep*; ma poule! = *ducky!*)	**poulet** (m) chick, chicken when eaten
préjudice (m) moral injury, wrong	**préjugé** (m) bias, prejudice

préparatifs (mpl) (only in pl)	**préparation** (f)

no clear distinction, although former more general than latter,
eg les préparatifs du mariage (= all the work concerned with
organising a wedding); la préparation au mariage (meeting(s)
with the priest before the marriage); la préparation du budget,
d'un plat, la préparation à la vie professionnelle

prévision (f)	**prévisionnel**	**provision** (f)	**provisoire**
forecast (eg la prévision météorologique)	planning for the future (eg coût prévisionnel)	provision, supply (eg un sac à provisions)	provisional

problème (m)	**problématique** (f)
problem (more precise and concrete than **problématique**) (eg partir aujourd'hui? – ça me pose un problème; le problème de la drogue; les problèmes sociaux)	series of issues (eg il existe toute une problématique à l'égard de nos rapports avec certains pays africains)

procédé (m)	**processus** (m)	**procès** (m)	**procédure** (f)
technique	process	trial (in law)	procedure

proche★	**prochain**	**prochain** (m)
near (lit and fig) (eg le village le plus proche; dans un proche avenir)	near, next (eg le prochain village)	neighbour (eg il faut aider son prochain)

prodige	**prodigue**
prodigious, prodigy (eg un enfant prodige)	prodigal (eg l'enfant/le fils prodigue)

programme (m)	**programmation** (f)
programme (eg un programme à la télévision, à la radio)	programme listings, planning

prolongation (f)	**prolongement** (m)
act of prolonging beyond normal time (eg la prolongation d'un congé, jouer les prolongations = to play extra time)	increase in length (eg le prolongement d'une rue); consequences (eg les prolongements d'une affaire)

pudibond	**pudique**
easily shocked, prudish	modest, chaste

rabattre	**rebattre**
to fold down, to reduce (eg une chaise)	to hit again (eg rebattre les oreilles à qn = to repeat)

radier	**rayer**
usu to cross off name on list (stronger than **rayer**)	to scratch, to score, to cross off name on list, to cross out (eg attention! tu vas rayer la table; rayer la mention inutile)

radoucissement (m)
softening of mood, voice;
movement towards milder
weather

redoux (m)
movement towards milder
weather

---

raie (f)
streak (general), parting in
hair, skate (fish) (eg un tissu
à raies)

rayure (f)
stripe (not wider than **raie**)
(eg une chemise à rayures)

---

raisonner
to reason, to make sb see
reason

résonner
to resound, to reverberate

---

rang★ (m)
row, rank (eg des soldats en
rang, les élèves se mettent en
rang = *in lines*)

rangée (f)
row (eg une rangée de
chaises, d'arbres, de carottes,
de salades, de vignes)

rangement (m)
putting away, tidying up (eg
le rangement du linge dans
une armoire)

---

reconstituer
to reform, to reconstitute
(more abstract than
reconstruire) (eg reconstituer
un crime, un dossier)

reconstruire
to rebuild (a house)

---

reconstitution
reconstruction, reshaping
(eg la reconstitution de la
vérité, d'un parti politique)

reconstruction
rebuilding (of a house)

---

recouvrer
R3/R2 to recover (eg
recouvrer son calme)
(**2.2.5.2**)

recouvrir
to recover, to cover again (eg
elle a recouvert l'enfant avec
une couverture)

---

refléter★
to reflect (lit and fig R3/R2)
(eg le soleil se reflète sur l'eau;
l'eau reflète le soleil; son
visage reflétait la joie)

réfléchir
to reflect at a certain angle (lit
R3/R2 and fig R2) (eg le soleil
se réfléchissait sur l'eau; l'eau
réfléchissait le soleil; laisse-
moi réfléchir un moment)

---

reformer
to re-form (eg soldiers' ranks);
to reshape (more concrete
than **réformer**)

réformer
to change sb's ideas, etc with
view to improvement; to
discharge a soldier
prematurely for health or
other reasons

régler	**régir**	**réglementer**	**régulariser**
to regulate, to adjust (eg machine)	R3 to rule, to govern	to make rules for	to regularise, to put into order (eg passport)

remplacer	**replacer**
to put sth in the place of sth else	to put back in place

renom (m)	**renommée** (f)
renown (less common than **renommée**) (eg le renom de d'Ecole Normale Supérieure)	renown (eg ce restaurant a une bonne renommée)

renoncement (m)	**renonciation** (f)
renunciation (eg son renoncement au projet)	R3 renunciation

repartir	**répartir**
to leave (once more) (eg il est arrivé pour repartir tout de suite)	to share out, to distribute (eg elle a réparti la cagnotte parmi toute la famille)

répons (m)	**réponse** (f)
R3 response (in church liturgy)	answer

résonner★	**sonner**
to reverberate, to ring out (suggesting an echo) (eg les pas résonnaient dans le couloir)	to ring (trans and intrans) (eg les cloches sonnent; Quasimodo sonnait les cloches)

(se) ressentir	**(se) sentir**
to feel (usu of emotions, intimate feelings) (eg dans son for intérieur, elle ressentait un profond mécontentement)	to feel (general but often physical, as with blow) (eg il sentit un violent coup sur la nuque)

restaurer	**restituer**
to repair (eg il a acheté cette vieille maison avec l'intention de la restaurer); to restore (eg le roi a été restauré au trône)	to restore to original state, to return (eg restituer une fresque, une toile, un texte; la police lui restitua tous les objets cambriolés)

retrait (m)	**retraite** (f)
withdrawal (of troops, not necessarily forced); withdrawal (eg faire un retrait dans une banque; le retrait d'un permis de conduire)	retreat (of troops, forced); religious retreat; pension, retirement (eg prendre sa retraite)

réunir★
to gather together (usu
suggesting an original
dispersal) (eg il a réuni tous
les étudiants, les documents;
la famille s'est réunie en fin
de semaine)

unir
to unite, to join together (eg
unir un pays; le prêtre a uni le
jeune couple = *married*)

---

rivage (m)
shore (eg le rivage de la mer)

rive (f)
bank (eg la rive d'un fleuve)

---

roc (m)
rock, the substance (eg le roc
de l'île était tellement dur
que . . .)

roche (f)
a stone, a rock (of granite,
chalk, etc with a geological
connotation) (eg creuser la
roche; il y a anguille sous
roche = *I smell a rat*)

rocher (m)
large rock (on mountain),
rock (on sea-shore) (eg les
enfants s'amusaient parmi les
rochers au bord de la mer)

---

roman
Romanesque/Norman
architectural style

romain
Roman (eg en chiffres
romains)

---

séculaire
century-old (eg une église
séculaire)

séculier
secular (eg des instances
ecclésiastiques ou séculières)

---

sécurité★ (f)
security, safety (although
interchangeable at times,
sécurité is more common
than **sûreté**) (eg la sécurité
routière; pour des raisons de
sécurité; la Sécurité Sociale;
une soupape de sécurité)

sûreté (f)
security, safety (eg une
soupape de sûreté; la sûreté
de l'Etat)

---

séducteur★
charming, attractive,
seductive (sometimes
suggests active and wilful
seduction) (eg ses paroles
séductrices; elle exerçait un
pouvoir séducteur sur le
jeune homme) (it may also be
used as a noun, eg la loi doit
protéger les mineurs contre
de tels séducteurs)

séduisant
charming, attractive (eg le
livre a une couverture
séduisante; elle a une grâce/
beauté séduisante)

---

sensé
possessing good sense

sensible
sensitive; perceptible

---

serveur (m)
waiter, server (in computing and tennis)

serviteur (m)
R3 servant, valet (eg votre très humble serviteur (at close of letter))

---

soir (m)
evening (eg on sort ce soir)

soirée (f)
evening (emphasis on duration); evening party (eg nous rentrerons tard dans la soirée)

(en) suspens
suspense (final *s* not pronounced) (eg son habileté à tenir le lecteur en suspens; la question reste en suspens)

suspense (m)
suspense (eg Hitchcock est le maître du suspense) (NB pronounced more or less as in English)

---

taper★
to knock (violently), to type (eg il l'a tapé si fort sur l'épaule qu'il est tombé par terre; taper à la machine)

tapoter
to tap (eg sa mère tapotait doucement l'enfant sur l'épaule)

---

teindre
to tint (hair, etc); to dye (eg teindre le linge)

teinter
to tinge (fig and lit), to tint (eg une philosophie teintée de pessimisme; les lunettes teintées)

---

teint (m)
colour/complexion (of face) (elle a le teint pâle, frais, éclatant)

teinte (f)
colour produced by mixing several colours; hue (eg les teintes de l'automne)

---

terrain★ (m)
piece of land (eg un terrain de foot = *pitch*; un terrain à construire)

terre (f)
land, earth (world and soil) (eg la terre est détrempée; elle possède d'immenses terres; sauter à terre; tomber par terre; la Terre = *planet Earth*)

terroir (m)
homeland (eg ce vin-là me donne le goût du terroir)

---

toit (m)
roof (eg il y a un chat sur le toit)

toiture (f)
roofing (ie roof + supports) (eg toute la toiture s'est écroulée pendant la tempête)

---

tombe (f)
grave, (eg être muet comme une tombe)

tombeau (m)
tomb (more imposing than **tombe**, suggests monument, often for family) (eg le tombeau familial)

---

tourment (m)	**tourmente** (f)
torment	R3 storm (lit and fig), upheaval, turmoil

tourner	**se tourner**	**retourner**	**se retourner**
to turn (eg une page; tourner à droite et à gauche)	to turn (of person)	to turn over (eg earth), to turn back (eg ils sont retournés à la maison)	to turn right round, to turn right over (eg la voiture a heurté le trottoir et s'est complètement retournée)

triomphal	**triomphant**
triumphal (of things) (eg une entrée triomphale; un accueil/un succès triomphal)	triumphant (of persons) (eg il est sorti triomphant de l'épreuve)

trou (m)	**trouée** (f)
hole, gap (eg tu as un trou dans ton pantalon; ce golf a dix-huit trous)	hole (in hedge, wall, wood) (eg tout le monde est passé par la trouée dans le mur)

val (m)	**vallée** (f)	**vallon** (m)
R3 large valley (restricted use eg Val de Loire)	valley (general)	small valley

valable	**valide**
valid (more common than **valide** in this sense) (eg votre raisonnement n'est pas valable; ce passeport est valable; une objection valable)	valid, able-bodied (eg tous les hommes valides sont priés de . . .), R3 = *valid* (eg une proposition/une suggestion valide)

veille (f)	**veillée** (f)	**réveillon** (m)
eve, day before; watch, vigil (eg la veille de Noël; à la veille de la Révolution russe)	staying up at night after evening meal (eg la veillée de Noël)	late night supper, celebration; Christmas Eve, New Year's Eve (eg ils ont passé le réveillon près de la Place de la Concorde)

vénéneux	**venimeux**
poisonous to eat (eg des champignons vénéneux)	capable of injecting poison (un serpent/un insecte venimeux), R3 fig (eg tenir des propos venimeux; une langue venimeuse)

vers (m)	**verset** (m)
line of poetry	verse in Bible

vigne (f)	**vignoble** (m)
vine (plant)	vineyard

vitrail (m)	vitre (f)
stained glass window (eg les vitraux d'une église)	pane of glass (eg attention! tu vas casser la vitre; baisse la vitre de la voiture, s'il te plaît)
vomissement (m)	vomissure (f)
action of vomiting	R3 what is vomited (usu pl)
voyageur (m)	voyagiste (m/f)
traveller (eg les voyageurs sont priés de regagner le car)	tour operator (eg consulter votre voyagiste pour des renseignements complémentaires sur la croisière)

2.4   Synonyms and words with related meanings

Every word in a language is connected to other words by a series of relationships, based particularly upon similarities of meaning and oppositeness of meaning. In this section attention is focused upon synonyms – words which are more or less equivalent to each other in meaning – and words which, while not being exact synonyms, are nonetheless linked to each other by a similarity of meaning. In order to present this aspect of the vocabulary as simply and clearly as possible, a series of tables, representing broad concepts or groups of closely-related objects, are used. The words or items are organised in the tables, first of all, according to their register, descending from the highest to the lowest and, secondly, within each register division, in alphabetical order. Accompanying the meanings in the second column are a number of indications of contexts in which the words or items commonly occur and collocations which they regularly form. Examples are provided in the third column. A fuller discussion and justification of this approach and additional synonymic families are to be found in the authors' *Using French Synonyms* (Cambridge University Press, 1992).

être d'accord

R3 agréer	to accept with approval (usu in letters) (trans)	veuillez agréer, madame, l'expression de mes sentiments les meilleurs
R3 convenir de	to agree to	les divorcés sont convenus de vendre la maison; elle a raison, j'en conviens, mais . . .
R2 être d'accord	to agree to	ils étaient d'accord pour partir aux Etats-Unis
R2 s'accorder	to agree, to suit	les deux gouvernements se sont accordés à respecter le cessez-le-feu; l'adjectif s'accorde avec le nom; votre cravate s'accorde bien avec votre chemise

R2 **tomber d'accord**	to agree to	ils tombaient d'accord pour partir en Afrique

aider

R3 **assister** R2 when passive	to assist (usu suggesting charitable intention)	la religieuse a assisté le malade dans ses derniers moments; le médecin était assisté de deux infirmiers
R2 **aider**	to help	j'ai aidé mon fils à faire ses devoirs
R2 **venir en aide à**	to come to the help of	'Médecins sans frontières' vient en aide aux réfugiés
R2 **secourir**	to help in danger (used in infin and pp only)	le SAMU (= Service d'assistance médicale d'urgence) a secouru les accidentés du carambolage
R2/1 **donner un coup de main à**	to give sb a hand	tu me donnes un coup de main au jardin ce matin?

amoureux (m)

R3 **bien aimé/aimée**	sweetheart	il/elle a envoyé un billet-doux à sa/son bien aimée/aimé
R2 **amant** (m)	lover (extramarital)	George Sand eut plusieurs amants au cours de sa vie
R2 **amoureux** (m)	sweetheart	'les amoureux qui se bécotent sur le banc public' (song by Georges Brassens); alors, les amoureux, vous sortez ce soir?
R2 **maîtresse** (f)	lover, mistress	c'est un drôle de coco, il a plusieurs maîtresses
R2 **petit ami** (m)	boyfriend	ton petit ami peut venir dîner ce soir
R2 **petite amie** (f)	girlfriend	alors, tu sors avec ta petite amie ce soir?
R2/1 **copain** (m)	boyfriend	elle est partie en week-end avec son copain
R2/1 **copine** (f)	girlfriend	sa copine aime aller aux discos, mais lui préfère les bars

apparition (f)

R3/2 **éruption** (f)	(sudden) appearance (fig)	une éruption de joie/de colère
R2 **apparition** (f)	(sudden) appearance	son apparition subite a surpris tout le monde; les catholiques croient à l'apparition de la Vierge Marie à Lourdes

R2 **comparution** (f)	appearance (in court, before a judge, etc)	sa comparution devant le tribunal; en cas de non-comparution vous risquez un mois de prison
R2 **entrée** (f)	entry	dès son entrée, tout le monde s'est levé
R2 **éruption** (f)	(sudden) appearance, outbreak	le petit a une éruption de boutons – il faut consulter le toubib

appeler

R2 **appeler**	to call (tr and intr)	tu m'appelles ce soir?; papa est au jardin, appelle-le; ça s'appelle comment, ce truc?
R2 **convoquer**	to summon officially	j'ai convoqué les candidats pour quatorze heures trente
R2 **héler**	to hail	héler un taxi
R2 **hurler**	to scream	elle hurlait de douleur
R2 **interpeller**	to call suddenly (tr) (of police)	plusieurs jeunes ont été interpellés par la police
R2 **rappeler**	to call back (on telephone)	rappelle-moi cet après-midi, je serai dans mon bureau
R1 **gueuler**	to bawl	arrête de gueuler, tu vas réveiller tout le monde

s'approcher

R2 **aborder**	to approach (with intention) (trans; lit and fig)	il m'a abordé dans la rue et m'a dit que . . .; elle a abordé le délicat sujet de leurs fiançailles
R2 **approcher**	to approach (trans; lit and fig)	approche la chaise, svp; elle approche la quarantaine
R2 **approcher de**	to approach (NB difference from **rapprocher**)	la voiture approchait de sa destination
R2 **s'approcher**	to approach (with intention) (tr)	elle s'est approchée de la porte
R2 **avancer**	to approach with intention (often used with a group or of a queue) (lit and fig)	elle a avancé vers lui d'un pas; avancez, svp; elle a avancé un argument incontournable

R2 s'avancer	to approach (with intention) (tr) (same as **s'approcher**, **avancer**)	elle s'est avancée vers lui
R2 **rapprocher**	to approach, to bring together, to unite (tr, lit and fig)	rapproche la chaise, svp; rapprocher ces deux idées est absurde

NOTE: the contrasts of reflexive–non-reflexive, transitive–intransitive, literal–figurative with this group of verbs.

argent (m)

R2 **argent** (m)	money	tu peux être idéaliste si tu veux, mais il te faut toujours de l'argent
R2 **cash** (m)	cash	tu paies cash, ils te font une ristourne
R2 **devises** (fpl)	(foreign) currency	la carte Visa, c'est pratique à l'étranger, mais il te faut toujours des devises
R2 **monnaie** (f)	small change	je prends un café à la machine – tu as de la monnaie?
R1 **fric** (m) **sous** (mpl) **pèze** (m) **pognon** (m)	dough	je peux pas aller au restau, j'ai plus de fric/de sous/de pèze/de pognon

attrayant

R2 **alléchant**	attractive, appetising	une suggestion/une proposition alléchante
R2 **appétissant**	appetising (food), tasty	un repas appétissant
R2 **attirant**	attractive (similar to **attractif**)	un endroit/un pays attirant
R2 **attractif**	attractive (similar to **attrayant**, but not used of a woman)	ce caméscope-là a un prix attractif; un voyage attractif
R2 **attrayant**	attractive	une femme/une maison attrayante; un voyage/un endroit/un pays/un prix attrayant; un cadre de vie attrayant
R2 **captivant**	captivating	un roman captivant; une histoire captivante
R2 **provocant**	provocative	un regard/un comportement provocant

R2 **séducteur**	seductive, which seduces (sexual)	elle le dominait avec un pouvoir séducteur
R2 **séduisant**	attractive	un aspect séduisant; une couverture/une femme séduisante
R2 **succulent**	succulent, tasty	des mets succulents; un repas succulent
R1 **appétissant**	appetising, tasty (fig)	une femme appétissante
R1 **succulent**	succulent, tasty (fig)	une femme succulente

augmenter

R3 **croître**	to grow (of plants) (intr) (only third person sg and pl)	les plantes/les mauvaises herbes croissaient en abondance
R2 **accroître**	to increase (trans) (only certain parts of this verb are used: infin, pp, imperfect, third person sg and pl)	elle a accru sa fortune en héritant d'une vaste propriété
R2 **s'accroître**	to increase (intr) (see **accroître** for usage)	la population s'est accrue de vingt mille habitants en cinq ans
R2 **agrandir**	to make bigger, to extend	ils ont l'intention d'agrandir leur maison
R2 **augmenter**	to increase	les prix ont augmenté de 10 pour cent; augmenter les salaires/le nombre d'élèves/la quantité de maisons
R2 **grandir**	to grow up, to grow tall (intr)	qu'il a grandi, le petit!
R2 **pousser**	to grow (intr)	tondre le gazon encore une fois? un peu de pluie et ça pousse
R2 **faire pousser**	to grow (tr) (but not fruit, which would be **cultiver**)	il fait pousser pas mal de légumes/de plantes/d'arbres; il a fait pousser sa barbe

balle (f)

R2 **balle** (f)	small ball	une balle de tennis
R2 **ballon** (m)	large ball, balloon	un ballon de foot; est-ce que les frères Montgolfier ont créé le premier ballon?
R2 **bille** (f)	marble	allez, les enfants, on joue aux billes?

R2 **boule** (f)	small ball, usu solid, bowl	une boule de billard/de cristal/de neige; t'as un jeu de boules?
R2 **boulet** (m)	cannon ball, large marble	un boulet de canon/de prisonnier; les enfants jouaient avec des boulets
R2 **boulette** (f)	small ball, usu of compressed material	les garçons balançaient des boulettes de pain/de poisson/de viande par la fenêtre
R2 **pelote** (f)	ball of wool, ball for game of **pelote**	une pelote de laine; faire sa pelote = *to make one's pile (money)*
R1 **balle** (f)	ball (for football)	une balle de foot

banlieue (f)

R2 **abords** (mpl)	outskirts (of town)	les abords des grandes villes sont souvent laids
R2 **alentours** (mpl)	surrounding area (see **environs**)	j'habite dans les alentours de Paris/de Nantes; je n'ai pas visité le centre de Bordeaux mais les alentours
R2 **banlieue** (f)	suburbs (around town)	ils habitent en banlieue; un train de banlieue
R2 **environs** (mpl)	surrounding area (same as **alentours**, but more common)	j'habite dans les environs de Paris/de Nantes; un petit village dans les environs d'Angers
R2 **faubourg** (m)	suburb (less common than **banlieue**; used of Paris)	le faubourg St Germain/Montmartre
R2 **zone** (f)	outer deprived area	pour rien au monde je n'habiterai ce quartier, c'est la zone

bateau (m)

R2 **barque** (f)	small rowing boat	on va faire une promenade en barque cet après-midi
R2 **bateau** (m)	boat	tu viens avec nous faire un petit tour de bateau?
R2 **bâtiment** (m)	large ship (as in navy)	un bâtiment de guerre
R2 **canoë** (m)	canoe	tu as les pagaies pour le canoë?
R2 **canot** (m)	small rowing boat	on a fait une partie de canot hier matin
R2 **embarcation** (f)	any small craft	toutes les embarcations ont quitté le port pour saluer le navigateur

R2 **ferry(boat)** (m)	ferry	la guerre des prix est rude entre le shuttle et les ferries
R2 **navire** (m)	ship	un navire de guerre/de commerce/de plaisance
R2 **paquebot** (m)	cruise liner	traverser l'Atlantique en avion est rapide, mais une croisière en paquebot est plus agréable
R2 **pétrolier** (m)	tanker	les pétroliers continuent à dégazer en mer, en dépit de la loi
R2 **vaisseau** (m)	large ship, vessel	plusieurs vaisseaux ont appareillé pour aider les milliers de réfugiés
R1 **rafiot** (m)	old boat	partir en mer dans un rafiot comme ça? jamais de la vie!

other boats: **bananier** (m) = banana boat, **catamaran** (m), **négrier** (m) = slave ship, **planche à voile** (f) = windsurfer, **trimaran** (m)

bâtiment (m)

R2 **bâtiment** (m)	building	ils veulent rénover ce bâtiment en maison d'habitation
R2 **bâtisse** (f)	building (st = **bâtiment**; st suggests old and broken down)	quelle belle bâtisse!; ils viennent de démolir cette vieille bâtisse
R2 **construction** (f)	construction, building (suggesting function)	il y a plusieurs constructions autour du parc
R2 **édifice** (m)	building (suggesting good quality or official)	le roi fit construire plusieurs édifices près de la rivière
R2 **immeuble** (m)	large building (in town, of several storeys)	mon père vient d'acheter un appartement au quatrième étage d'un immeuble près de la gare
R2 **local** (m)	premises	les locaux du parti socialiste ont été réhabilités
R2 **monument** (m)	monument	on va faire demain le tour des monuments à Paris

se battre

| R2 **agresser** | to mug | elle a été agressée dans la cage de l'ascenseur |

R2 **se battre**	to fight	il a un œil au beurre noir, ils se sont battus dans la cour; elle s'est battue avec sa meilleure copine
R2 **combattre**	to fight (in a group) (lit and fig)	les gladiateurs combattaient dans les arènes; je combats toutes les idées extrémistes
R2 **lutter**	to struggle (intr) (lit and fig)	lutter contre une idéologie; elle a lutté contre le cancer de toutes ses forces

billet (m)

R2 **billet** (m)	ticket (has cultural associations, except for plane!; compare **ticket**)	un billet de cinéma/de théâtre/d'opéra; un billet d'avion
R2 **bulletin** (m)	slip, report	un bulletin de paie/de vote/scolaire/médical
R2 **étiquette** (f)	tab, price tag	tu as vu le prix sur cette étiquette?; l'enfant a mis son nom sur une étiquette
R2 **fiche** (f)	slip, card	une fiche de renseignements
R2 **récépissé** (m)	receipt (has administrative connotation; a slip you sign for, as with postman)	j'ai signé le récépissé et la factrice m'a donné le colis
R2 **reçu** (m)	receipt	il me faut un reçu pour me faire rembourser
R2 **ticket** (m)	ticket (utilitarian; compare **billet**)	un ticket de bus/de train/de métro; un carnet de tickets

blesser

R2 **blesser**	to hurt (lit and fig)	elle s'est blessée au bras; il l'a blessé dans son amour-propre
R2 **léser**	to harm (fig)	le partage n'étant pas équitable, je m'estime avoir été lésé; léser les intérêts d'une personne
R2 **faire (du) mal à**	to hurt (lit and fig)	ne saute pas, tu vas te faire (du) mal; la nouvelle de leur divorce m'a fait (du) mal
R2 **nuire à**	to hurt (more formal than **blesser, faire (du) mal à**; lit and fig)	le tabac nuit beaucoup à la santé; cet acte nuit à ses intérêts

bouchée (f)

R2 **bouchée** (f)	mouthful (lit (of solid food) and fig)	allez, mon petit, il ne te reste qu'une bouchée à avaler; une bouchée de pain; faire les bouchées doubles = *to work really hard*
R2 **gorgée** (f)	mouthful (of liquid)	elle a bu son lait à petites gorgées
R2 **lapée** (f)	mouthful (of liquid)	il a terminé son assiette de soupe à grandes lapées

NOTE: whereas English would use *mouthful* for all three French words, they are distinct in French.

briller

R2 **briller**	to shine	le soleil brille; ses yeux brillaient de convoitise
R2 **chatoyer**	to shimmer (usu suggesting movement)	la soie/l'eau chatoie; un diamant chatoyait à son doigt
R2 **étinceler**	to sparkle (usu of light)	les étoiles étincellent; astiquez-moi tout ça, je veux que ça brille, que ça étincelle!
R2 **flamboyer**	to flash, to blaze	l'incendie de forêt flamboyait à l'horizon
R2 **luire**	to shine (with one's/its own light)	le soleil luit; la transpiration faisait luire sa peau
R2 **miroiter**	to reflect light	ébloui par la mer qui miroite
R2 **pétiller**	to sparkle	ses yeux pétillaient d'intelligence
R2 **reluire**	to shine (after polishing, not like **luire**)	l'argenterie/le cuivre reluit; les casseroles reluisent; rien de tel pour faire reluire l'argenterie
R2 **resplendir**	to shine, to beam	le soleil resplendit; son visage resplendissait de bonheur
R2 **scintiller**	to shine intermittently, to twinkle, to sparkle, to glisten	les étoiles scintillent; ses yeux scintillaient; des gouttes d'eau scintillaient dans ses cheveux

brouillard (m)

R2 **brouillard** (m)	fog (lit and fig)	le *Titanic* a violemment heurté un iceberg à cause du brouillard; je suis dans le brouillard
R2 **brume** (f)	mist	la brume s'élevait lentement au petit matin; la corne de brume = *foghorn*

| R2 **buée** (f) | steam (on window, etc) | mes lunettes sont couvertes/pleines de buée |
| R2 **embrun** (m) (usu pl) | sea–spray | le visage du pêcheur était couvert d'embruns |

bureau (m)

R2 **bureau** (m)	office, study	veuillez vous présenter au bureau numéro cent dix; elle a demandé à l'étudiant d'aller la voir dans son bureau; j'ai passé toute la journée dans mon bureau à corriger des copies
R2 **cabinet** (m)	office, surgery	un cabinet d'avocat/de dentiste/de docteur
R2 **cabinet d'étude** (m)	office	le cabinet d'étude d'un architecte/d'un notaire

casser

R3 **rompre**	to break (lit only) (see below)	rompre un morceau de pain; la corde a rompu
R3 **se rompre**	to break (lit only) (see below)	la chaîne s'est rompue; tu vas te rompre le cou
R3/2 **briser**	to break, to shatter (lit only) (see below)	briser un/du verre; des voyous ont brisé la vitrine du magasin
R3/2 **se briser**	to break, to shatter (lit only) (see below)	mes lunettes se sont brisées sous le choc; le miroir s'est brisé en mille morceaux
R3/2 **fracturer**	to break (violently)	fracturer une porte/une serrure; les cambrioleurs ont fracturé le coffre-fort
R3/2 **se fracturer**	to break (violently)	il s'est fracturé la jambe; son bras s'est fracturé dans l'accident
R2 **briser**	to break (fig only)	elle a le cœur brisé; le départ de son fils lui a brisé le cœur; nos espoirs de le voir libéré sont brisés
R2 **se briser**	to break (fig only)	nos espoirs de le voir libéré se sont brisés
R2 **casser**	to break (lit only)	il a cassé son jouet; la corde a cassé
R2 **se casser**	to break (lit only)	il s'est cassé la jambe; l'assiette s'est cassée
R2 **fracasser**	to shatter, to smash	je vais te fracasser la mâchoire

R2 **rompre**	to break, to break off (fig only)	ils ont rompu leurs fiançailles; les relations diplomatiques ont été rompues; on est sorti ensemble pendant deux ans et puis on a rompu
R1 **casser**	to break up (fig only)	ils vivaient ensemble, mais ça a cassé

chaise (f)

R2 **banc** (m)	bench (much rougher than **banquette**; usu found outside)	les amoureux s'assirent sur un banc au parc
R2 **banquette** (f)	seat, bench (often upholstered)	une banquette de piano; la banquette arrière d'une voiture
R2 **bergère** (f)	wing chair	see **voltaire**
R2 **canapé** (m)	sofa	je vais m'étendre sur le canapé
R2 **escabeau** (m)	stool (often at a bar), small stepladder	elle a pris l'escabeau pour atteindre les casseroles
R2 **fauteuil** (m)	armchair	qu'est-ce qu'il est confortable, ce fauteuil!
R2 **selle** (f)	saddle	j'arrive pas à rester en selle (d'un cheval); les coureurs du Tour de France passent des heures sur la selle
R2 **siège** (m)	seat, the actual part for sitting on, see (ecclesiastical)	attention, le siège est mouillé; un siège éjectable; le Saint Siège; elle passe des heures sur le siège (du wc) à lire son journal
R2 **strapontin** (m)	foldaway seat (formerly common on buses and in cinemas and theatres; still used on Paris Métro)	on voit rarement des strapontins de nos jours, question de sécurité
R2 **trône** (m)	throne; toilet	le petit est sur le trône
R2 **voltaire** (m)	upright armchair	les voltaires et les bergères sont toujours très recherchés

chemin (m)

R2 **artère** (f)	main road (in a big town)	les grandes artères de la ville sont très fréquentées aux heures de pointe
R2 **autoroute** (f)	motorway	pendant les vacances les autoroutes sont encombrées

R2 **axe routier** (m)	main road (linking towns)	évitez les grands axes routiers à cause des grands départs en vacances
R2 **bretelle (d'accès)** (f)	slip road	je n'ai pas trouvé la bretelle d'accès pour l'autoroute
R2 **chaussée** (f)	roadway, carriageway	ne reste pas dans la chaussée, tu vas te faire renverser; il faut entretenir la chaussée pour les voitures, autrement il y aura des nids de poule
R2 **chemin** (m)	road, way (leading somewhere)	ce chemin ne mène nulle part; c'est là le chemin de Niort?
R2 **passage** (m)	way, path, road	passage interdit; les deux rues étaient reliées par un petit passage; ils se sont frayé un passage dans la foule
R2 **périphérique** (m)	ring road (not only in Paris, as originally, but also in other large towns, such as Nantes)	je suis passé par le périphérique pour éviter la circulation
R2 **rocade** (f)	ring road	la rocade est beaucoup plus pratique, elle évite les embouteillages aux heures de pointe
R2 **route** (f)	road (often main road linking towns)	demande à ce monsieur la route vers la montagne/la route de Cannes
R2 **rue** (f)	road, street	la rue est trop étroite pour le passage des voitures
R2 **ruelle** (f)	lane, alley	les petites ruelles de la vieille ville
R2 **voie** (f)	route, way	une voie privée; les grandes voies de communication reliant les capitales européennes
R2 **voie express** (f)	dual carriageway	la voie express rive gauche; les deux quartiers sont reliés par une voie express
R1 **périf** (m)	= **périphérique**	

cloche (f)

R2 **bourdon** (m)	large church bell	le bourdon de la cathédrale
R2 **cloche** (f)	bell	la cloche a sonné sept fois
R2 **clochette** (f)	small bell	réveille-toi, j'entends la clochette du steward (dans un bateau)

R2 **grelot** (m)	small bell (for dog, goat, sleigh, etc)	si vous campez dans le Massif Central vous entendrez les grelots des brebis/des vaches
R2 **sonnette** (f)	small bell, hand bell, door bell	Maman, j'ai entendu la sonnette
R2 **timbre** (m)	small bell (with striking hammer, for bicycle, etc)	quand j'étais jeune, j'avais un timbre de bicyclette

colline (f)

R2 **ballon** (m)	rounded-top hill, mountain (especially in the Vosges)	le ballon de Guebwiller
R2 **butte** (f)	small hill	au milieu de la plaine se dressait une butte avec un château dessus; j'habitais près des Buttes Chaumont quand j'étais à Paris
R2 **colline** (f)	hill	au loin se voyaient des collines boisées
R2 **côte** (f)	slope (up or down) (often associated with vines, eg **les Côtes du Rhône**)	il montait la côte à vélo et transpirait à mi-côte (= *half-way up the hill*)
R2 **coteau** (m)	small hill	les coteaux étaient couverts de vignes
R2 **descente** (f)	downward slope, descent	la descente est dangereuse pour un vélo
R2 **montée** (f)	upward slope, ascent, rise (lit and fig)	c'était une courte étape avec de nombreuses montées (dans le cyclisme); contrairement à ce que l'on pense, une descente est plus difficile qu'une montée (dans l'alpinisme); la montée des eaux; la montée des prix
R2 **raidillon** (m)	short steep hill	ce raidillon est plus dur que je ne le pensais

combustible (m)

R2 **alcool à brûler** (m)	methylated spirits	pour amorcer mon réchaud à pétrole j'utilisais de l'alcool à brûler
R2 **bois** (m)	wood	à la campagne ils se chauffent encore au bois
R2 **brut** (m)	crude oil	à combien s'est élevé le baril de brut?
R2 **carburant** (m)	liquid fuel, petrol	le prix du carburant monte sans cesse
R2 **charbon** (m)	coal	la première tâche de l'instituteur était d'allumer le poêle à charbon
R2 **combustible** (m)	combustible fuel	le combustible nucléaire

R2 **diesel** (m)	diesel	le diesel a toujours été moins cher en France
R2 **électricité** (f)	electricity	on dit que l'électricité est plus chère que le gaz
R2 **courant** (m)	(synonym for) electricity	on a une coupure de courant
R2 **essence** (f)	petrol	un moteur/une pompe à essence; il faut que je prenne de l'essence
R2 **fioul/fuel** (m)	oil (for central heating) (former spelling more common)	on se chauffe au fioul
R2 **gaz** (m)	gas	maintenant, nous, on se chauffe au gaz
R2 **huile** (f)	oil (for lubrication, cooking)	cuisiner à l'huile d'olive; je garde toujours un bidon d'huile dans le garage
R2 **mazout** (m)	= **fioul/fuel**	on se chauffe au mazout, mais ça pue
R2 **pétrole** (m)	unrefined oil, paraffin	des gisements de pétrole; un réchaud à pétrole (= *paraffin stove*)

ne pas tenir compte de

R3 **faire abstraction de**	to ignore	faire abstraction des propos de Mme la directrice, c'est risqué
R3 **passer sous silence**	to ignore	passer sous silence les propos de M. le proviseur, c'est risqué
R3/2 **ignorer**	not to know	j'ignore la date de son retour
R2 **ne pas tenir compte de**	not to take into account	elle n'a pas tenu compte des conseils qu'on lui avait donnés
R2 **ignorer**	to ignore (sb)	il m'a ignoré toute la soirée
R2 **négliger**	to ignore	elle a négligé les consignes de sécurité
R2 **omettre**	to omit	elle a omis son nom sur la copie

concours (m)

R2 **compétition** (f)	competition (usu sporting)	une compétition sportive
R2 **concours** (m)	competitive examination, competition	un concours hippique/de cartes/de boules/d'échecs; pour avoir un poste permanent dans le secteur public/pour être fonctionnaire, il faut avoir le concours (CAPES/agrégation pour l'enseignement)

R2 **concurrence** (f)	rivalry, competition (in commerce)	le nouveau supermarché va faire concurrence aux petits commerçants; la concurrence européenne
R2 **rivalité** (f)	rivalry	la rivalité entre les deux coureurs cyclistes fut intense

coquillage (m)

R2 **carapace** (f)	shell (of insect, tortoise, etc)	la carapace d'un insecte/d'une tortue
R2 **coque** (f)	shell (of nut)	la coque d'une noix
R2 **coquillage** (m)	shell (outer and inner parts)	ramasser des coquillages
R2 **coquille** (f)	shell (outer part)	la coquille d'un œuf
R2 **écaille** (f)	shell (of oyster), scale (of fish)	l'écaille du crocodile/de l'huître

couper

R2 **couper**	to cut (lit (but not lawn, see **tondre**) and fig)	couper le pain/l'herbe; elle m'a coupé la parole; il m'a coupé l'herbe sous les pieds; je vais me faire couper les cheveux; couper la gorge à une personne
R2 **découper**	to cut out, cut up	découper un article dans le journal; découper de la viande
R2 **élaguer**	to prune	les arbres sont un peu longs, il faut les élaguer
R2 **entamer**	to cut into, to start (eg loaf of bread)	tu peux prendre ce pain-là, il est déjà entamé; elle a entamé le livre/sa conférence
R2 **sectionner**	to cut through (sth metallic, eg cable)	l'avion a sectionné le câble du téléphérique
R2 **tailler**	to cut, to trim (eg rosebush, hedge)	tailler les rosiers/la haie du jardin; il s'est taillé la barbe
R2 **tondre**	to cut closely (eg hair, lawn)	papa a fini de tondre la pelouse/le gazon
R2 **trancher**	to slice (lit, eg loaf of bread), to decide (fig)	les terroristes ont tranché la gorge aux soldats; on ne va pas rester indécis, il faut trancher

cueillir

R2 **assembler**	to put together (eg pieces; suggesting order)	il a assemblé toutes les pièces du mécano pour faire une tour
R2 **cueillir**	to pick (eg fruit)	cueillir des fruits/des raisins/des champignons
R2 **ramasser**	to pick, to gather (eg mushrooms), to pick up (eg stones), to tidy up	en automne on ramasse des champignons en forêt; allez, ramasse tes affaires avant de partir
R2 **rassembler**	to collect, to bring together	la prof a rassemblé tous les élèves dans la cour
R2 **recueillir**	to gather together (eg poems)	l'auteur a recueilli ses poèmes dans un seul ouvrage

délit (m)

R2 **attentat** (m)	bomb outrage	un attentat à la bombe
R2 **cambriolage** (m)	burglary	ils ont été victimes d'une douzaine de cambriolages ces dernières années
R2 **chantage** (m)	blackmail	contrairement à ce que tu penses, le chantage est un délit sérieux
R2 **contravention** (f)	breaking of any kind of rule or law (eg traffic) (often the result of breaking the law)	tu brûles les feux et tu es en contravention
R2 **crime** (m)	crime (suggesting sth more serious than the English word)	elle a été condamnée à trente ans de prison pour son crime; commettre un crime
R2 **délit** (m)	crime (more serious than **infraction**)	le délit d'adultère/de vol/de cambriolage; elle a été prise en flagrant délit
R2 **enveloppe** (f)	bribe	en échange de la signature du contrat, le député avait reçu plusieurs enveloppes
R2 **forfait** (m)	serious, heinous crime	commettre/expier un forfait; il a commis d'affreux forfaits
R2 **fraude** (f)	fraud	la fraude fiscale
R2 **homicide (involontaire)** (m)	manslaughter	elle a été condamnée à trois ans de prison pour homicide involontaire
R2 **infraction** (f)	breaking of the law	commettre une infraction à la loi/au règlement

R2 **pot-de-vin** (m)	bribe	les pots-de-vin sont monnaie courante dans certains pays
R2 **sévice sexuel** (m) (usu pl)	child abuse	il a été accusé de sévices sexuels
R2 **viol** (m)	rape	les étudiantes sont armées d'une alarme pour se protéger contre le viol
R2 **vol** (m)	theft, robbery	j'ai souscrit une assurance contre le vol; le vol à la tire; le vol à main armée

discours (m)

R2 **allocution** (f)	short formal speech	une allocution télévisée du Président de la République
R2 **causerie** (f)	talk, chat	ils organisent une causerie autour de son dernier ouvrage
R2 **conférence** (f)	special lecture	la prof donne une conférence sur Proust en amphi A
R2 **cours** (m)	lesson in class	ses cours sur l'histoire sont passionnants; j'ai cours ce matin à dix heures
R2 **discours** (m)	formal speech	le premier ministre a prononcé un discours sur l'Union Européenne
R2 **oraison** (f)	speech at funeral	Malraux prononça une oraison funèbre pour le transfert des cendres de Jean Moulin au Panthéon
R2 **topo** (m)	talk	Pierre va faire un topo sur son séjour aux USA
R1 **laïus** (m)	spiel	elle a fait tout un laïus sur son voyage en Afrique
R1 **speech** (m)	aggressive telling off, lecture	le proviseur nous a fait tout un speech sur notre comportement au lycée

donner

R3 **conférer**	to confer	en vertu des pouvoirs qui me sont conférés (*an official expression*)
R3/2 **octroyer**	to grant	on lui a octroyé une prime exceptionnelle/une semaine de congé supplémentaire

R2 **accorder**	to grant	accorder un droit/une faveur/une interview/de l'importance à qn/qch; on lui a accordé une dérogation
R2 **attribuer**	to attribute, to award	ce morceau est attribué à Telemann; elle a attribué à chacun la part qui lui revient
R2 **décerner**	to bestow	le jury lui a décerné le premier prix
R2 **donner**	to give	je vous donne ma parole d'honneur; tu·peux me donner un coup de main?
R2 **remettre**	to hand in, to hand over	l'étudiante lui a remis sa traduction
R2 **valoir**	to earn, to bring	qu'est-ce qui me vaut leur visite?; cela m'a valu quelques compliments
R1 **filer**	to slip, to hand, to dish out	elle m'a filé du fric/une baffe

échouer

R3 **faillir à**	to fail (intr), to break (one's word), not to keep	elle a failli à son devoir/à sa parole
R3 **faire défaut**	to be lacking	je ne puis écrire l'article, les documents me font défaut
R2 **échouer à**	to fail (intr) (eg an exam)	elle a échoué au bac; le recordman a échoué dans sa tentative de battre son propre record
R2 **manquer à**	to fail (intr), to break, not to keep	elle n'a pas manqué à sa parole/à sa promesse/à ses engagements
R2 **manquer de**	to lack (intr)	le petit ne boit pas assez de lait, il manque de calcium
R2 **ne pas manquer de**	not to fail to	ne manquez pas de venir; je ne manquerai pas d'envoyer la lettre
R2 **ne pas réussir à**	to fail (tr and intr)	elle n'a pas réussi au bac; *also* elle n'a pas réussi son bac; je n'ai pas réussi à gagner le prix
R1 **flancher**	to fail, to give way (intr)	lorsque le coeur flanche, ce n'est pas toujours la fin ces jours-ci

école (f)

R2 **cours** (m)	private institution (often religious; usu accompanied by a proper name)	elle assiste au Cours Prétôt; en ville les cours privés sont très chers
R2 **collège** (m)	school (for 11 to 15 year olds)	après le collège, j'irai au lycée Victor Hugo
R2 **école** (f)	primary school (for 6 to 11 year olds)	à partir de six ans, tous les enfants vont à l'école
R2 **école libre**	private primary school	c'est une famille très catholique, ils envoient leurs enfants à une école libre
R2 **lycée** (m)	(nearest equivalent) comprehensive school	le lycée Henri Quatre à Paris a un énorme prestige
R2 **lycée professionnel** (m)	school offering vocational training (of quite advanced level)	si tu vas au lycée professionnel, tu suivras des cours en atelier
R2 **(école) maternelle** (f)	nursery school	la plupart des tout petits vont à la/en maternelle
R1 **bahut** (m)	school	tu enseignes dans quel bahut, toi?
R1 **boîte** (f)	school	qu'est-ce que tu penses des profs de ta boîte?

employé de maison (m)

R2 **bonne** (f)	maid (with literary connotation)	dans les anciennes familles on avait des bonnes
R2 **domestique** (m/f)	servant (with literary connotation)	dans les anciennes familles on avait des domestiques
R2 **employé de maison** (m)	servant	il est employé de maison chez les Durand
R2 **femme de chambre** (f)	chambermaid (in private house or hotel)	beaucoup d'immigrés travaillent comme femmes de chambre dans les hôtels
R2 **femme de ménage** (f)	cleaning lady	mon épouse a un emploi exigeant, on a donc embauché une femme de ménage
R2 **garçon** (m)	waiter	garçon, une bière s'il vous plaît!
R2 **homme d'entretien** (m)	helper, odd job man	je ne suis jamais à la maison, heureusement que nous avons un homme d'entretien
R2 **jardinier** (m)	gardener	le jardin a plus de trois mille mètres carrés, il faut absolument embaucher un jardinier

R2 **servant/ servante** (m/f)	servant	la plupart des familles bourgeoises au XIXe siècle avaient des servants/servantes
R2 **serveur** (m)	waiter (in restaurant)	appelle le serveur, le vin n'est pas bon
R2 **sommelier** (m)	wine waiter	pour le vin, il faut faire confiance au sommelier
R1 **bonniche** (f)	maid (pej)	la bonniche n'a pas encore passé la serpillière
R1 **larbin** (m)	servant, flunkey (pej)	je ne suis pas son larbin

endroit (m)

R2 **emplacement** (m)	site (of church, school, etc)	ils cherchent un emplacement pour un nouveau parking/restaurant
R2 **endroit** (m)	place	je ne voudrais pas vivre dans un endroit pareil, c'est trop près d'une usine
R2 **lieu** (m)	place	on va passer nos vacances en Dordogne, c'est un lieu charmant
R2 **localité** (f)	precise district, village	Peyrat-le-Château est une localité en Limousin
R2 **parages** (mpl)	area, place, vicinity	je ne trouve pas un supermarché dans les parages
R2 **place** (f)	space, room, seat (in theatre, etc), position	il y a une place pour ma voiture sur le parking?; il y a encore des places au théâtre?; à ta place, j'y irais demain
R2 **site** (m)	site (of church, school, etc)	c'est un site touristique très fréquenté; un site archéologique

ennuyer

R3 **importuner**	to trouble, to bother	j'en ai assez d'être importuné tous les jours par les représentants de commerce
R3 **incommoder**	to inconvenience, to make (sb) feel uncomfortable	ce bruit/cette chaleur/cette odeur m'incommode
R2 **contrarier**	to annoy (suggesting sudden upset)	le retard de sa fille l'a contrarié
R2 **déranger**	to disturb	prière de ne pas déranger; ne dérange pas ta maman, tu vois bien qu'elle est occupée
R2 **embêter**	to trouble, to annoy	arrête d'embêter ta sœur!

R2 **ennuyer**	to trouble, to bore	cela m'ennuierait d'arriver en retard; c'est un professeur qui ennuie ses étudiants chaque fois qu'il ouvre la bouche
R2 **gêner**	to trouble, to get in the way	est-ce que ça vous gêne si je fume?; enlève cette chaise – elle me gêne
R2 **tracasser**	to bother (less strong than **gêner**)	tout de même, ça me tracasse qu'elle n'ait pas encore téléphoné
R1 **énerver**	to get on (sb's) nerves	qu'est-ce qu'il m'énerve, à traîner comme ça!
R1 **enquiquiner**	to get on (sb's) nerves	ça enquiquine un peu, mais ce n'est pas grave
R1 **taper sur les nerfs à qn**	to get on sb's nerves	ça me tape sur les nerfs, ce genre de disque
R1★ **casser les couilles à qn**	to give sb a pain in the arse	il me casse les couilles à vouloir me doubler
R1★ **faire chier**	to give (sb) a pain in the arse	ça me fait chier de les voir ensemble
R1★ **emmerder**	to give (sb) a pain in the arse	elle m'emmerde avec ses histoires
R1★ **foutre les boules/les glandes à qn**	to give sb a pain in the arse	ça m'a foutu les boules/les glandes de la voir avec lui

enseignant (m)

R2 **directeur/ directrice** (m/f)	headteacher (of **école maternelle**/**primaire**)	un directeur/une directrice a des tâches administratives de plus en plus pressantes
R2 **enseignant** (m)	teacher	les enseignants ont plus de vacances que leurs homologues anglais; la grève des enseignants
R2 **instituteur/ institutrice** (m/f)	primary school teacher (now being replaced by **professeur d'école**)	les instituteurs/institutrices sont progressivement remplacés/remplacées par les professeurs d'école
R2 **maître d'école** (m)	primary school teacher (disappearing)	le maître d'école joue un rôle important dans *Le Grand Meaulnes* d'Alain Fournier
R2 **maîtresse** (f)	school mistress (mainly used as title)	qu'est-ce que tu as fait avec la maîtresse aujourd'hui?
R2 **principal** (m)	headteacher (of **collège**)	le principal préside les conseils de classe en collège

R2 **professeur** (m)	teacher (from secondary level onwards, male or female)	pour avoir un poste permanent le professeur doit avoir le concours
R2 **proviseur** (m)	headteacher (of **lycée**)	le proviseur doit organiser la répartition des salles d'examen au lycée
R1 **instit** (m/f)	primary school teacher	il est instit au village
R1 **prof** (m/f)	teacher	il est mon/elle est ma prof de maths/de chimie

enseigner

R3 **professer**	to teach	elle professait le latin dans un cours privé
R3/2 **former**	to train (child, pupil)	elle s'est formée à l'ENA (=Ecole Nationale d'Administration)
R2 **apprendre**	to teach	on lui a appris l'anglais dès son plus jeune âge
R2 **éduquer**	to educate	ils ont mal éduqué leurs enfants
R2 **élever**	to bring up	ils font de leur mieux pour élever leurs enfants, mais tu les as vus dans la rue?
R2 **enseigner**	to teach	qu'est-ce que tu enseignes? j'enseigne les arts plastiques; elle enseigne la physique aux étudiants en classes préparatoires
R2 **instruire**	to instruct	ils instruisent leurs enfants à la maison et ne les envoient pas à l'école

entretien (m)

R3/2 **entrevue** (f)	interview (suggesting a formal situation)	le premier ministre a eu une entrevue avec le Président de la République
R2 **entretien** (m)	interview (usu word for job interview)	pour obtenir ce poste-là il m'a fallu me présenter à l'entretien
R2 **interview** (f)	interview (usu in journalism and radio)	le chanteur a accordé une interview aux journalistes
R2 **tête-à-tête/ tête à tete** (m)	interview (with a literary connotation) (invariable in pl.)	ils se sont retrouvés en tête à tête pendant une heure; la dame rêvait de tendres têtes-à-têtes avec son ami

essayer

R3 **s'efforcer à**	to strive to, to strive for	elle s'est efforcée à l'aider; il s'efforce à l'abstinence
R3 **s'évertuer à**	to strive	c'est ce que je m'évertuais à t'expliquer
R2 **s'efforcer de**	to strive to	devant les autres, elle s'efforçait d'être sérieuse
R2 **essayer de**	to try to	tais-toi, j'essaie de regarder la télé
R2 **faire de son mieux pour**	to do one's best to	elle a fait de son mieux pour élever quatre enfants toute seule après le décès de son mari
R2 **tâcher de**	to try (same as **essayer**, but of slightly higher register)	je tâcherai de venir ce soir avant 19h
R2 **tenter de**	to attempt to (often suggesting possible failure; less common than **tâcher**)	j'ai déjà tenté de lui en parler à plusieurs reprises; je vais tenter ma chance = *I'm going to try my luck*

examiner

R2 **analyser**	to analyse	le médecin a analysé les résultats; le professeur analyse le sujet
R2 **contrôler**	to check (often with an official connotation)	les véhicules doivent être régulièrement contrôlés; les services de police contrôlent l'afflux des étrangers à la frontière
R2 **examiner**	to examine (book, patient etc; *not* a candidate)	examiner des documents/des papiers; il a examiné le patient dans son cabinet
R2 **faire passer un examen à un étudiant**	to examine a student	phew! ce matin on fait passer l'épreuve orale aux étudiants
R2 **vérifier**	to check	le technicien vérifie l'état de la machine/des pneus

facture (f)

R2 **addition** (f)	bill (in restaurant)	le consommateur doit payer l'addition à la caisse

R2 **facture** (f)	invoice	les factures arrivent souvent à la fin du mois; le garagiste m'a présenté une grosse facture à payer
R2 **note** (f)	bill (in restaurant, for doctor, etc)	mon ami a payé la note au restaurant; je n'ai pas encore payé la note du médecin
R2 **quittance** (f)	bill (for water, gas, electricity, etc)	les quittances d'eau/d'électricité/de gaz et de loyer arrivent en même temps
R2 **traite** (f)	account with tradesman	le fournisseur a réclamé la dernière traite à son client

fermier (m)

R2 **agriculteur** (m)	farmer (suggesting profession, replacing **fermier**; grows fruit and vegetables, rears animals)	l'Union Européenne réglemente le travail des agriculteurs à travers la Politique Agricole Commune (PAC)
R2 **cultivateur** (m)	farmer (fruit and vegetables but no animals)	les cultivateurs ont déversé tous leurs produits sur la chaussée pour protester contre la décision du gouvernement
R2 **fermier** (m)	farmer	le fermier commence sa journée par la traite des vaches
R2 **laboureur** (m)	person ploughing or cultivating land	le laboureur commence son travail à l'automne
R2 **maraîcher** (m)	market gardener	le maraîcher prend soin de ses plantes et de ses arbres fruitiers
R2 **métayer** (m)	tenant farmer	le métayer travaille dur pour régler le loyer à son propriétaire
R2 **paysan** (m)	farmer (low social class)	les paysans quittent de plus en plus la campagne
R2 **vigneron** (m)	wine grower	le vigneron cultive vingt hectares de vignes

feu (m)

R2 **embrasement** (m)	large fire (lit and fig)	l'embrasement de la broussaille a été anéanti par les pompiers; l'embrasement du pays s'est traduit par des émeutes quotidiennes
R2 **feu** (m)	fire (lit and fig)	le pyromane a mis le feu à la forêt; il n'y a pas le feu (= *there's no rush*)

R2 **flambée** (f)	flare-up (usu fig)	la flambée des prix/de la colère
R2 **incendie** (m)	large fire (causing damage)	un incendie s'est déclaré sous les combles de l'immeuble

figure (f)

R3 **face** (f)	countenance, face (often in set expressions)	il y a eu face à face à la télévision entre les deux hommes politiques; elle a été photographiée de face et de profil
R2 **figure** (f)	face	sa figure est aussi belle que son corps; il a reçu un coup en pleine figure
R2 **tête** (f)	face (as opposed to head)	elle a une tête sympathique; une sale tête; sa tête ne me revient pas = *I can't place him/her*
R2 **visage** (m)	face (lit and fig)	cet institut de beauté est spécialisé dans les soins de visage; il a un visage long/allongé/agréable; le visage du capitalisme/de la justice
R1 **binette** (f)	mug	elle a une drôle de binette, celle-là
R1 **bouille** (f)	mug	elle a une bonne bouille = *she's good looking*
R1 **gueule** (f)	mug (the R1 words are not easily interchangeable)	attention ou je te casse la gueule; il a une sale gueule; il a une grosse gueule = *he shouts a lot*

file (f)

R2 **file** (f)	row (of people, trees, etc) (occ fig)	une file de voitures/de clients; il n'y a pas de place – je me mets en double file; un chef de file (d'un parti politique)
R2 **ligne** (f)	row (of soldiers, trees)	une ligne de soldats/d'arbres/de vignes/de carottes
R2 **rang** (m)	row (of soldiers, lettuce, beans)	des soldats en rang; les élèves étaient en rangs dans la classe
R2 **rangée** (f)	row (of soldiers, chairs, bottles)	des rangées de carottes/de vignes/de soldats

fille (f)

R2 **demoiselle**(f)	female (up to 25 years)	elle a engagé une demoiselle de vingt ans dans son entreprise

R2 **fille** (f)	girl (until married), daughter	il n'y avait que des filles de vingt ans au bal; une vieille fille (= *spinster*); j'ai une fille de 30 ans
R2 **jeune fille** (f)	girl (from 15 to 25 years)	jeune fille cherche du travail dans le secrétariat (*in a newspaper*)
R2 **petite fille** (f)	girl (up to 12 years)	elle avait l'air d'une petite fille alors qu'elle avait seize ans
R2 **jeune femme** (f)	female (up to 30 years)	entra une jeune femme ravissante qui portait un beau tailleur
R2 **gamine** (f)	girl, daughter	il y avait une gamine au magasin qui pleurait, je sais pas pourquoi; je vais chercher ma gamine à l'école
R1 **gonzesse** (f)	chick, bird	la gonzesse a du toupet
R1 **nana** (f)	chick, bird	la nana a du toupet
R1 **nénette** (f)	chick, bird (the most *chic* of the R1 words)	c'est une belle nénette

fleuve (m)

R3 **ru** (m)	rivulet, brook	j'entendais tout près le clapotement d'un ru
R3 **ruisselet** (m)	rivulet, brook	j'entendais tout près le clapotement d'un ruisselet
R2 **cours d'eau** (m)	river	tous les cours d'eau sont secs après la sécheresse de l'été dernier
R2 **fleuve** (m)	large river	la Loire est un fleuve long d'au moins huit cents kilomètres; quel est le fleuve le plus long du monde?
R2 **rivière** (f)	river	la rivière serpentait parmi les arbres
R2 **ruisseau** (m)	stream	un ruisseau souterrain alimentait le lac

gel (m)

R2 **gel** (m)	frost (the phenomenon in general)	le gel est un phénomène climatique; le grand gel de l'hiver de cinquante-cinq est mémorable
R2 **gelée** (f)	frost (specific)	une forte gelée; la gelée de cette nuit a endommagé les cerisiers

R2 **givre** (m)	hoar frost, white frost (on trees, windows), frost (eg in refrigerator)	le givre du matin a couvert les pare-brises de la voiture
R2 **verglas** (m)	ice, black ice (on road)	attention au verglas sur la route

goinfre

R3 **cupide**	greedy (usu for money) (usu fig)	lorsqu'il s'agit de gagner de l'argent, il est cupide
R2 **avide**	greedy (lit and fig), eager	les yeux avides, elle pensait au banquet du soir; il est avide de voyages
R2 **glouton**	greedy (stronger than **gourmand**)	il est tellement glouton, c'est presque une maladie
R2 **goinfre**	greedy (= **glouton**)	quand il voit une table bien garnie il devient goinfre
R2 **goulu**	greedy (= **glouton**, but st with comic connotation)	le regard goulu, il s'est rué vers la table chargée de mets délicats
R2 **gourmand**	appreciative of good food (rather than greedy)	elle est très gourmande avec le chocolat

grand

R2 **colossal**	colossal (lit and fig)	après un effort colossal ils sont arrivés en haut de la montagne; une tâche colossale
R2 **démesuré**	inordinately large (usu fig)	elle a pris des dispositions démesurées; il a une ambition démesurée
R2 **énorme**	enormous (lit and fig)	le catcheur était énorme, au moins deux cents kilos; fournir un effort énorme/un énorme effort
R2 **grand**	big (usu implying height or importance; lit and fig)	c'est un grand gaillard de deux mètres; elle est un grand écrivain/une grande cantatrice
R2 **gros**	big (implying volume, weight; lit and fig)	il était tellement gros, qu'il avait des difficultés à enfiler son pantalon; elles sont grosses, ces pommes de terre; il a retiré une grosse somme d'argent
R2 **immense**	immense (lit and fig)	le terrain était immense; le travail qui reste à faire est immense

R2 **monumental**	monumental	elle a commis une erreur monumentale
R2 **volumineux**	voluminous, bulky, very large	le chargement (=*load on lorry*) était volumineux

impôt (m)

R2 **contributions** (fpl)	tax	les taxes locales font partie des contributions diverses
R2 **impôt** (m)	tax	l'impôt sur le revenu a tendance à augmenter; il est impossible d'éviter de payer des impôts, qu'ils soient directs ou indirects
R2 **prélèvement fiscal** (m)	tax paid at source	le prélèvement fiscal représente une part primordiale du budget de l'Etat
R2 **taxe** (f)	tax (on goods)	la taxe sur les véhicules est très élevée; à l'aéroport on peut acheter quantités d'articles hors taxe; encore une taxe!; la TVA = taxe à la valeur ajoutée

jambe (f)

R2 **cuisse** (f)	thigh, leg (of poultry etc)	elle s'est fait mal à la cuisse en tombant
R2 **gigot** (m)	leg of lamb	le gigot d'agneau est succulent
R2 **jambe** (f)	leg	elle s'est cassé la/une jambe, elle ne peut plus marcher
R2 **patte** (f)	leg (of animal), paw	ne laisse pas entrer le chien – il a les pattes sales
R1 **gambette** (f)	leg (usu of female, suggesting shapeliness)	elle a de belles gambettes, cette nana
R1 **guibolle** (f)	leg (of human; less attractive than **gambette**)	ses guibolles sont tellement minces qu'on se demande comment il fait pour se tenir debout
R1 **patte** (f)	leg (of human)	pourquoi tu rampes à quatre pattes?

jeter

R2 **jeter**	to throw	ne jette pas les déchets par la fenêtre

R2 **lancer**	to throw (suggesting more distance and precision than **jeter**; used in athletics)	il a lancé une pierre sur le chien; elle a lancé le javelot/le disque/le poids très loin
R1 **balancer**	to chuck	elle a balancé de l'eau sur la tête de son copain
R1 **bazarder**	to chuck (usu sth old) away	il a bazardé son vieux meuble
R1 **virer**	to chuck away (lit), to chuck out (fig)	prends ces livres-là et vire-les; il ne travaille pas bien – il faut le virer

joindre

R2 **intégrer**	to join, to get into	elle a intégré l'entreprise à vingt-cinq ans; j'ai intégré l'université de Princeton l'année dernière; intégrer une association/un club
R2 **joindre**	to join together (persons, things), to talk to (on the telephone)	elle a joint les deux parties du puzzle; je n'arrive pas à la joindre par téléphone; joindre les deux bouts (= *to make ends meet*) n'est pas si simple que ça
R2 **se joindre à**	to join, to meet up with	on est parti le matin et ils se sont joints à nous vers midi
R2 **réintégrer**	to rejoin, to return to	il a réintégré son régiment/le lieu/le lycée
R2 **rejoindre**	to join, to meet up with	si tu pars maintenant, je te rejoins plus tard
R2 **rencontrer**	to meet	j'ai rencontré ton frère dans la rue
R2 **réunir**	to gather together (eg people)	on a réuni toute la famille pour les obsèques
R2 **unir**	to join together (things, people)	le prêtre les a unis par le mariage

lac (m)

R2 **bassin** (m)	artificial lake or pond (as in garden)	le bassin d'eau est tellement grand qu'ils peuvent y pratiquer la planche à voile; le petit bassin du jardin public est dangereux pour les tout petits
R2 **étang** (m)	large pond (much larger than **mare**)	l'étang encourage les touristes à camper; tu as visité l'Etang de Berre près de Marseille?
R2 **lac** (m)	lake	les enfants se baignaient dans le lac; as-tu vu le Lac d'Annecy/du Bourget?

R2 **mare** (f)	pond (eg in village)	la mare attire les canards du village; j'ai lu récemment *La Mare au diable* de George Sand

se lever

R2 **se lever**	to get up	elle s'est levée à sept heures
R2 **s'élever**	to rise up (eg smoke)	la fumée s'élevait lentement dans le ciel
R2 **se soulever**	to rise (from a low level with effort)	il était étendu par terre et s'est soulevé péniblement

lointain

R2 **distant**	distant (lit and fig)	les deux villages sont distants d'une centaine de kilomètres; elle est si distante que je ne lui ai jamais parlé
R2 **éloigné**	far away, far removed (lit and fig)	la poste est éloignée de la place du village; il reste éloigné de ma position
R2 **lointain**	distant, far away (lit and fig)	le sommet de la montagne est encore lointain; j'adore les pays lointains; à une époque lointaine
R2 **reculé**	isolated, far off (lit and fig)	c'est un coin reculé du site touristique; à une époque reculée les choses étaient différentes

magasin (m)

R2 **boutique** (f)	stylish shop (eg for clothes)	la boutique de vêtements a fermé très rapidement par manque de clients
R2 **centre commercial** (m)	shopping centre	le centre commercial comprend une cinquantaine de magasins et même deux restaurants
R2 **débit** (m)	shop (eg for wine; becoming less used)	un débit de boissons/de tabac
R2 **échoppe** (f)	small general store	la petite échoppe rend service aux habitants du quartier
R2 **hypermarché** (m)	hypermarket	l'hypermarché est tellement immense qu'on ne peut le parcourir en une journée
R2 **magasin** (m)	shop	les magasins ferment/ouvrent à quelle heure?

R2 **grand magasin** (m)	department store	je ne vais jamais le week-end aux grands magasins – il y a trop de monde
R2 **supérette** (f)	small supermarket, self-service shop	il y a une supérette tout près – elle est très utile, surtout le dimanche
R2 **supermarché** (m)	supermarket	on peut tout acheter au supermarché
R2 **grande surface** (f)	supermarket	en grande surface, il y a aussi une galerie marchande (=*shopping arcade*) avec des petits commerçants

se marier

R2 **épouser**	to marry (less common than **se marier**)	elle a épousé le fils du banquier
R2 **marier**	to marry, to give in marriage, to conduct a wedding	le prêtre les a mariés samedi dernier
R2 **se marier à/avec**	to marry	il y a dix ans elle s'est mariée avec un médecin; je suis mariée à/avec un ingénieur

matériel (m)

R2 **équipement**	equipment	l'équipement d'un soldat/d'une armée; l'équipement de chasse/de pêche/de ski; équipements (*on a notice* = *facilities and equipment required for public works, roads* etc)
R2 **matériau** (m)	material one works on (eg paper, plastic, wood)	un matériau naturel/synthétique; un matériau très résistant
R2 **matériel** (m)	material one works with (eg tools, equipment)	je n'ai pas le matériel qu'il faut
R2 **matière** (f)	matter, substance (lit and fig)	les matières premières (=*raw materials*); la matière grise (=*grey matter, intellectual capacity*); la matière grasse (=*fat content*); c'est une usine qui utilise de nombreuses matières dans la construction de ses produits

mince

R2 **chétif**	puny	elle est devenue chétive depuis qu'elle suit un régime amincissant
R2 **fluet**	slender (less pejorative than **maigre**)	son corps fluet lui donne l'air d'être malade
R2 **frêle**	frail (more fragile than **mince**)	il est tellement fragile qu'il tombe souvent malade
R2 **maigre**	thin, skinny	elle est trop maigre – il faut qu'elle mange plus
R2 **mince**	slim	sa taille mince lui permet de porter de beaux vêtements
R2 **svelte**	slender (suggesting elegance; tends to be used of females)	elle a un corps svelte et élégant

monter

R2 **escalader**	to climb (trans) (suggesting vertical ascent, of wall, rock face etc)	les alpinistes ont escaladé la paroi du versant nord
R2 **gravir**	to climb (tr and intr) (implying effort, eg up a mountain slope)	ils ont mis trois heures à gravir à la cime de la montagne
R2 **grimper**	to climb (tr and intr) (lit and fig; implying effort, eg up a tree)	les enfants ont tous grimpé sur les arbres; de tous les coureurs cyclistes c'est lui qui grimpe le mieux; les prix ne cessent de grimper
R2 **monter**	to go up (lit and fig)	elle a rapidement monté les marches des escaliers; maman est montée mais elle redescend tout de suite; il a monté les échelons en peu d'années

morceau (m)

R2 **fragment** (m)	fragment (part of whole)	il a récupéré un fragment de sa dent
R2 **lopin** (m)	small piece of land	il a acheté un lopin de terre pour construire une maison
R2 **morceau** (m)	piece	tu as un morceau de pain là?

R2 **parcelle** (f)	piece of land (for administrative or building purposes)	les parcelles de terrain étaient redistribuées	
R2 **pièce** (f)	piece (of jigsaw puzzle, engine etc)	il me manque une pièce (d'un puzzle); le mécanicien a mis en place toutes les pièces du moteur	
R2 **portion** (f)	fragment (part of whole)	elle a pris une portion de fromage au goûter	
R1 **bout** (m)	bit	il y avait des bouts de ficelle par terre	

mot (m)

R3 **vocable** (m)	term	son vocabulaire est tellement fin que les vocables qu'elle utilise sont très recherchés
R2 **mot** (m)	word (usu written, but also used with **dire**)	elle utilise des mots difficiles que je ne comprends pas; Antoine, n'emploie pas ces gros mots-là (= *vulgar expressions*); sans mot dire, elle est repartie
R2 **parole** (f)	spoken word (eg of song, speech)	elle a pris la parole devant tout le monde
R2 **terme** (m)	term	c'est un terme qui s'emploie assez rarement

mouillé

R2 **humide**	humid, damp, moist	le temps est humide et le linge ne va pas sécher dehors; l'émotion était tellement forte qu'elle avait les yeux humides; un climat humide
R2 **mouillé**	wet	l'éponge est très mouillée, il faut l'essorer (= *to wring out*)
R2 **trempé**	soaked	elle est trempée jusqu'aux os – elle doit changer de vêtement

mur (m)

R2 **mur** (m)	wall	il a construit le mur en une demi-journée
R2 **muraille** (f)	big, solid wall (of fortress, etc)	as-tu vu les murailles de St Malo?
R2 **muret/ murette** (m/f)	small low wall	une voiture a dû rentrer dans le muret/la murette du jardin?

R2 **pan de mur** (m)	section of wall	le pan de mur s'est écroulé – heureusement qu'il n'y avait personne
R2 **paroi** (f)	face (of mountain), side (of drinking glass, etc)	la paroi du vase est fêlée; la paroi d'une casserole; ils ont escaladé la paroi du versant nord
R2 **rempart** (m)	(circular) wall, ramparts (like **muraille**), (often used in pl)	les soldats défendirent les remparts de la ville

nouveau

R2 **neuf**	(brand) new	la maison qu'ils viennent d'acheter est toute neuve; ils ont acheté un service de table neuf
R2 **nouveau**	(brand) new, another	il a engagé un nouveau technicien; ils ont acheté un nouveau service de table
R2 **récent**	recent	c'est un ouvrage récent qui est sorti il y a à peine une semaine

odeur (f)

R3 **fumet** (m)	smell (of fish, ham, etc)	le fumet du gibier est apprécié par les chasseurs
R3 **senteur** (f)	scent, perfume	les senteurs matinales sont très agréables quand on se réveille
R2 **arôme** (m)	aroma, pleasant smell	le café dégage un bon arôme
R2 **bouquet** (m)	bouquet of wine, scent of flowers	ce vin a un excellent bouquet
R2 **odeur** (f)	smell	il y a une bonne odeur de cuisine
R2 **parfum** (m)	scent, perfume	ça sent le bon parfum; j'ai acheté du parfum hors taxe
R2 **puanteur** (f)	stench, stink	les ordures dégagent une puanteur insupportable
R2 **relent** (m)	persistent, unpleasant smell (eg of bad cooking)	les relents de l'ancienne décharge sont à éviter; c'est nauséabond, les relents de la cuisine

orage (m)

R2 **bourrasque** (f)	squall, gust	la bourrasque n'a duré que cinq minutes
R2 **giboulées** (fpl)	sudden wind with rain, hail, even snow	au cours du mois de mars, il y a souvent des giboulées; les giboulées de mars (= *April showers*)
R2 **grain** (m)	squall, gust	je reste pas sur la plage – il y a un grain qui arrive
R2 **intempéries** (fpl)	bad weather (usu with wind)	au cours de cet hiver, on a eu de fortes intempéries
R2 **orage** (m)	storm (accompanied by lightning and thunder)	les éclairs annoncent l'orage
R2 **tempête** (f)	storm (with violent wind)	la tempête a fait de gros dégâts; une tempête de neige

ordures (fpl)

R3 **immondices** (mpl)	refuse	les rats tournaient autour des immondices
R2 **déchets** (mpl)	rubbish	le recyclage des déchets est de plus en plus perfectionné
R2 **décombres** (m)	building rubbish	le bombardement a provoqué de nombreux décombres
R2 **détritus** (m)	waste (from factories etc)	les poubelles du restaurant sont pleines de détritus
R2 **épluchures** (fpl)	rubbish (food etc)	les épluchures des fruits et légumes sont données aux animaux
R2 **ordures** (fpl)	domestic rubbish	tu mets les ordures dans la poubelle, s'il te plaît
R2 **rebut** (m)	thing of little value	les usines évacuent une grande quantité de rebuts; c'est bon pour le rebut (= *scrapheap*)

NOTE: all these nouns, except for **rebut**, are used more frequently in the plural.

passager (m)

R2 **passager** (m)	passenger (on coach, plane, train, boat, in car)	une dizaine de passagers ont quitté le car à Grenoble; au cours de l'accident, deux passagers ont eu de légères blessures

R2 **voyageur** (m)	passenger (on coach, plane, boat, train)	les voyageurs sont remontés dans le car; après une courte pause, les voyageurs ont été priés de monter dans l'avion; les voyageurs ont passé la nuit à l'hôtel

NOTE: **passager** and **voyageur** seem interchangeable except for car (**voiture**); and in last example of **voyageur**, **passager** could not be used.

passionner

R2 **émouvoir**	to move, to touch (fig)	elle était émue à la pensée de retrouver sa fille
R2 **éveiller**	to awaken	l'ouvrage a éveillé mon intérêt pour l'Alaska
R2 **exciter**	to excite, to stimulate	les cadeaux de Noël excitent les enfants; les films pornographiques n'excitent pas mon imagination; le café m'excite, donc je n'en prends pas le soir
R2 **motiver**	to motivate	il faut motiver les jeunes, autrement ils perdent tout intérêt
R2 **passionner**	to thrill, to stir	le film/la course m'a vraiment passionnée
R2 **provoquer**	to stimulate, to provoke (eg interest)	cette injure a provoqué mon indignation
R2 **stimuler**	to stimulate	une bonne randonnée à la montagne stimule l'appétit
R2 **surexciter**	to excite (stronger than **exciter**; only used in passive)	les enfants étaient surexcités à la veille des vacances
R2 **susciter**	to arouse	cette injustice suscita sa colère; ce roman a suscité beaucoup d'intérêt

peinture (f)

R2 **aquarelle** (f)	water colour	ce peintre a exposé quantité d'aquarelles au Musée Laffont
R2 **fresque** (f)	fresco	les fresques de Michel-Ange à Florence
R2 **gravure** (f)	print	la gravure avait des couleurs pastel
R2 **peinture** (f)	painting	ce qui m'intéresse surtout, ce sont les peintures du dix-neuvième siècle
R2 **retable** (m)	altar piece	le retable *L'enterrement du Comte d'Orgaz* du Greco à Tolède

R2 **tableau** (m)	painting (on canvas)	les tableaux de Delacroix au Louvre sont vraiment impressionnants
R2 **toile** (f)	painting (on canvas)	la toile de Van Gogh a rapporté plusieurs millions aux enchères

plancher (m)

R2 **carrelage** (m)	tiled floor	en hiver le carrelage est glacé
R2 **dallage** (m)	tiled floor (large tiles)	le dallage qu'il a étalé n'est pas très solide
R2 **parquet** (m)	wooden floor, parquet	je cire le parquet une fois par an
R2 **parterre** (m)	floor	il faut nettoyer le parterre tous les jours
R2 **plancher** (m)	boarded floor	il a complètement refait le plancher de sa maison

poids (m)

R3 **faix** (m)	load	courbée sous le faix qu'elle portait
R2 **charge** (f)	load (lit, fig, technical); responsibility	la charge maximale d'un poids-lourd; j'avais la charge de trois enfants
R2 **chargement** (m)	load (of lorry, car)	le chargement du camion déborde
R2 **fardeau** (m)	load (lit and fig)	comment arrive-t-elle à porter ce fardeau sur sa tête?; le fardeau des années
R2 **poids** (m)	weight (lit and fig)	le poids du sac à provisions est trop lourd; je ne supporte pas le poids de mes responsabilités

poignée (f)

R2 **anse** (f)	handle (usu curved, eg of vase, basket)	l'anse du panier s'est brisée sous le poids des courses
R2 **manche** (m)	handle (usu straight, eg of broom)	le manche du balai est à changer; le manche du couteau ne tient pas bien
R2 **manivelle** (f)	crank-handle	pour changer la roue de la voiture on a besoin d'un cric et d'une manivelle
R2 **poignée** (f)	handle (fitting hand, eg of door, bag)	la poignée de la porte ferme mal

policier (m)

R2 **agent de police** (m)	policeman (more or less the same as **gardien de la paix, policier**; slightly more formal) (ellipsis of **de police** once identity established)	un agent de police affecté à la circulation (**policier** not used here)
R2 **CRS** (m)	member of special police force (used to control demonstrations etc)	les CRS sont intervenus lors d'une émeute
R2 **gardien de la paix** (m)	policeman (see **agent de police**)	le gardien de la paix est intervenu à la suite de l'agression
R2 **gendarme** (m)	member of police militia (associated with the countryside)	les gendarmes ont arrêté les voleurs du village
R2 **îlotier** (m)	community policeman	les îlotiers ont interpellé les trois truands
R2 **policier** (m)	policeman (see **agent de police**)	le policier interrogeait les témoins après l'accident
R1 **barbouze** (m)	secret police agent	les barbouzes étaient impliqués dans une histoire louche
R1 **flic** (m)	cop, fuzz	le flic m'a collé un P.-V. (=*booked me*)
R1 **poulet** (m)	cop, fuzz	le poulet m'a collé un P.-V.

porte (f)

R2 **barrière** (f)	gate (of wood, metal)	le champ était accessible en passant par une barrière
R2 **grille** (f)	gate (of metal)	le château était protégé par une grande grille
R2 **portail** (m)	large gate (often in garden)	le portail du jardin est resté ouvert toute la nuit
R2 **porte** (f)	door, gateway (to walled city)	la porte de la maison est bien fermée; la Porte St Denis
R2 **portillon** (m)	barrier (in Paris Métro)	tout le monde se bousculait au portillon

prison (f)

R2 **bagne** (m)	prison (stronger than **prison** but becoming outdated) (lit and fig)	Dreyfus était condamné au bagne de Cayenne; quel bagne! (= *this work is hell!*)
R2 **centre de détention** (m)	detention centre (for young offenders)	le délinquant n'avait que treize ans lorsqu'il a été placé en ce centre de détention
R2 **maison d'arrêt** (f)	remand centre	l'accusé s'est trouvé à la maison d'arrêt de Fresnes près de Paris
R2 **prison** (f)	prison	elle a été condamnée à vingt ans de prison ferme
R1 **ballon** (m)	nick	pour un vol de rien je veux pas repartir au ballon
R1 **bloc** (m)	nick (same as **ballon**)	
R1 **taule/tôle** (f)	nick (same as **ballon**)	
R1 **violon** (m)	one night's custody	il s'est tellement soûlé qu'on l'a mis au violon pour vingt-quatre heures

privé

R2 **particulier** (m)	private person, individual	cette loi doit clarifier les rapports entre l'Etat et les particuliers
R2 **particulier** (adj)	private (of lessons etc), special, odd	il a des cours particuliers en physique; elle a un caractère particulier
R2 **privé** (adj)	private	une propriété privée; un parking privé; puis-je vous parler en privé?

raconter

R3 **conter**	to relate (more literary than **raconter**)	la gouvernante contait tous les soirs des anecdotes aux enfants
R3 **relater**	to relate (eg a story)	elle avait l'habitude de relater des faits extraordinaires
R2 **raconter**	to tell, to relate	chaque soir elle racontait des histoires aux enfants; qu'est-ce que tu racontes là? (= *what yarn are you spinning now?*)
R2 **rapporter**	to report (an event)	elle a rapporté des détails précis/ l'événement tel quel

rapport (m)

R2 **bulletin trimestriel** (m)	school report (for term)	l'enfant attendait avec impatience son bulletin trimestriel
R2 **compte-rendu** (m)	report, account; review (of film, book etc)	la réunion se terminait toujours par un compte-rendu; le compte-rendu d'un spectacle/d'un livre/d'une pièce
R2 **exposé** (m)	report, account	l'étudiant présente son exposé devant le professeur
R2 **procès-verbal** (m)	official, legal report; fine (often reduced to **p.v.** with this sense)	l'agent de police a dressé un procès-verbal à l'automobiliste; j'ai trouvé un procès-verbal/p.-v. sur mon pare-brise
R2 **rapport** (m)	summary, report	le soldat présenta son rapport à son supérieur
R2 **relevé de compte** (m)	statement of account	la banque envoie chaque mois un relevé de compte à tous ses clients
R2 **résumé** (m)	summary, account	l'enseignant a demandé un résumé du livre à tous les étudiants

refléter

R3/2 (**se**) **réfléchir**	to reflect (at a certain angle) (more technical than **refléter**) (tr; intr when fig)	le soleil se réfléchissait sur l'eau; son visage réfléchissait le soleil; laisse-moi réfléchir un moment
R2 (**se**) **refléter**	to reflect (lit and fig)	le soleil se reflète sur l'eau; l'eau reflète le soleil; son visage reflétait la joie
R2 **renvoyer**	to reflect	le miroir renvoyait son profil sur le mur

réfrigérateur (m)

R2 **congélateur** (m)	freezer	il faut sortir la viande du congélateur aujourd'hui si on veut la manger demain
R2 **frigidaire** (m)	refrigerator (more common than **réfrigérateur**)	je me demande comment on se passait de frigidaires il y a cinquante ans
R2 **réfrigérateur** (m)	refrigerator	mets le lait et les œufs au réfrigérateur
R1 **frigo** (m)	fridge	le vin est dans le frigo

représentation (f)

R2 **exécution** (f)	performing (of music)	l'exécution de l'œuvre musicale fut parfaite
R2 **performance** (f)	performance (in sport)	les rugbymen ont réalisé une performance sportive exceptionnelle
R2 **réalisation** (f)	creation	la réalisation de l'ouvrage porte bien le cachet de son auteur
R2 **représentation** (f)	theatrical performance	la représentation théâtrale commence à vingt heures
R2 **séance** (f)	cinema performance	au cinéma, il y a trois séances quotidiennes

retourner

R2 **faire demi-tour**	to go back, to make an about turn	à mi-chemin, nous avons fait demi-tour parce qu'il commençait à faire nuit
R2 **regagner**	to return, to go back	elle a regagné son pays après plusieurs années d'exil; après mon séjour à Marseille, je regagne Paris tout de suite
R2 **rentrer (à la maison)**	to return (home) (**à la maison** is in fact redundant, but often heard, unless an infinitive follows)	écoute, je suis fatigué, je rentre (à la maison); allez, on va rentrer dîner
R2 **retourner**	to return, to go back	elle a été obligée de retourner en Italie parce que sa mère était malade
R2 **revenir**	to come back	nous sommes revenus des Etats-Unis fin juillet

rude

R2 **âpre**	rough (of wine), tart (of fruit)	je n'apprécie pas le goût âpre de ce fruit
R2 **dur**	hard, harsh (lit and fig)	le pain est trop dur pour mes dents; la prof est dure – elle ne donne jamais de bonnes notes
R2 **rauque**	harsh (of voice)	j'ai la voix rauque – j'ai passé l'après-midi au match de foot et c'était la demi-finale!
R2 **rêche**	rough (of surface, eg skin)	le vêtement est devenu rêche après le lavage

R2 **rigoureux**	harsh (of weather) (lit and fig)	un hiver rigoureux; le prof est rigoureux envers ses élèves
R2 **rude**	harsh (of experience, weather)	un hiver rude; une rude épreuve
R2 **sévère**	severe (fig only)	des parents sévères; un juge sévère; prendre des mesures sévères

rusé

R2 **astucieux**	astute, clever, sly	qu'est-ce qu'il est astucieux – il est plein de combines; une réponse astucieuse; c'est là un raisonnement astucieux; un projet astucieux
R2 **espiègle**	prankish (of children)	ce garçon est espiègle – il cherche toujours à se cacher
R2 **filou**	crooked rascal	qu'est-ce qu'il est filou – il a trompé tout le monde
R2 **futé**	clever	il est futé – il a construit la maison lui-même; chaque été la sécurité routière met en place le système de 'bison futé' (= *alternative routes during the tourist season*)
R2 **malin**	crafty (F rarely used)	c'est un petit garçon malin – il gagne toujours au jeu
R2 **rusé**	sly	il est rusé comme un renard
R2 **sournois**	cunning	méfie-toi – elle est sournoise
R1 **roublard**	fly	il est roublard – il cherche toujours à profiter de la situation

saisir

R3 **se saisir de**	to grasp	elle s'est saisie de la plume pour écrire des vers
R2 **s'emparer de**	to take/to get hold of	les policiers se sont emparés du voleur
R2 **empoigner**	to take hold of (suggesting violence)	la femme a empoigné la barre de fer pour se défendre
R2 **étreindre**	to clasp with one's arms	après de longues années d'absence, la mère a étreint son enfant dans ses bras
R2 **prendre**	to take (hold of)	elle a pris son manteau et est sortie; elle a pris l'enfant dans ses bras

R2 **saisir**	to seize, to take hold of	il a saisi le couteau pour couper le pain; j'ai saisi une branche pour éviter de tomber; le truand a saisi le pistolet et s'est enfui
R2 **serrer**	to hold tightly, to tighten one's grip	au passage du train, elle a serré l'enfant contre sa poitrine

salaire (m)

R2 **honoraires** (mpl)	fees (of doctor, solicitor)	les honoraires d'un médecin sont fixés par l'Etat
R2 **paie** (f)	pay (monthly)	je touche ma paie à la fin du mois
R2 **paiement** (m)	one single payment	aussitôt la traduction terminée, le paiement sera versé à mon compte
R2 **rémunération** (f)	remuneration, any sum of money given for work done	la rémunération des ouvriers représente le tiers du budget de notre entreprise
R2 **salaire** (m)	pay (monthly) (same as **paie**)	je touche mon salaire à la fin du mois
R2 **solde** (f)	military pay	la solde des militaires sera majorée de trois pour cent
R2 **traitement** (m)	salary (monthly, for civil servants, teachers etc)	le traitement des fonctionnaires est réglé par le trésor public

sale

R3 **immonde**	foul	ce coin est immonde – il est plein de détritus
R3 **ordurier**	foul (especially fig)	il m'a tenu des propos orduriers que je ne puis accepter
R2 **crasseux**	mucky	le mécanicien a les mains crasseuses
R2 **impur**	impure (lit and fig)	cette eau est impure – on ne peut la boire; des idées impures
R2 **infect**	filthy (lit and fig)	cette nourriture est infecte – je ne peux pas la manger; les toilettes dégagent une puanteur infecte; un individu/un temps infect
R2 **sale**	dirty (lit and fig)	la maison est sale – il faut la nettoyer; c'est un sale type – on ne peut pas se fier à lui

| R2 **stagnant** | stagnant (lit and fig) | de l'eau stagnante; le commerce est stagnant |
| R1* **dégueulasse** | filthy, revolting (lit and fig) | cette bouffe est dégueulasse; il m'a fait un tour dégueulasse |

sécurité (f)

R2 **salut** (m)	(Christian) salvation	l'éternel salut est le but de tous les chrétiens; l'Armée du Salut entreprend une œuvre charitable exemplaire
R2 **sécurité** (f)	safety, security (often in fixed expressions)	la sécurité routière/sociale; une soupape de sécurité; la sécurité des citoyens
R2 **sûreté** (f)	safety, security (often in fixed expressions)	voyager en sûreté; la sûreté nationale; la sûreté de ce système n'est pas garantie; en sûreté

série (f)

R2 **assortiment** (m)	set (of tools, the same items but with slight differences in shape etc)	un assortiment de couteaux/de serviettes
R2 **batterie** (f)	set (of kitchen utensils)	une batterie de cuisine/de casseroles
R2 **jeu** (m)	set (of chess pieces, golf clubs, spanners etc), pack (of cards)	le mécanicien dispose d'un jeu de clefs; les joueurs ont mis plusieurs jeux de cartes sur la table; un jeu d'échecs
R2 **série** (f)	set (of chairs, numbers etc), serial (on television)	une série de chiffres/de chemises/de casseroles; une série télévisée
R2 **trousse** (f)	kit (eg medical), gear	la trousse de l'enfant qui part en colonie de vacances a été préparée par sa mère; la trousse médicale est dans l'ambulance
R2 **trousseau** (m)	bunch (of keys)	mince, alors, je trouve pas mon trousseau de clefs

sommet (m)

R2 **apogée** (m)	apex (fig)	l'apogée de la civilisation européenne
R2 **cime** (f)	top (of tree, mountain)	la cime de la montagne est très élevée
R2 **faîte** (m)	top (not very common)	le faîte d'une maison
R2 **haut** (m)	top (lit and fig)	le haut de la montagne est éloigné; il a connu des hauts et des bas

R2 **sommet** (m)	top (lit (of tree, mountain) and fig)	ils atteignirent le sommet de la montagne après dix heures d'ascension; une conférence au sommet; elle atteignit le sommet de sa carrière à l'âge de trente ans
R2 **summum** (m)	apex (fig)	la neuvième symphonie de Beethoven est le summum de la musique européenne

sort (m)

R2 **chance** (f)	chance, good luck	on n'a pas eu de chance – le bateau était déjà parti; bonne chance!
R2 **destin** (m)	destiny (usu of an individual)	le destin de l'homme est de mourir; le destin de cet individu est marqué par la religion
R2 **destinée** (f)	destiny (usu of a nation, tribe, religious group)	la destinée de ce peuple est tragique
R2 **fortune** (f)	(usu good) fortune	sa bonne fortune était de retrouver son travail; faire contre mauvaise fortune bon cœur (= *to put a brave face on it*)
R2 **hasard** (m)	chance	le hasard fait bien les choses; le bel hasard (NB the form of the adj)
R2 **sort** (m)	fate	on lui a jeté un mauvais sort; le héros se lamentait sur son sort
R1 **pot** (m)	(usu good) luck	il a eu du pot – il s'en est bien sorti; un coup de pot; pas de pot! (= *I'm/you're out of luck*)
R1 **veine** (f)	(usu good) luck	il a eu de la veine; un coup de veine; pas de veine!

tapis (m)

R2 **descente de lit** (f)	bedside rug	il y a une descente de lit dans chaque chambre
R2 **moquette** (f)	carpeting (wall-to-wall)	la moquette a été posée par un spécialiste dans toutes les pièces
R2 **paillasson** (m)	door mat	tu frottes bien les pieds sur le paillasson!
R2 **tapis** (m)	carpet	le tapis persan coûte très cher

terre (f)

R2 **sol** (m)	ground, floor, surface, soil	ce sol est riche en humus; des avions ont été retenus au sol en raison du brouillard
R2 **terrain** (m)	piece of land (suggesting dimension)	ce terrain est réservé à la construction; un terrain de foot
R2 **terre** (f)	earth (world and soil), land (ie property)	la Terre fait partie de l'univers; cette terre n'est pas très cultivable/fertile; le seigneur possédait de vastes terres
R2 **terroir** (m)	one's region, homeland	ce fruit a le goût du terroir; ce sont les meilleurs produits du terroir

toucher

R2 **effleurer**	to brush past (lit), to occur (fig)	l'eau de la rivière effleurait les branches; l'idée de ne pas rendre l'argent ne m'a jamais effleuré
R2 **frôler**	to brush past (lit), to almost touch, to just miss (fig)	la voiture m'a frôlé, j'ai eu de la veine; il a frôlé la mort; la valeur du dollar frôle six francs
R2 **manier**	to handle (suggesting care) (rarely used fig)	elle manie l'épée avec dextérité
R2 **manipuler**	to handle (suggesting care) (lit and fig)	manipuler une arme/un poignard; il a su manipuler tout le monde pour ses fins
R2 **palper**	to feel (suggesting exploration or appreciation)	elle a palpé le tissu en velours
R2 **tâter**	to feel, to grope (lit and fig)	il a tâté le terrain pour voir s'il était stable; je vais tâter le terrain pour voir s'ils acceptent de nous accueillir; le médecin a tâté le pouls au petit
R2 **toucher**	to touch (lit and fig)	ne touche pas (à) la casserole – elle est très chaude; ce qui m'a vraiment touché, c'était la réunion de toute la famille

travail (m)

R2 **besogne** (f)	task (harder than **tâche**)	quelle besogne! m'occuper du bébé jusqu'au retour de ses parents

R2 **corvée** (f)	task (harder than **besogne**; suggesting unpleasant work)	quelle corvée! laver la voiture de mon père
R2 **emploi** (m)	job (both practical and abstract), work	je cherche un emploi dans le bâtiment; offres/demandes d'emploi (in newspaper); l'emploi est fondamental pour l'équilibre de l'homme
R2 **œuvre** (f)	piece of work, work of art	c'est une œuvre architecturale grandiose
R2 **ouvrage** (m)	piece of work, work of art	un ouvrage d'art; lorsque l'ouvrage sera terminé, je t'enverrai un tirage
R2 **poste** (m)	job	elle a quitté son poste; il a été nommé à un poste aux Etats-Unis; elle est en poste à Bangkok
R2 **situation** (f)	job, position	elle a une belle situation à Paris
R2 **tâche** (f)	task	le lundi matin tout le monde s'en va à sa tâche hebdomadaire; ma tâche aujourd'hui, c'est de classer mes livres
R2 **travail** (m)	job, work	j'ai retrouvé un/du travail après plusieurs mois de chômage; le travail? – je préfère les vacances
R1 **boulot** (m)	job	elle a un petit boulot dans un restaurant
R1 **job** (m)	job	il a un petit job dans l'atelier de son oncle

trembler

R3/2 **tressaillir**	to shake	elle tressaillit comme si elle eût été frappée par la foudre
R2 **frémir**	to shudder (often at danger)	elle frémissait à la pensée qu'elle pouvait tomber
R2 **frissonner**	to shiver (from cold, pleasure)	il frissonnait de froid/de fièvre/d'émotion
R2 **trembler**	to tremble (from cold, emotion etc)	elle a tremblé de colère/de froid/de peur

usager (m)

R2 **abonné** (m)	consumer (of gas, water), user (of telephone)	les abonnés d'eau/de gaz/d'électricité sont priés de relever leurs compteurs (= *to take a meter reading*); les abonnés de téléphone reçoivent une facture tous les deux mois
R2 **consommateur** (m)	consumer (of gas, water; but not telephone)	les consommateurs d'eau/de gaz/d'électricité
R2 **usager** (m)	user (of road, rail etc)	les usagers des transports en commun/de la route/d'Internet/de la bibliothèque
R2 **utilisateur** (m)	user (often of machines)	les utilisateurs de l'ordinateur ont besoin d'un code personnel; les utilisateurs de ce système

vacances (fpl)

R2 **congé** (m)	short break (from school, work)	l'employé a pris quelques jours de congé
R2 **congé annuel/payé** (m)	holiday entitlement (usu a month)	tu vas où pour tes congés annuels?
R2 **fête** (f)	festival	la fête du quatorze juillet; les fêtes de Noël
R2 **jour férié** (m)	public holiday	le premier mai est un jour férié
R2 **permission** (f)	military leave	le soldat est en permission pour le weekend
R2 **vacances** (fpl)	holidays, vacation	comment vas-tu passer les grandes vacances/les vacances de Noël?
R1 **perm** (f)	military leave	le soldat est en perm pour le weekend

verre (m)

R2 **carreau** (m)	pane of glass	le carreau de la fenêtre est fêlé
R2 **fenêtre** (f)	window	j'ai demandé à tous les enfants qui avait cassé la fenêtre
R2 **rosace** (f)	rose window	la rosace de Notre Dame est magnifique
R2 **verre** (m)	glass (substance and container)	ce verre est trop fragile – je vais en acheter d'autres; je préfère un verre dépoli pour la salle de bains; le vase est en verre
R2 **verrière** (f)	glass covering, glass conservatory	les plantes poussent sous une verrière (= *under glass*); ils ont agrandi le restaurant avec une verrière

| R2 **vitrail** (m) | stained glass window | les vitraux de la cathédrale ont été rénovés |
| R2 **vitre** (f) | pane of glass (like **carreau** but also of car) | baisse la vitre un peu – il fait trop chaud dans la voiture |

vieux

R2 **âgé**	old (of person; more polite than **vieux**)	bien qu'elle soit âgée, elle est toujours capable de nager un kilomètre; il faut toujours respecter les personnes âgées
R2 **ancien**	old	ces meubles anciens seront vendus chez l'antiquaire
R2 **antique**	old (suggesting long ago)	ces faits remontent à la période antique
R2 **caduc**	out-of-date (of law, custom)	cette loi est caduque depuis longtemps
R2 **périmé**	old, out-of-date	mon passeport/ce médicament est périmé
R2 **ringard**	behind the times	auprès des jeunes, il est très ringard
R2 **vétuste**	old (of building)	ce bâtiment abandonné est vétuste
R2 **vieux**	old	ce pain est trop vieux, il faut le jeter; elle est extrêmement vieille – elle a quatre-vingt-dix ans

ville (f)

R2 **agglomération urbaine** (f)	built-up area	il ne faut pas dépasser cinquante km/heure en agglomération urbaine
R2 **capitale** (f)	capital	quelle est la capitale du Pérou?
R2 **cité** (f)	city (implying historic importance, old centre), housing estate (usual meaning nowadays)	la cité de Carcassonne; l'Ile de la Cité; les cités en banlieue parisienne posent de plus en plus de difficultés aux instances municipales
R2 **métropole** (f)	metropolis	Tokyo est une grande métropole avec plus de douze millions d'habitants
R2 **ville** (f)	town	Mexico est la ville la plus peuplée du monde

voler

R3/2 **soustraire**	to steal (eg money, jewels, documents)	le cambrioleur a soustrait une grosse somme d'argent et des bijoux
R2 **dérober**	to steal (eg money, jewels, documents)	le voleur s'est introduit par une porte vitrée et a dérobé d'importantes sommes d'argent
R2 **subtiliser**	to steal, to spirit away (suggesting skill and dexterity)	le voleur a subtilisé mon portefeuille sans que je m'en rende compte
R2 **voler**	to steal	quelqu'un a volé mon stylo/ma voiture
R1 **chaparder**	to pinch	le jeune a chapardé des produits dans le supermarché
R1 **chiper**	same as **chaparder**	
R1 **piquer**	same as **chaparder** but the most common of the R1 verbs	

2.5   Complex verbal expressions

There exist in French many verbal expressions which, as a result of their apparently complicated structure, students tend to be reluctant to use. This is unfortunate because these expressions often convey important shades of meaning, which it is impossible to express otherwise, and also because some of them are very common in current usage. By listing some of the most frequently employed expressions and by giving examples of them in use, it is hoped that students will be prepared to absorb some of them into their workaday vocabulary, and that they will be able to recognise the others. Again, it should be remembered that unless there is an indication to the contrary, all these expressions are R2.

il s'agit de = it is a question of

il s'agit de comprendre l'idée principale du texte
it is a question of understanding the main idea in the text
il s'agissait de le faire correctement
it was a question of doing it correctly
il s'agira de récrire la lettre
it will be a question of rewriting the letter
NOTE: this is an impersonal expression, and the subject can only ever be **il**, never a noun. However, **s'agissant de** is permissible

s'agissant de son retour, je lui ai dit que je ne serais pas à la maison
as far as her return was concerned, I told her that I wouldn't be at home

s'attendre à ce que + subj = to expect
je m'attends à ce qu'elle revienne sous peu
I expect she will return soon
on s'attend du prof qu'il fasse les copies dans la semaine
the teacher is expected to mark the scripts within a week

NOTE: **attendre** can also mean 'to expect':
il est attendu dans la soirée
he is expected this evening

avoir beau faire qch = to do sth in vain
elle a beau faire, elle n'aura pas ses examens
whatever she does she will not pass her examinations

avoir l'interdiction/la défense de faire qch (R3) = to be forbidden to do sth
ils ont eu l'interdiction de fumer en cours
they were forbidden to smoke in class

avoir à cœur de faire qch = to be anxious to do sth
j'ai à cœur d'accomplir cette tâche
I am anxious to complete this task

se défendre d'être (R3) = to refuse to admit, to deny being
il se défend d'être anti-européen
he refuses to admit that he is anti-European
elle s'est toujours défendue de vouloir créer un nouveau parti politique
she has always refused to admit that she wanted to create a new political party
je ne m'en défends pas
I do not deny it

défrayer la chronique de = to be the talk of the town
le désastre ferroviaire/l'enlèvement des touristes a défrayé la chronique de tous les journaux
the rail accident/the kidnapping of the tourists has been all over the papers

se disputer le droit/privilège de faire qch = to argue over the right/privilege to do sth
les deux frères se disputaient le droit de conduire la voiture
the two brothers argued over who would drive the car

(il) n'empêche que + indicative = nevertheless
on avait une bonne défense; (il) n'empêche qu'ils ont marqué trois buts
we had a good defence but they still scored three goals

NOTE: the expression is more familiar if the impersonal **il** is omitted

comme si de rien n'était = as if nothing had happened

> **après notre querelle elle est revenue comme si de rien n'était**
> after our quarrel she came back as if nothing had happened

s'ennuyer de qn (R1) = to miss sb

> **je m'ennuyais de mes amis que j'avais laissés au village**
> I missed my friends whom I left behind in the village

s'entretenir avec qn de qch = to hold discussions with sb about sth

> **le ministre s'est entretenu avec le président de la politique agricole**
> the minister discussed the agricultural policy with the president

se faire faute de (R3) = to feel guilty or responsible

> **après cet accident, je me ferai toujours faute de ne pas avoir été plus prudent**
> after this accident I shall always feel guilty over not having been more cautious

en faire autant = to do the same thing

> **elle a fait de belles études; j'aimerais en faire autant**
> she has done very well in her studies; I should like to do the same

faire connaissance avec/la connaissance de = to come to know

> **elle a fait connaissance avec/la connaissance de mon frère sans que je le sache**
> she came to know my brother without my knowing about it

faire défaut = to be lacking

> **l'argent me fait défaut**
> I need money

faire exprès de = to do (sth) deliberately

> **elle a fait exprès d'arriver tard**
> she deliberately arrived late

avoir vite fait de faire qch = to be quick in doing sth (suggesting 'too quickly')

> **on a vite fait de juger cette personne**
> this person was judged (too) quickly

faire fi de qch (R3) = to scorn sth

> **il fait fi de mon autorité**
> he defies/scorns my authority

se faire fort de = to be confident about

> **je me suis fait fort de remporter le premier prix**
> I was pretty certain I'd walk off with the first prize

faire honte à qn = to make sb feel ashamed

> **par son impolitesse à table il fait honte à son père**
> his poor table manners make his father feel ashamed

faire peu de cas de qch = to ignore sth

> **il fait peu de cas de ce qu'on lui dit**
> he ignores what is said to him

peu s'en faut que (R3) + subj: suggests the idea of 'almost'

> **il est venu s'excuser; mais peu s'en faut que le directeur aille le dire à son pere**
> he came to apologise; but the headmaster almost feels like going to tell his father

il s'en faut de beaucoup que + subj = to be far from

> **il s'en fallait de beaucoup qu'il soit heureux**
> he was far from being happy

se féliciter de qch = to express satisfaction over sth

> **je me félicite de vous voir venir**
> I am happy to see you come

se garder de = to take care *not* to

> **j'ai mes propres opinions mais je me garderai de les exprimer**
> I have my own opinions but I shall be careful not to express them

en imposer à qn = to fill sb with respect

> **avec sa carrure le boxeur en a imposé à son adversaire**
> with his enormous build the boxer made his opponent feel inferior

intenter un procès à qn (R3) = to take sb to court

> **elle a intenté un procès à son voisin**
> she took her neighbour to court

manquer à qn = to be lacking to sb

> **le soleil me manque en Angleterre**
> I miss the sun in England

> NOTE: **manquer de** contains the idea of 'almost' doing sth **dans sa précipitation il a manqué de renverser le vase** in his hurry he almost knocked over the vase

> NOTE: **ne pas manquer de** = not to fail to
> **ne manque pas de venir** = don't fail to come
> **manquer de**, however, in the positive form does not mean 'to fail to' (3.4.3)

se passer de qch = to do without sth

> **tu te passeras de ton livre pendant ton examen**
> you will do without your book when you take your examination

passer en revue = to review or go through

> **la reine a passé les troupes en revue**
> the queen reviewed the troops
> **elle a passé en revue sa garde-robe avant de partir en vacances**
> she went through her wardrobe before going on holiday

porter atteinte à qch (R3) = to damage sth, to affect sth adversely

> **cet acte a porté atteinte à l'honneur du ministre**
> this act cast a slur on the minister's honour

s'en prendre à qn = to criticise sb

> **les journalistes s'en sont pris au gouvernement**
> the journalists criticised the government

s'en rapporter à qch = to rely on sth

> **il s'en est rapporté à son jugement**
> he put faith in his judgement

se réclamer de qch/qn (R3) = to cite the authority of sth/sb

> **il se réclame du marxisme pour défendre sa cause**
> he appeals to Marxism to defend his cause

s'en remettre à qn = to rely on sb

> **je m'en remets à vous**
> I rely on you

se répercuter sur = to have repercussions upon

> **les hausses de salaire se sont répercutées sur les prix**
> the increases in wages had an effect upon prices

se ressentir de qch = to feel the effects of sth

> **il se ressent toujours de l'accident**
> he still feels the effects of his accident

ne pas savoir à quoi s'en tenir = not to know what to believe

> **puisqu'il blague toujours, je ne sais pas à quoi m'en tenir**
> since he is always joking I never know what to believe

savoir gré à qn (R3) = to be grateful to sb

> **je lui sais gré de m'avoir averti**
> I am thankful to him for warning me

> NOTE: **je lui *suis* gré** R1

souhaiter la bienvenue à qn = to welcome sb

> **je lui ai souhaité la bienvenue**
> I welcomed him

> NOTE: **vous êtes le (la) bienvenu(e)** = you are welcome

tenir à = to be anxious to

> **je tiens à le faire**
> I am anxious to do it

tenir rigueur à qn de qch = to hold it against sb for sth

> **je tiendrai toujours rigueur à cet étudiant de ne pas avoir fait son travail**
> I shall always hold it against this student for not doing his work

tenir tête à = to defy

> **les jeunes du quartier ont tenu tête aux îlotiers**
> the local youth defied the community police

traiter qn de qch = to call sb sth (pej)

> **il a traité son père de tyran**
> he called his father a tyrant

trouver à redire à qch (R1 **de/sur**) = to criticise sth
> **elle trouve toujours à redire sur ce que je fais**
> she always finds fault with what I say

veiller à ce que + subj = to see to it that
> **veillez à ce que le travail soit fait en temps voulu**
> see to it that the work is done in the agreed time

venir en aide à qn = to come to sb's aid
> **il nous est venu en aide lors de notre accident**
> he came to our aid when we had the accident

en vouloir à qn = to hold it against sb
> **il m'en veut de ne pas lui avoir écrit**
> he is angry because I did not write to him

2.6   Idioms, similes and proverbs

'Honestly, I can't make head nor tail of it.' — 'What d'you mean? It's as easy as ABC.'

Idioms, similes and to a lesser extent proverbs, add colour to our speech. The following is a list, in alphabetical order of the pivotal words, of some of the most common French idioms; a small number of similes and proverbs is also given. There are also selections of expressions involving colours and numbers.

2.6.1   Idioms

		Register	
A	**expliquer de A à Z**	2	to explain logically
	démontrer par A plus B	2	to demonstrate logically
	ne savoir ni A ni B	2	not to have a clue
	être aux abois	2	to be in extreme difficulty
	abonder dans le sens de qn	3	to be entirely of sb's opinion
	battre de l'aile	2	to flounder
	prendre des airs	2	to put on airs and graces
	parler sans ambages	3	to speak without beating about the bush
	être aux anges	2	to be in seventh heaven
	filer à l'anglaise	1 + 2	to take French leave
	avoir une araignée au plafond	1	to have a screw loose
	passer l'arme à gauche	1	to die
	être un as	1	to be an ace (eg sportsman)
	ne pas être dans son assiette	1 + 2	not to be in good form

Register

	se faire l'avocat du diable	3	to play devil's advocate
B	plier bagage	2	to set off
	renvoyer la balle	2	to put the ball in sb else's court
	faire un ballon d'essai	3	to have a trial run
	un ballon d'oxygène	2	a life saver or anything which gives you an extra lift
	c'est là que/où le bât blesse	2	that's where the shoe pinches
	mettre des bâtons dans les roues	2	to put a spoke in the wheel
	parler à bâtons rompus	2	to talk in a disconnected way
	chercher la petite bête	1	to be over-critical
	toucher du bois	1	to touch wood
	mettre les bouchées doubles	2	to work hard
	avoir sur les bras	1	to have on one's hands
	battre en brèche	3	to attack violently
	colmater la brèche/les brèches	3	to fill in the gap
	revenir bredouille	2	to come home empty-handed
	à brûle-pourpoint	3	point blank
C	boire le calice jusqu'à la lie	3	to drain the cup to the dregs
	la balle est dans son camp	2	the ball is in his court
	battre la campagne	1	to be delirious
	il fait un froid de canard	1	it's freezing cold
	passer un cap difficile	2	to weather an awkward situation
	avoir carte blanche	2	to have a free hand
	à tout bout de champ	1	all the time
	donner le change à qn	3	to deceive sb
	démarrer en chapeaux de roue	2	(lit and fig) to shoot off at top speed/to get off to a cracking start
	la foi de charbonnier	3	simple faith
	venir de Charenton	1	to be mad
	il n'y a pas un chat	1	there's not a soul about
	appeler un chat un chat	2	to call a spade a spade
	ne pas réveiller le chat qui dort	3	to let sleeping dogs lie
	avoir un chat dans la gorge	1	to have a frog in one's throat

	Register	
donner sa langue au chat	1 + 2	to give in/up (eg in guessing game)
bâtir des châteaux en Espagne	2	to build castles in Spain
avoir d'autres chats à fouetter	1	to have other fish to fry
prendre le chemin des écoliers	2 + 3	to take the longest way round
ne pas y aller par quatre chemins	2	not to beat about the bush
couper les cheveux en quatre	2	to split hairs
tiré par les cheveux	2	far-fetched
ménager la chèvre et le chou	2	to sit on the fence
vivre comme chien et chat	2	to live a cat and dog's life
il fait un froid à ne pas mettre un chien dehors	1	it's freezing cold
remuer ciel et terre	2	to move heaven and earth
faire un pas de clerc	3	to make a blunder
être collet monté	3	to be prim and proper
prêcher un converti	2	to preach to the converted
il pleut des cordes	1 + 2	it's raining cats and dogs
remuer le couteau dans la plaie	2	to twist the knife in the wound
être à couteaux tirés avec qn	2 + 3	to be at daggers drawn with sb
donner le coup d'envoi	2	to set things in motion
un honnête courtier	3	an honest broker
battre qn à plate couture	2 + 3	to beat sb hollow
être un crack	1	to be an ace (eg sportsman)
pendre la crémaillère	2	to have a house-warming
faire un créneau	1	to park between two cars
verser des larmes de crocodile	1 + 2	to weep crocodile tears
va te faire cuire un œuf	1	go and take a running jump/ get stuffed
D le système D	1	ability to get out of a difficult situation
être sur les dents	1	to be worn out
tirer le diable par la queue	1	to be in difficult financial circumstances

Register

	Register	
un conte à dormir debout	2	a very boring story, a tall story
avoir bon dos	1	to be accused instead of another
faire le gros dos	1	to get angry
être dans de beaux draps	1	to be in a sorry state

E
porter de l'eau à la rivière	3	to carry coals to Newcastle
une douche écossaise	2	sth unpleasantly unexpected
être gêné aux encoignures	2 + 3	to feel awkward
jeter l'éponge	1	to throw in the towel, to give up
avoir l'esprit de l'escalier	3	to be witty when the opportunity has passed
brûler une étape/les étapes	2	to go fast
être dans tous ses états	1	to be in a stew

F
sauver la face	2	to save face
il n'y a pas le feu	2	there's no rush
mettre le feu aux poudres	2	to bring things to a head
brûler les feux/une gare	2 + 3	to go through red traffic lights/a station without stopping
donner le feu vert	1	to give the green light
donner du fil à retordre à qn	2 + 3	to give sb trouble
faire un four	1	to be a flop
ne pas avoir froid aux yeux	1	to be brazen
avoir la frousse	1	to have the wind up

G
en avoir gros sur le cœur	2	to be unhappy

H
il pleut des hallebardes	3	it's raining cats and dogs
couper l'herbe sous le pied à qn	2	to cut the ground from beneath sb's feet
voilà le hic	3	there's the rub/the snag
jeter de l'huile sur le feu	2	to add fuel to the fire
faire tache d'huile	2	to spread (of strike, etc)

J
être gros Jean comme devant	1 + 2	to be tricked

Register

L	**y perdre son latin**	2	not to be able to make head nor tail of sth
	lâcher du lest	1	to become freer (with children, etc)
	tenir les leviers de commande	2	to hold the reins, to be in control
	se tailler la part du lion	2	to give oneself the lion's share
	il fait un froid de loup	1	it's freezing cold
	il y a belle lurette qu'il le fait (pres tense)	1	he's been doing it for a long time
	il y a belle lurette qu'il l'a fait (pft tense)	1	it's a long time since he did it
M	**faire machine arrière**	2	to go into reverse
	avoir maille à partir avec qn	3	to have a bone to pick with sb
	avoir plus d'un tour dans la manche	2	to have a trick up one's sleeve
	une autre paire de manches	2	another kettle of fish
	par-dessus le marché	1 + 2	into the bargain
	faire la grasse matinée	2	to lie late in bed
	vendre la mèche	2	to let the cat out of the bag
	ça ne mène à rien	2	that doesn't get us anywhere
	être le point de mire de tout le monde	2 + 3	to attract attention (involuntarily)
	être monnaie courante	2 + 3	to be common knowledge
	être au point mort	2	to be at a standstill (eg in negotiations)
	le mot de Cambronne	1 + 2	crap
	manger ses mots	1	to speak indistinctly
	retournons/revenons à nos moutons	1	let's get back to the point
	employer les grands moyens	2	to take extreme measures
N	**être en nage**	2	to be in a sweat
	faire la navette	2	to shuttle back and forth
	trancher le nœud gordien	3	to cut the Gordian knot
	perdre le nord	1	to get confused
O	**faire de l'œil à qn**	1	to ogle sb
	tourner de l'œil	1	to faint
	tuer dans l'œuf	2	to nip in the bud
	se faire tirer l'oreille	1 + 2	to be persuaded with difficulty (to do sth)

		Register	
P	avoir du pain sur la planche	1 + 2	to have a lot on one's plate
	une vérité de la Palice	2	an obvious truth, a commonplace
	être dans les bons/petits papiers de qn	1 + 2	to be in sb's good books
	se sentir bien/mal dans sa peau	1	to feel at ease/not at ease with oneself
	ramasser une pelle	1	to come a cropper
	faire sa pelote	1	to feather one's nest
	payer de sa personne	3	to sacrifice oneself
	être dans le pétrin	2	to be in a mess
	ne pas savoir sur quel pied danser	1 + 2	to be indecisive
	avaler la pilule	1	to swallow the pill, to allow oneself to be tricked
	dorer la pilule	1	to sugar the pill
	casser sa pipe	1	to kick the bucket
	être à côté de la plaque	1	to be completely mistaken/ way off the mark
	battre son plein	2	to be in full swing
	parler de la pluie et du beau temps	2	to talk about nothing in particular
	dormir à poings fermés	2	to sleep like a log
	mettre au point	2	to perfect
	faire le point sur qch	2	to give a report on sth
	faire un poisson d'avril à qn	2	to play an April Fools' Day trick on sb
	une pomme de discorde	2	a bone of contention
	tomber dans les pommes	1	to faint
	tourner autour du pot	1 + 2	to beat about the bush
	payer les pots cassés	2	to pick up the pieces
	donner un coup de pouce à qn	2	to encourage sb to complete sth (at the last moment)
	jeter de la poudre aux yeux à qn	2	to amaze, dazzle sb
	tuer la poule aux œufs d'or	2	to kill the goose that laid the golden egg
	aux frais de la princesse	2	on the house, free
	pour des prunes	1	for little
	mettre la puce à l'oreille à qn	2	to hint at sth
Q	à la queue leu-leu	1	in single file
	faire une queue de poisson	1	to overtake a car and then pull in suddenly

R	mettre au rancart	1	to cast aside
	la règle d'or	2	the golden rule
	cela n'a ni rime ni raison	2	there's neither rhyme nor reason in it
	franchir le Rubicon	3	to cross the Rubicon
S	avoir plus d'un tour dans son sac	2	to have more than one trick up one's sleeve
	ne pas savoir à quel saint se vouer	2	to be at one's wits' end
	passer un savon à qn	1	to reprimand sb
	être/mettre qn sur la sellette	1 + 2	to be/put sb on the carpet
	un dialogue de sourds	2	a dialogue between two people who refuse to understand each other
T	passer qn à tabac	1	to beat sb up
	faire table rase	2 + 3	to make a clean sweep
	arriver tambour battant	2	to come bustling up
	faire qch tambour battant	2	to hustle sth along
	sans tambour ni trompette	2	quietly
	crier sur tous les toits	2	to shout from the roof tops
	avoir du toupet	2	to have cheek
	avoir le trac	2	to get the wind up
	aller son petit train-train	2	to jog along in the usual way
	servir de tremplin	2	to act as a spring-board
V	brûler ses vaisseaux	3	to burn one's boats
	renverser la vapeur	2	to go into reverse
	tirer les vers du nez à qn	1	to worm secrets out of sb
	les choses tournent au vinaigre	1	things are turning sour
	un violon d'Ingres	3	a hobby
	virer de l'œil	1	to pass out
	à vol d'oiseau	2	as the crow flies
	en vrac	2	higgledy-piggledy
Y	faire les gros yeux	2	to glare at

2.6.2 Similes

Register

A **fier comme Artaban** 2 as proud as a peacock

B **rire comme une baleine** 1 to laugh like a drain
   c'est simple comme 1 it's as easy as ABC
   bonjour
   rire comme un bossu 1 to laugh like a drain

C **il s'en moque comme de** 1 he couldn't care less
   sa première chemise
   être malade comme un 1 to be as sick as a dog
   chien

E **clair comme de l'eau de** 2 as clear as crystal
   roche

F **trembler comme une** 2 to tremble like a leaf
   feuille
   pleurer comme une 2 to cry floods of tears
   fontaine

L **s'entendre comme** 2 to be as thick as thieves
   larrons en foire
   parler comme un livre 2 to speak with eloquence
   dormir comme un loir 2 to sleep like a log
   être connu comme le 2 to be known by everyone
   loup blanc

M **être vieux comme le** 2 to be as old as Methuselah
   monde

P **ça se vend comme des** 2 it's selling like hot cakes
   petits pains
   fier comme un paon 2 as proud as a peacock
   il est bête comme ses 1 he's as daft as a brush
   pieds
   soûl comme un Polonais 1 as drunk as a lord
   se coucher comme les 1 to go to bed early
   poules

S **dormir comme une** 1 to sleep like a log
   souche

V **parler français comme** 1 to murder the French
   une vache espagnole language

2.6.3   Proverbs

Register

le jeu n'en vaut pas la chandelle	3	the game is not worth the candle
mettre la charrue devant les bœufs	2	to put the cart before the horse
chat échaudé craint l'eau froide	2	once bitten twice shy
la nuit tous les chats sont gris	1+2	everyone looks the same in the dark
à bon chat bon rat	2+3	tit for tat
le chat parti, les souris dansent	2	when the cat's away, the mice will play
une fois n'est pas coutume	2	one swallow doesn't make a summer
il faut battre le fer pendant qu'il est chaud	2	you must strike while the iron's hot
la goutte d'eau qui fait déborder le vase	1	the straw that breaks the camel's back
l'habit ne fait pas le moine	2	it's not the cowl that makes the monk
une hirondelle ne fait pas le printemps	2	one swallow doesn't make a summer
à chaque jour suffit sa peine	3	sufficient unto the day is the evil thereof
on parle du loup, on en voit la queue/il sort du bois	2	speak of the devil
ce n'est pas la mer à boire	1	it's not so very difficult to do
il ne faut pas vendre la peau de l'ours (avant de l'avoir tué)	2	don't count your chickens (before they are hatched)
il partira quand les poules auront des dents	1	he'll be here until the cows come home
mieux vaut prévenir que guérir	2	prevention is better than cure

2.6.4   Expressions involving colours

Register

blanc		
la traite des blanches	2	the white slave trade
ce garçon est blanc comme un cachet d'aspirine	1	this boy is lily white

Register

elle est blanche comme le linge	1	she's as white as a sheet
il n'est pas blanc	2	he's not innocent
il est blanc comme neige pure	2	he's as pure as the driven snow
elle est connue comme le loup blanc	2	she's well known
c'est bonnet blanc et blanc bonnet	2	it's six of one and half a dozen of the other
elle a abordé son ami de but en blanc	2	she came straight out with it to her boyfriend
ils se sont saignés à blanc	2	they were bled dry (financially)
je lui ai donné carte blanche	2	I gave him/her a free hand
c'est un mariage blanc	2	an unconsummated marriage
une voix blanche	2	a toneless voice
j'ai passé une nuit blanche	2	I spent a sleepless night
quelle oie blanche!	2	what a goose of a girl, a naive girl!
elle a montré patte blanche avant d'entrer	2	she proved herself acceptable before going in
cet événement/ce jour est à marquer d'une pierre blanche	2	it's a red letter day
il a fait chou blanc	1	he's drawn a blank
ils se sont regardés dans le blanc des yeux	2	they stared at each other
elle dit tantôt noir, tantôt blanc	2	she says contradictory things
elle passe du blanc au noir	2	she's inconsistent
c'est écrit noir sur blanc	2	it's there in black and white

bleu

la grande bleue	2	the sea
Sophie, bas-bleu	2	blue stocking
les casques bleus	2	United Nations troops
une colère bleue	2	red with fury
un véritable cordon bleu	2	a real *cordon bleu* chef
être fleur bleue	2	to be starry-eyed/romantic (suggests naivety)
avoir une peur bleue	2	to be scared stiff, to be in a blue funk

gris

il fait gris	1	it's dull outside
faire grise mine	2	to look down in the dumps

Register

jaune		
un rire jaune	1	a forced laugh
jaune comme un citron/ un coing	2	as yellow as can be
noir		
il voit les choses en noir	1	he looks on the black side, he sees things in a sad light
c'est noir comme l'encre	2	it's as black as ink
il y faisait noir comme dans un four	2	it was as black as pitch
avoir l'âme noire	2	to be angry
une bande noire	1	a criminal bunch, a bad lot
elle est ma bête noire	1	she's my bugbear
broyer du noir	2	to be in the doldrums
les blousons noirs	1	rockers
ils ont une caisse noire	1	they've got a slush fund
elle a les cheveux noirs comme l'ébène	2	her hair is as black as ebony
on lisait dans ses yeux une colère noire	1	he/she looked as black as thunder
elle est d'une humeur noire	1	she's in a bad mood
avoir des idées noires	1	to be in the doldrums
il est sur la liste noire	2	he's on the black list
cela se vend au marché noir	2	you can buy that on the black market
une marée noire	2	an oil slick
ils sont dans une misère noire	2	they're in dire poverty
les pieds noirs	2	white settlers in Algeria
elle a lancé un regard noir	1	she looked as black as thunder
la série noire	2	a thriller (novel)
une série noire	1	a run of bad luck
le travail noir/travailler au noir	1	moonlighting/to moonlight
dire tantôt noir, tantôt blanc	2	to contradict oneself
elle passe du blanc au noir	2	she's inconsistent
c'est écrit noir sur blanc	2	it's there in black and white
or		
le silence est d'or	2	silence is golden
tout ce qui brille n'est pas or	2	all that glitters is not gold

Register

	Register	
être tout cousu d'or/ rouler sur l'or	1	to be rolling in it/money
ne pas rouler sur l'or	1	to be poor
je ne le ferais pas pour tout l'or du monde	2	I wouldn't do it for all the tea in China
l'âge d'or	2	the golden age (eg of cinema)
avoir un cœur d'or	1	to have a heart of gold
valoir son pesant d'or	2	to be worth one's weight in gold
tuer la poule aux œufs d'or	1	to kill the goose that laid the golden egg
le Siècle d'Or	2	The Golden Age (of Spain)
rose		
être frais comme une rose	2	to have a radiant complexion
ne pas sentir la rose	1	to stink
voir la vie/tout en rose	1	to see life through rose-coloured spectacles
tout n'est pas rose	1	not everything is OK
un roman/un film à l'eau de rose	1	a sentimental/schmaltzy novel/film (suggests mediocrity)
la Messagerie Rose	2	sex chat line (on Minitel)
rouge		
être dans le rouge	2	to be in the red (banking)
être rouge de colère	2	to get hopping mad/all steamed up
se fâcher tout rouge	2	to get hopping mad/all steamed up
rouge comme un coquelicot/une écrevisse	1	as red as a beetroot (after excessive sun, unexpected emotion – shame etc)
rouge comme du feu	2	to be fiery red
la lanterne rouge/les lanternes rouges	2	the last in a classification (in a competition)
dérouler le tapis rouge	2	to roll out the red carpet
vert		
les verts	2	environmentalists/Greens
se mettre au vert	2	to take a break (originally in the country, not necessarily so now)
en bailler/dire/voir des vertes et des pas mûres	1	to tell/hear dirty/scandalous jokes/stories

	Register	
elle nous en a donné de bien vertes	1	she really did deceive us
être vert de peur/de terreur	1	to be petrified/scared stiff

NOTE: for *to be green with envy* there is no exact equivalent with a colour term in French

une carte verte	2	a green card (for travelling abroad)
avoir/donner le feu vert	1	to have/to give the go ahead
la langue verte	2	slang, vulgar language
le numéro vert	2	free number (telephone)
une verte réprimande/semonce	2	a sharp telling off
être dans la verte saison	2	to be in one's prime (ie youthfulness)

2.6.5   Idioms/expressions involving numbers

These are numerous in modern French, some of which are just as odd in French as their English equivalents:

eg **apprendre le français à la six-quatre-deux** = to learn French in a slip-shod way

Consequently what follows is simply a selection. Some are genuine idioms; some are fixed expressions; others have been included to illustrate how to use numbers in various situations

	Register	
zéro		
avoir les boules/les avoir à zéro	1	to feel really low
avoir le moral à zéro	2	to feel really low
partir à zéro	2	to start from scratch
zéro pour cent de matière grasse	2	fat free
un tiers		
je suis assuré en tiers/ tierce collision	2	I've got third party (insurance) only
le Tiers Etat	2	the Third Estate (French history)
le tiers monde	2	the third world
le tiercé	2	system of betting on three placed horses
un quart		
le quart d'heure de Rabelais	3	the moment of reckoning (eg when it comes to paying the bill in a restaurant)

Register

le quart monde	2	the fourth world
un quart de seconde	2	a split second
passer un sale/un mauvais quart d'heure	2	to have a difficult time
demi/moitié		
et un demi, s'il vous plaît	2	a pint of beer (more or less)
à moitié/à mi-chemin	2	half way (to somewhere)
à moitié prix	2	half price
trois quarts		
il l'a fait aux trois quarts	2	he did three quarters of it
un		
un! deux! un! deux!	2	left! right! left! right!
un partout	2	one all (in sport/a game)
de deux choses l'une	2	it's one of two things
être en CM1/CE1	2	to be in the first year of *cours moyen/élémentaire* (primary school)
d'un seul coup	2	all in one go
encore un que les Boches n'auront pas!	1	that's another (drink) the Jerries won't have!
en un mot	2	in a word
une fois n'est pas coutume	2	one swallow doesn't make a summer
ne pas en perdre une/ ne pas en louper une	2	not to miss a trick
une de perdue, dix de retrouvées	2	there are plenty of fish in the sea (eg if your girl has left you)
avoir un pied dans la tombe	2	to have one foot in the grave
faire d'une pierre deux coups	2	to kill two birds with one stone
ne pas pouvoir en placer une	2	not to be able to get a word in edgeways
un tiens vaut mieux que deux tu l'auras	2	a bird in the hand is worth two in the bush
premier/première		
le premier de l'an	2	New Year's Day
le premier venu/la première venue	2	the first to arrive

Register

de premier choix/ordre	2	first choice, top quality
de première classe	2	first class
le premier de la classe	2	top of the class
du premier coup	2	at (the) first go
en premier lieu	2	in the first place
à première vue	2	at first sight
deux		
être plié en deux	2	to be creased/folded up (with pain/laughter etc)
couper la poire en deux	2	to have half each
avancez deux par deux	2	off you go in twos, forwards in twos/pairs
jamais deux sans trois	2	if it's happened twice it'll happen again/a third time, things come in threes
un homme averti en vaut deux	2	forewarned is forearmed
joindre les deux bouts	2	to make ends meet
être assis entre deux chaises	2	to fall between two stools
vouloir sa tartine beurrée des deux côtés	2	to want to have your cake and eat it
de deux choses l'une	2	one of two things, either one or the other
être en CM2/CE2	2	to be in the second year of *cours moyen/cours élémentaire*
prendre son courage à deux mains	2	to pluck up courage
être à deux doigts de	2	to be within an ace of (suggests danger)
il ne faut pas me le dire deux fois	2	you don't need to say it again/to tell me twice
je vais lui dire deux mots	2	I'll have a word with her/him
c'est à deux pas d'ici	2	it's a short distance from here/ it's not far
vous y serez en deux secondes	2	you'll be there in a jiffy
deuxième/second		
elle a retrouvé sa deuxième jeunesse	2	she's found her second youth
le deuxième sexe	2	the fair sex, womankind
ma fille est en seconde	2	in the lower sixth, year 11
retrouver un second souffle	2	to get a second breath/wind

Register

trois

frapper les trois coups	2	signal for beginning of play in French theatre
en trois D/dimensions	2	in 3-D
un hôtel à trois étoiles	2	three star hotel
c'est trois fois rien	2	it's nothing at all, it's not important
une barbe de trois jours	2	three-days' (beard) growth
ma voiture avance sur trois pattes	1	my car's firing on three plugs/cylinders
un costume trois-pièces	2	a three-piece suit
haut comme trois pommes	2	to be knee-high to a grasshopper

troisième

mon fils est en troisième	2	my son's in the fourth form/year 10
le troisième âge	2	the elderly, senior citizens
l'Université du troisième âge	2	University of the third age (for retired/older people)

quatre

il mange comme quatre	2	he's got a colossal appetite
couper les cheveux en quatre	2	to split hairs
se mettre en quatre pour . . .	2	to kill oneself to . . .
c'est clair comme deux et deux font quatre	2	it's as clear as crystal
monter/descendre un escalier quatre à quatre	2	to race up/down the stairs
ne pas y aller par quatre chemins	2	not to beat about the bush
être tiré à quatre épingles	2	to be dressed up to the nines
prendre son quatre heures	2	to have an afternoon snack
marcher à quatre pattes	2	to walk on all fours
les quatre points cardinaux	2	the cardinal points (of the compass)
une marchande de quatre saisons	2	(open air) fruit and vegetable merchant
je n'irai pas par quatre saisons	2	I'll not beat about the bush
l'Opéra de Quat'sous de Brecht	2	*The Threepenny Opera* (Brecht)

Register

se saigner les quatre veines pour . . .	2	to kill oneself to . . .
dire ses quatre vérités à qn	2	to tell sb what you think of them
faire les quatre volontés de qn	2	to be at someone's beck and call
quand je rentrerai en quatrième, je choisirai espagnol LV2	2	in year 9 I'll take Spanish

cinq		
je vous reçois cinq sur cinq	2	I'm receiving you loud and clear
moins cinq, ça y était	1	almost (eg just avoiding an accident)
le mouton à cinq pattes	2	a rare bird (as of an antique)
en cinq secondes	1	in a jiffy
la classe de cinquième est importante	2	second form, year 8, is an important year
être la cinquième roue du carrosse	2	to be a doormat

six		
faire qch à la six-quatre-deux	2	to do sth in a slip-shod way
le sixième sens	2	the sixth sense
mon petit dernier va rentrer en sixième	2	the first year, year 7

sept		
de sept à soixante-dix-sept ans	2	everyone
une K7 audio/vidéo	2	audio/video cassette
être laid comme les sept péchés capitaux	2	to be as ugly as sin
le septième art	2	the cinema
être au septième ciel	2	to be on cloud nine

huit		
faire les trois huit	2	to do shift work (right round the clock)
le Grand Huit	2	rollercoaster
dans huit jours	2	in a week's time
je te verrai dimanche en huit	2	I'll see you Sunday week
le huitième art	2	television

Register

neuf
neuf fois sur dix	2	nine times out of ten
le neuvième art	2	comics
(la bande dessinée)		

dix
les dix Commandements	2	the Ten Commandments
ne pas savoir quoi faire	2	to be cackhanded
de ses dix doigts		

douze
les douze coups de	2	the moment of high drama
minuit		
les douze travaux	2	the twelve labours of Hercules
d'Hercule		

treize
être treize à table	2	to be thirteen at table (to be avoided)
treize à la douzaine	2	baker's dozen (originally thirteen oysters given for twelve)
le vendredi treize	2	Friday 13th
avoir le treizième mois	2	to have a month's pay/bonus above the statutory twelve

quatorze
c'est reparti comme en quatorze!	2	here we go again!
chercher midi à quatorze heures	2	to complicate matters
il a fait quatorze dix-huit	2	he was in the First World War
fêter le 14 juillet	2	to celebrate 14th July

quinze
dans quinze jours	2	in a fortnight's time
tous les quinze jours	2	every fortnight
lundi en quinze	2	two weeks (from) Monday
dans une quinzaine	2	in a fortnight's time

vingt
vingt sur vingt	2	brilliant!
on n'a pas tous les jours vingt ans	2	you're not twenty for ever

NOTE: whereas in English adulthood begins at eighteen, it begins at twenty in France

	Register	
vingt dieux de vingt dieux!	1	heavens above!
miscellaneous 22–80		
vingt-deux, v'là les flics	1	careful! watch it! here come the cops
je te l'ai dit vingt-cinq fois!	2	I've told you hundreds of times!
être/se mettre sur son trente-et-un	2	to be dressed up to the nines/to put one's glad rags on
dites trente-trois	2	open wide (at the doctor's)
(en) voir trente-six chandelles	2	to see stars
faire trente-six choses à la fois	2	to be doing too many things at the same time
il n'y a pas trente-six solutions	2	there's not a million ways of doing/solving it
la semaine de trente-neuf heures	2	the thirty-nine-hour week
s'en moquer comme de l'an quarante	2	not to care a toss
à remettre sous (les) quarante-huit heures	2	to put off for a time (in French administration with respect to a decision)
les années cinquante/ les fifties	2/1	the fifties
je te l'ai répété cinquante fois	2	I've told you hundreds of times
être heureux comme un cinquante-et-un dans l'eau	2	to be as happy as a sandboy (with reference to the Pastis advert)
les années soixante/les sixties	2/1	the sixties
(faire (le)) soixante-neuf	1	soixante-neuf/sixty-nine (erotic position)
les années soixante-dix/les seventies	2/1	the seventies
Putain! c'est encore un 75!	1	bloody hell! another Parisian! (behind the wheel) (75 is the number plate for Paris)
les années quatre-vingts	2	the eighties
cent		
je te le donne en cent	2	I'll give you three guesses
gagner des mille et des cents	2	to win a fortune

Register

ma voiture fait six litres aux cent	2	my car does forty miles to the gallon
cent pour cent matière grasse	2	full fat
être aux cent coups	2	to be in a state, to be worried sick
faire les cent coups	2	to paint the town red
Maman te l'a dit cent fois	2	Mummy's told you a hundred times
il y en a cent fois trop	2	there's far too much
tu me feras cent lignes	2	you will write out one hundred lines
ce n'est pas à cent mètres d'ici	2	it's just round the corner
faire les cent pas	2	to pace up and down

miscellaneous 107–400

on va pas attendre cent sept ans!	2/1	we're not going to wait an eternity!
trois cent soixante-cinq jours par an	2	every single day
faire les quatre cents coups	2	to be up to no good

mille

et paf, en plein dans le mille!	1	and bang, spot on!
taper dans le mille	1	to hit (it) spot on
elle a fait mille conneries dans sa vie	1	she's done some stupid things in her life
mille fois merci	2	a thousand thanks
un mille-pattes	2	a centipede, millipede

2.7 Proper names

2.7.1 Personal names

Although there are French equivalents for a number of English personal names (Peter = *Pierre*, Stephen = *Etienne*, Joan = *Jeanne*, Mary = *Marie*) the names of individuals are not translated from one language to the other: John Smith remains John Smith in French, and Pierre Dupont likewise remains Pierre Dupont in English.

The names of famous or notorious historical personages often have a peculiar French form. Although this does not apply to English names, Latin, Greek and Italian names are particularly affected. There

153

are also special French forms for some modern-day Russian names as well as historical ones.

Greek

Alexandre	Homère	Périclès	Pythagore
Aristote	Léandre	Platon	Sophocle
Euripide			

NOTE: *in* Pâris (*in the story of Helen of Troy*) *the final –s is pronounced*

Latin

Auguste	Cicéron	Marc-Aurèle	Scipion
Caton	Lavinie	Néron	Tibère
Jules César		Ovide	

Biblical

Elie (*Elijah*)	Moïse	Jean-Baptiste
Esaïe (*Isaiah*)	Barthélemy	Lazare
Esdras (*Ezra*)	(*Bartholomew*)	Zachée (*Zachaeus*)
Jérémie	Hérode	

NOTE: *the Old Testament character 'Saul' becomes* Saül *in French, whereas the New Testament 'Saul' is* Saul

Italian

Sometimes the names of Italian artists and writers are preceded by le *in French, translating the Italian 'il'.*

Arioste	Léonard de Vinci	Le Tasse
Boccace	Machiavel	Le Tintoret
Le Caravage	Pétrarque	Le Titien
Le Corrège	Michel-Ange	

NOTE: *When names of painters, usually Italian, involving* Le *and also of the architect* Le Corbusier *are preceded by* de, le *and* de *combine to form* du (*eg* les toiles du Caravage/du Titien). *This does not apply in the case of the politician* Le Pen.

Russian

Borodine	Soljenitsyne	*'Catherine the Great'*
Dostoïevski	Staline	*is normally*
Eltsine	Tchaïkovski	*translated as* la
Lénine	Tolstoï	Grande Catherine
Raspoutine	Tourgueniev	

The Spanish painter 'El Greco' is Le Greco (*eg* les peintures du Greco). *The Emperor 'Charles V' is known as* Charles Quint *in French.*

For matters of gender and number of proper names, see **3.1** Gender and **3.2.1.4** Proper names.

2.7.2   Names of towns

Many towns in Europe and elsewhere have a particular French form.
Below is a list of the most common ones.

Europe	Autriche	Vienne	Grèce	Athènes
	Belgique	Anvers		Thessalonique
		(*Antwerp*)	Hollande	La Haye
		Bruxelles	Italie	Gênes (*Genoa*)
		Gand (*Ghent*)		Livourne
	Chypre	Nicosie		(*Leghorn*)
	Danemark	Copenhague		Padoue
	Espagne	Barcelone		Rome
		Cordoue		Sienne
		La Corogne		Venise
		(*Corunna*)		Vérone
		Saint-Sébastien	Malte	La Valette (elle
		Salamanque		est à La
		Saragosse		Valette)
		Séville	Pologne	Cracovie
		Tarragone		Varsovie
		Tolède	Portugal	Lisbonne
		Valence	Russie	Moscou
		(*Valencia*)	Sicile	Palerme
	Grande	Cantorbéry	Suisse	Genève
	Bretagne	Douvres		
		Edimbourg		
		Londres		
Afrique	Afrique du Sud	Le Cap (elle est	Ethiopie	Addis–Abéba
		au Cap)	Ghana	Khoumassi
	Algerie	Alger (un	Maroc	Marrakech
		Algérois =		Tanger
		inhabitant of	Tunisie	Bizerte
		Algiers)		
	Egypte	Alexandrie		
		Le Caire (il		
		est au Caire;		
		un Cairote =		
		inhabitant of		
		Cairo)		
Asie	Afghanistan	Kabou/Kabul	Malaisie	Singapour
	Chine	Chang-hai	Népal	Katmandou
		Pékin	Philippines	Manille
	Corée	Séoul	Tibet	Lhassa

Moyen Orient	Arabie Séoudite	La Mecque (il est à La Mecque) Médine	Iran Liban Syrie	Téhéran Beyrouth Alep Damas
Amérique du Nord	Canada	Montréal /mɔ̃real/		
	Etats-Unis	La Nouvelle Orléans (elle est à La Nouvelle Orléans) Philadelphie		
Amérique Centrale	Cuba	La Havane (il est à La Havane)		
	Mexique	Mexico (*Mexico City*)		
Amérique du Sud	Argentine	Buenos Aires /bɥenɔs ɛr/		

2.7.3   Pronunciation

Personal names

Generally speaking personal names are pronounced in an orthodox French manner, and even if the spelling of foreign names remains the same, their pronunciation conforms to French principles, eg Dante /dãt/, Samson /sãsõ/, Romulus /rɔmylys/. There are, however, a few peculiarities of pronunciation which should be noted:

Jésus–Christ /ʒesykri/, but le Christ /lə krist/
Pierre Boulez (*composer and conductor*) /pjɛr bule/ *or* /bulɛz/
les Broglie (*an eminent French family*) /le brœj/
Albert Camus (*French author*) /albɛr kamy/
Machiavel (*Italian politician*) /makiavel/
Michel-Ange (*Italian painter and sculptor*) /mikɛlãʒ/
Robespierre (*French politician*) /rɔbɛspjɛr/
George Sand (*French author*) /ʒɔrʒ sãd/

Place names

Here is a sample of some French and Belgian place names whose pronunciation gives difficulty:

Auxerre /ɔksɛr/ *or* /ɔsɛr/
Bruxelles /bryksɛl/ *or* /brysɛl/
Chamonix /ʃamɔni/ *or* /ʃamɔniks/
Le Doubs /lə du/
Laon /lã/
Lot /lɔt/
Metz /mɛs/
Rodez /rɔdɛz/
Saint-Gaudens /sɛ̃ godɛs/

Saint-Jorioz (*Alpine village*) /sɛ̃ ʒɔrio/ *or* /sɛ̃ ʒɔriɔz/
Saint-Tropez /sɛ̃ trope/ *or* /sɛ̃ tropɛz/

2.8   Abbreviations

2.8.1   General

With the proliferation of numerous types of organisations –
international, political, scientific, economic and so on – it has
become necessary to distinguish between them by the use of precise,
but often long, titles. Inevitably, in an age when speed and efficiency
are at a premium, these long titles become truncated or, more often,
reduced to their initial letters. Abbreviations are now so widespread
in French that they have become, to quote one French person, a
maladie!

The desire for conciseness leads in a number of cases to the initial
letters themselves forming a word in its own right: in the following list
such words are indicated by a ⋆. The other abbreviations are
pronounced as a series of individual letters except for those marked ^,
which need to be pronounced in their full form. The former are
known as *acronyms*, the latter as *sigles*. The list contains the most
widely used French abbreviations.

The gender of the abbreviation is determined by the first word: eg
le CAPES, le CES, la BNP.

Abbreviation	Full form	English equivalent (or explanation)
ADN	acide désoxyribonucléique	*DNA*
AF	allocation familiale	*family allowance*
arr^	arrondissement	*postal district (of large town)*
ASSEDIC⋆	Association pour l'emploi dans l'industrie et le commerce	*(organisation managing unemployment contributions and payments)*
guide A–Z de Paris		*A–Z guide to Paris*
bac⋆	baccalauréat	*GCE 'A' levels or school leaving certificate*
BCBG	bon chic, bon genre	*smart and stylish*
bd^	boulevard	*boulevard*
BD	bande dessinée	*comic strip*
BNP	Banque Nationale de Paris	*(French bank)*
BT	brevet de technicien	*(vocational diploma)*
BTS	brevet de technicien supérieur	*(advanced vocational diploma)*
BU	bibliothèque universitaire	*university library*
CAPES⋆ /kapɛs/	certificat d'aptitude au professorat de l'enseignement secondaire	*Diploma of Education*

Abbreviation	Full form	English equivalent (or explanation)
CCP	compte chèque postal	*Giro account*
CD	disque compact	*CD, compact disk*
CDD	contrat à durée déterminée	*fixed-term contract*
CDI	contrat à durée indéterminée	*open-ended contract*
CE	Communauté européenne	*EC, Common Market*
CE1	Cours élémentaire 1	*(syllabus for 7–8 year olds in primary school)*
CE2	Cours élémentaire 2	*(syllabus for 8–9 year olds)*
CEDEX★	Courrier d'entreprise à distribution exceptionnelle	*(special state postal system)*
CEG	collège d'enseignement général	*secondary school (up to 16 years)*
CES	collège d'enseignement secondaire	*secondary school (up to 18 years)*
CET	collège d'enseignement technique	*technical secondary school*
CFDT	Confédération française et démocratique du travail	*(French trades union)*
CGT	Confédération générale du travail	*(French trades union)*
Cie^	compagnie	*Co, company*
CL	Crédit Lyonnais	*(French bank)*
CM1	cours moyen 1	*(for 9–10 year olds)*
CM2	cours moyen 2 eg la petite est en CP/CM1 etc	*(for 10–11 year olds)*
CNED	Centre national d'enseignement à distance	*Open University*
CNPF	Conseil national du patronat français	*CBI, Confederation of British Industry*
CP	cours préparatoire	*(syllabus for 6–7 year olds)*
CROUS★	Centre régional des œuvres universitaires et scolaires	*(university body dealing with student welfare matters)*
CRS	Compagnies républicaines de sécurité	*riot police*
un CRS	membre des Compagnies . . .	*riot policeman*
CV	curriculum vitae	*curriculum vitae*
le système D (R1)	le système débrouillard	*(one's ability to get out of a difficult situation)*
DAEU	diplôme d'accès aux études universitaires	*Access Diploma*
DCA	Défense contre avions	*anti-aircraft defences*
dép^	département	*department*
DES	diplôme d'études supérieures	*M.Phil.*
DESS	diplôme d'études supérieures spécialisées	*higher degree taken after Master's*
DEUG★	diplôme d'études universitaires générales	*(university diploma after two years' study)*
DOM★– TOM★	départements d'outre-mer et territoires d'outre-mer	*(French overseas possessions)*

Abbreviation	Full form	English equivalent (or explanation)
Dr^	docteur	*doctor*
DST	Direction de la surveillance du territoire	*secret service, MI5*
EDF	Electricité de France	*Electricity Board*
E–M G	état-major général	*GHQ, general headquarters*
ENA★	Ecole nationale d'administration	*(a Grande Ecole producing France's administrative élite)*
EU	Etats–Unis	*USA*
exp^	expéditeur	*sender*
F	franc(s)	*franc*
FC	formation continue	*adult continuing education*
FEN★	Fédération de l'éducation	*(trades union grouping all national teachers)*
FMI	Fonds monétaire international	*IMF, International Monetary Fund*
FN	Front National	*(French political party)*
FNAC★	Fédération nationale des achats des cadres	*(chain of shops selling cultural goods, books, records, music in nearly all large towns)*
FO	Force Ouvrière	*(trades union)*
le point G		*G-spot (female orgasm)*
GDB (R1)	'gueule de bois'	*hangover*
GDF	Gaz de France	*Gas Board*
GPL	gaz de pétrole liquéfié	*LPG liquefied petroleum gas (found at petrol stations)*
elle fume du H (R1)		*she smokes hashish*
la bombe H		*H-bomb*
l'heure H		*zero hour*
HLM	habitation à loyer modéré (Note: m or f in abbreviated form, but f in full form)	*council house; social housing estate/flats/low cost accommodation*
le point I	le point Information	*Information bureau*
IFOP★	Institut français d'opinion publique	*(opinion research organisation)*
INSEE★	Institut national de la statistique et des études économiques	*(centre for study of statistics and economics)*
IUFM	Institut universitaire de formation des maîtres	*School of Education*
IUT	Institut universitaire de technologie	*(University devoted exclusively to technology)*
le jour J		*D-Day*
JO	les Jeux Olympiques	*Olympic Games*
kg^	kilogramme	*kilogram*
km^	kilomètre	*kilometre*
KO	knock out	*knock out*

Abbreviation	Full form	English equivalent (or explanation)
LEA	langues étrangères appliquées	*university vocational language course (especially with reference to business and management)*
LV1, LV2, LV3	langues vivantes	*modern languages, years 1, 2, 3*
M.^	monsieur	*Mr, sir*
Me^	maître (avocat)	*(title for lawyer)*
ME	moyennes entreprises	*(middle-size businesses)*
MF/FM	modulation de fréquence	*high frequency*
Mgr^	monseigneur	*monseigneur (title for cardinal)*
MLF	Mouvement de libération de la femme	*Women's Liberation Movement*
Mlle(s)^	mademoiselle, mesdemoiselles	*Miss, misses*
MM^	messieurs	*gentlemen*
Mme(s)^	madame, mesdames	*Mrs, ladies*
M–P	mandat-poste	*postal order*
NDLR	note de la rédaction (pour) la énième fois	*(editorial note in newspaper) for the umpteenth time*
OLP	Organisation de la libération de la Palestine	*PLO, Palestine Liberation Organisation*
OM	Olympique de Marseille	*Marseille Football Club*
ONU★	Organisation des Nations Unies	*UNO, United Nations Organisation*
OPEP★	Organisation des pays exportateurs de pétrole	*OPEC, Oil Producing and Exporting Countries*
ORSEC★	Organisation des secours, *usually* le plan ORSEC	*(national accident service, operating in summer)*
ORTF	Office de la radiodiffusion et télévision français	*(French equivalent of BBC)*
OS	ouvrier spécialisé	*unskilled worker*
OTAN★	Organisation du traité de l'Atlantique du Nord	*NATO, North Atlantic Treaty Organisation*
OUA	Organisation de l'unité africaine	*OAU, Organisation of African Unity*
OVNI★	objet volant non-identifié	*UFO, unidentified flying object*
PAC★	la Politique agricole commune	*Common Agricultural Policy*
PACA★	Provence–Alpes–Côtes d'Azur (eg la région PACA)	*(Administrative region of southern France)*
PC	Parti communiste	*Communist party*
PC	poste de commandement	*(military base, any centre for an official organisation)*
PCV	percevoir; téléphoner en PCV	*to reverse the charges for a phone call*
PDG	président-directeur général	*managing director*
PE	petites entreprises	*(small businesses)*

Abbreviation	Full form	English equivalent (or explanation)
PEL	plan d'épargne logement	*(savings scheme entitling saver to cheap mortgage)*
PEP★	plan d'épargne personnalisé	*personal equity plan*
PME	petites et moyennes entreprises	*(small and middle-size businesses)*
PMU	pari mutuel urbain	*(French betting system, tote)*
PNB	produit national brut	*gross national product*
PQ (R1)	papier à cul	*toilet paper*
PS	Parti socialiste	*French socialist party*
PSG	Paris Saint Germain	*Paris Saint Germain Football Club*
PTT	Postes, Télégraphes, Téléphones	*Post Office*
PV	procès-verbal	*(booking, by policeman)*
PVD	pays en voie de développement	*developing countries*
QI★/kyi/	quotient intellectuel	*IQ, intelligence quotient*
les mois en R		*months containing the letter R (eg il faut acheter des huîtres les mois en R (ie when they are safe to eat))*
RAS	rien à signaler	*nothing to report*
RATP	Régie autonome de transports parisiens	*(Parisian transport system)*
RED	rez-de-chaussée	*ground floor (in many large public buildings eg hospitals)*
RER	Réseau express régional	*(Parisian surburban rail service connecting with the Metro)*
RF	République française	*French Republic*
RMI	revenu minimum d'insertion	*income support*
RPF	Rassemblement du peuple français	*(French political party)*
RPR	Rassemblement pour la République	*(French political party)*
RSVP	répondez, s'il vous plaît	*RSVP*
RTF	Radiodiffusion et télévision françaises	*French equivalent of BBC*
RU★	restaurant universitaire	*University dining-hall/canteen*
SAMU★	Service d'assistance médicale d'urgence	*mobile accident unit*
SARL★	société à responsabilité limitée	*limited company*
SDF	sans domicile fixe	*of no fixed abode*
SICAV★	Société d'investissement à capital variable	*unit trust*
SIDA★	syndrome immuno-deficitaire acquis	*AIDS, acquired immune deficiency syndrome*
SME	système monétaire européen	*ERM = exchange rate mechanism*
SMIC smic★	salaire minimum interprofessionnel de croissance	*guaranteed minimum income*
SMIG smig★	salaire minimum interprofessionnel garanti (*same as* SMIC *but less common*)	*guaranteed minimum income*

161

Abbreviation	Full form	English equivalent (or explanation)
SN	Service national (– militaire)	*National Service*
SNCF	Société nationale des chemins de fer français	*British Rail*
SNES	Syndicat national des enseignants du secondaire	*National Union of Teachers, NUT*
SNE sup★ /snesyp/	Syndicat national de l'enseignement supérieur	*Association of University Teachers, AUT*
SNI	Syndicat national des instituteurs	*(Primary school-teachers' trades union)*
SOFRES★ /sɔfrɛs/	Société française d'enquêtes par sondages	*(opinion research organisation)*
SS	Sécurité sociale, also la Sécu★ (R1)	*Social Security*
STAPS★	Sciences et techniques des activités physiques et sportives	*College for teachers studying physical education*
SVP	s'il vous plaît	*please*
un T-shirt		*a T-shirt*
TD	travaux dirigés	*main lecture*
TGV	train à grande vitesse	*high speed train*
TNP	Théâtre national populaire	*(French national theatre)*
TP	travaux pratiques	*tutorial*
TSF	télégraphie sans fil	*radio*
TSVP	tournez, s'il vous plaît	*PTO, please turn over*
TTC	toutes taxes comprises	*including tax*
TVA	taxe à la valeur ajoutée	*VAT, value added tax*
UDF	Union pour la démocratie française	*(French political party)*
UE	Union européene	European Union
UFR	Unité de formation et de recherche	*Faculty (as in UFR sciences / lettres)*
UNEF★	Union nationale des étudiants de France	*National union of students*
URSS★	Union des Républiques Socialistes Soviétiques	*USSR, Union of Soviet Socialist Republics*
USA	Etats Unis	*USA*
à vitesse grand V		*at top speed*
VO	version originale (voir en VO)	*original version*
VPC	vente par commande	*mail order*
VTT	vélo tout terrain	*mountain bike*
VTT	véhicule tout terrain	*off-road type vehicle / 4 × 4*
WC (pl)	water closet, les double VC, les VC (R1)	WC
un film (classé) X		*an X (rated) film*
porter plainte		*to lodge a complaint against*

Abbreviation	Full form	English equivalent (or explanation)
contre X		*persons/a person unknown*
ZEP★	zone d'éducation prioritaire	*area of educational priority*
ZI	Zone industrielle	*industrial estate/complex*
ZUP	zone à urbaniser en priorité/zone d'urbanisation prioritaire	*(new suburb, comprising mainly low-cost housing)*

2.8.2   Petites annonces

Penetrating the language of *les petites annonces* in newspapers and magazines may be a bewildering task. The most esoteric examples seem to be those relating to accommodation, *immobilier*, and it is also in this area that the grammar appears at its most 'strangled'. The following is a short glossary of the most frequently encountered abbreviations and more obscure expressions.

	Abbreviation	Full form	English equivalent
position of accommodation:	**2 arrdt**	dans le deuxième arrondissement	*in the 2nd postal district*
	banl	en banlieue	*in the suburbs*
	ttes banl	toutes les banlieues	*easy access to the suburbs*
	camp	à la/de campagne	*in the country*
	M° Gare du Nord	Métro Gare du Nord	*nearest Métro station Gare du Nord*
accommodation:	**asc./ascens.**	ascenseur	*lift*
	bains/bns/s.d. bns	salle de bains	*bathroom*
	balc	balcon	*balcony*
	ch	chambre	*bedroom*
	chauf. centr.	chauffage central	*central heating*
	tt/tout cft	tout confort	*all mod cons*
	pte cour	petite cour	*small backyard*
	cuis.	cuisine	*kitchen*
	cuis. amén.	cuisine aménagée	*well-equipped kitchen*
	dche	douche	*shower*
	2e	au deuxième étage	*on the second floor*
	s. d'eau	salle d'eau	*bathroom/shower room*
	entrée	salle d'entrée	*entrance hall*
	gar.	garage	*garage*
	habit. + dép.	habitations et dépendances	*tenant houses and outhouses (eg of farm)*
	imm.	immeuble	*building*
	moq.	moquette	*with fitted carpets*

	Abbreviation	Full form	English equivalent
	1 p.	une pièce	*one-roomed flat (excluding kitchen and bathroom)*
	3 + 4 ps.	trois et quatre pièces	*flats with three and four rooms (excluding kitchen and bathroom)*
	park.	parking	*space for car*
	s/rue	donnant sur la rue	*overlooking the road*
	s-sol	sous-sol	*basement*
	vue dég.	vue dégagée	*uninterrupted view*
condition of accommodation:	eau EGDF	eau, électricité et gaz de France	*water, gas and electricity*
	ensol.	ensoleillé	*sunny*
	imm. ravalé	immeuble ravalé	*modernised building (exterior)*
	imm. réc.	immeuble récent	*new building*
	m. à rén.	maison à rénover	*house in need of renovation*
	poss.	possibilités	*with possibilities*
	tr. b. rénovat. en cours	très belle rénova-tion en cours	*outstanding renovation in progress*
	terrain 1000 m² entièrement viab.	terrain de 1000 m² entièrement viabilisé	*1,000 m² plot with all services laid on*
selling/buying process	ach.	achète	*wishes to purchase (viewing) after 6 pm*
	apr. 18h	après 18 heures	
	cpt	comptant	*cash sale*
	libre de ste	libre de suite	*immediate occupation*
	p. à p./part. à part.	particulier à particulier	*private sale*
	pptaire	propriétaire	*house-owner*
	px 530 000 F à débattre	prix de 530 000 F à débattre	*price 530,000 F or nearest offer*
	vd	vend	*wishes to sell*
	vend.–sam. 15–18h	vendredi à samedi entre 15 et 18 heures	*(viewing) Friday and Saturday between 3 and 6 pm*
	vis.	visiter	*viewing (recommended)*

2.8.3 Truncation

Truncation is the process whereby a word is shortened by one or more syllables or simply one or two sounds. It has become a passion in current spoken French, and with a few exceptions most of the truncated forms fall into the R1 category. Exceptions which have become part of standard (R2) French are:

métro, photo, topo, vélo

Others are also of long standing but have not been raised to R2 status; most are formed by young people:

eg **auto (automobile), bac (baccalauréat), dac (d'accord), diapo (diapositive), dico (dictionnaire), disserte (dissertation), fac (faculté), maths (mathématiques), philo (philosophie), prof (professeur), rab (rabiot), rédac (rédaction), sympa (sympathique)**

The following list presents some more recent creations and illustrates the wide-ranging nature of the phenomenon:

un accro (accroché) = fanatic (eg *les accros du téléphone mobile*)

l'amphi (amphithéâtre) = lecture theatre (eg *la conférence aura lieu en amphi 1*)

un anar (anarchiste)

un apéro (apéritif) (eg *on prend un apéro?*)

un appart (appartement)

cet aprem (après-midi)

un aristo (aristocrate)

le bénéf (bénéfice) (eg *faire du bénéf* = to make profit)

une bio (biographie)

le calva (calvados) (eg *tu prends du calva?*)

la cata (catastrophe) (eg *c'est la cata!*)

le champ (champagne) (eg *tu prends du champ?*) (p is pronounced)

le ciné (cinéma)

la clime (la climatisation = air-conditioning) (eg *s'il fait trop chaud on met la clime*)

un collabo (collaborateur)

une compo (composition) (eg *je dois faire une compo ce soir*)

une conf (conférence) (eg *j'ai une conf ce matin*)

un croco (crocodile)

D un/deux (division un/deux) (eg *c'est une excellente équipe, ils sont en D un depuis vingt ans; ils ne sont pas très solides, ils sont en D deux*)

la dactylo (dactylographe/dactylographie)

sans déc (sans déconner = no kidding)

les arts déco (décoratifs), la déco (décoration)

le petit déj (déjeuner) (eg *allez, on prend le petit déj*)

la dém (démission) (eg *donner sa dém*)

la dép (dépression) (eg *faire une dép*)

un dino (dinosaure)

le dirlo (directeur, of a school/business) (eg *on a une réunion avec le dirlo*)

une disco (discothèque) (eg *de la musique disco*)

un docu (documentaire) (eg *ils passent un docu à la télé ce soir*)

un édito (éditorial)

un expat (expatrié)

une expo (exposition)

un fana (**fanatique**)

le foot (**football**) (eg *jouer au foot*)

un frigo (**frigidaire**) (eg *mets-le au frigo*)

le gaspi (**gaspillage**) (eg *la chasse au gaspi*)

la géo (**géographie**)

la gym (**gymnastique**) (eg *elle est prof de gym*)

un hebdo (**hebdomadaire** = weekly newspaper)

un hélico (**hélicoptère**) (eg *ils ont fait l'excursion en hélico*)

hétéro (**hétérosexuel**) (eg *il n'est pas hétéro*)

un imperm (**imperméable**) (eg *où est-ce que t'as mis mon imperm?*)

les infos (**informations** = news) (eg *on va regarder les infos*)

un intello (**intellectuel**); **intello** (adj)

une interro (**interrogation** = short test) (eg *j'ai une interro ce matin*)

la Place d'It (**la Place d'Italie** in Paris)

le kiné (**kinésithérapeute** = physiotherapist) (eg *j'ai mal au mollet, je vais voir le kiné*)

le labo (**laboratoire**) (eg *je suis des cours de japonais en labo*)

Libé (*Libération* French daily newspaper) (eg *t'as lu Libé ce matin?*)

McDo/McDos (McDonald's fastfood restaurants)

une manif (**manifestation** = demonstration) (eg *ça va barder, il y a une manif en ville*)

maso (**masochiste**)

le max (**maximum**) (eg *je fais le max pour finir aujourd'hui*)

un mécano (**mécanicien**)

faire du mélo (**mélodrame**) (eg *c'est du pur mélo* = it's a real tear jerker)

un mémo (**mémorandum**)

un métallo (**métallurgiste**)

une mob (**mobylette**)

le Nouvel Obs (*Le Nouvel Observateur* French news magazine) (eg *je suis abonné au Nouvel Obs*)

l'occas (**occasion**) (eg *il faut profiter de l'occas*)

otorino (**oto-rhino-laryngologiste** ENT, ears, nose and throat specialist)

parano (**paranoïaque**)

un pédé (**pédéraste**)

une perf (**performance**) (eg *il a réalisé une belle perf*)

le périf (**périphérique** = ring road) (eg *prends le périf, c'est plus rapide*)

la perm (**permission** = leave (for soldiers)) eg *on est en perm ce week-end*)

une photocop (**photocopie**) (eg *je fais combien de photocops?*)

les Sciences Po (**Politiques**) (eg *elle est en Sciences Po*)

la polio (**poliomyélite**)

un polycop (**polycopié** = handout) (eg *le prof a distribué des polycops*)

un porno (**un film pornographique**) (eg *on va voir un porno ce soir*)

la porno (**pornographie**) (eg *ce livre-là, c'est de la porno*)

la prépa (classe préparatoire for the *Grandes Écoles*) (eg *elle est en prépa*)

un projo (projecteur)

les prolos (prolétaires = the plebs)

une promo (promotion) (eg *il y a plusieurs produits en promo*)

les pros (professionnels) (eg *je peux pas faire la planche à voile comme les pros*)

la psycho (psychologie) (eg *elle est en fac de psycho*)

la pub (publicité = advertising, advertisement) (eg *il y a trop de pub à la télé; c'est une drôle de pub*)

un pull (pullover)

le pyj (pyjama) (eg *Antoine, t'as mis ton pyj?* (mother to a child))

la radio (radiographie = X-ray unit) (eg *j'ai passé une radio des poumons*)

rapido (rapidement) (eg *fais-le, et rapido!*)

un Rasta (= Rastafarian (there seems to be no accredited full French form))

réac (réactionnaire) (eg *les gens réac*)

réglo (réglementaire) (eg *il est réglo* = he's straight)

restau(-U) (restaurant (universitaire)) (eg *on va au restau(-U) à quelle heure?*)

rétro (rétrospective) (eg *la mode rétro*)

un rhino (rhinocéros)

les rollers (roller skates)

sado (sadique)

la Sécu (Sécurité Sociale)

sensass (sensationnel) (eg *c'est sensass!*)

un sous-off (officier = non-commissioned officer)

une (chaîne) stéréo (stéréophonique; une chaîne may also be used by itself)

les Stups (stupéfiants; la Brigade des Stups = Drugs Squad)

sup (supplémentaires) (eg *elle fait souvent des heures sup*)

le super (supercarburant = 4 star petrol) (eg *je prends toujours du super*)

un survêt (survêtement = track suit) (eg *il était en survêt*)

tel (téléphone – only in writing)

la télé (télévision; à la télé = on telly)

un toxico (toxicomane = drug addict)

un travelo (transvesti = transvestite)

2.9   Latin expressions

Educated French people will occasionally use Latin expressions in their fairly formal R3 speech. They may also, but less frequently, introduce certain ones into more relaxed R2 speech. However, *etc* (*et cetera, et caetera*), *illico, ex aequo* and *grosso modo* are probably the only Latin expressions that find their way into the most informal

register. There follows a list of the more common expressions, with
their meanings and, where they exist, their French-language
counterparts. Expressions marked with an asterisk are also used in
English.

	Latin	French	Meaning
R3	ad hoc★	destiné expressément à cet effet	*arranged for this purpose*
	a fortiori★	à plus forte raison	*with all the more reason*
	a posteriori★	par la suite	*after the event*
	cum grano salis	il ne faut pas l'accepter tel quel	*with a pinch of salt*
	desiderata★	ce qui est nécessaire	*desiderata, requirements*
	de visu	pour l'avoir vu	*as an eye witness, at first hand*
	ex cathedra★	officiellement; d'un ton doctoral	*with the highest authority*
	ex-voto★	vœu	*ex voto, offering made in pursuit of a vow*
	in situ★	dans l'endroit même	*in the very place*
	ipso facto★	par le fait même	*by the very fact*
	modus vivendi★	arrangement	*working agreement*
	(le) nec plus ultra	le meilleur	*the best*
	persona non grata★	(personne) indésirable	*unwelcome person*
	(une condition) sine qua non★	indispensable	*indispensable*
R3/R2	idem★	de même	*idem/ibid*
	in extremis★	à l'extrême limite	*at the last extremity, if pushed*
	in vitro★	en milieu artificiel/ en laboratoire	*in vitro*
	manu militari	par la force des armes	*by force of arms*
	primo, segundo, tertio	premièrement, deuxièmement, troisièmement	*in the first, second, third place*
	summum	le plus haut point (fig) (eg le summum de la littérature européenne)	*the apogee*
R2	alias★	autrement appelé	*alias*
	alibi★	prétexte	*alibi*
	a priori★	avant/auparavant	*before the event*
	mea culpa	c'est ma faute	*mea culpa; it is my fault*
	(un) mea culpa	repentir	*repentance*

	Latin	French	Meaning
	quiproquo	malentendu	*mistake (NB = not quid pro quo)*
	statu quo	dans l'état actuel	*unchanged position,*
	(*note spelling*)	des choses	*status quo*
	les ultras	les extrémistes	*extremists*
	via★	au moyen de	*via*
	vice versa★	inversement	*vice versa, conversely*
R1 and R2	**ex aequo**	à égalité	*equal, level*
	(eg il etait deuxième ex aequo)		*pegging (as in a race)*
	grosso modo	en gros	*in broad detail*
	illico	immédiatément	*immediately*

NOTE: *in the following combinations* **ès** *is a survival from Old French* (**ès = en les**), eg docteur ès lettres, licencié ès sciences. *Also from Old French* **nonobstant** (R3) = *despite*

2.10 Interjections, fillers, transition words and forms of address

2.10.1 Interjections

In the measured, self-conscious speech of R3, interjections are by definition rare. On the other hand, at the other end of the formality-informality scale, in the more spontaneous speech of R1, interjections (like slang expressions and colloquialisms) are very common indeed, occurring frequently as involuntary, emotional reflexes. R2 speech, lying between R1 and R3, also contains a certain number of interjections, but is more selective in its usage of them. In the following table an attempt has been made to grade the interjections according to intensity and decency; that is to say, the interjections are placed on a continuum, one end of which is termed 'respectable usage', and covers the expressions in the R2 column and to a lesser extent the first two of the R1 columns, and the other end of which is termed 'indecent usage' and covers the expressions in the last column.

It is accepted that 'respectable' and 'indecent' are relative terms; attitudes towards indecency and swearing are naturally highly subjective. It should be stressed that the use of interjections by non-native speakers needs to be exercised with extreme caution, as an inappropriate usage may lead to deep offence at the worst, or at the very least to embarrassment. In fact, it may be wiser for such speakers to avoid many R1 interjections altogether. It is sufficient to appreciate their force without necessarily using them oneself. Interjections of surprise and annoyance are quite often interchangeable, the emotion expressed depending entirely upon intonation and the attitude of the speaker. Popular speech and slang, including interjections, are often subject to the whims of fashion, and there is a constant gain and loss of expressions. However, the expressions in the table, which are often preceded by *c'est* and followed by an exclamation mark or question mark when written, are all in contemporary use.

	Respectable usage			Indecent usage
	R2		**R1**	**R1★**
Admiration	excellent	ça assure, Max	hyper cool	bandant
	formidable	la bombe (of girl)	méga trop cool	enculé
	parfait	c'est de la bonne	l'panard	hyper bien foutu
	parfaitement	(of girl)	le pied	joussif
		canon (of girl)	ça roule	
		ça, c'est la classe	tip top	
		clean	top	
		cool	top méga top	
		eh bien dis donc	ça tope	
		d'enfer	trop bon	
		génial		
Agreement	d'accord	d'acc	y a pas photo	
	c'est clair	ben oui	pourquoi pas?	
	entendu	bonnard	va (*occurs after a*	
	impeccable	ça boom	*statement*: je	
		ça colle, Anatole	t'aime, va!)	
		et comment	ça va	
		cool ton plan	vas-y, fais comme	
		mais ne te gêne pas	chez toi	
		impec	si tu veux, ma	
		OK	poule	
		OK, y pas		
		d'embrouille		
Annoyance	bigre	casse-toi	tu vas te prendre	berk (*disgust, eg at*
	fichtre	elle (*subject*)	une beigne	*rotten food*)
		m'empoisonne	tu me prends la	bordel
		espèce d'idiot	tête?	bordel de merde
		flûte	punaise	il me fait caguer/chier

	Respectable usage		
			Indecent usage

	R2	**R1**	**R1★**
Annoyance (*cont.*)	ça me gave/gonfle lâche-moi les baskets mince alors nom d'un chien sacré nom de Dieu (*strong*)	la purée bon sang va te faire shampooiner zut (alors)	ha, tu fais chier va chier espèce de con quel con/connard quelle conne (*F*) couillon je t'emmerde va te faire enculer/ foutre/mettre merde (alors) putain (de merde) résidu de capote salaud
Disbelief	sans blague	arrête de bourrer arrête ton char/ charre (Ben Hur) je n'y crois pas c'est dingue	mais alors mon œil pas possible? t'as vu la vierge? c'est pas vrai	tu déconnes sans déc/déconner rien à foutre putain, pas possible putain, tu rigoles

Joy	chic alors	ça baigne
		bath
		c'est la bombe
		bon Dieu de bon
		   Dieu
		bonnard
		chouette alors
		c'est l'extase
		c'est giga
		ça fait hyper du
		   bien
			c'est méga
			le pied
			roule, ma poule
			sensass
			super
			super bien
			super génial
			c'est top
			top clean
			top cool
				décontracter du gland
				je pète le feu/la forme

Objection	mais tout de
	   même
		et après?
		ben quoi?
		cacahuète
		   camembert
		qu'est-ce que tu
		   embrouilles, toi
		tu te fous de moi
		n'importe quoi
			tu rêves?
			tu rigoles
			et ta sœur?
			tu tapes dans les
			   boîtes ou quoi?
			(et) toc
			ça va pas la tête?
			ça va pas ou quoi?
				bordel
				merde
				putain
				putain de bordel de
				   merde

Relief		ouf		

	Respectable usage			Indecent usage

←———————————————————————————————————————→

	R2		**R1**	**R1★**
Surprise	grands Dieux	ça alors	délire	
	ma foi	ah ben, ça alors	(eh ben) dis/dites	
	parbleu	ah, non alors	donc	
	(mille)	ben quoi	j'hallucine	
	tonnerre(s)	eh ben	ouf	
	de Dieu	bondieu	pas possible	
		quel con	tu rigoles	
		cool	non, je suis vert	
		tu déconnes	c'est zarbi	
		sans déc/déconner		

NOTE: R3 pardi, R3/R2 ma foi

Warning	attention	défie-toi, mec	tu vas t'en prendre	va te faire foutre
		faire gaffe	une	j'vais t'tuer
		fais gaffe à ta	je te préviens, ça	vire ton cul
		gueule	vas pas le faire	
		gare/gare–gare	je suis vert	

NOTE: R3/R2 prends garde

2.10.2 Fillers

In informal speech, where hesitation is common and the right word is slow in coming to mind, sentences are rarely completely formed, and fillers, such as the following, presented in alphabetical order, are called upon to bridge the gaps:

allez	**bref**	**eh bien**	**quoi**
	(passons)		
allons donc	**c'est-à-dire**	**enfin**	**remarque**
alors	**déjà**	**euh**	**tu vois**
ben	**disons**	**ma foi**	**vous voyez/**
bof	**écoute(z)**	**un peu**	**voyez-vous**
bon			

allez   Allez, tu dis ça pour me faire rire.
allons donc   Allons donc, vous plaisantez.
alors   Alors, raconte! qu'est-ce qui s'est passé?
    Alors, tu viens?
    Il parlait tout le temps, alors je lui ai dit de se taire.
    Et alors, que veux-tu que je fasse?
ben   Ben, je sais pas.
bof   Tu penses que cette cravate va avec mon costume? Bof! Pourquoi pas?
bon   Allons bon! Il pleut.
    Vous voulez connaître la vérité? Bon, je vais tout vous dire.
    Bon! Ne te fâche pas!

bref	J'ai passé la journée à courir d'un magasin à l'autre. Bref, je suis épuisé.
c'est-à-dire	Etes-vous sûr de l'avoir vue? C'est-à-dire, tout le monde peut se tromper.
	Je ne peux pas vous aider. C'est-à-dire, je n'en ai pas le droit.
déjà	C'est combien, déjà?
disons	Disons, (que) je ne me rappelle plus.
écoute(z)	Oh, écoute, il faut pas le faire comme ça.
	Qu'est-ce que vous pensez de ce film? – Ecoutez, il n'est pas très bon.
eh bien	Comment allez-vous? – Ça va beaucoup mieux, merci. – Eh bien, c'est parfait.
enfin	Ce meuble est très cher, mais enfin je peux peut-être l'acheter.
	Je vous ai dit ce que je pensais. Enfin, c'est à vous de décider.
euh	La rue Victor Hugo? Euh . . . Je crois que c'est la première à gauche.
ma foi	Cette maison est bien située et, ma foi, je pense qu'elle vous plaira.
un peu	Tu as des nouvelles, un peu?
	Dis-moi, un peu, tu as des nouvelles?
quoi	Allons, quoi, faut pas te décourager.
	Alors quoi, on joue?
remarque	Remarque, tu peux mettre le bouquin là.
tu vois	C'est quelqu'un de très bien, tu vois. Je l'aime beaucoup.
vous voyez/ voyez-vous	Vous voyez, il ne faut jamais désespérer.
	C'est un monsieur très important, voyez-vous.

2.10.3   Transition words

In R3 speech and writing, where careful organisation of structure is essential, particularly when a discussion is taking place, transition words, marking the steps and points of an argument, are very common. They also occur quite frequently in R2 usage.

alors que	Il a plu tout l'été, alors que cet hiver nous n'avons pas eu une goutte d'eau.
au contraire	Elle a dit que ce problème de maths était tres simple. Moi, au contraire, je l'ai trouvé très difficile.
aussi	J'ai raté mon train. Aussi a-t-il fallu que je prenne l'autocar.
car	Il n'a pas pu se baigner car il avait trop mangé.
en conséquence/ par consé- quent	Elle n'a pas gagné beaucoup d'argent. En conséquence/par conséquent, elle n'a pas pu partir en vacances.
en effet	Ils ont dit que votre équipe allait gagner. En effet, c'est ce qui s'est passé.
en fait/en réalité	On a cru que Delvaux était un bon sculpteur. En fait/en réalité, il est plutôt un peintre.
en résumé	Les règles de la grammaire française sont tres nombreuses. En résumé, ce manuel pourra vous aider.
en revanche/	Nous n'avons pas pu visiter le château. En revanche/par contre, nous

par contre	sommes allés au musée.
or	Les restrictions budgétaires devraient réduire l'inflation. Or, celle-ci continue à monter.
partant (R3)	Les études littéraires sur l'œuvre de Camus sont de plus en plus nombreuses. Partant, l'intérêt des lecteurs s'est accru.
quant à	Quant à Madame Dupont, je dirais qu'elle . . .
voire (R3)	Nous pourrons peut-être étudier les romans de Butor, voire même ceux de Pinget.

In addition to transition words, also frequently used in discussions and debates are balancing words, which allow contrasts and comparisons to be made more effectively.

d'un côté . . . **de l'autre** **(côté)**	La critique contemporaine se divise en deux clans. D'un côté les traditionnalistes, de l'autre (côté) les modernistes.
d'une part . . . **d'autre part**	Dans un travail de rédaction, il faut faire attention d'une part au contenu et d'autre part à la forme.

In a carefully reasoned argument the following series of terms frequently occur:

premièrement . . .   deuxièmement . . .   troisièmement . . .

en premier lieu . . .   en second lieu . . .   troisièmement . . .

2.10.4 Forms of address

When meeting someone or when writing a letter to him/her, it is important, from the very beginning of the encounter, to strike the right chord on the register scale: first words create first impressions, and will therefore affect the subsequent attitude of the addressee. Consequently, an appropriate opening gambit should ensure a favourable hearing thereafter. The following table illustrates the various formulae that are used in contemporary French:

in speech	R1	R2	R3
on meeting	salut	bonjour, Monsieur/ Madame/ Mademoiselle/ jeune homme, etc	
	tu vas bien?	comment vas-tu?	
	vous allez bien?	comment allez-vous?	Monsieur/Madame se porte bien?
	(comment) ça va?		
	ça marche?		
	ça boum?		
	ça gaze?		
	ça fait un bail/une paie qu'on ne s'est pas vu		
	quoi de neuf?		

in speech	R1	R2	R3

on leave-taking	salut
	ciao
	tchao
	à la revoyure
		au revoir/adieu
		au plaisir (de
		  vous revoir)
		à bientôt
		à tout de suite
		à la semaine
		  prochaine, etc
		bon retour
		bon voyage
		bonne route
		bonne chance	

in letter	R1	R2	R3

introduction	Chère Jeanne	Cher Monsieur/
		  Chère Madame/
		  Mademoiselle
		(Mon) cher Jean/(Ma)
		  chère Jeanne
			Monsieur/Madame/
			  Mademoiselle
			
			Monsieur le Dir-
			  ecteur/le Premier
			  Ministre/le
			  Président

in letter	R1	R2	R3

conclusion	à bientôt
	grosses bises
	salut
		affectueusement
		  (eg *niece to uncle*)
		amitiés
		bien à toi/vous
		amicalement
		toutes mes amitiés à
		  tes parents
			je vous prie de/
			  veuillez agréer
			  (l'expression de)
			  mes salutations
			  distinguées/mes
			  respectueuses
			  salutations/mes
			  sentiments les
			  meilleurs/
			  distingués/
			  respectueux

2.11   Differences in measurements, etc

Metrication has a long history in France, its use having become legal in 1795 and compulsory from 1840. In Britain, on the other hand, two systems of weights and measures, metric and imperial, coexist in certain domains, whereas in others either the metric or imperial system has the upper hand. The result of this is not only that hesitation occurs in the minds of English-speakers using their own language, but also that on many occasions different standards prevail in the two countries. In the series of tables that follow, accepted

175

approximations for the two systems are stated (exact equivalents are generally not essential in speech), certain norms are mentioned and 'records' are given to ease comparison. It is, of course, important, when translating from English to French, to change imperial to metric measurement.

2.11.1   Distance

metric	imperial	metric	imperial
10 centimètres	4 in	100 mètres	100 yards
50 cms	1½ ft	1 kilomètre	½ mile
1 mètre	1 yard	2 kilomètres	1 mile

Height   **un enfant de quatre-vingt-dix centimètres** = a child three-foot tall

un homme d'un mètre quatre-vingts = a man six-foot tall
un homme de deux mètres = a man six-foot-six tall
France's highest mountain: **Mont Blanc: 4807 mètres** = 15,782 feet
the world's highest mountain: Mount Everest: **8880 mètres** = 29,002 feet

world record high jump: **2,38 mètres** = 7 feet 8 inches
Length   world record long jump: **8,95 mètres** = 29 feet 5 inches
the French use the term **mille** in the following expression only: **un mille marin** = a nautical mile: **1852 mètres** = 2,027 yards
Speed   **100 kilomètres/heure** = 60 mph
speed of light: **300 000 kilomètres/seconde** = 186,000 miles/second
speed of gravity: **981 centimètres/seconde carrée** = 32.2 feet/second squared
world record for car (*Thrust*) **1232 kilomètres/heure** = 770 mph
world record for aeroplane: **3 529 kilomètres/heure** = 2,113 mph

Length, height, depth and width

The following ways of expressing measurements are available:

long   un mur long de deux mètres
un mur de deux mètres de long
ce mur a deux mètres de long
ce mur est long de deux mètres

haut   un poteau haut de trois mètres
le poteau a trois mètres de haut
le poteau est haut de trois mètres

profond   un trou profond de deux mètres
le trou a deux mètres de profondeur
le trou est profond de deux mètres

large   une route large de quatre mètres
cette route a quatre mètres de large/de largeur
cette route est large de quatre mètres

2.11.2 Weight

metric	imperial
un quart de kilogramme un quart de kilo 250 grammes une demi-livre	½ pound
un demi-kilo (gramme) 500 grammes	1 pound
un kilo(gramme)	2 pounds

un homme de soixante kilos = a ten-stone man
un homme de quatre-vingts kilos = a thirteen-stone man

2.11.3 Area

metric	imperial
6 centimètres carrés	1 square inch
1 mètre carré	1 square yard
1000 mètres carrés	a quarter of an acre
1 hectare 10000 mètres carrés	2½ acres
50 hectares	125 acres
250 hectares 2½ kilomètres carrés	1 square mile

une ferme de 40 hectares = a 100-acre farm

2.11.4 Volume

metric	imperial
1 litre	2 pints
4 litres	1 gallon
16 litres	4 gallons
24 litres	6 gallons

ma voiture fait six litres aux cent (kilomètres) = my car does fifty (miles) to the gallon
ma voiture fait onze litres aux cent = my car does twenty-five to the gallon
un demi de bière = a pint of of beer

2.11.5 Temperature

Centigrade	Fahrenheit
0	32
10	50
20	68
30	86

The following formulae convert the temperature scales:
Centigrade/Celsius to Fahrenheit:

$$C \times \frac{9}{5} + 32 = F$$

Fahrenheit to Centigrade/Celsius:

$$F - 32 \times \frac{5}{9} = C$$

Body temperature: 37°C = 98.4°F. One should consult a doctor when one's temperature rises above 40°C or 104°F!

In France, degrees Celsius are used in official circumstances, in education and the media. Consequently in France **C** = **Celsius**, although ordinary French people still tend to understand the **C** as = **Centigrade**. Use of **Celsius** evokes a higher register than use of **Centigrade**.

2.11.6   Currency

The unit of currency is the *franc* (*lourd*), frequently designated F to avoid confusion with the 'old' franc, now called *centime*. However, many French people still speak in terms of old francs, ie *centimes*: thus, *gagner vingt-cinq millions* is equivalent to 250000 F or, at an exchange rate of 10 F to £1, it represents £25,000.

NOTE: **milliardaire** = millionaire

une brique (R1) = 10000F (ie 1000000 centimes) = £1,000

Euro

France and most of its European partners adopted the *euro* on 1 January 1999. The *euro* is used in the financial markets and stock exchanges, but will not replace national currencies (*les monnaies nationales*) until January 2002. In the meantime prices will be increasingly displayed in both *francs* and *euros*, in order to enable people to become familiar with the new currency. The present value of the *euro* is **1 euro = 6.56 francs**; consequently **1 franc = 0.15 euros**. The *euro* consists of 100 *centièmes* or *cents*. When it comes into operation in 2002, it will circulate in notes (*billets*) of seven different values (5, 10, 20, 50, 100, 200 and 500 *euros*) and coins (*pièces*) of eight different values (1, 2, 5, 10, 20, 50 *cents* and 1 and 2 *euros*). A 10 *euro* note will equal 65F and a 20 *cent* coin 1.30F. The French coins will be distinguished from the coins of other countries in that they will bear the initials *RF* on the national side. The *franc* will disappear from circulation after July 2002.

2.11.7   Time

The twenty-four hour system is used not only for official business – time-tables, the radio, etc – but sometimes also in daily speech:

il vient à dix-sept heures/dix-sept heures trente = he's coming at 5 o'clock/half past 5

2.11.8   Telephone

France is divided into five zones. For phone calls made within France, each number consists of five sets of two digits (10 in all). A number in Nantes, for instance, could have the following number: 02 (code for Nantes) 40 25 69 83 (zéro deux – quarante – vingt-cinq – soixante-neuf – quatre-vingt-trois). To phone Nantes from the United

Kingdom the initial 0 is dropped and 00 33 added, so the same number above would be 00 33 240 25 69 83 (zéro zéro – trente-trois – deux cent quarante – vingt-cinq – soixante-neuf – quatre-vingt-trois). To phone a number in the United Kingdom from France, again the initial 0 is dropped and 00 44 added: consequently, a number in Nottingham phoned from Grenoble, for example, might be 00 44 115 9259322.

For Paris the code is 01 plus 8 figures

For Minitel the code is 36 11 . . . (eg 36 11 + code for TF1 (Canal))

Free number – **le numéro vert** = 0800 + number.

2.11.9   Clothing sizes

Here are some examples of equivalents:

dress sizes	France	38	40	42	44				
	UK	10	12	14	16				
shoe sizes	France	37	38	39	40	41	42	43	44	45
	UK	4	5	6	7	8	9	10	11	12
shirt collar sizes	France	30	33	35	38	41	43	46		
	UK	12	13	14	15	16	17	18		

2.11.10   Numerals

Presentation of decimals, thousands and millions is different on the continent from in Britain.

For decimals a comma, *virgule, is* used instead of the British 'point':

10,1 = dix virgule un   29,7 = vingt-neuf virgule sept

For thousands and millions, instead of punctuation marks, the numerals are spaced out thus:

4 321 quatre mille, trois cent vingt-et-un

7 654 321 sept millions, six cent cinquante-quatre mille, trois cent vingt-et-un

2.12   Semi-technical vocabulary

Today's, and certainly tomorrow's, world requires ordinary citizens to acquire expertise in subjects which a generation ago would not have impinged upon them. In order to participate fully in the life of our society, to be able to talk intelligently about the latest developments, to be in a position to utilise the most recent facilities, an adequate vocabulary is necessary. Dictionaries do not always organise their lists of words in the most convenient way – alphabetical ordering is ideal if you know what you are looking up, but if you want to know what words you are likely to need in a certain situation, a different means of grouping words is preferable. In what follows, tables of the key words appropriate to a range of topics are provided. These key words constitute the essential or core vocabulary to enable the user to engage in meaningful conversation in the chosen domains.

2.12.1 La Banque

ouvrir un compte en banque	to open a bank account	un relevé bancaire un solde créditeur un solde débiteur	a bank statement a balance in credit a balance in the red
un compte bancaire un compte courant un compte d'épargne un compte sur livret un compte chèques postal	a bank account a current account a savings account a deposit account a giro account	faire un virement payer par virement automatique un prélèvement automatique	to make a transfer to pay by standing order a direct debit
le numéro de compte le code bancaire de tri	bank account number bank sort code	un prêt bancaire une traite bancaire un prêt au logement/ un emprunt immobilier	a loan a banker's draft a home loan/ mortgage
un carnet de chèques/ un chéquier	a cheque book	le distributeur automatique de billets (DAB) le code confidentiel	cash dispenser/cash point personal identification number (PIN)
un chèque en blanc un chèque barré le talon/la souche	a blank cheque a crossed cheque the stub	une carte bancaire/ de retrait bancaire une carte de crédit/ une carte bleue une carte d'achat une carte à mémoire	a bank card/debit card a credit card a charge card a smart card
émettre un chèque déposer un chèque encaisser/toucher un chèque endosser un chèque	to write/draw a cheque to pay in a cheque to cash a cheque to endorse a cheque	la prestation de service bancaire le taux d'escompte/ d'intérêt	bank service charge the interest rate
débiter son compte alimenter/ approvisionner son compte/verser de l'argent sur son compte	to debit your account to pay money into your account	le taux de base des banques/bancaire une baisse/ diminution des taux d'intérêt une hausse/ augmentation des taux d'intérêt	the bank base lending rate a cut in interest rates a rise in interest rates

un bordereau de versement	pay-in slip	une action	a share
		une obligation	a bond
un bordereau de retrait	withdrawal slip	des valeurs	securities
		des titres	stocks and shares
retirer de l'argent en espèces	to withdraw in cash	le marché de l'immobilier	the property market
payer cash/comptant	to pay cash	les placements immobiliers	property investments
un compte sans provision	an overdrawn account	les investissements fonciers	investment in land and property
être à découvert	to be overdrawn		
un découvert	an overdraft		

2.12.2   Les Assurances

un assureur	an insurer	la cotisation annuelle est déductible du revenu soumis à l'impôt	the annual payment/ subscription is deductible against tax
un agent d'assurance	an insurance agent		
un courtier	a broker		
		un abattement de 10% sur la première prime	a 10% discount on the initial premium
l'assurance automobile	car insurance	faire assurer qch	to have sth insured
l'assurance maladie	health insurance		
l'assurance invalidité	disability allowance		
l'assurance vie	life assurance		
l'assurance des biens	contents insurance		
l'assurance tous risques	fully comprehensive insurance	la valeur à neuf	new for new replacement value
l'assurance au tiers	third party insurance	la valeur de reconstitution	
la couverture	cover	indemniser	to compensate
la garantie	guarantee	les indemnités journalières	compensation by the day
les conditions	conditions		
souscrire une police/ un contrat d'assurance	to take out an insurance policy	en cas de décès	in the case of death
		en cas d'invalidité	in the case of disability
remplir une proposition d'assurance	to fill in an insurance proposal form		

la prime	premium	une demande	a claim
la cotisation	contribution	d'indemnité	
une cotisation	a supplementary	une déclaration de	a claim
supplémentaire	contribution	sinistre	
la franchise	excess	un formulaire de	a claim form
		déclaration de	
		sinistre	

l'échéance	date due	demander une	to make/put in a
le renouvellement	renewal	indemnité	claim

le bonus	bonus	la protection	legal protection
le malus	penalty	juridique	
les exclusions	exclusions	l'insolvabilité des tiers	insolvency of third
			parties

annuler/résilier un	to cancel a contract	l'incendie	fire
contrat		l'explosion	explosion
		le bris de glaces	broken windscreen
		les dommages	damage
		des frais de	breakdown and
		dépannage et	towing expenses
		remorquage	

les prestations de	sickness benefit	les régimes de	pension funds/
maladie		retraite/les caisses	pension schemes
une pension	disability pension	de retraite	
d'invalidité			

se faire rembourser à	to be reimbursed by	une pension de	old age pension
la Sécurité sociale	Social Security	retraite	
le remboursement	reimbursement of	la pension d'Etat	state pension
des frais médicaux	medical expenses	une pension de veuve	widow's pension
le remboursement	reimbursement in	une retraite	occupational pension
intégral	full	complémentaire	
		le minimum vieillesse	basic pension

cotiser à une	to contribute to a	le préretraite	early retirement
mutuelle	mutual insurance	partir en retraite	to take early
	company/friendly	anticipée	retirement
	society		

2.12.3 Les Impôts

le fisc	Inland Revenue	un abattement	tax allowance
		une remise/une	tax cut/reduction
		diminution	

un centre des impôts	tax office	une dispense	exemption
le contrôleur/ inspecteur des impôts	tax inspector	une exception déduction faite de	exception after deduction of
le revenu imposable	taxable income	donnant droit à abattement	eligibility for tax relief
un contribuable	a taxpayer		
remplir une feuille d'impôts	to fill in one's income tax return	les charges de famille	dependants
remplir une déclaration des revenus annuels	to declare one's annual income		
le premier volet/la première rubrique de la déclaration	first section of tax return	avoir droit à une pension/à une retraite/à une rente	to be entitled to a pension
un justificatif de salaires antérieurs	proof of previous earnings	un relevé de pension d'invalidité	a statement of entitlement to a disabled person's pension
le taux de fiscalité de la tranche médiane	basic rate of income tax	des revenus des valeurs et capitaux mobiliers	income from stocks and shares
la contribution directe	direct tax		
la contribution indirecte	indirect tax		
l'impôt sur les grandes/grosses fortunes	supertax/wealth tax		
le montant imposable/de l'imposition	taxable amount	la TVA/taxe à valeur ajoutée	VAT/value added tax
le barème de l'impôt sur le revenu	income tax rates	les droits de succession	death duties
le seuil minimum d'imposition	tax threshold		
la majoration des seuils d'exonération	raising tax bands		
tomber dans une tranche supérieure	to pay tax at a higher rate	la retenue à la source sur salaire	PAYE/Pay As You Earn tax system
tomber dans une tranche inférieure	to pay tax at a lower rate		

les revenus de professions non salariées	unearned income	l'abattement à la base	basic personal allowance
les revenus fonciers (loyers et fermages)	income from property	l'abattement pour couples mariés	married couples' allowance
un allègement/dégrèvement fiscal	tax relief	les impôts locaux	council tax

2.12.4   L'Informatique

l'informatique	information technology/data processing/computing	un programme	a program
		un programmeur (sur ordinateur)	a programmer
l'informatisation	computerisation	la programmation	programming
l'ordinateur	computer	la fonte	font
le portable	laptop	un caractère de 10 points	10 point type
		en romain	in roman
		en italique	in italics
		en gras	in bold
le télécopieur	fax machine	un tableau	a table
le photocopieur/la photocopieuse	photocopier	une colonne	a column
		un rang	a row
la machine à traitement de texte	word processor	l'infographie	graphics
l'imprimante	printer		
le terminal	terminal	la mise en page	layout
		le tableur	spreadsheet
		le tirage	print-out
le matériel	hardware	le format	format
le logiciel	software	formater	to format
une puce (électronique)	a microchip	le formatage	formatting
le clavier	keyboard	la télécopie/le fax	fax
la touche	key	le courrier électronique/le e-mail/la messagerie électronique	e-mail
		la toile	the world wide web
		l'Internet	the Internet

l'unité/le lecteur de disquettes	the hard drive	l'enseignement assisté par ordinateur	computer-assisted learning/CAL
le disque (dur)	the hard disk	l'apprentissage des langues assisté par ordinateur	computer-assisted language learning/CALL
une disquette (souple)	floppy disk	la conception assistée par ordinateur	computer-assisted design
sauvegarder sur disque	to save on disk	une banque de données/un fichier central	computer/data bank
emmagasiner	to store		
effacer	to delete		
sortir	to exit		
une console	console	la téléconférence informatisée	computer conferencing
le moniteur	monitor		
un écran de visualisation	visual display unit/VDU		
une souris	a mouse	un informaticien	a computer expert/engineer
cliquer	to click		
un curseur	a cursor	les services en informatique	computer services
		la sécurité informatique	computer security
		un pirate informatique	a hacker

2.12.5 La Sécurité sociale

la Sécurité sociale/la Sécu R1	the social security system	avoir droit à des prestations	to be entitled to benefits
l'Etat-providence	the Welfare State	les ayants droit	those eligible
les budgets sociaux/les dépenses sociales	expenditure on social services	revendiquer/réclamer son droit à une allocation	to claim an allowance
cotiser à la Sécurité sociale	to pay national insurance contributions	verser une allocation/une prestation	to pay an allowance/a benefit
les cotisants	NI contributors		
les cotisations versées par l'employeur et les salariés	NI contributions paid by employer and employees		

le prélèvement social	NI deductions	se faire rembourser à	to be reimbursed by
les prélèvements	compulsory	la Sécurité sociale	Social Security
obligatoires	deductions		
le relèvement des	increase in NI		
cotisations	contributions		

les prestations sociales	social benefit	les services sociaux	social services
	payments	un assistant social	social worker
une prestation en cas	sickness benefit	une assistante sociale	social worker
de maladie		un éducateur social	youth worker
une prestation pour	disability benefit		(including
incapacité			children)
		l'aide sociale	social welfare
		l'aide sociale à	child welfare
		l'enfance	

une allocation	an allowance	en fonction de	means-tested
l'allocation familiale	family allowance	ressources	
l'allocation postnatale	maternity allowance	au-dessus/au-delà	above a certain
l'allocation de parent	single parent benefit	d'un certain	ceiling
isolé		plafond	
l'allocation de	housing allowance	au-dessous/en deçà	below a certain
logement		d'un certain	ceiling
l'allocation de loyer	rent allowance	plafond	
une allocation	unemployment	dépasser un plafond	to exceed an
chômage	benefit	de ressources de	earnings ceiling
		revenu	

2.12.6   Le Commerce

le marché financier	the financial stock	le marketing/la	marketing
	market	mercatique	
la Bourse des valeurs	the French Stock	l'image de marque	brand image
	Exchange	le circuit de	(chain of)
le marché boursier	the stock market	distribution	distribution

une action	a share	à terme	on credit
une obligation	a bond	à tempérament	on hire purchase/
des valeurs	securities		HP/in instalments
des titres	stocks and shares	les conditions de	credit terms
		crédit	

les transactions	share dealing	un acompte	a deposit/
boursières			downpayment
les plus-values sur les	increases in the prices	un versement	an instalment
cours des actions	of shares		

la cotation en Bourse	being quoted on the Stock Exchange	un bon	a voucher
		un bon de commande	an order form
être coté en Bourse	to be quoted on the Stock Exchange	une facture	invoice
		une quittance	an acknowledgement/ a receipt
un actionnaire	a shareholder	une entreprise	a business/a firm
un agent de change	a stockbroker	la société mère	parent company
un cambiste	foreign exchange broker	une filiale	a subsidiary company
		une succursale	a branch
		le siège social	head office
		la raison sociale	corporate/company name
le pouvoir d'achat	purchasing power	une SARL/société à responsabilité limitée	a limited liability company/Ltd
l'économie de marché	market economy	une SA/société anonyme	a limited company/ plc
		les PME/petites et moyennes entreprises	small and medium-sized firms
l'offre et la demande	supply and demand	le chef d'entreprise	the head of a company
le rapport qualité-prix	value for money	le président	chairman
		le président-directeur général/PDG	chairman and managing director
		le manager	manager
		la gestion/le management	management
		le conseil d'administration	board of directors
		le directoire	board of directors
		la direction	management
		l'assemblée générale	annual general meeting/AGM
le chiffre d'affaires	turnover	l'ordre du jour	agenda
un bénéfice	profit	les délibérations	proceedings
rentable	profitable	le procès-verbal	minutes
		une note de service	memo
		le rapport annuel	the annual report
un rabais/une remise	reduction/rebate/ discount	l'actif	assets
		l'actif immobilisé	fixed assets
l'escompte	discount	le passif	liabilities
		les amortissements	depreciation/paying off (of a debt)

une crise économique	an economic crisis	un arriéré	an amount overdue
un recul/un repli économique	slump/a downturn in the economy	une traite non honorée	an overdue bill
une reprise économique	an upturn in the economy	une créance	a debt
		une créance irrécouvrable	a bad debt

l'indice des prix	price index	la comptabilité	accounting
la fourchette des prix	price range	le bilan	balance sheet
le prix de revient	cost price	la vérification des comptes	auditing
		le planning budgetaire	budgetary planning
		le cash-flow	cash flow

2.12.7 La Justice

le tribunal de grande instance/la cour d'appel	Crown court	le témoin à charge	witness for the prosecution
		le témoin à décharge	witness for the defence
le tribunal d'instance/ le tribunal correctionnel	magistrates' court	la partie défaillante	party failing to appear in court
la cour d'assises	criminal court	faire une déposition	to testify/to give evidence
la cour de cassation	final court of appeal		
le tribunal pour enfants	juvenile court		
la cour martiale	court martial		
le parquet	the public prosecutor's department		

le procureur de la République	Attorney General	une infraction au code de la route	a driving offence
le procureur général	director of public prosecutions	un excès de vitesse	breaking the speed limit
un juge	a judge	le non-respect d'un stop	ignoring a halt sign
un juge d'instruction	an examining magistrate	l'absence de feux par temps de brouillard	failure to use lights in fog
un juge d'instance/de paix	a justice of the peace	le tapage nocturne	disturbance of the peace at night
un magistrat/une magistrate	a magistrate	le tapage diurne	disturbance of the peace in the day
un juré/une jurée	a juror		
le jury	jury		
un avocat/une avocate	a lawyer/solicitor/ barrister		
un notaire	a solicitor		
Maître X	Mr X, QC		

la police	the police/police force	les délits	(non-indictable) offences
la gendarmerie	the police (usu in rural areas)	le vol	robbery/theft
un agent de police/ un gendarme	a policeman	l'abus de confiance	breach of trust
		la banqueroute/la faillite	bankruptcy
les forces de l'ordre	the law-enforcement agencies	l'escroquerie/la fraude	fraud
		coups et blessures	assault and battery
		entrer par effraction dans la maison	breaking and entering
		subir un préjudice financier	to suffer a financial loss
		subir un préjudice matériel	to suffer damage
la partie publique/ poursuivante/ principale	the Crown	les crimes	crimes
		le vol à main armée	armed robbery
la partie civile	private party/plaintiff	l'enlèvement/le kidnapping	kidnapping
se constituer partie civile	to act with the public prosecutor	contrefaire des billets de banque	to forge bank notes
un plaignant	a plaintiff	un attentat à la bombe	bomb attack
un accusé/un inculpé	an accused/defendant	l'assassinat/le meurtre	murder
la partie lésée	the injured party	le meurtre avec préméditation	premeditated murder
la victime	victim	l'homicide involontaire	manslaughter
		la violation de la propriété privée	forcible entry into private property
interpeller	to stop for questioning	un criminel/un malfaiteur	a criminal (guilty of serious crime)
un mandat d'arrêt	a warrant	un cambrioleur	a burglar
arrêter	to arrest	un bandit/un escroc	a swindler/crook
traduire en justice	to prosecute/to bring before the court	un assassin/un meurtrier	murderer
		un pickpocket	a pickpocket
		être en infraction	to be caught breaking the law
		être pris en flagrant délit	to be caught in the act/red-handed
		commettre/perpétrer un crime	to commit a crime

l'inculpation/le chef d'accusation	indictment/charge	une peine	a sentence/ punishment
une allégation	an allegation	une amende	a fine
intenter une action contre	to bring an action against	être passible d'une amende	to be liable for a fine
déposer une plainte contre	to bring a charge against	être sommé de verser une amende	to be summoned to pay a fine
engager un procès contre	to take to court	le retrait du permis de conduire	having your driving licence withdrawn
intenter un procès à	to institute legal proceedings		
une action civile	a civil action		
une action en diffamation	an action for libel		
un litige	litigation/dispute		
un procès	a trial		

siéger	to sit	se faire écrouer	to be imprisoned
juger	to judge	être mis sous les verrous	to be put behind bars
instruire l'affaire	to set up an inquiry		
recevoir une déposition	to hear a witness	être condamné à six mois de prison	to be sentenced to six months' imprisonment
prononcer/rendre un verdict	to give/pronounce a verdict	une peine avec sursis	a suspended sentence
infliger une peine	to pass sentence	un sursis simple	a conditional discharge
renvoyer le cas en/ devant la cour de cassation	to take a case to the Appeal Court	purger sa peine en prison	to serve time in prison
mettre le cas en délibéré	to adjourn the case	être mis en prison	to be put in prison
		être mis en cabane R1	to be put in clink
		la réclusion à durée déterminée	a prison sentence with specific time
		la réclusion à perpétuité	life imprisonment

défendre	to defend	la peine capitale/de mort	capital punishment
citer un témoin	to subpoena a witness		
soumettre à un interrogatoire	to cross-examine/to question	condamner à mort	to condemn to death
		être gracié	to be pardoned
présenter un pourvoi en cassation	to take/refer a case to the Appeal Court		
faire appel	to appeal		
faire appel d'un jugement	to appeal against a decision		
une pièce à conviction	exhibit		

comparaître en justice	to appear in court/to put in a court appearance	être relaxé/remis en liberté/libéré	to be released/freed
être appelé à comparaître	to be summoned to appear in court	être placé sous contrôle judiciaire	to be put on probation
passer en jugement/ justice	to be on trial/to stand trial	être condamné à huit mois de détention	to be sentenced to eight months' imprisonment
être au box des accusés	to be in the dock	être placé en garde à vue	to be held in police custody
plaider non-coupable	to plead not guilty	être condamné par défaut/par contumace	to be sentenced in absentia/for contempt of court
plaider coupable	to plead guilty		
être acquitté	to be acquitted		
être innocenté	to be found innocent		

2.13 Miscellaneous matters concerning vocabulary

2.13.1 Frequency of occurrence

Very often words that are cognates in English and French, that is words that bear a very strong resemblance to each other, both in form and meaning, are used in exactly the same way in the two languages. In other words, they are used in identical contexts and with identical frequency. For example the French word **machine** is used just as frequently as the English word *machine*, **pilote** as *pilot*, **illustrer** as *to illustrate*. However, there are also cases where the frequency of use varies between the two languages, and it is important for a non-native speaker to be aware of such differences. There is a danger of a word being overused and therefore inappropriately used in the second language simply because its cognate is common in the first language. This would appear odd to a native speaker of the second language.

In the following cases the French word is used more often than the English cognate:

aberrant (*aberrant*)
accéder (*to accede*)
annuler (*to annul*)
apothéose (*apotheosis*)
autonomie (*autonomy*)
camarade (*comrade*)
commencer (*to commence*)
se désister (*to desist*)
divers (*diverse*)
émettre (*to emit*)
époque (*epoch*)
évoluer (*to evolve*)
inscrire (*to inscribe*)
intégrer (*to integrate*)
interlocuteur (*interlocutor*)
interroger (*to interrogate*)
juriste (*jurist*)
(se) manifester (*to manifest (oneself)*)
multiple (*multiple*)
pédagogique (*pedagogic(al)*)
proposer (*to propose*)
renoncer (*to renounce*)
saluer (*to salute*)
transmettre (*to transmit*)
vérifier (*to verify*)

This situation also functions in reverse, and the following is a brief list of English words that occur more frequently than their French cognates:

appropriate (**approprié**)   *erratic* (**erratique**)
to blame (**blâmer**)   *fragrant* (**fragrant**)
dense (**dense**)   *magnitude* (**magnitude**)
disadvantage (**désavantage**)   *substantial* (**substantiel**)
disappointment (**désappointement**)

A corollary of the above is that very often a more frequently used English word is used instead of the cognate term:

eg **dans un but pédagogique** would regularly correspond to *with an educational objective*
il faut vérifier les pneus to *tyres should be checked*
émettre une opinion to *to express an opinion*

2.13.2   Spelling

There are cases where cognate words in the two languages appear identical in form – see **2.13.1**. On the other hand, there are also cases where there are slight differences between the two languages. These differences often concern single/double consonants, the presence of final **-e** in French but not in English, a difference of vowels. Although the differences are often slight, it is important to note them and to learn them! It would be a good idea to produce a personal list of such items. The following examples present a small selection of common differences.

adresse – *address*
calme – *calm*
caractère – *character*
circulaire – *circular*
courrier – *courier*
développement – *development*
entreprise – *enterprise*
enveloppe – *envelope*
environnement – *environment*
exemple – *example*
extase – *ecstasy*
groupe – *group*
(im)personnel – *(im)personal*
(in)dépendant – *(in)dependent*
(in)dépendance – *(in)dependence*
liqueur – *liquor*
liquide – *liquid*

littéral – *literal*
littéraire – *literary*
littérature – *literature*
mouvement – *movement*
responsable – *responsible*
responsabilité – *responsibility*
ressources – *resources*
ressusciter – *resuscitate*
rime – *rhyme*
rythme – *rhythm*
seconde (of time) – *second*
sentinelle – *sentinel*
sollicitude – *solicitude*
tarif – *tariff*
transfert – *transfer*
ustensile – *utensil*

2.13.3   Creation of compound words

A highly noticeable characteristic of word formation in contemporary French is the use of increasing numbers of compound words. This is an indication of the trend towards efficiency and economy of effort in the language. Such creations also have an air of being right up-to-date about them, of being racy, of the gimmick:

eg formerly a second-hand car was **une voiture d'occasion**; now **des voitures occasions** are advertised.

This trend is not without its problems. It is clear from consulting the standard French-language dictionaries that in many cases usage is not yet fixed. Indeed it fluctuates in three areas: gender, plural formation and spelling:

eg originally the French for bar code was **code à barres**, but now the almost universal form is **code barre(s)**; one dictionary gives **code (à) barres** (which is to be interpreted as **code barres** as well as **code à barres**), whereas another gives **code à barres**, then **code barre**.

In what follows it has not been possible to guarantee a rule for these compounds in the three areas mentioned above. The most straightforward way to proceed is to divide the examples into two categories, according to whether they are hyphenated or not (but even this is not always certain). Since the plural forms are more controversial than the singular, and since the latter may be derived from the former, the lists present the plural forms, where applicable; the gender is also indicated.

The lists provide both old and new examples, but all are common.

Hyphenated compounds
albums-photos m – allers-retours m – bateaux-mouches m – bébés-éprouvette m – camions-citernes m – centres-villes m – cocottes-minute f – contacts-radio m – écrans-vidéos m – émissions-phares f – émissions-radio f – films-culte m – hommes-grenouilles m – idées-force f – idées-clefs f – jumbos-chèques m – machines-outils f – opérations-commandos f – plateaux-repas m – pochettes-surprises f – points-clefs m – points-fidélité m (= *reward points*) – portraits-robots m – projets-phares m – réponses-modèles f – rôles-clefs m – scénarios-catastrophes m – serviettes-éponges f (= *terry towel*) – stations-services f – talkies-walkies m – timbres-poste m – villes-lumières f – villes-tests f – volte-face f

Unhyphenated compounds
années disco – années fac f – appartements témoins m (= *show flats*) – arguments chocs m – autoradio m – cassettes audio/vidéo f – code barres m – côté éducation/température (= *with respect to . . .*) m – dates butoirs f – dates limites f – ensembles jogging m –

gouvernements fantoches m – grandeur nature f (= *life size*) – images chocs f – jeux miniature m – maisons témoins f (= *show houses*) – meetings monstre m – mots pièges m – niveau éducation/température (= *with respect to* . . .) m – les parties chansons f (*of a show*) – pommes frites f – programmes télé m – rencontres chocs f – satellites espions m – services maximum m – seuils minimum m – soirées cabarets f – sommes records f – top modèles m – top secrets m – trains miniature m – voitures occasions f

Fleuve is regularly used to denote an ongoing, continuing saga: eg discours/procès/romans fleuve m

2.13.4   Verlan

Another feature of contemporary French is the emergence of words formed by transposing the syllables or sounds of the standard forms; the process is known as **verlan** and is to be particularly found amongst young people in disadvantaged areas of major cities, although some terms have also been adopted by adults. Ten of the most frequent examples are:

auche (= **chaud** = ready, dangerous), **beur** (= North African second/third generation French person, generally Algerian), **féca** (= **café**), **feuj** (= **Juif**), **keuf** (= **flic**), **keum** (= **mec**), **meuf** (= **femme**), **rem** (= **mère**), **rep** (= **père**), **tromé** (= **métro**)

3 Grammar

3.1 Gender

Gender constitutes a basic ingredient of French grammar. It is, therefore, crucial to assign the correct gender to a particular noun.

3.1.1 Rules of gender

3.1.1.1 *Simple nouns (ie non-compounds)*

Masculine gender:

Type of noun	examples	exceptions
names of days of the week	dimanche, lundi	
names of months	janvier, février	
names of seasons	hiver, printemps	
names of languages	français, swahili	
names of trees	chêne, lilas	
names of metals	cuivre, plomb	
names of human agents ending in **-eur**, **-ien**	facteur, mécanicien	
nouns ending in **-acle**	cénacle, obstacle	
nouns ending in **-ail**	détail, éventail	
nouns ending in **-at**	assassinat, secrétariat	
nouns ending in **-eau**	chapeau, seau	eau, peau
nouns ending in **-ège**	collège, sacrilège	
nouns ending in **-eil**	soleil, sommeil	
nouns ending in **-ème**	chrysanthème	crème
nouns ending in **-er**	goûter, fer	cuiller, mer
nouns ending in **-ice**	sacrifice, bénéfice	justice, malice, police; *for usage with* délice *see later*; immondices (pl)

Masculine gender:	Type of noun	examples	exceptions
	nouns ending in **–ier**	**calendrier, papier**	
	nouns ending in **–in**	**poulain, requin**	**fin, main**
	nouns ending in **–isme**	**gaullisme, prisme**	
	nouns ending in **–ment**	**commencement, monument**	**jument** (*mare*)
	nouns ending in **–o**	**numéro, zéro**	**dynamo**
	nouns ending in **–oir**	**arrosoir, miroir**	
	nouns ending in **–ou**	**genou, hibou**	
	nouns ending in **–our**	**four, tambour**	**cour, tour** (2.2.1)
	nouns with two or more syllables ending in **–age**	**sondage, virage**	**image**

Feminine gender:	Type of noun	examples	exceptions
	names of sciences	**chimie, physique**	**droit** (*law*)
	names of F agents ending in **–esse, –euse, –ière, –trice**	**maîtresse, ouvreuse, fermière, actrice**	
	nouns ending in **–ade**	**bourgade, limonade**	
	nouns ending in **–aie**	**haie, plaie**	
	nouns ending in **–aille**	**canaille, paille**	
	nouns ending in **–aine**	**haine, plaine**	
	nouns ending in **–aison**	**raison, saison**	
	nouns ending in **–ance/anse**	**assistance, danse**	
	nouns ending in **–ée**	**gorgée, matinée**	**apogée, musée, scarabée, trophée**
	nouns ending in **–ence/ense**	**magnificence, défense**	**silence**
	nouns ending in **–elle**	**ombrelle, sauterelle**	
	nouns ending in **–esse**	**petitesse, sagesse**	
	nouns ending in **–ette**	**allumette, baguette**	**squelette**
	abstract nouns ending in **–eur**	**hauteur, grandeur**	**honneur, labeur**
	nouns ending in **–ie**	**furie, partie**	**génie, incendie, parapluie**
	nouns ending in **–ière**	**prière, tanière**	**cimetière**
	nouns ending in **–ille**	**famille, grille**	*for usage with* **pupille** *see* 2.2.1
	nouns ending in **–ine**	**pénicilline, quinine**	
	nouns ending in **–ise**	**expertise, mise**	

Feminine gender:	Type of noun	examples	exceptions
	nouns ending in **-sion/tion**	**attention, compréhension**	
	nouns ending in **-té**	**beauté, rareté**	**comité, comté, côté, été**
	nouns ending in **-tié**	**moitié, pitié**	
	nouns ending in **-tude**	**habitude, solitude**	
	nouns ending in **-ue**	**charrue, grue, mue**	
	nouns ending in **-ure**	**bigarrure, tournure**	**murmure**
	monosyllabic nouns ending in **-age**	**cage, plage**	*nouns denoting males,* eg **mage, page** (**2.2.1**), **sage**

3.1.1.2   *Compound nouns (unhyphenated and hyphenated)*

type of compound	gender	examples and comments	
		M	F
noun + noun	assigned according to gender of head-word (ie first word if both nouns are of equal importance, eg *un spectateur-auditeur*, or, if one noun qualifies the other, the noun (usually the first), which is qualified, eg *un mot-clé, une idée-choc*)	*chou-fleur* *homme-grenouille* *timbre-poste*	*loi-programme* *ville-fantôme* *porte-fenêtre* (**3.2.1.2**)
adjective + noun *or* **noun + adjective**	assigned according to gender of noun	*coffre-fort* *rond-point*	*basse-cour* *chauve-souris* exceptions: *rouge-gorge, rouge-queue* are M
verb + noun	always M	*chauffe-eau* *pare-brise* *porte-avions* *portefeuille*	
invariable word + noun	assigned according to gender of noun, but always M if noun is plural	*avant-bras* *contrepoids* *haut-parleur* *deux-pièces* *mille-pattes*	*arrière-pensée* *contre-partie*
verb + verb	always M	*laissez-passer* *savoir-vivre*	
phrase	always M	*sauve-qui-peut* *va-et-vient*	

3.1.2 Difficult cases

However even native French-speakers are not always certain about the gender of some nouns, such as the following.

M gender

abîme	dédale	interrogatoire	pastiche
âge	delta	intervalle	pétale
aléas	deltaplane	labyrinthe	phoque
alinéa	dialecte	légume	quelque chose
amalgame	dilemme	liquide	quota
antidote	disco	lobe	reproche
apogée	dividende	luxe	réquisitoire
artifice	échange	magma	reste
astérisque	édifice	manque	rêve
atome	effluve	mascara	rire
autoradio	élastique	masque	saxophone
axe	éloge	mausolée	scarabée
bermuda	emblème	média(s)	schéma
boom	épisode	mérite	scrupule
cadavre	espace	micro-ondes	service
calme	estuaire	mime	sévices
caractère	exemple	minuit	silence
carrosse	exode	molécule	sourire
casque	fantoche	monopole	squelette
châle	fascicule	morse	suicide
le Petit	fleuve	moustique	swastika
Chaperon	formulaire	multimédia	symptôme
Rouge	générique	mythe	terre-plein
charme	geste	obélisque	thermos
chaume	gouffre	ongle	tonnerre
chèvrefeuille	groupe	opuscule	trapèze
choix	hectare	orchestre	trombone
choléra	hémisphère	organe	trophée
cobaye	holocauste	pactole	tuba
comble	humour	panache	uniforme
conciliabule	iguane	panorama	ustensile
crible	incendie	parachute	vice
crime	insecte	parapente	violoncelle
culte	intermède	parapluie	

F gender

alcôve	cendre	dynamo	forêt
ancre	cible	énigme	fourmi
annexe	cime	épigramme	garden-party
artère	circulaire	épitaphe	(R3/2)
atmosphère	contagion	épithète	Gestapo
basket	croix	équivoque	horreur
BBC	crypte	espèce	idole
boum	dent	étoile	idylle
caractéristique	dupe	extase	libido

liqueur	pédale	stratosphère
mappemonde	pénicilline	superbe (R3)
mimique	primeur	surface
mosquée	recrue	toux
moustiquaire	réglisse	variable
noix	sentinelle	victime
oasis	sphère	vidéo
ombre	SS	vis
orbite	stalactite	vodka
pantomime	stalagmite	

NOTES:

1 There are a number of M nouns which normally refer to females: **mannequin**, **nu**, **(top-)modèle**, and a number of F ones which regularly refer to males: **canaille** (= foul person), **coqueluche** (= darling/idol), **dupe** (= dupe), **grosse légume** (= big wig, fat cat), **ordure** (= foul person), **recrue** (= recruit), **sentinelle** (= sentry), **victime** (= victim). **Etoile** and **star**, F, are used of both male and female 'stars'.

2 When **basket** and **tennis** refer to footwear and not types of sport, they are F.

3 **Hémisphère** is M but **atmosphère** and **sphère** F.

3.1.3 Doubtful and variable genders

It should be noted that a small number of nouns are of doubtful or variable gender:

amour and **délice** are M in sg but F in pl

après-midi, **pamplemousse**, **perce-neige**, **sandwich**, have varied in gender but are now usually M

an excellent illustration of this M/F problem is the word **bic**

bic M = biro (pen) but F = name of a sail board (made by the Bic company).

espèce   is F, but in R1 is M when followed by a M noun:

eg **un espèce de bâtiment**

gens   adjectives are feminine when they precede **gens**:

certaines gens, de vieilles gens

when they follow **gens** they are masculine:

des gens malheureux, des gens très bavards

holding   both M and F

Pâques   is treated as Msg when it is unaccompanied by an article:

Pâques fut célébré avec beaucoup de solennité

when it is accompanied by an article or any other qualifier it is treated as Fpl:

toutes les Pâques précédentes ont été célébrées avec beaucoup de solennité

photocopieuse   and **photocopieur** both exist, but F is used more.

putain   as with **espèce**:

eg **ce putain de livre**

3.1.4 Names of boats, cars, aeroplanes and watches, letters and numbers, etc

Boats

Despite controversy amongst grammarians, M gender is usually assigned to the names of boats:

eg **le France, le Normandie, le Reine Elizabeth, le Torrey Canyon**

Cars

All names of makes of cars are F.:

eg **une Renault, une deux-chevaux (Citroën), une Ford, une Jaguar**

Turbo, diesel, turbo-diesel are F when referring to the car but M when referring to the engine. The gender of **semi-remorque** is particularly controversial: the majority view is that it is F when = articulated lorry and M when = semitrailer.

(However, types of cars may be M: eg **un break** = an estate car, **un 4×4 (quatre-quatre), un cabriolet, un coupé**)

Aeroplanes

As with names of boats, there is also controversy here.

Usage assigns M gender to all names of aeroplanes except for **la Caravelle**:

eg **le Boeing, le Concorde, le Jaguar, le Mig**

Watches

All names of watches are F:

eg **la Rolex, la Seiko**

Companies

All names are F:

eg **la Philips, la Fiat, la BMW, la General Motors**

Holidays and festivals

Those involving saints' names are F:

eg **à la Saint Valentin, la Saint Sylvestre** (= New Year's Eve), **la Saint Jean** (= mid-summer's day), **la Saint Martin, la Toussaint**

Hotels with stars are M:

eg **un trois étoiles**

Cheeses and wines

Names of cheeses and wines are M:

eg **du brie, du camembert, du cantal**

eg **du champagne, un côtes du Rhône, un beaujolais**

Students

Les première/deuxième, etc année when referring to first year/second etc year students would be M unless they were all female.

NOTE: **première/deuxième année** is invariable for number:

eg **les première année sont plus intelligents que les deuxième année**

Letters

All names of letters are M:

eg **le m, le a, le f**

Numbers

When a specific page number is being referred to **un** may be M or F:

eg **prenez vos livres à la page un/une**

but when a collection of pages is being referred to, the F form is used:

eg **vingt-et-une pages**

In sporting classification the numeral follows the noun in the M even if the noun is F:

eg **la France est en poule un** (= pool 1)

Paris Saint Germain est en division un

3.1.5   Names of towns

Towns provide a more difficult problem. Generally, they are masculine, as in **le tout Paris**, and **Copenhague est grand**. A few are feminine as in **Rome la belle**. The gender of some varies, eg **Marseille est grand**(e). Usage with names of countries is illustrated in **3.9**.

3.1.6   Sex and gender

Certain nouns denoting persons change their gender according to the sex of the person denoted:

eg **un/une camarade, un/une complice, un/une élève, un/une enfant** (but it is always **un bébé**), **un/une esclave, un/une pensionnaire, un/une touriste**

In recent years there has been much controversy over the feminisation of professional names. A *commission de terminologie* on the subject reported in 1984, but its recommendations have not been universally accepted, let alone adopted, and practice is chaotic.

In certain cases it is sufficient, as with the previous group of examples, simply to change the article from the normal masculine to the feminine to indicate that a female is being referred to:

eg **une dentiste, une juge, une journaliste, une ministre, une photographe, une propriétaire**

(Edith Cresson was **la première premier ministre!**)

In other cases the addition of a final **–e** or a standard F form is acceptable:

eg **une avocate, une députée, une magistrate, une ambassadrice, une directrice, une poétesse**

Doctoresse is normal French when speaking to children but not amongst adults and especially professionally:

eg **allez, mon petit, on va voir la doctoresse**

This does not apply to all nouns which potentially belong to this class; for example **chercheur** = research worker, **éleveur** = cattle breeder, **professeur** (see below), **témoin** = witness are always M:

eg **elle est chercheur au CNRS**

No F form for **proviseur** exists and both **Madame le Proviseur** and **Madame la Proviseur** occur.

In some further cases, the choice of gender is a matter of status, with M gender denoting high status and F gender lower status: thus **secrétaire** remains M when it refers to a woman holding a position at the top of the organisational hierarchy:

eg **Madame le secrétaire du parti . . .**

but **la secrétaire** is also being used here. The same applies to **conseiller:**

eg **elle est conseiller en économie**

conseillère exists (as in **conseillère municipale**) but is used in more lowly domains. Although **académicienne** exists, the first female member of the **Académie Française** (Marguerite Yourcenar) did not succeed in having the F form applied to her and is known as **un académicien** (but in Belgium female members of the **Académie Royale de Belgique** are known as **académiciennes**; cf below). **Procureur géneral** (equivalent to Director of Public Prosecutions) remains adamantly M:

eg **Louise Arbour, procureur géneral, chargé de . . .**

However, in other cases where a new form would be required, the French of France are much more reluctant to indicate the gender specifically, unlike French-speakers in Canada, Belgium and Switzerland. Consequently, whereas female writers, doctors, teachers, engineers and so on have special terms to refer to them in Canada, Belgium and Switzerland – **écrivaine, docteure, professeure, ingénieure** (as indeed do the Spaniards). Such terms are not used in France itself. The issue is a contentious one and one which is in a state of evolution: for example some women refer to themselves as **autrice** but generally French people, even women, reject the word.

Others are preceded by the word **femme** to denote a woman exercising the profession in question:

eg **une femme auteur, une femme ingénieur, une femme médecin, une femme politique**

Coiffeur, M, is used in a general sense, whether the hairdresser is male or female:

eg **Je vais chez le coiffeur**

but **coiffeuse** is used to refer specifically to a female hairdresser:

eg **ma coiffeuse m'a dit que . . .**

As far as **professeur** is concerned the following possibilities exist: **une femme professeur, elle est mon professeur préféré** and R1 **elle est ma prof préférée**

Maître produces particular problems because of the sexual associations of **maîtresse**. Consequently the M form is used with reference to females in non-sexual situations:

eg **elle est passé maître** = *expert*; **elle est maître de recherche au CNRS**

The French government has called for a new *commission* (cf above) to be established to investigate further the feminisation of professional names.

3.2   Number

3.2.1   Formation of plurals

3.2.1.1   *Simple words (ie non-compounds)*

The following table summarises the procedures for plural-formation for simple words.

words ending in	plural ending	examples and comments	exceptions and comments
-ail	+ s	ails, chandails, détails, éventails	*a certain number of exceptions have pl in* **-aux**: corail, émail, travail, vitrail
-al	-aux	*the majority of* **-al** *words*: eg chenaux, fluviaux, idéaux, illégaux, immémoriaux, légaux, moraux, rivaux, signaux, sociaux, spéciaux	*the plural of* final, *either* finals *or* finaux, *is avoided and replaced by* dernier, ultime, définitif etc
	or + s	bals, banals, carnavals, chacals, fatals, festivals navals, récitals	
-au, -eau	+ x	boyaux, noyaux, beaux, eaux	*a few rare words*
-eu	+ x	cheveux, feux	bleus, pneus
-ou	+ s	fous, trous	*7 words take* **x** *in pl*: bijou, caillou, chou, genou, hibou, joujou, pou
-s, -x, -z	*none*	mois, croix, nez	*none*
all other words	+ s	amis, langues	*none*

If a plural-form sounds awkward, as in *final*, a French person avoids the word.

A very small number of words have two plural forms:

aïeul	aïeuls aïeux	grandparents ancestors
ciel	ciels cieux	skies in painting (semi-technical); roof of 4-poster bed skies, heavens (general)
œil	œils yeux	in compounds, eg **œils-de-boeuf** = small round windows eyes

3.2.1.2 *Compound words*

type of compound	plural ending	examples and comments	exceptions and comments
unhyphenated compounds	*according to criteria outlined in* **3.2.1.1**	entresols, portemanteaux	bonshommes (*but* bonhommes R1), gentilshommes, mesdames, mesdemoiselles, messieurs, messeigneurs
hyphenated compounds:			
noun + noun	*both elements take ending according to criteria outlined in* **3.2.1.1**	choux-fleurs, oiseaux-mouches	*none*
noun + adjective	*as above*	coffres-forts, états-majors	*none*
adjective + noun	*as above*	basses-cours, francs-maçons	*in the case of certain F nouns preceded by* grand *in M form, the adjective is sometimes invariable in the plural and sometimes not: eg* grands-mères *or* grand-mères; grands-tantes *or* grand-tantes (grands-pères, grands-oncles *are compulsory*)
verb + noun	*noun remains invariable or noun varies according to criteria outlined in* **3.2.1.1**	des garde-manger, des perce-neige	*in certain cases the singular form already involves a plural noun:* un porte-avions, un presse-papiers
invariable word + noun	*noun varies according to criteria outlined in* **3.2.1.1**	haut-parleurs, sous-marins	*usage varies with* après-midi: des après-midi *or* après-midis
verb + verb	*both invariable*	des laisser-aller, des faire-valoir	*none*

type of compound	plural ending	examples and comments	exceptions and comments
phrase	*plural formation depends upon nature of elements involved*	des vêtements prêts-à-porter, des va-et-vient	*none*

The foregoing analysis accounts for the following anomalies:
des porte-parole, where **porte** is a verb, but **des portes-fenêtres**, where **porte** is a noun
des garde-manger, where **garde** is a verb, but **des gardes-malades**, where **garde** is a noun

Compound adjectives of colour
These are invariable for both number and gender:
eg **une robe bleu clair, une chemise jaune clair, un pantalon gris foncé, une chevelure châtain clair**

Numbers
80 = **quatre-vingts** (with **-s**), but 81 etc = **quatre-vingt-un** etc (without **-s**)
200 = **deux cents**, 300 = **trois cents** etc (with **-s**), but 201 etc = **deux cent un** etc (without **-s**)
2000 = **deux mille** (never with **-s**)

NOTE: **le cent mètres** = the 100 metres (race), **le quatre cents mètres** = the 400 metres (race)

3.2.1.3   *Foreign words*

It is possible here to suggest only the broadest categories (many foreign words being somewhat rarely used), and it should be remembered that usage is often variable:

English
As far as English words adopted by French are concerned, problems occur where English and French plural-forming patterns diverge. However, those who have a reasonable knowledge of English tend to use authentic English plurals; consequently R2 users would opt for:
eg **des boxes, des flashes, des matches, des sandwiches, des smashes** (in tennis), **des sketches, des lobbies, des tories, des rugbymen, des tennismen**
whereas R1 users would opt for forms without **-es**:
eg **des boxs, des flashs, des matchs, des sandwichs, des smashs**
Where the plural-forming patterns are the same, there is no difficulty:
eg **des scoops, des sex-shops**
It should be noted that this distinction is masked in speech for those words ending in **-(e)s**, as the **-(e)s** is not pronounced in any case.

Even so, there are still anomalous forms of English plurals created in French:

eg **des pin-up** (without **-s**) and both **média** and **médias** occur as plural forms.

Usually a well-established foreign word, which may well have lost some of its foreign appearance, conforms to the French pattern by adding **-s** in the plural:

eg **des biftecks, des boléros, des panoramas, des référendums**

Some, on the other hand, remain invariable; this applies especially to words of Latin origin:

eg **des amen, des forum, des lapsus, des veto**

Italian: **des broccoli, des concerti, des confetti, des graffiti** (also **du graffiti**), **des macaroni, des spaghetti**

(consequently any verb with these nouns as subject should be in the plural-form).

un graffiti = a piece of graffiti (cf **3.2.2.**)

NOTE: **du vermicelle** (sg); **prima donna** remains invariable in the pl

Use of a foreign plural-form is frequently a mark of R3 speech or is simply affectation (musicians etc like to show that they know the Italian plurals):

eg **des concertos/des concerti, des sanatoria/des sanatoriums, des scenarii/des scenarios, des soprani/des sopranos**

In the case of **addendum** and **erratum**, the Latin plural-form may be used as a singular noun, with a collective value, thus producing the following distinctions of meaning:

un addendum = a single addition to be made (to a book)

un addenda/ = a list/lists of such additions
   des addenda

un erratum = a single mistake to be corrected (in a book)

un errata/des errata = a list/lists of such mistakes

3.2.1.4   Proper names

Generally, proper names are invariable in the plural:

eg **les Dupont, les Morand**
   il a acheté deux Peugeot
   plusieurs Caravelle sont retenues au sol à Orly
   les deux Angleterre, la protestante et la catholique

With the names of certain famous families, **-s** is added in the plural (but agreement as to the degree of fame necessary before such an honour is conferred upon a proper name is far from general):

eg **les Césars, les Bourbons, les Condés, les Stuarts**

and certain geographical names also have **-s** in the plural:

eg **les deux Amériques, les Guyanes, les Flandres;** also **la Flandre**

When an artist's name is applied to his paintings, an author's to his books, or a film director's to his films, and so on, usage varies, but normally no **-s** is used:

eg **j'ai vu un grand nombre de Monet au Grand-Palais**
  j'ai acheté trois Simenon chez un bouquiniste
  deux Buñuel viennent d'être montrés pour la deuxième fois
  la soprano a chanté dans plusieurs *Carmen*

3.2.1.5   *Singular subject but plural verb*

Normally subject and verb agree in number, but occasionally a
singular subject is followed by a plural verb:

eg **le tiers/le quart/la moitié des voitures sont toutes neuves**
  une quarantaine de touristes sont arrivés
  cinq pour cent des étudiants sont Japonais
  la plupart des bureaux sont trop petits

In the first three cases (ie not for **la plupart**) use of a sg verb would
indicate a higher register

eg **une quarantaine de touristes est arrivée** R3

3.2.2   Differing usages between English and French

Sometimes a singular in English is conveyed by a plural in French:

les agressions	= aggression
NOTE: **une agression**	= an act of aggression
dans les airs (R3)	= in the air
les applaudissements	= applause
les arènes	= arena

NOTE: pl more common than sg, but when fig, sg only occurs, eg
dans l'arène politique

les bagages	= luggage
les blés (R3)	= (fields of) corn
les buts	= goal (the place)

eg **qui est dans les buts ce soir?**

NOTE: **un but** = goal (scored)

à ses côtés	= by his/her side
les couverts	= cutlery
les crampes	= cramp

NOTE: pl more common than sg

des cris	= shouting
les eaux (R3)	= water
les embruns	= spray (from water)
les équipements (also sg)	= equipment
les fiançailles	= engagement
les Finances	= the Treasury
les forces	= strength
les funérailles	= funeral
les informations	= the (pieces of) information
les intempéries	= bad weather
les intérêts	= (financial) interest
les labours (R3)	= ploughed land

les neiges (R3)	= snow
les nuisances	= nuisance (environmental)
eg **les nuisances de la circulation urbaine**	
les obsèques	= funeral
les orges (R3)	= (fields of) barley
les pluies passagères	= patchy rain
les précipitations	= rainfall
NOTE: sg is used but rarely	
faire des progrès	= to make progress
avoir des remords	= to have remorse
faire des révisions	= to revise, to do revision
les rhumatismes	= rheumatism
NOTE: pl more common than sg	
les sévices sexuels	= physical (usu sexual) abuse
les ténèbres (R3)	= darkness
les violences	= violence
eg une flambée de violences urbaines; la femme a subi des violences (**la violence** = violence as a concept)	

Conversely, sometimes a plural in English is conveyed by a singular in French:

le bermuda	= Bermuda shorts
la bouche	= lips (sometimes)
du changement	= changes
NOTE: but also used in pl	
le collant	= tights
le dimanche	= on Sundays
être dans son droit	= to be within one's rights
le générique	= credits (for film, play etc)
un jean	= jeans
le pantalon	= trousers
la pince	= pincers
le pyjama	= pyjamas
rencontrer le regard de qn	= to meet sb's eyes
le short	= shorts
le slip	= (under)pants
la troupe	= troops, also **les troupes**

Many 'apparent' plurals in English have a corresponding singular term in French:

le diabète	= diabetes	**la physique**	= physics
la dialectique	= dialectics	**la polémique**	= polemics
la dynamique	= dynamics	**la politique**	= politics
l'économie	= economics	**la statistique**	= statistics
la linguistique	= linguistics	(see below)	
l'optique	= optics	**la tactique**	= tactics

The most important exception is: **les mathématiques/maths.**

NOTE: **la moustache** and **les moustaches** may be used interchangeably.

In French certain words have a singular–plural duality unlike their English equivalents:

la drogue	drugs (narcotics)
les drogues (R1, R2)	drugs (medicaments)
un fruit	a 'piece' of fruit
des fruits	fruit, stressing individual fruit
un pain	a loaf of bread
des pains	loaves
du pain	bread, general
un raisin	type of grape
des raisins	different types of grapes
du raisin	grapes, general
un grain de raisin	grape
la recherche	practice of research, research, the concept
les recherches	detailed research
une statistique	single set of statistics
des statistiques	series of statistics
un toast	a piece of toast
des toasts	some toast, some slices of toast

Allied to this is the case of **musique**, although the noun is not often used in the plural:

une musique	a piece of music (eg **voici une musique qui vous plaira**)
des musiques	pieces of music, different types of music (eg **mes musiques préférées**)
de la musique	some music (eg **j'ai écouté de la musique ce matin**)
la musique	music (the concept as well as the activity) (eg **j'adore la musique/la musique de Beethoven**)

One or two other nouns have a different meaning in the plural from in the singular:

le devoir	usu duty
les devoirs	usu homework
l'enfer	hell
les enfers	the underworld
	eg **Orphée aux enfers**

NOTE: **les polices** as well as = policies also = police forces

3.2.3   Use of the partitive article before an adjective preceding a plural noun

With most adjectives **de** is used, but this is tending now to be R3 usage:

eg **après de longues années; de vieux vêtements**
j'ai recu de très bonnes notes

Thus an R2, as well as an R1, speaker would easily say:

des vieux vêtements; des très bonnes notes

Des is also used when the adjective and noun form a group which may be considered a single unit; this is perfectly normal R2 usage:

eg **des jeunes filles/gens; des petits pains/pois**

3.3   Word order

The position which a word occupies in a sentence, in French as in English, is very often a matter of style, personal preference or register. Speakers or writers sometimes deliberately use unconventional or unexpected sequences of words in their speech or writing, in order to achieve certain effects. They may carefully balance one part of a sentence against another, striving for symmetry or asymmetry; they may wish to introduce a certain rhythm, harmony or euphony into what they say or write, or they may wish to underline a certain word or phrase by placing it in a prominent position in the sentence. There is, therefore, as far as word order is concerned, a certain degree of flexibility but obviously only within the limits permitted by grammar and intelligibility. On the other hand, certain word orders are fixed and may not be altered.

In this section it is not so much style as grammatical constraints and usages which are treated, although it has to be admitted that it is not always possible to dissociate style and grammar.

3.3.1   Adjectives and word order

The position of an adjective in relation to the noun it qualifies is one of the most subtle aspects of French. The following sub-sections indicate the major considerations to be borne in mind in this connection.

3.3.1.1   Normal usage

The following diagram illustrates 'normal' usage for the positioning of adjectives with respect to the noun they qualify. Normal usage means language unaffected by particular considerations of style, emphasis and so on.

types of adjectives which normally precede the noun	types of adjectives which normally follow the noun	examples
short, very common: *bon* (**3.3.1.2**) *gentil* *grand* (**3.3.1.2**) *gros* *jeune* *long* *mauvais* (**3.3.1.2**) *méchant* (**3.3.1.2**) *petit* *vieux* *vilain*	colour nationality arts and sciences religion the quality denoted by the adjective is stressed	*un livre noir* *une voiture française* *une étude littéraire* *l'acide sulfurique* *un pays musulman* *une maison solide* *une serviette inutile*
adjectives forming a unit with the noun: eg *une jeune fille* *un petit pain* *un grand garçon*	long adjectives past participles used as adjectives	*un paysage pittoresque* *un homme fatigué*

3.3.1.2   *Adjectives which change their meaning according to their position*

The meaning of certain adjectives changes according to their position with respect to the noun they qualify, often becoming more specialised. It should also be realised that in some cases the meaning of the adjective is conditioned in part by the meaning of the noun and will only be used in a certain position with a limited number of nouns (eg *bon, faux*).

ancien	
before noun	after noun
former **un ancien forçat**	old **une coutume ancienne**

brave	
before noun	after noun
obliging, honest **un brave homme**	courageous **un homme brave**

bon	
before noun	after noun
good, nice **un bon homme**	kind, thoughtful **un homme bon**

certain	
before noun	after noun
certain (indefinite adjective) **un certain fait**	unquestionable **un fait certain**

cher

before noun	after noun
dear, beloved **mon cher Jean**	expensive **une voiture chère**

dernier

before noun	after noun
last of series **le dernier mois de l'année**	last, preceding **le mois dernier**

différent

before noun	after noun
various **différentes maisons**	different **des maisons différentes**

divers

before noun	after noun
various **diverses opinions**	diverse, distinct **des opinions diverses**

faux

before noun	after noun
false, not genuine **la fausse monnaie**	untrustworthy, hypocritical **un homme faux**

galant

before noun	after noun
well-mannered **un galant homme**	attentive to women **un homme galant**

grand

before noun	after noun
great **un grand homme**	tall **un homme grand**

haut

before noun	after noun
high, open (of sea) **la haute mer**	high (of tide) **la mer haute**

honnête

before noun	after noun
of good breeding **un honnête homme**	honest, honourable **un homme honnête**

jeune

before noun	after noun
young **un jeune homme**	youthful **un homme jeune**

léger

before noun	after noun
slight (fig) **une légère reprise /baisse** (eg in economic activity)	light (of weight) **une armoire légère**

mauvais

before noun	after noun
bad **une mauvaise réputation**	evil **avoir l'air mauvais** = to look evil

méchant

before noun	after noun
disagreeable **une méchante affaire**	spiteful, naughty **un enfant méchant**

même

before noun	after noun
same **le même nom**	very, even **les enfants mêmes**

pauvre

before noun	after noun
poor (pitiful) **un pauvre homme**	poor (impecunious) **un homme pauvre**

présent

before noun	after noun
the one in question **le présent ouvrage/ auteur** **la présente émission vous propose une discussion sur . . .**	present (of time) **le moment présent**

propre

before noun	after noun
own, very **ses propres paroles**	clean; appropriate **le linge propre;** **le mot propre**

pur

before noun	after noun
simple, plain **la pure vérité**	pure, free from impurity **l'or pur**

sacré

before noun	after noun
(intensifying adj R1) **sacré nom de Dieu**	holy, sacred **le nom sacré de Dieu**

sale

before noun	after noun
nasty **un sale chien**	dirty **un chien sale**

seul

before noun	after noun
only, single, sole **un seul homme** **la seule France est capable de résister à la pression internationale** = only France	lonely, alone, on one's own **un homme seul** **la France seule n'est pas assez puissante** = France by itself

simple

before noun	after noun
ordinary, only **une simple question de temps**	simple, unsophisti-cated **un plaisir simple** **un billet simple**= a single ticket

seul (*cont.*)		triste	
before noun	after noun	before noun	after noun
le film *Titanic* a rapporté trente milliards (de francs) sur le seul marché américain = just the American market		inauspicious, dull **un triste visage**	sad **un visage triste**
pour la seule (et même) raison que . . . = for the one and only reason that . . .			

3.3.1.3   *Adjectives which may occur either before or after a noun*

Certain adjectives may be placed before or after the noun without changing their meaning.

adjective	examples	preferred position, if any
bas	de bas nuages = des nuages bas	*after noun*
bref	un bref entretien = un entretien bref	
charmant	un charmant tableau = un tableau charmant	
court	une courte histoire = une histoire courte	*after noun*
double	un double programme = un programme double	
énorme	un énorme lion = un lion énorme	
excellent	une excellente machine = une machine excellente	
fort	une forte économie = une économie forte	
futur	les futures générations = les générations futures	
gros	un gros homme = un homme gros	
innombrable	d'innombrables livres = des livres innombrables	
long	il a de longs cheveux = il a les cheveux longs	
magnifique	une magnifique voiture = une voiture magnifique	
modeste	une modeste somme = une somme modeste	
principal	la principale ville = la ville principale	
rapide	un rapide coup d'œil = un coup d'œil rapide	
terrible	un terrible accident = un accident terrible	

On the other hand it should be noted that usage fixes certain expressions:

bas	charmant	chaud
un bâtiment bas	un livre charmant	un point chaud = *dangerous place* (neighbourhood, town or country), *stall selling quickly prepared, hot food*
un coup bas = *dirty trick, low blow* (in boxing)	un film charmant	
une table basse		
des talons bas		un chaud lapin = *sexy bloke*

double	droit	faux
un mot à double entente	le droit chemin (*metaphorical*)	une fausse déclaration
faire coup double = *to kill two birds with one stone,*	la ligne droite (*literal*), en ligne droite	un faux billet = *counterfeit*
un agent double		un faux départ = *false start* (in swimming, athletics)
		un homme faux
		un faux mouvement = *an awkward movement* (which could damage a muscle)

fort	franc	futur
de fortes chances (pour) que	un homme franc	ma future épouse
un homme fort	une franche horreur	ma future maison

gros	léger	libre
une grosse tête	un livre léger	la libre entreprise
	un léger rhume	l'école libre

long	lourd	modeste
une longue journée	une lourde responsabilité	une femme modeste
une longue rue	un poids lourd	
une jupe longue	l'industrie lourde	

moyen	premier	saint
un cours moyen	sa vocation première = *her fundamental vocation*	un saint homme
un avion moyen courrier		
le Moyen Age		

second
seconde nature
second souffle = *second wind*

However, there is an increasing tendency to place adjectives which normally follow the noun before it. This tendency is particularly noticeable in the media – newspapers, advertising, television, radio. Placing the adjective before the noun in these circumstances focuses attention upon it because it is unusual and arresting and therefore lends extra weight to what is being said. Register level is also involved:

215

register level is raised if an adjective which is traditionally placed after the noun, precedes it. The following examples (from a short article in *Les Echos* of 18 August 1998) illustrate the phenomenon:

Et l'on y suit ainsi une longue et finalement très cohérente existence . . .

jusqu'à l'extrême mais toujours lucide vieillesse d'un monstre sacré de la littérature . . .

R2 – adjective follows noun	R3 –adjective precedes noun
des parents anxieux	d'anxieux parents
un geste brusque	un brusque geste
un produit dangereux	un dangereux produit
les années difficiles de la guerre	les difficiles années de la guerre
une journée dure	une dure journée
un risque éventuel	un éventuel risque
ce drame horrible	cet horrible drame
la protection mutuelle	la mutuelle protection
un accord possible	un possible accord
une bataille rude	une rude bataille
une idéologie stupide	une stupide idéologie
des images sublimes	de sublimes images

For **dernier**, **meilleur** and **premier**, which normally precede the noun, the situation is reversed:

R2 – adjective precedes noun	R3 – adjective follows noun
ces derniers jours	ces jours derniers
le meilleur livre	le livre le meilleur
le premier chapitre	le chapitre premier

3.3.1.4 *Miscellaneous matters*

Word position is also sometimes dictated by considerations of what is known as 'cadence majeure'; that is, in French there is a preference for phrases to be constructed with words which increase in length, and a reluctance to form phrases with a long adjective preceding a short noun:

eg **une vue magnifique** rather than: **une magnifique vue**

However, it is also true to say, in the light of the remarks made at the end of **3.3.1.3**, that the register in the former case is higher than in the latter:

eg **une magnifique vue** R3/2 – **une vue magnifique** R2/1
un excellent film R3/2 – **un film excellent** R2/1

When two adjectives follow a noun, the adjective immediately after the noun relates to it more intimately than the second adjective (unless they are joined by *et*, in which case they both apply equally):

eg **la littérature française contemporaine**
l'opinion politique populaire
les partis communiste et socialiste

Because of the desire for 'cadence majeure', as defined above, when a series of adjectives follows a noun, it is preferable for the longer or longest to be placed last:

eg **des murs gris et délabrés** is preferred to: **des murs délabrés et gris**

When a numeral is combined with an adjective preceding the noun, the order is: numeral + adjective + noun:

eg **les six derniers livres que j'ai lus**

Usage with *demi* and *nu*: when they precede the noun there is no agreement (and the adjective and noun are hyphenated), whereas when they follow it, agreement occurs:

before the noun	after the noun
une demi-heure	**une heure et demie**
nu-pieds	**les pieds nus**

The presentation of dates differs in French from English:

eg **le samedi deux janvier**
le mardi 21 août

3.3.2   Adverbs and word order

In a sentence consisting of a subject, verb, object and adverb, the adverb normally precedes the object. However, when it is stressed it follows the object. The usage with adverbs of time and place is somewhat different. Adverbial phrases (rather than simple adverbs) normally follow the object, whatever the circumstances.

		examples
normal order (other than adverbs of time and space)	subject + simple tense of verb + simple adverb + object	*j'aime beaucoup le cidre* *il attend patiemment la voiture*
	subject + compound tense of verb (auxiliary verb + simple adverb + past participle) + object	*j'ai longuement regardé le paysage* *elle a soigneusement nettoyé sa chambre*
	subject + verb + object + adverbial phrase	*j'ai lu le livre encore une fois*

		examples
order with stress on adverb	subject + verb + object + adverb	*il attend la voiture patiemment* *elle a nettoyé sa chambre soigneusement*
normal order with adverbs of time and place	subject + verb + object + adverb	*je suis allé à la bibliothèque aujourd'hui* *j'ai vu un film de Barrault hier* *je ferai mon travail demain* *il achète son journal ici/là*
order with stress on adverb of time	adverb + subject + verb + object	*aujourd'hui je suis allé à la bibliothèque* *hier j'ai vu un film de Barrault* *demain je ferai mon travail*
order with stress on *là*	subject + verb + *là* + object	*elle fait là son travail*

The position of certain common short adverbs, such as *bien* and *mieux*, as well as *tout* as a direct object, is flexible in relation to an infinitive preceded by an unstressed object pronoun:

adverb and *tout*	**normal order**	**less frequently found order**
bien	pour bien me comprendre	pour me bien comprendre pour me comprendre bien
mieux	pour mieux le faire	pour le mieux faire pour le faire mieux
trop	sans trop en prendre	sans en prendre trop
tout	je vais tout vous dire	je vais vous dire tout

The addition of an adverb like *bien* to an expression like *parler français* has certain repercussions upon the form of the expression as can be seen by the following examples:

parler français   parler bien le français
parler français   extrêmement bien

When *bien is* combined with *vouloir*, the varying orders sometimes reflect a contrast of register:

structure	example	register
bien + finite form of *vouloir*	**je veux bien t'aider**	all registers
	il a bien voulu me prêter de l'argent	all registers
bien + infinitive of *vouloir*	**je vous demande de bien vouloir m'excuser**	R1 + R2
	je vous demande de vouloir bien m'excuser	R3

The position of adverbs in conjunction with a negative expression also requires comment: certain adverbs precede the negative particle *pas* rather than follow it:

eg **il ne pleut** $\begin{cases} \textbf{donc} \\ \textbf{même} \\ \textbf{toujours} \end{cases}$ **pas**   **je ne l'ai** $\begin{cases} \textbf{donc} \\ \textbf{même} \\ \textbf{toujours} \end{cases}$ **pas fait**

With *encore* and a simple tense, the norm is:
il ne pleut pas encore
But with a compound tense there are two possibilities:
je ne l'ai encore pas fait
je ne l'ai pas encore fait (more usual)
For inversion with adverbs, see **3.3.4.**

3.3.3   Personal pronouns and word order

The order of unstressed pronouns excluding subject pronouns with respect to the verb is as follows:

me					le				
te	**le**				**le**	**lui**			all tenses and moods
nous	**la**	**y**	**en**		**la**		**y**	**en**	+ of the verb, except
vous	**les**				**les**	**leur**			the positive imperative
se									

examples
elle nous le donne	= she gives it to him/her
elle me le donne	= she gives it to me
elle te le donne	= she gives it to you
elle le lui donne	= she gives it to him/her
elle nous le donne	= she gives it to us
elle vous le donne	= she gives it to you
elle le leur donne	= she gives it to them
il leur en donne	= he gives them some
il y en a	= there is/are some

| positive imperative + | le
la
les | moi
toi
lui
leur | m'
t'
lui
leur | y en | nous
vous | le
la
les | y en |

examples	donne-le-moi	= give it to me
	donne-m'en	= give me some
	donne-nous-en	= give us some

NOTE: it is not acceptable to combine the direct objects *me, te, nous, vous, se,* with the indirect objects *lui, leur.* Instead the indirect object figures after the verb:

eg **il me présente à elle**

elle se fie à eux

la question qui se pose à nous, c'est . . .

3.3.4 Inversion

Whereas normal word order in French requires that the subject precede the verb, inversion involves the placing of the subject after the verb. Inversion, it should be noted, is frequently a mark of formal, refined language. Inversion is used in the following circumstances:

Often in the official variety of French, when a long subject, usually consisting of an enumeration of nouns, occurring in its normal position, would delay the appearance of the verb and thus impair comprehension:

eg **se sont qualifiés les numéros douze, treize, quinze, etc**

ont été augmentés le pain, le lait, le beurre

With verbs of movement and *rester* to provide an intimate link with the previous sentence or to focus attention on the noun or the verb:

eg **suivit un vacarme assourdissant**

voilà deux tâches bien faites; reste une troisième

In sentences in R3 usage, introduced by adverbs and adverbial phrases of time (eg *alors, aujourd'hui, bientôt, enfin*) and place (eg *de là, ici, là*):

eg **de là découlent grand nombre de nos problèmes actuels**

au jardin poussait un arbre

ensuite arrivèrent des renforts

also, occasionally, in sentences introduced by an adjective:

eg **rares sont les écrivains qui . . .**

telle est ma volonté

In R2 and R3 usage with concessive clauses of the following type:

quelles que soient les causes, cela ne changera rien au problème

With relative clauses:

eg **une charrette que tiraient deux chevaux**
une voiture que conduisait un vieux monsieur

With *que*-clauses:

eg **ce que dit le président doit être bien noté**

With 'incises' (ie references to speakers occurring after passages of direct speech):

eg **j'ai soif, dit-il**
je ne fais rien, a répondu mon père

In R2 and R3 usage after initial *à peine, ainsi, aussi, du moins, encore,* and in R3 usage after initial *tout au plus*:

eg **à peine semblait-il écouter ce que disait le professeur**
à peine la nuit était-elle venue que . . .

Usage with *peut-être, sans doute* demands particular comment:

R1	R3	R1–R3
peut-être + **que** + direct order **sans doute**	**peut-être** + inversion **sans doute**	**peut-être** verb + **sans doute**
eg **peut-être/sans doute qu'il va venir**	eg **peut-être/sans doute va-t-il venir**	eg **il va venir peut-être/sans doute** **il va peut-être/sans doute venir**

Inversion may take the following forms:

		examples
pronoun	simply placed after the verb	**dit-il**
noun	sometimes placed after the verb, for stylistic reasons, such as balance	*dans le parc se dressait un monument*
	sometimes remains before the verb and a pronoun repeats it after the verb	*aussi la jeune fille s'était-elle décidée à partir*

To summarise, inversion may occur in the following circumstances:

grammatical circumstances	register
in enumerations	R3
with verbs of movement and *rester*	R3
in sentences introduced by adverbs and adverbial phrases of time and place	R3
in sentences introduced by an adjective	R3
in concessive, relative and *que*-clauses	R2 and R3
in 'incises'	R2 and R3
after initial *à peine, encore, ainsi, aussi, du moins, peut-être, sans doute*	R2 and R3
after initial *tout au plus*	R3

221

3.3.5 Interrogatives and word order

French interrogative sentences may be of two types:

1 those which involve an interrogative word and which invite a detailed reply (*qui, que, quoi, comment, où*, etc)
2 those which do not involve an interrogative word and which invite a yes/no answer.

Questions may be expressed in the following ways, considerations of register being an important factor:

type of question	form of question	register	examples
questions without interrogative word (see NOTE A)	inversion of subject + verb	R2, R3	*allez-vous manger maintenant?*
			mon père, vous a-t-il téléphoné?
	use of *est-ce que* + direct order	R2	*vous y allez maintenant?*
			est-ce que mon père vous a téléphoné?
	addition of *n'est-ce pas* at end of direct order (see NOTE B)	R2	*vous allez manger maintenant, n'est-ce pas?*
			mon père vous a téléphoné, n'est-ce pas?
	direct order + rising intonation	R1	*vous allez manger maintenant?*
			mon père vous a téléphoné?
questions with interrogative word *combien, comment, lequel, où, pourquoi, quand, qui/que/quoi*	interrogative word + inversion	R2, R3	*pourquoi êtes-vous sorti?*
			pourquoi votre père est-il sorti?
	interrogative word + *est-ce que* + direct order; *est-ce qui* in the case of *qui* subject (see NOTE C)	R2	*pourquoi est-ce que vous êtes sorti?*
			pourquoi est-ce que votre père est sorti?
			qui est-ce qui va venir ce soir?
			qui est-ce que vous avez invité?

type of question	form of question	register	examples
	direct order with interrogative word placed at end of question	R1	*vous sortez quand?* *votre père sort quand ?*
	interrogative word + direct order	R1	*où tu vas?* *comment tu fais ça?*
	interrogative word + *c'est que*	R1	*quand c'est que vous sortez?*
	highlighting by placing noun or stressed form of pronoun before interrogative word or at end of question in direct order (**3.3.7**)	R1	*votre père, pourquoi il est sorti?* *lui, pourquoi il est sorti?* *pourquoi votre père il est sorti?* *pourquoi il est sorti, lui?*

NOTE A: *Si* and not *oui* is used for an affirmative reply to a negative question or suggestion:

eg **Vous n'allez pas manger maintenant, n'est-ce pas? – Si!**

NOTE B: The use of *n'est-ce pas* implies agreement with the statement contained in the question.

NOTE C: *Qui* alone is more common as subject than *qui est-ce qui*. On the other hand the long forms of the other interrogative pronouns are more frequently used than the short forms:

eg **qui est-ce que vous voyez?** rather than: **qui voyez-vous?**

eg **qu'est-ce que tu fais?** rather than: **que fais-tu?**

3.3.6   Exclamations and word order

form of exclamation	register	examples
inversion of subject pronoun	R3	*est-elle jolie!*
inversion of noun with repetition by pronoun	R3	*est-elle jolie, cette fille!*
comme/que + direct order with pronoun and highlighting of noun (**3.3.7**)	R2, R3	*comme elle est jolie!* *qu'elle est jolie, cette fille!*
ce que/qu'est-ce que + direct order and highlighting (**3.3.7**)	R1	*ce que/qu'est-ce que c'est bête, ce film!*
intonation	R2	*elle est jolie!*

3.3.7 Highlighting

Highlighting is the means whereby a certain element of a sentence is brought into prominence and has attention focused upon it. It is naturally a very common process in everyday speech when it is essential for the person addressed to appreciate immediately what is the most significant point in what is being said to him or her. Highlighting is achieved by adjusting 'normal' word order:

$$\text{subject} + \text{verb} + \begin{cases} \text{adjective} \\ \text{adverb} \\ \text{object} \\ \text{prepositional phrase} \\ \text{etc} \end{cases}$$

An element that is being highlighted is called a focal element; elements of a sentence may be highlighted in the following ways:

means of highlighting	examples
by isolating the focal element in front of the sentence and, if appropriate, repeating it by a pronoun	*lui, il a écrit ce livre* *ce livre, il l'a écrit* *penser aux vacances, j'ose pas/je ne l'ose pas* *Paris, j'en rêve souvent*
by isolating the focal element after the sentence, and, if appropriate, heralding it by a pronoun	*il a écrit ce livre, lui* *il l'a écrit, ce livre* *j'en rêve souvent, de Paris* *il y en a, des voitures*
by using **c'est . . . qui/que**	*c'est lui qui a écrit ce livre* *c'est ce livre-ci qu'il a écrit* *c'est à Paris que je pense souvent* *c'est demain que je dois aller chez le médecin*
by using the passive voice if appropriate	*ce livre a été écrit par Camus*
double focus may be achieved by combining means of highlighting	*ce livre, c'est lui qui l'a écrit*

In **si** clauses, in speech as well as in writing, an object may become the focal element without repetition by a pronoun; the register level is higher than for the unhighlighted order:

eg **si accord il y a**

si harmonie tu vois en tout cela

si indifférence ils montrent

3.4   Prepositions

Competent and accurate handling of prepositions is as sure a mark as any of a speaker's ease in a foreign language. The main problem for an English-speaker speaking French is knowing when to use the same preposition as in English, when to use a different one, or whether to use one at all.

Reduced to its most basic function, a preposition is a linking word, which may express a relationship between what precedes and what follows it. The relationship may be one of place, time, aim, means, manner, possession, quantity, measurement, cause, purpose, accompaniment, support/opposition, concession, exception, reference. It is well known that there is not a one-to-one correspondence between relationship and preposition (see in particular **3.4.4**). Certain prepositions have a constant value in themselves, eg *avec, devant, environ, parmi* (**3.4.4.1**), whereas others in isolation have a more indeterminate value, which may become defined to a certain extent by the meaning of the construction or context in which they occur, eg *à, de, en*. This latter series of prepositions may lose their identity altogether and become fully integrated into compound words: compare, for example, *une pomme de terre* and *la pomme de Jean, un sac à main* and *une canne à pommeau sculpté*.

Prepositions may link different types of words:
adjective/noun to noun
verb to infinitive
verb to noun
adjective/noun to infinitive
adverb to noun

and these groups of words function in a variety of ways, principally to introduce:

an adverbial expression:	**agir par jalousie**
an indirect object:	**donner à quelqu'un**
a complement of a verb in the passive mood:	**mordu par un chien**
an adjectival expression:	**la voiture de mon père**
an infinitival expression:	**j'ai fini par me coucher**
a prepositional phrase:	**à cause de mon mal de tête**

Just as there is not a one-to-one correspondence between relationship and preposition, neither is there a one-to-one correspondence between English and French prepositions, and herein lies the major difficulty for the student of French: which preposition to use? The most obvious illustration of this is the simple problem of knowing which preposition to use to link a verb and an infinitive in French (**3.4.1**). In English the situation is straightforward: verb + *to* + infinitive (except for modal verbs), but in French the possibilities are wider:

$$\text{verb} + \begin{matrix} \text{à} \\ \text{de} \\ \text{par} \\ \text{pour} \\ \text{no preposition } (\ldots) \end{matrix} \quad + \text{infinitive}$$

The symbol (. . .) will be used to indicate that no preposition is required to link the infinitive (or noun, or pronoun) to the verb.

In the following sections an attempt is made to provide a systematic analysis of the use of prepositions in French.

NOTE: It is necessary to repeat the preposition before coordinated nouns, pronouns and verbs which are not closely related in sense:

eg **j'ai parlé** *avec* **sa mère et** *avec* **la directrice de l'école**

On the other hand, it is not normally necessary to repeat it before coordinated nouns, pronouns and verbs which are closely related in sense:

eg **j'ai parlé** *avec* **sa mère et** (*avec*) **son père**
faire part de l'événement *à* **ses amis et connaissances**

3.4.1   verb + preposition

3.4.1.1   verb + preposition + infinitive

$$\text{verb} + \begin{matrix} \text{à} \\ \text{de} \\ \text{par} \\ \text{pour} \\ (\ldots) \end{matrix} \quad + \text{infinitive}$$

à

eg
il s'est abaissé *à* **fréquenter des gens méprisables**
elle s'acharne *à* **le terminer ce soir**
il tarde *à* **venir**
nous nous sommes employés *à* **le mettre à son aise**

s'abaisser à	s'attacher à
aboutir à	s'attendre à (**3.4.3**)
s'accorder à (R3) (**3.4.3**)	s'avilir à (R3)
s'acharner à	avoir à
s'adonner à	se borner à
aimer à (R3)	se buter à
s'amuser à	chercher à
s'animer à	commencer à (**3.4.3**)
s'appliquer à	se complaire à
apprendre à	concourir à
s'apprêter à	se consacrer à
arriver à	consentir à
aspirer à	consister à
s'assujettir à (R3)	conspirer à
s'astreindre à	se consumer à

continuer à (**3.4.3**)
contribuer à
se décider à (**3.4.3**)
demander à (**3.4.3**)
se déterminer à
se dévouer à
se disposer à
se divertir à
s'efforcer à (R3) (**3.4.3**)
s'employer à
s'engager à
s'enhardir à (R3)
s'ennuyer à (**3.4.3**)
s'entraîner à
équivaloir à
s'essayer à
s'évertuer à (R3)
exceller à (R3)
s'exposer à
se fatiguer à
s'habituer à (**3.4.3**)
se hasarder à
hésiter à
incliner à (R3)
s'ingénier à
insister à (**3.4.3**)
s'intéresser à (**3.4.3**)
se mettre à
s'obstiner à

s'occuper à (**3.4.3**)
s'offrir à
s'opiniâtrer à (R3)
parvenir à
passer son temps à
peiner à
perdre son temps à
persévérer à
persister à
se plaire à
se plier à
se prendre à
prendre plaisir à
se préparer à
se refuser à (**3.4.3**)
renoncer à
répugner à (R3) (**3.4.3**)
se résigner à
se résoudre à (**3.4.3**)
réussir à (**3.4.3**)
revenir à
servir à (**3.4.3**)
songer à
tarder à (**3.4.3**)
tendre à (R3)
tenir à (**3.4.3**)
travailler à
veiller à
venir à (R3) (**3.4.3**)

de

eg
il s'abstient *de* **commenter l'événement**
il s'avise *de* **partir tout de suite**
l'armée menaçait *de* **franchir la frontière**
vous méritez *de* **recevoir une médaille**
vous avez raison *de* **venir**

s'abstenir de
accepter de
s'accuser de
achever de (**3.4.3**)
affecter de
s'affliger de
ambitionner de (R3)
s'applaudir de (R3)
s'arrêter de
attendre de (**3.4.3**)
s'aviser de

avoir peur de
brûler de
cesser de
se charger de
choisir de
commencer de (R3) (**3.4.3**)
comploter de
continuer de (**3.4.3**)
convenir de (**3.4.3**)
craindre de
décider de (**3.4.3**)

dédaigner de (cf daigner *below*)

mériter de

se dépêcher de

négliger de

désespérer de (R3)

être obligé de (**3.4.3**)

se devoir de (R3)

s'occuper de (**3.4.3**)

discontinuer de (R3)

offrir de (R3)

disconvenir de (R3)

omettre de

se disculper de

oublier de

s'efforcer de (**3.4.3**)

parler de

s'empêcher de

se piquer de

s'empresser de

prendre garde de

s'ennuyer de (**3.4.3**)

(= *to take care not to*)

entreprendre de

se presser de

envisager de

prévoir de (**3.4.3**)

espérer de (R3) (**3.4.3**)

projeter de

essayer de

promettre de

s'étonner de

se proposer de

éviter de

avoir raison de

s'excuser de

redouter de

exulter de (R3)

refuser de (**3.4.3**)

bien faire de

regretter de

faire semblant de

se repentir de

se féliciter de

résoudre de (**3.4.3**)

finir de (3.4.3)

se retenir de

se flatter de

risquer de

être forcé de (**3.4.3**)

rougir de

se garder de

simuler de

se glorifier de (R3)

souhaiter de (**3.4.3**)

se hâter de

se souvenir de

s'indigner de

suffire de (**3.4.3**)

jurer de

supporter de

manquer de (**3.4.3**)

tâcher de

en avoir marre de (R1)

tenter de

méditer de

avoir tort de

se mêler de (**3.4.3**)

se vanter de

menacer de

venir de (**3.4.3**)

par

achever par (**3.4.3**)

finir par (**3.4.3**)

commencer par (**3.4.3**)

terminer par

pour

attendre pour (**3.4.3**)

insister pour (**3.4.3**)

hésiter pour (**3.4.3**)

suffire pour (**3.4.3**)

verb +
infinitive
ie (. . .)

With certain verbs no preposition is required to link the verb with the following infinitive:

eg **j'aime le faire**

je peux y aller

nous pensions lui envoyer une lettre

adorer (. . .)

aimer (. . .)

aimer mieux (. . .)

aller (. . .)

avoir beau (. . .)

compter (. . .)

daigner (. . .)

détester (. . .)

devoir (. . .)

entendre (. . .) R3 = *to intend*

entrer (. . .)

espérer (. . .) (**3.4.3**)

faillir (. . .) (**3.4.3**)

falloir (. . .)

manquer (. . .) (**3.4.3**)

oser (. . .)

penser (. . .) (**3.4.3**)

pouvoir (. . .)

préférer (. . .)

savoir (. . .)

souhaiter (. . .) (**3.4.3**)

valoir mieux (. . .)

venir (. . .) (**3.4.3**)

vouloir (. . .)

Usage with *faire, entendre, laisser* and *voir* + infinitival group: in the group, the infinitive may have a subject and an object (which may be a *que*-clause) of its own:

eg **j'ai vu** *une jeune fille* **sortir de la salle**

(subject of the infinitive)

j'ai entendu *la jeune fille* **chanter** *des chansons* **à la guitare**

(subject of the infinitive)　　(object of the infinitive)

The following diagram illustrates the various constructions:

structure	notes	examples
faire + **infinitive with pronoun subject only**	if the subject is a noun, it precedes the infinitive; if it is a pronoun, the pronoun precedes the finite verb	*elle a entendu son père arriver* *il l'a entendu crier*
faire, etc + **infinitive with object only**	if the object is a noun, it follows the infinitive; if it is a pronoun, it precedes the finite verb	*elle a fait réparer sa voiture* *j'ai entendu dire que . . .* *j'ai entendu chanter des chansons* *elle l'a fait réparer*
faire, etc + **infinitive with subject and object**	the subject figures as an indirect object; *faire* + following verb has a variety of values: = to make, to force, to get to, to have	*elle lui a fait lire le journal* *il a fait admettre à sa mère que . . .* = he had his mother admit that . . . *je lui ai fait voir la ville* = I took her round the town *je lui ai fait comprendre que . . .*
entendre, laisser, voir + **infinitive with noun subject only**	the subject may precede or follow the infinitive	*elle a entendu son père crier* *il a entendu crier sa mère*
entendre, laisser, voir + **infinitive with subject and object**	verb + subject + infinitive + object	*nous avons entendu des garçons chanter des cantiques* *j'ai vu plusieurs ouvriers construire la maison*

3.4.1.2   *verb* + *preposition* + ^{noun} / pronoun

$$verb + \begin{matrix} à \\ de \\ avec + \end{matrix} \begin{matrix} \\ \\ noun \\ pronoun \end{matrix}$$
dans
sur

à

NOTE: Whereas in English it is possible for an indirect object in an active clause to become the subject of a passive voice clause (eg my father gave *me* a book = *I* was given a book by my father), in French such a transformation is not permitted and has to be avoided. (In other words, French active voice *la réception me plaît* has no passive equivalent.)
Exceptions to this general rule are specified below.

Examples of verb + à + ^{noun} / pronoun:
je m'attends *à* son arrivée
il pare *à* tout danger
elle a survécu *à* l'explosion
il a renoncé *à* sa carrière

assister à
s'attendre à
se confier à (**3.4.3**)
être confronté à (**3.4.3**)
consentir à (**3.4.3**)
convenir à (**3.4.3**)
croire à (**3.4.3**)
déplaire à
désobéir à
NOTE: désobéir *can be used in the passive voice with persons or things*
échapper à (**3.4.3**)
faillir à (**3.4.3**)
faxer à
se fier à (**3.4.3**)
insulter à (R3) (**3.4.3**)
manquer à (**3.4.3**)
se mêler à (**3.4.3**)
nuire à
obéir à
NOTE: *as with* désobéir: *eg il est obéi; mon ordre sera obéi*
pardonner à
NOTE: pardonner *can be used in passive voice*
parer à
participer à (**3.4.3**)

penser à (**3.4.3**)
plaire à
prendre part à
profiter à
NOTE: *used impersonally:* eg cela profite à l'homme
remédier à
renoncer à
répondre à (**3.4.3**)
répugner à (R3) (**3.4.3**)
résister à
ressembler à
ressortir à (R3) = *to be under the jurisdiction of* (**3.4.3**)
réussir à (**3.4.3**)
satisfaire à (R3) (**3.4.3**)
servir à (**3.4.3**)
songer à
subvenir à (eg aux besoins de qn)
succéder à
suffire à (**3.4.3**)
surseoir à (R3)
survivre à
téléphoner à
toucher à
NOTE: *occ, as in* toucher à sa fin
vaquer à

de

eg
elle a accouché de trois enfants
je conviens *de* mon erreur
il se méfie même *de* ses amis

abuser de (**3.4.3**)	s'inquiéter de
s'accommoder de (**3.4.3**)	s'inspirer de
s'accompagner de	se jouer de (R3) (**3.4.3**)
accoucher de	jouir de
s'aider de	manquer de (**3.4.3**)
s'alimenter de	médire de
s'alourdir de	se méfier de
s'apercevoir de	se mêler de (**3.4.3**)
(s')approcher de	se moquer de
s'armer de	s'occuper de (**3.4.3**)
avoir besoin/honte/peur de	s'offenser de
changer de	s'offusquer de
se charger de	s'orner de
convenir de	se parer de (R3)
se défier de (cf **3.4.3** fier)	partir de
se démettre de (R3)	se passer de
démissionner de	penser de (**3.4.3**)
dépendre de	profiter de
se dorer de (R3)	répondre de (**3.4.3**)
se douter de (**3.4.3**)	rire de (R3)
s'échapper de (**3.4.3**)	se saisir de
écoper de (R2/1)	se servir de (**3.4.3**)
s'embellir de	sortir de
s'émerveiller de	se souvenir de
s'emparer de	se targuer de (R3)
s'ennuyer de (**3.4.3**)	témoigner de
s'enrichir de	triompher de
s'entourer de	se tromper de (**3.4.3**)
s'envelopper de	user de (R3) (**3.4.3**)
s'évader de	se vanter de
s'excuser de	vivre de (**3.4.3**)
s'indigner de	

avec

s'accorder avec	rivaliser avec (**3.4.3**)
se familiariser avec	se solidariser avec

dans

s'embarquer dans

sur

s'accorder sur	insister sur (**3.4.3**)
brancher sur (**3.4.3**)	se renseigner sur

There is sometimes the possibility of choice of preposition with certain verbs:
eg **l'Assemblée Nationale a débattu/a discuté (*de*) la question**
   juger (*d'*) une personne

qu'est–ce que tu fais avec/de la voiture? tu la mets au
garage?

anticiper + (. . .)/sur	juger + (. . .)/de = *to estimate*
débattre + (. . .)/de	juger + sur/par = *to judge by*
délibérer + (. . .)/de (R3)	méditer + (. . .)/sur
discuter + (. . .)/de	se passionner de/pour (**3.4.3**)
faire + avec/de (**3.4.3**)	présider + (. . .)/à (R3)
s'identifier + à/avec (*less common*)	réfléchir + sur/à
informer + sur/de	rêver + à/de (*more common*)
inscrire + dans/sur	sauver la vie + de/à qn
(s')intégrer + dans/à	traiter + (. . .)/de

3.4.1.3 verb + direct object + preposition + infinitive

verb + direct object + $\begin{matrix} à \\ de \end{matrix}$ + infinitive

à

eg

les autorités l'ont autorisée *à* partir
cette idée m'amène *à* dire que . . .

aider . . . à	déterminer . . . à
amener . . . à	encourager . . . à
appeler . . . à	engager . . . à
autoriser . . . à	entrainer . . . à
condamner . . . à	exhorter . . . à (R3)
conduire . . . à (R3)	forcer . . . à (**3.4.3**)
contraindre . . . à (**3.4.3**)	inviter . . . à
convier . . . à	obliger . . . à (**3.4.3**)
décider . . . à (**3.4.3**)	pousser . . . à

de

eg

la police l'accuse *de* tuer un homme
je vous remercie *de* m'avoir aidée

accuser . . . de	implorer . . . de
avertir . . . de	intéresser . . . de (impers)
conjurer . . . de (R3)	(**3.4.3**)
contraindre . . . de (**3.4.3**)	menacer . . . de
convaincre . . . de	persuader . . . de (**3.4.3**)
décourager . . . de	prier . . . de
défier . . . de	remercier . . . de
dissuader . . . de	sommer . . . de (R3)
empêcher . . . de	soupçonner . . . de
féliciter . . . de	supplier . . . de

3.4.1.4 verb + preposition + $\begin{matrix} noun \\ pronoun \end{matrix}$ + preposition + infinitive

verb + à + $\begin{matrix} \textbf{noun} \\ \textbf{pronoun} \end{matrix}$ + de + infinitive

eg **je (dé)conseille** *à* **la femme** *de* **le faire**
   elle sait gré *à* **son père** *de* **l'aider au dernier moment**
   il pardonne *à* **son ami** *de* **l'avoir omis**
   il lui tarde *de* **le revoir**

The comment about active–passive transformation under **3.4.1.2** is also relevant here.

à . . . *de*		
	appartenir (impers) à . . . de	permettre à . . . de
	arriver (impers) à . . . de	peser à . . . de (impers)
	commander à . . . de	plaire (impers) à . . . de
	conseiller à . . . de	proposer à . . . de
	déconseiller à . . . de	reprocher à . . . de
	défendre à . . . de	répugner (impers) à . . . de (R3)
	demander à . . . de (**3.4.3**)	(**3.4.3**)
	dire à . . . de (**3.4.3**)	savoir gré à . . . de (R3)
	imposer à . . . de	faire signe à . . . de
	être impossible/possible	souhaiter à . . . de (3.4.3)
	à . . . de	suggérer à . . . de
	incomber (impers) à . . . de (R3)	tarder (impers) à . . . de (R3)
	interdire à . . . de	(**3.4.3**)
	ordonner à . . . de	en vouloir à . . . de
	pardonner à . . . de	

$$\text{verb} + à + \frac{\textbf{noun}}{\textbf{pronoun}} + à \text{ infinitive}$$

eg **le professeur apprend/enseigne** *à* **l'élève** *à* **lire le français**

à . . . *à*		
	apprendre à . . . à	enseigner à . . . à

$$\text{verb} + de + \frac{\textbf{noun}}{\textbf{pronoun}} + pour + \text{infinitive}$$

de . . . *pour*	
	s'inspirer de . . . pour

3.4.1.5 *verb + direct object + preposition +* $\frac{noun}{pronoun}$

$$\text{verb} + \text{direct object} + \begin{matrix} \textbf{à} \\ \textbf{de} \\ \textbf{avec} \\ \textbf{dans} \\ \textbf{par} \end{matrix} + \frac{\textbf{noun}}{\textbf{pronoun}}$$

**verb + direct
object + à
+ noun
+ pronoun**

eg
cette action lui aliène toutes les sympathies
la sœur a caché la lettre *à* **son frère**
il évite *à* **son fils la tâche de le récrire**
le capitaine imposa le silence *à* **ses hommes**
j'ai acheté des œufs au fermier
NOTE: acheter qch à qn *is ambiguous, as* à *can mean 'for' or 'from'.*

accommoder . . . à (R3)
   (**3.4.3**)
accorder . . . à
acheter . . . à
aliéner . . . à
apprendre . . . à
arracher . . . à (**3.4.3**)
assigner . . . à (R3)
associer . . . à
cacher . . . à
chercher . . . à
commander . . . à
communiquer . . . à
comparer . . . à (**3.4.3**)
conférer . . . à (R3)
confier . . . à (**3.4.3**)
coûter . . . à
décerner . . . à
défendre . . . à
demander . . . à (**3.4.3**)
dérober . . . à
devoir . . . à (**3.4.3**)
dissimuler . . . à
donner . . . à
emprunter . . . à
enlever . . . à (**3.4.3**)
enseigner . . . à
envier . . . à
envoyer . . . à
épargner . . . à
éviter . . . à
exprimer . . . à
extorquer . . . à
fournir . . . à

garantir . . . à
imposer . . . à
imprimer . . . à
inspirer . . . à
interdire . . . à
intéresser . . . à (**3.4.3**)
manifester . . . à
montrer . . . à
octroyer . . . à (R3)
ôter . . . à (**3.4.3**)
pardonner . . . à
payer . . . à (**3.4.3** and **3.4.5**)
permettre . . . à
prêcher . . . à
prendre . . . à (**3.4.3**)
préparer . . . à
présenter . . . à
prodiguer . . . à (R3)
rappeler . . . à (**3.4.3**)
réclamer . . . à
recommander . . . à
refuser . . . à (**3.4.3**)
reprendre . . . à
reprocher . . . à
réserver . . . à
restituer . . . à
retirer . . . à
retrancher . . . à
souhaiter . . . à (**3.4.3**)
soustraire . . . à
substituer . . . à
transmettre . . . à
voler . . . à

**verb + direct
object + *de*
+ noun
   pronoun**

eg

**on l'a accusée *de* vol
assurez-le *de* mon respect**

absoudre . . . de (R3)
accabler . . . de
accuser . . . de
approcher . . . de
arracher . . . de (**3.4.3**)
assurer . . . de (**3.4.3**)
avertir . . . de
aviser . . . de
bombarder . . . de

charger . . . de
complimenter . . . de
débarrasser . . . de
décharger . . . de
dégouter . . . de
délivrer . . . de
détourner . . . de
dispenser . . . de
écarter . . . de

	éloigner . . . de	libérer . . . de
	enlever . . . de (**3.4.3**)	menacer . . . de
	excuser . . . de	ôter . . . de (**3.4.3**)
	exempter . . . de	persuader . . . de (**3.4.3**)
	féliciter. . . de	prévenir . . . de
	frapper . . . de	remercier . . . de
	informer . . . de	traiter . . . de (= *to call sb sth*)
avec	comparer . . . avec (Rl) (**3.4.3**)	
dans	glaner . . . dans	puiser . . . dans
	prendre . . . dans (**3.4.3**)	
par	remplacer . . . par	
pour	inspirer . . . pour	

3.4.2   noun / adjective + preposition + infinitive

3.4.2.1   **noun + preposition + infinitive**

noun + à / de + infinitive

à   **son acharnement *à* compléter la tâche**
son habileté *à* défendre la cause

acharnement à	hésitation à
aisance à	impuissance à
aptitude à	insistance à (**3.4.3**)
ardeur à	intérêt à (**3.4.3**)
avidité à	persistance à
détermination à	regret à
difficulté à	répugnance à
facilité à	retard à
habileté à	

NOTE: un homme *à* craindre
un homme *à* tout faire

de   **je me trouvais dans l'impossibilité *de* partir**
sa volonté *de* l'emporter m'étonna

autorisation de	nécessité de
besoin de	obligation de
capacité de	occasion de
désir de	permission de
droit de (**3.4.3**)	plaisir de
honte de	rage de
impossibilité de	volonté de
incapacité de	

NOTE: *use of* de + *infinitive with:* avoir honte, les moyens, peur, raison, le temps, tort, faire semblant. Raison *is normally followed by* de *not* pour *with a noun or pronoun:*

eg la raison de son départ

however: la raison pour laquelle + *relative clause*

merci de *is more formal than* merci pour

3.4.2.2 *adjective + preposition + infinitive*

$$\text{adjective} + \frac{\grave{a}}{de} + \text{infinitive}$$

à

eg
il est lent *à* raisonner
elle est prompte *à* répondre
il était assis *à* lire son journal

apte à	long à
assis à	préparé à
décidé à	prêt à
déterminé à	prompt à
disposé à	propre à
enclin à	quitte à
fondé à (R3)	résolu à
habile à	réticent à (R3)
habilité à = *to be empowered to*	unanime à, *also* pour
lent à	

NOTE: c'est lourd *à* porter (**3.8.2.1**)
c'est facile *à* faire
c'est agréable *à* entendre
il est le seul/premier/deuxième, etc/dernier *à* arriver

de

eg
je suis curieux *de* le savoir
vous êtes libre *de* partir

avide de	libre de
capable de	mécontent de
certain de	ravi de (R3)
content de	reconnaissant de (R3)
curieux de	responsable de
désireux de (R3)	satisfait de (**3.4.3**)
heureux de	sûr de

NOTE: être content/heureux de qch, *but* être content/heureux avec qn
eg j'étais heureux *de* sa réponse/*de* partir demain
je suis heureuse *avec* mon mari

NOTE: *also the use with past participles:* aimé, estimé, apprécié, etc
eg il est aimé *de* tout le monde
il est estimé *de* tous les critiques

When the agent is active, however, par *is often used:*
eg il a été mordu *par* son chien (NB **3.4.4.2** BY)

accompagné *may be followed by* de *or* par

pour *must be used after* trop *and* assez:

　eg il est trop/assez grand *pour* le faire

3.4.3 Varying prepositions

In certain cases, depending upon meaning, register, euphony, context or construction, the preposition following a verb or related expression varies. It is vital to fit the right preposition with the right set of circumstances. The following list is an attempt to highlight the most important verbs and expressions involved in these prepositional variations.

abuser	**il abuse** (R3) **le public** he deceives . . . **elle abuse** *de* **la bonté de son ami** she takes advantage of . . . **le père a abusé** *de* **sa fille** the father abused his daughter
(s')accommoder	**il accommode** (R3) **sa conduite** *à* **toutes les circonstances** he adapts his conduct . . . **je m'accommoderai** *de* **ce logement modeste** I shall accept as suitable . . .
s' accorder	**tout le monde s'accorde** (R3) *à* **reconnaître que** . . . everyone agrees in . . . **le verbe s'accorde** *avec* **le nom** **ils se sont accordés** *sur* **le traité de paix**
achever	**il acheva** *de* **se ruiner** he finally . . . **il commença par rire, acheva** *par* **pleurer** (here one action is added to another)
aimer	**j'aime** *à* (R3) **croire que** . . . **elle aime jouer de la guitare** **j'aime mieux travailler que** *de* **jouer** 　(NOTE: *de* after second verb)
arracher	**il arracha sa chemise** *à* **son frère** (*à* with persons) **il l'arracha** *de* **son fauteuil** (*de* with things, although *à* is possible)
assurer	**je lui ai assuré qu'il n'y avait rien à craindre** (suggests affirmation) **assurez-le** *de* **mon respect** (suggests guarantee)
attendre	**elle attendait** *pour/de* (R3) **partir** **je ne m'attendais pas** *à* **un pareil traitement** I did not expect . . .

je m'attends *à* ce qu'il revienne
I expect . . .
elle attend le bateau
she waits for . . .

avoir   **avoir affaire *à* qn**
(more common and general than **avoir affaire avec qn**)
> NOTE: the difference between *avoir mal à la tête* and *avoir un mal de tête*

se battre   **il s'est battu *avec* son frère**
(ie on his brother's side or against his brother)
il s'est battu *contre* l'ennemi
(ie against)

changer   **il faut le changer**
je change *de* vêtements
(ie one set of clothes for another)
elle a changé ses meubles *contre* des tableaux
she exchanged . . .

commencer   **il a commencé *par* dire que . . .**
il a commencé sa conférence en disant que . . .
ii commença *à/d'*avoir des regrets
> NOTE: *de* (R3) is often used instead of *à* to avoid two or more similar sounds occurring in quick succession

comparer   **il compare une chose *à/avec* (R1) une autre**
> NOTE: *en comparaison de*, never *avec*

compter   **elle comptait partir**
je compte *avec* lui
I take him into consideration
je compte sur lui
I count on him
> NOTE: *escompter un résultat* = to count on a result

(se) confier   **elle se confie *à* lui**
j'ai confiance *en* eux

connaître/   **elle s'y connaît**
se connaître she is an expert on the matter
elle se connaît *en* tableaux
she is an expert . . .
j'ai connu mon épouse à Rome
I came to know my wife . . .
> NOTE: *j'ai fait la connaissance de Pierre l'an dernier*
> *il a fait connaissance avec elle il y a deux semaines*

consentir   **consentir un traité**
(ie to authorise)
je consens *à* tout ce que vous voulez
(ie to consent to)

construire   in *une maison construite de pierre* less attention is fixed on the material than in *une maison construite en pierre* (**3.4.4.** DE)

continuer	*à* and *de* are equally common with *continuer* (see note to *commencer*)
contraindre	**il la contraint** *à*/*de* **partir**

convenir	**cet arrangement n'a pas convenu** *à* **Jean**
	(ie did not suit)
	elle est convenue *de* **venir**
	she agreed . . .
	    NOTE: when *convenir* means 'to suit' it is conjugated with *avoir*.
	    When it means 'to agree', it is conjugated with *être*. This difference
	    is not observed by many French people.

courir	**le petit passe son temps** *à* **courir dans le jardin** **courir le cent mètres** **il court** (*après*) **les filles tous les week-ends** **elle court les universités pour trouver un cursus qui lui** **plaît**
croire	**il croit** *à* **la médecine** he thinks medicine is a valid discipline **il croit** *en* **Dieu**/*en* **l'avenir**/*en* **l'homme** (suggests trust)
décider	**cette raison m'a décidé** *à* **partir** (persuaded me) **c'est à vous de décider** *de* **ma fortune** (to make a decision over) **j'ai décidé** *de* **le faire** (here, the decision is arrived at more quickly than with *se décider à*) **elle s'est décidée** *à* **quitter l'école** she made up her mind after careful consideration **elle s'est décidée** *pour* **le parti socialiste** she declared herself in favour of . . .
demander	**elle demande** *à* **partir** **son ami lui demande** *de* **partir**
devoir	**elle doit faire ses devoirs** **elle doit dix livres** *à* **son père** **vous vous devez à vous-même** *de* (R3) **bien travailler** you owe it to yourself . . .
dire	**je lui dis** *de* **partir** **j'ai dit avoir lu le livre**
divorcer	**divorcer** (intr) to get a divorce **ils ont divorcé** they got a divorce **divorcer** *avec*/*d'avec* (R3) **qn** to divorce sb **être divorcé** to be divorced
douter	**je ne doute pas** *de* **son honnêteté** I do not doubt . . .

se douter *de*
to suspect
je m'en doutais
I suspected it

droit   **avoir droit** *à* + noun
avoir le droit *de* + infinitive

échapper   **il a échappé** *à* **la mort/***à* **la police**
(ie to avoid)
ils se sont échappés *de* **l'embuscade**
(ie to get clear from)
> NOTE: *s'échapper de is* not normally used for prison; use *s'évader de.*

s'efforcer   usu **s'efforcer** *de*
s'efforcer *à* (R3)

enlever   as **arracher**

ennuyer   **elle s'ennuie** *à/d'***attendre**
il s'ennuyait *d'***elle**
he missed her
(impers: **il m'ennuie** *d'***être si longtemps séparé de vous**)

entendre   **elle entend le bruit**
il s'entend *à* (R3) **la peinture/***en* **peinture**
he is an expert on painting
je m'entends (bien) *avec* **lui**
I get on well . . .
ils se sont entendus *pour* **lui tendre un piège**

entrer   **il est entré** *dans* **l'école**
(ie he entered the school buildings)
il est entré *à* **l'école septembre dernier**

espérer   **j'espère arriver ce soir**
je ne puis espérer de (R3) **recevoir cette réponse**

se fâcher   **elle se fâche** *avec* **son frère**
she quarrels with . . .
il se fâche *contre* **elle**
he gets angry with her

faillir   **j'ai failli gagner à la loterie nationale**
I almost won . . .
j'ai failli *à* **mon devoir**
I failed in . . .

faire   **qu'est-ce qu'il a fait** *de/avec* **son livre?**
il le fait *de/par* **lui-même**
he does it by himself
elle ne fait que jouer
all she does is play
elle ne fait que *d'***entrer/que** *d'***arriver/que** *de* **s'éveiller**
she has only just . . .

se familiariser/ être familier	il se familiarise *avec* le français il est familier *de/avec* plusieurs langues
se fier/ confier/ défier/méfier	je me fie *à* mon ami elle lui a confié une lettre il faut se défier/se méfier *de* ses ennemis
finir	elle a fini *par* dire . . . il a fini sa conférence en disant . . . (cf *commencer*) elle a fini *d'*écrire sa lettre
forcer	son père le force *à* étudier (ie active voice) je suis forcé *de* lire toute la journée (ie passive voice, cf *obliger*)
habituer/ avoir l'habitude	il faut s'habituer *à* parler en public elle a l'habitude *de* se coucher tôt
hésiter	il n'hésite pas *à* (st *pour*) répondre hésiter *entre* le vice et la vertu elle hésite *sur* le choix d'une profession
insister	j'insiste *à/pour* le faire j'insiste *pour* qu'il le fasse le professeur a insisté *sur* le fait que la lecture est importante son insistance *à* travailler toute la journée . . .
insulter	il l'a insultée he insulted her insulter *à* (R3) eg le luxe insulte *à* la misère publique
intéresser/ avoir intérêt/se désintéresser	je m'intéresse *à* y aller vous avez intérêt *à* faire des économies it is in your interest to . . . il y a intérêt *à* payer maintenant elle m'y a intéressé she interested me in it je suis intéressé *par* ce que tu dis elle est inintéressée/peu intéressée *par* vos idées cela m'intéresse *d'*écrire un roman il cultive un intérêt *pour* l'histoire il est intéressant *de* . . . je me désintéresse *de* ses propos I am uninterested in . . .
jouer	il joue Hamlet elle joue un air de Mozart *au* piano nous jouons *du* violon (ie instrument) ils jouent *au* football (ie sport)

se jouer *de* qn (R3)

to make fun of sb

elle lui a joué un mauvais tour

she played a nasty trick on him

manquer	**il manque *de* pain**

he lacks bread

le pain manque *à* la famille

(literally) bread is lacking in the family (ie the family needs bread)

il a manqué (*de*) tomber

he almost fell (**2.5**)

ne manque pas *de* venir

don't fail to come

> NOTE: *manquer de* does not mean 'to fail to'

elle a manqué *à* la consigne

she failed in/disregarded orders

elle a manqué le train

she missed the train

marier	**le prêtre a marié les jeunes**

elle s'est mariée *avec* le fils du maire

il est marié *à/avec* une Espagnole

elle a marié sa fille *à/avec* un ingénieur

mêler	**il se mêla *à* la foule et disparut**

he mingled with . . .

elle se mêle *de* la politique

she is concerned with politics

voilà qu'elle se mêle *de* nous donner des conseils

there she goes, giving us advice

obliger	as with **forcer**
occuper	**la mère s'occupe *de* l'enfant**

il était occupé *à* écrire une lettre

elle s'occupait *à/de* l'habiller

ôter	as **arracher**
participer/ participation	**elle participe *à* ma joie**

she shares in . . .

le mulet participe *de* (R3) l'âne et *du* cheval

the mule is of the same nature as . . .

sa participation *au/dans* le débat m'étonna

passionner/ passion	**il se passionne *pour* le football**

(suggests passive interest)

elle est passionnée *de* natation

(suggests active interest)

elle éprouvait une passion profonde *pour* lui

payer	**il a payé le livre**

he paid for the book (**3.4.5**)

il a payé dix francs *à* l'homme

il a payé dix francs le livre *à* l'homme

pénétrer	**elle a pénétré** *dans* **le jardin** in figurative usage *dans* does not occur: **elle pénétra le mystère/le marché**
penser	**elle pense** *à* **sa mère** she thinks of her mother **que pensez-vous** *de* **ce peintre?** what is your opinion about . . . ? **elle pense partir en vacances** she's thinking of going . . .
prendre	**elle le prend** *à* **sa sœur** she takes it from her sister **il le prend** *dans* **le tiroir** he takes it from/out of the drawer **il le prend** *sur* **la table** he takes it from/off the table
prevoir	**le mariage était prévu** *pour* **février** **je prévois** *de* **partir demain**
profiter	**il faut profiter** *de* **l'occasion** **la France lui a profité énormément**
rappeler	**j'ai rappelé l'incident** *à* **mon père** I reminded my father of . . . **je me rappelle le livre:** ie rappeler qch *à* soi-même NOTE: *je me rappelle du livre* is often used, on analogy *with je me* *souviens du livre*, but is condemned by purists
refuser	**il refuse** *d'***y aller** **il se refuse** *à* **le faire** **elle refuse le droit** *à* **son collègue de . . .**
répondre	**je réponds** *à* **la question** **il doit répondre** *de* **ses actes** he must take responsibility for his actions
répugner	**je répugne** *à* (R3) **le faire** I find it repugnant to do it **cet homme répugne** *à* (R3) **mon père** my father finds that man repugnant **cela me répugne** *de* **lui écrire**
résoudre	**j'ai résolu la question** I solved the question **résoudre** *de***/se résoudre** *à***:** as **décider**
ressortir	**il ressort** *de* **chez lui** he comes out again . . . **mon affaire ressortit** *au* **juge de paix** (R3) my case falls within the jurisdiction of . . . NOTE: in this latter meaning *ressortir* is conjugated like *finir* (cf **2.2.4**). This is not observed by many French people.

réussir	**elle a réussi un grand exploit** she brought off . . . **nous avons réussi _à_ le terminer** **tout lui réussit** everything succeeds with him
satisfaire	**il satisfait son maître** **satisfaire _à_** (R3) **une promesse/un besoin/une obligation** (the use of _à_ suggests fulfilment, completion) **je suis satisfaite _de_ ton travail**
servir	**le moteur peut encore servir** the engine is still fit for use **la lecture sert _à_ la formation des étudiants** reading helps in . . . **un moteur sert _à_ faire marcher une voiture** an engine is used to . . . **il ne sert _à_ rien de l'écrire ce matin** it serves no purpose to . . . **les tables servent _de_ pupitres** the tables are used as desks **elle s'est servie _du_ livre** she used the book **servir qn** to serve sb
souhaiter	**j'ai souhaité (_de_) le voir** (usage with or without _de_ is acceptable) **je te souhaite _d_'être en bonne santé** I hope you are . . . **elle lui a souhaité la bienvenue**
souscrire	**elle a souscrit une assurance/un plan d'épargnement/un abonnement** she has taken out . . . **j'ai souscrit _au_ journal _Le Monde_/_à_ une œuvre (charitable)** **je ne souscris pas _à_ cette opinion-là** I don't subscribe to . . .
suffire	**dix minutes ont suffi _pour_ le terminer** **cinq jours ont suffi _à_ l'écrivain _pour_ composer son roman** **il suffit _de_ peu de chose _pour_ . . .** **il suffit _de_ le faire tout de suite**
tarder	**il tarde _à_ venir** he is slow in coming **il lui tarde _de_ revoir ses parents** (impers) he is keen to see his parents again
tenir	**l'élève tient _à_ ses livres** the pupil values his books **j'y tiens/je tiens _à_ le faire** I am keen on it/to do it, etc

il tient *de* son père
he takes after his father

se tromper   je me suis trompé *d'*adresse
I was mistaken over . . .
elle m'a trompé
she deceived me

user   il use ses vêtements
he wears his clothes out
elle use *d'*un style recherché
she uses a refined style
 NOTE: *user de*: R3 but common

venir   je viens vous dire que . . .
je viens *de* lui envoyer une lettre
I have just. . . (cf **3.6.1.5**)
 NOTE: *venir de* cannot be followed by *revenir*. Say, for example, *il est*
 revenu à l'instant.
une voiture vint *à* (R3) passer
a car happened to pass (this expression is normally used with the ph)

viser   il vise un grand marché
he is aiming at . . .
il vise *à* créer un nouveau système

vivre   le retraité vit *de* sa pension
the pensioner lives off . . .

3.4.4 Prepositional expressions

It is in this section that the differences between patterns in English and
French appear most clearly. It is absolutely impossible to legislate on
the translation of prepositional expressions from one language to
another: very few clear tendencies emerge. That is why it seems best
to present for both languages as many examples as possible for as many
prepositions as possible. An attempt has been made, where
appropriate, to classify the examples according to the relationship
expressed between the preposition and the noun.

3.4.4.1 *French prepositions*

A
expressing
position

à l'équateur (cf **sous**)	*at/on* the equator
au pôle nord	*at* the north pole
aux Tropiques (cf **sous**)	*in* the Tropics
à l'horizon	*on* the horizon
à Paris	*in* Paris
à la maison	*at* home
à l'hôtel	*at* the hotel
à la faculté/*à* la fac (R1) (cf **EN**)	*at* university
des peintures pendues *au* mur	pictures hanging *on* the wall
au tableau noir/blanc (cf **SUR**)	*on* the blackboard/whiteboard

travailler *à* la mine	to work *in* the mines

NOTE: for a discussion on the use of A rather than DANS in this and the following six examples, see **3.4.4.2** IN

à la campagne (cf EN)	*in* the country
à la montagne (cf DANS and EN)	*in* the mountains
aux champs	*in* the fields
au jardin	*in* the garden
au salon	*in* the drawing room
à la cuisine	*in* the kitchen
au plafond	*on* the ceiling
à la ferme (cf DANS)	*on* the farm
travailler *à* un ranch	to work *on* a ranch
au téléphone	*on* the telephone
au paradis	*in* paradise
entrer *au* paradis	to go *to* paradise
au soleil	*in* the sun
à l'ombre (cf DANS)	*in* the shade
à terre (R3) (cf PAR)	*on* the ground
tomber *à* terre (cf PAR)	to fall *to* the ground (from a height)
tomber *à* l'eau (cf DANS)	to fall *in* the water
au contact de l'eau	*in* contact with the water
à bord d'une voiture/un avion/un train	*in* a car/plane/train
être *à* bicyclette/vélo (cf EN and SUR)	to be *on* a bicycle
blessé *au* bras, etc	wounded *in* the arm, etc
tomber *aux* mains de qn (cf ENTRE)	to fall *into* sb's hands
avoir la pipe *à* la bouche	to have a pipe *in* one's mouth
tenir un livre *à* la main	to hold a book *in* one's hand
avoir qch *aux* pieds, etc (not SUR)	to have sth *on* one's feet, etc
à la première page	*on* the first page
(point) – *à* la ligne	a new paragraph (in dictation)
à la place de/*au* lieu de	*in* place of/*instead* of
aller *à* sa rencontre	to meet sb

expressing time	*à* l'heure actuelle	*at* the present time
	à notre époque	*in* our time
	au 21ᵉ siècle	*in* the 21st century
	au printemps	*in* the spring
	à l'automne (cf EN)	*in* the autumn
	à la mi-avril	*in* mid-April
	à la Saint Sylvestre/*à* la Toussaint	New Year's Eve/All Saints' Day
	au bout d'un mois	a month later
	au début de l'après-midi (cf EN)	*at* the beginning of the afternoon/in the early afternoon

à la fin de la séance (cf EN)	*at* the end of the meeting
à la mi-temps (cf EN)	*at* half-time
à mon arrivée/retour	*on* my arrival/return
au temps des Pharaons (cf DE)	*in* the time of the Pharaohs
la date *à* laquelle il a envoyé ...	the date *on* which ...
elle est arrivée *à* temps	she arrived *on* time
à l'avance (cf DE and PAR)	*in* advance

figurative
usage

à ce que je vois	*from* what I can see
à ce que je sache	*from* what I know
à ce que j'ai entendu	*from* what I've heard
je ne comprends rien *à* ce qu'il dit	I don't understand a thing *of* what he says
il ne comprend rien *au* problème	he doesn't understand anything *about* the problem
à son avis	*in* his opinion
à mon point de vue	*from* my point of view
à ce point de vue-là	*from* that point of view
reconnaître qn *à* sa voix	to recognise sb *by* his voice
rouler *à* bicyclette/vélo (cf EN and SUR)	to travel *by* bicycle
aller *à* moto (cf EN)	to travel *by* motorbike
à cheval	*on* horse back
à dos de chameau	*on* camel back
à la radio (cf 3.4.4.2 ON)	*on* the radio
à la télé (cf 3.4.4.2 ON)	*on* TV
écrire *à* l'encre/*au* crayon	to write *in* ink/pencil
lire *à* la lumière d'une lampe	to read *by* the light of a lamp
un instrument *à* cordes/*à* cuivre/ *à* vent	a string/brass/wind instrument
à partir de cette idée	*from* this idea
au nom du roi (cf EN)	*in* the king's name
ce livre vient de paraître *aux* éditions Gallimard (cf CHEZ)	this book has just been published *by* Gallimard
le gouvernement *au* pouvoir	the government *in* power
il l'a abattu *à* coups de poing/bâton/hâche/ revolver/couteau	he punched him until he fell to the ground, etc
elle l'a emporté *à* coups de pédale	she pedalled off with it
à sa manière (cf DE)	*in* his way
à pas lents/de géant/de loup/feutrés	slowly/*with* giant strides/ stealthily/noiselessly
à la dérobée	stealthily/secretly
à reculons	backwards
à regret	regretfully
à la rigueur	if need be
au secours/voleur	help/thief

	une boîte *à* lettres	a letter box
	une boîte *à* archives	a file box
	un pot *à* beurre/eau/fleurs (cf DE)	a butter dish/water jug/ flower pot

NOTE: A indicates that the two nouns together form a single entity, whereas with DE a more lax connection is marked

	un verre *à* bière/vin (cf DE)	a beer/wine glass

NOTE: see previous note

	côte *à* côte	side *by* side
	mot *à* mot	word *by* word
	pas *à* pas	step *by* step
	un *à* un	one *by* one
	travailler *aux* PTT (cf DANS)	to work *for* the Post Office
	travailler *aux* chemins de fer (cf DANS)	to work *for* the railway
	être *au* chômage (cf EN)	to be *out of* work
	à son intention	*for* him/her
	faire une remarque *à* son égard/son propos/ son sujet	*with* respect to him/her
	au moins dix mètres	*at* least ten metres
	elle a *au* moins le mérite de . . .	*at* least she's got the merit of . . . (cf DE)
expressing measurement	*à* une vitesse de 80 kms *à* l'heure	*at* a speed of 50 miles an hour
	il lit *à* raison de 10 pages *à* l'heure	he reads *at* a rate of 10 pages an hour
	louer *à* l'heure	to hire *by* the hour
	vendre *au* litre/mètre	to sell *by* the litre/metre
AU-DESSOUS DE (R3) expressing position	il jeta la balle *au-dessous de* la table (cf EN DESSOUS DE)	he threw the ball *under* the table
figurative usage	il a trouvé un poste *au-dessous de* ses compétences	he found a post *beneath* his qualifications
AU-DESSUS DE expressing position	l'église est située *au-dessus du* village	the church stands *above* the village
	il y avait une enseigne *au-dessus de* nos têtes	there was a sign *above* our heads
	l'oiseau vola *au-dessus du* mur (cf 3.4.4.1 OVER for comment)	the bird flew *over/along* the wall
figurative usage	épouser *au-dessus de* soi	to marry *above* one's station

CHEZ expressing position	*chez* **nous**	*in* our country
	chez **nous/lui, etc**	*at* home
	chez **le docteur**	*at* the doctor's
figurative usage	*chez* **les Français il y a une coutume**	*amongst* the French there is a custom
	chez **lui**	*in* his case
	ce livre vient de paraître *chez* **Gallimard** (cf A)	this book has just been published by Gallimard
CONTRE figurative usage	**échanger une chose** *contre* **une autre** (cf POUR)	to exchange one thing *for* another
	être fâché *contre* (**3.4.3 se fâcher** and **3.4.4.2 WITH**)	to be angry *with* sb
DANS expressing position	*dans* **l'air/les airs** (R3) (cf **3.2.2** and EN)	*in* the air
	dans **l'espace**	*in* space (of astronaut)
	dans **la lune** (cf SUR)	*on* the moon
	aller *dans* **la lune** (cf SUR)	to go *to* the moon
	dans **les Alpes, etc**	*in* the Alps, etc
	dans **la montagne** (cf A and EN)	*in* the mountains
	dans **la région parisienne** (cf EN)	*in* the Paris area
	dans **la capitale**	*in* the capital (Paris)
	dans **le 19e arrondissement**	*in* the 19th district (of Paris)
	dans **la rue**	*in* the street
	dans **l'avenue/le boulevard**	*in* the avenue/boulevard
	dans **l'allée**	*on* the path
	dans **le square** (but *sur* **la place**)	*in* the square (small public square with garden)
	tomber *dans* **l'eau** (cf A)	to fall *in* the water
	dans **une tente** (cf SOUS)	*in* a tent
	dans **la maison**	*in* (as contrasted with outside) the house

NOTE: for a discussion of the use of **DANS** and **A** in such contexts, see **3.4.4.2 IN**

dans **le stade**	*in* the stadium (of spectator)
dans **les buts**	*in* goal
dans **la ferme** (cf A)	*in* the farmhouse
dans **l'aéroport** (cf SUR)	*at* the airport (in the buildings)
dans **le parking** (cf SUR)	*in* the carpark (enclosed or multi-storied)
travailler *dans* **la mine**	to work *in* a mine

NOTE: for a discussion on the use of **DANS** rather than **A** in this and the following two sets of examples, see **3.4.4.2 IN**

dans **la campagne/les champs/le jardin**	*in* the country/fields/garden

249

	dans le salon/la cuisine	*in* the drawing room/kitchen
	dans la chambre	*in* the bedroom
	NOTE: only DANS may be used here	
	dans les coulisses	*in* the wings (lit and fig)
	dans l'escalier	*on* the stairs
	dans le train	*on* the train
	il est *dans* la voiture de son père	he's *in* his father's car
	NOTE: DANS is used when *voiture* is qualified; otherwise EN is used	
	monter *dans* un avion	to get *into* a plane
	dans un carnet (cf SUR)	*in* a note-book
	dans le journal (cf SUR)	*in* the paper
	être assis *dans* un fauteuil	to sit *in* an armchair
	mettre qch *dans* une assiette	to put sth *on* a plate
	boire *dans* un verre	to drink *from* a glass
	se refléter *dans* le soleil	to be reflected *in* the sunlight
	dans l'ombre (cf A)	*in* the shade
	dans l'espace de dix mètres (cf EN for time)	*in* the space of ten metres
expressing time	*dans* le même temps (R3) (cf EN)	*at* the same time
	dans la semaine (cf EN)	*during* the week
	dans la matinée/après–midi/ soirée	*in* (the course of) the morning/afternoon/evening
	je le ferai *dans* dix jours	I'll do it *in* ten days (in ten days' time)
	dans le temps	some time ago, a long time ago
	être *dans* les temps	to be *on* schedule
	dans les prochains jours/ les trois jours	*in* the next few days/*in* the next three days (from this point in time)
figurative usage	*dans* une forme littéraire (cf SOUS)	*in* a literary form
	dans la situation actuelle	*in* the present situation
	dans le secret/privé (cf EN)	*in* secret/private
	travailler *dans* les chemins de fer (cf A)	to work *for* the railway
	travailler *dans* les PTT (cf A)	to work *for* the Post Office
	dans les limbes	*in* limbo
	être *dans* la lune	to be *in* the clouds
	être/rester *dans* l'expectative	to wait and see
DE expressing position	le chemin *de* la gare	the road *from*/*to* the station
	le train *de* Paris	the train *from*/*to* Paris
	de Londres *à* Paris (cf 3.4.4.2 FROM)	*from* London *to* Paris

de ville *en* ville	*from* town *to* town
de porte *en* porte	*from* door *to* door
une rue *de* Marseille	a street *in* Marseilles
du haut du balcon/*des* remparts	*from* the balcony/ramparts (suggesting height)
de ce côté	*on* this side
de l'autre côté	*on* the other side
du côté de la gare	*in* the direction of the station
voir *de* dos/*de* face/*de* profil/*de* derrière/*de* côté	to see (sb) *from* the back/face on/*in* profile/*from* the back/the side

<table>
<tr><td rowspan="4">expressing usage with materials (cf EN)</td><td colspan="2">NOTE: DE is less concrete than EN in such expressions; EN stresses the material</td></tr>
<tr><td>un cheval *de* bois</td><td>a wooden horse</td></tr>
<tr><td>une chemise *de* coton</td><td>a cotton shirt</td></tr>
<tr><td>une barrière *de* métal</td><td>a metal gate</td></tr>
</table>

expressing time	*de* notre temps/nos jours	*in* our time
	de temps *en* temps	*from* time *to* time
	*d'*heure/année *en* heure/année	*from* hour/year *to* hour/year
	de 10 heures *à* midi	*from* 10 o'clock *to* midday
	du temps des Pharaons (cf A)	*in* the time of the Pharaohs
	différer/remettre/reporter *de* 10 jours	to postpone *for* 10 days
	une jeune fille *de* 15 *à* 16 ans	a girl *between* 15 *and* 16 years old
	*d'*avance (cf A and PAR)	*in* advance
	la semaine *d'*avant/*d'*après	the previous/following week

figurative usage	*d'*une voix heureuse/triste	*in* a happy/sad voice
	*d'*un ton heureux/triste (cf SUR)	*in* a happy/sad tone
	*d'*une façon/manière étrange (cf A)	*in* a strange way
	de l'avis de Jean	*in* John's opinion
	de la part de M. Henri	*on* behalf of M. Henri
	dites-le-lui *de* ma part	tell him *on* my behalf
	connaître qn *de* vue	to know sb *by* sight
	un pot *de* beurre/lait/fleurs (cf A)	a pot *of* butter/milk/flowers
	un verre *de* bière/vin (cf A)	a glass *of* beer/wine
	je suis inquiet *de* (R3) lui (cf POUR)	I'm worried *about* him
	il est *de* mon côté	he's *on* my side
	de toutes façons (cf EN)	*at* any rate
	de l'autre côté	*on* the other hand/side
	de part et *d'*autre	*on* both sides

de tout mon cœur	*with* all my heart
de bon cœur	sincerely
de son/leur vivant	while s/he was/they were still alive
de toutes mes forces	*with* all my strength
*d'*une main tremblante	*with* a trembling hand
battre *des* mains	to clap
frapper *du* pied	to kick
cligner *des* yeux	to wink
un chauffage *d'*appoint	an extra heating appliance
un livre *d'*emprunt	a borrowed book
un film *d'*exception	an exceptional film
un avocat/un expert *d'*office	an official lawyer/expert
la pièce *d'*origine (not **original**)	the original part (of a car, machine etc)
*d'*après le roman d'Emile Zola	*after* the novel by Emile Zola
du moins (not used with numbers (cf **A**))	*at* least

expressing measurement	avancer *de* 10 jours	to bring forward *by* 10 days
	augmenter/majorer *de* 10 francs	to increase *by* 10 francs
	réduire *de* 10 francs	to reduce *by* 10 francs
	battre qn *de* 10 mètres	to beat sb *by* 10 metres
	être plus intelligent *de* beaucoup	to be more intelligent *by* far
	la durée est *de* 7 heures	it lasts 7 hours
	le prix est *de* 3 euros	the price is 3 euros
	la distance est *de* 10 kilomètres	the distance is 10 kilometres
	gagner 300 euros *de* l'heure	to earn 300 euros an hour

expressing passive agent in passive voice	mourir *d'*un cancer	to die *from* cancer
	souffrir *d'*une bronchite	to suffer *from* bronchitis
	être suivi *d'*un chien (cf **PAR**)	to be followed *by* a dog

NOTE: a subtle register distinction may be made when **de** occurs before the indefinite article or a name beginning with **h** or before the plural definite article in book titles etc:

R2	R3/2
le règne d'Henri quatre	le règne de Henri quatre
augmenter d'un pour cent	augmenter de un pour cent
la dictature d'Hitler	la dictature de Hitler
Victor Hugo, l'auteur des *Misérables*	Victor Hugo, l'auteur de *Les Misérables*

DURANT expressing time	**des heures/journées** *durant* (R3)	*for* hours/days

EN expressing position	EN is becoming more and more common as a preposition (probably because it is an economical way of avoiding longer constructions such as **dans le/la, au/à la** etc.)

eg **on peut acheter ce roman** *en* **librairie** (instead of *dans* **une**)
   je l'ai rencontrée *en* **Gare du Nord** (instead of *à la*)
   lire *en* **page 6** (instead of *à la*)
   rouler *en* **Renault** (instead of *à bord d*'**une**/*dans* **une**)

EN has a more general value than A or DANS:

eg **l'ouvrage peut s'acheter** *en* **librairie dès demain**
   l'ouvrage peut s'acheter *dans* **cette librairie-là**
   mon père travaille *en* **faculté** (his regular work)
   mon père est *à la* **faculté** (today)

en **l'air** (cf DANS)	*in* the air
en **République Française** (R3)	*in* the French Republic
en **Avignon/***en* **Arles** (used of southern towns; to avoid hiatus; but not of northern towns, eg *à* **Arras**)	*in* Avignon/Arles
en **région parisienne** (cf DANS)	*in* the Paris area
en **métropole** (cf DANS)	*in* the capital (Paris), *in* France
en **banlieue** (see note to **3.4.4.2** IN)	*in* the suburbs
en **périphérie parisienne**	*in* the Paris suburbs
en **montagne** (cf A and DANS)	*in* the mountains
en **car**	*in* a coach
en **rade**	*in* the roads (of a harbour)
en **mer** (cf SUR) (see note to **3.4.4.2** AT)	*at* sea
en **orbite basse** (cf SUR)	*in* a low orbit
aller *en* **paradis** (R3) (cf A)	to go *to* paradise
aller *en* **enfer/purgatoire**	to go *to* hell/purgatory
aller *en* **classe**	to go *to* school
en **coulisses**	*in* the wings (lit and fig)
en **lycée**	*at* school
en **faculté/***en* **fac** (R1) (cf A)	*at* university
aller *en* **expédition**	to go *on* an expedition
aller *en* **ville**	to go *to* town
en **campagne** (cf A)	*in* the country
en **pleine campagne**	*in* the depths of the countryside/*in* the midst of a campaign
en **pleine rue**	*in* the middle of the road
en **brousse**	*in* the bush
en **usine**	*in* a factory
en **milieu hospitalier**	*in* a hospital environment

en **milieu universitaire/scolaire/ rural/sportif**	*in* a university/school/ country/sports environment
en **conseil des ministres**	*in* the cabinet
en **librairie**/*en* **pharmacie**/*en* **bibliothèque**	*in* a bookshop/ a chemist's/ a library
en **résidence surveillée**	*under* house arrest
en **grande surface** (but *au* **supermarché**)	*in* a supermarket
en **salle**	*in* a sports centre/cinema
en **pleine salle**	*in* the middle of the room
en **centre sportif/nautique**	*in* a sports centre/water sports centre
en **ligue des champions**	*in* the champions' league (European football)
en **pole position**	*in* pole position
en **salle d'opération/d'examen**	*in* an operation theatre/ examination room/hall
en **studio**	*in* a recording studio
en **zone occupée**	*in* occupied territory
en **amont de**	upstream from/before (lit and fig R3)
en **aval de**	downstream from
le drapeau est *en* **berne**	the flag is *at* half-mast
en **plein vol**	*in* full flight
en **plein soleil**	*in* the full sun
il l'a cogné *en* **pleine figure**	he smashed him right *in* the face
avoir une idée *en* **tête**	to have an idea *in* your mind
en **ballon**/*en* **montgolfière**	*in* a balloon
monter *en* **avion**	to go up *in* a plane
voyager *en* **avion** (cf PAR)	to travel *by* plane
être *en* **vélo** (R1) (cf A)	to be *on* a bicycle
rouler *en* **vélo** (R1) (cf A and SUR)	to travel *by* bicycle
aller *en* **moto** (cf A)	to travel *by* motorbike
en **scooter**	*on* a scooter
rouler *en* **deux roues**	to ride a bike
NOTE: *en* is more common than *à*	
voyager *en* **voiture/auto** (cf DANS)	to travel *by* car
rouler *en* **Peugeot**	to drive a Peugeot
voyager *en* **train** (cf PAR)	to travel *by* train
voyager *en* **bateau** (cf PAR)	to travel *by* boat
en **radeau**	*on* a raft
en **selle** (cf SUR)	*in* the saddle (of a horse)
en **première page** (cf A)	*on* the first page

expressing usage with materials (cf **DE**)	**un cheval** *en* **bois**	a wooden horse
	une chemise *en* **coton**	a cotton shirt
	une barrière *en* **métal**	a metal gate

expressing time	*en* **même temps** (cf DANS)	*at* the same time
	en **(l'an) 1950**	*in* 1950
	en **été/hiver**	*in* the summer/winter
	en **automne** (cf A)	*in* the autumn
	en **avril**	*in* April
	en **semaine**	*during* the week, *in* the week (as opposed to the weekend)
	en **début d'après-midi** (cf A)	*at* the beginning of the afternoon
	en **fin de séance** (cf A)	*at* the end of the meeting
	en **l'espace de trois semaines**	*in* the space of three weeks
	je l'ai fait *en* **dix jours**	I did it *in* ten days
	en **première/deuxième mi-temps** (cf A)	*in* the first/second half (of sports match)
	en **période électorale**	*during* the elections
	en **période de sécheresse**	*during* a drought
	un match *en* **nocturne**	an evening match
	partir *en* **weekend**	to go away *for* the weekend
	l'expérience/l'année *en* **cours**	the present/current experiment/year
	la dernière publication *en* **date**	the latest publication *to* date
	en **milieu de journée**	*at* midday
	en **ce temps-là**	*at* that time
	en **retard**	late (after a specified time; **tard** = late in general)
figurative usage	**se changer/se transformer** *en* **simple spectateur**	to change/be transformed *into* a mere spectator
	se déguiser *en* **prêtre**	to disguise oneself *as* a priest
	un assassin *en* **série**	a serial killer
	se comporter *en* **invité**	to behave *like* a guest
	une femme *en* **cheveux** (R3)	a woman *without* a hat
	être *en* **danger**	to be *in* danger
	dormir *en* **paix**	to sleep *in* peace
	rester assis *en* **silence**	to sit *in* silence
	être *en* **deuil**	to be *in* mourning
	en **catimini** (R3)/**sourdine**	quietly/secretly
	en **clair**	clearly
	être *en* **string**	to be wearing a G-string
	être *en* **uniforme**	to be *in*/wearing a uniform
	en **maillot de bain/bikini**	*in* trunks/a bikini
	en **smoking/tenue de soirée**	*in* a dinner jacket/evening dress
	en **secret/privé** (cf DANS)	*in* secret/private
	en **état de guerre/siège/crise, etc**	*in* a state of war/siege/crisis, etc
	partir *en* **tournée**	to go *on* tour

en mission d'enquête/ information	*on* an enquiry mission
les professeurs sont *en* réunion	the teachers are *at* a meeting
une édition *en* livre de poche	*in* paper back
notre équipe est *en* poule 2	our team is *in* pool 2
il est *en* âge d'aller à l'école	he's *of* school age
être *en* chômage (cf A)	to be *out of* work
rester *en* course	to stay *on* track/*in* the race
en version originale/VO	*in* the original (of a film)
en récital	*at* a concert
entrer/sortir *en* masse	to pour in/to flood/to spill out (of a crowd)
descendre *en* catastrophe	to crash land (of a plane)
en mal de vitesse	losing speed (of a car)
l'évadé est *en* cavale	the fugitive is *on* the run
en promotion	on special offer (of product)
en quête de (eg *Six personnages en quête d'auteur* (Pirandello))	*in* search for/of
en cure de désintoxication	*on* a drying out course
en moyenne	*on* average
en première lecture	*on* a first reading
être *en* ligne	to be *on* line (IT)
avoir un livre *en* chantier	to have a book *in* hand (in a state of preparation)
être *en* permission	to be *on* leave
des valeurs cotées *en* Bourse	shares quoted *on* the Stock Exchange
en la situation actuelle (R3) (cf DANS)	*in* the present situation
en sa faveur	*in* his favour
en l'honneur de	*in* honour of
en l'occurrence	*as* it turns/turned out
en mon nom (cf A)	*in* my name
en l'absence de	*in* the absence of
en présence de	*in* the presence of
en finale	*in* the final(s) (of a sport)
en direct	live (of transmission by radio or television, of sport etc)
en différé	recording (of transmission by radio or television, of sport etc)
en jeu	*at* stake
en tout cas (cf DE)	*at* any rate

EN DESSOUS DE expressing position	il jeta la balle *en dessous de* la table (cf AU-DESSOUS DE)	he threw the ball *under* the table

ENTRE expressing position	*entre* les maisons	*between* the houses
	tomber *entre* les mains de qn (cf A)	to fall *into* sb's hands
figurative usage	*entre* parenthèses	*in* parenthesis
HORS DE expressing position	*hors de* la maison, je me sens bien	*out of* the house, I feel fine
figurative usage	*hors de* danger	*out of* danger
	*hors d'*haleine	*out of* breath
	c'est *hors de* doute	it is *beyond* doubt
JUSQU'A expressing time	*jusqu'à* sept heures	*until* 7 o'clock
expressing position	il m'a accompagné *jusque* chez moi	he accompanied me home
	il m'a accompagné *jusqu'au* village	he accompanied me *as far as* the village
figurative usage	ils ont incendié *jusqu'aux* voitures	they even burnt the cars
PAR expressing position	il s'est promené *par* les champs	he walked *across* the fields
	par terre (cf A)	*on* the ground
	tomber *par* terre (cf A)	to fall *to* the ground (from a standing position)
	par-ci, *par*-là	hither and thither
	par ici/là	this/that way
expressing time	*par* un temps pareil	*in* such weather
	par le temps qui court	*as* it is
	par mauvais temps	*in* bad weather
	par un jour froid d'hiver	*on* a cold winter's day
	deux fois *par* semaine	twice a week
	par avance (cf A and DE)	*in* advance
figurative usage	*par* l'intermédiaire/ entremise de	*by* means of (a person)
	par une tierce personne	*by* a third party
	voyager *par* chemin de fer	to travel *by* rail
	voyager *par* le train (cf EN)	to travel *by* train
	voyager *par* avion (cf EN)	to travel *by* plane
	voyager *par* bateau (cf EN)	to travel *by* boat
	par écrit	*in* writing
	par parenthèse (R3) (cf ENTRE)	*in* parenthesis

	par **compassion/amitié/** **ignorance/amour, etc**	*out of* compassion/friendship/ ignorance/love, etc
	condamné/jugé *par* **contumace**	condemned/judged in one's absence
expressing active agent in passive voice	**être mordu** *par* **un chien** (cf DE)	to be bitten *by* a dog
PAR–DESSUS expressing position	**il regarda** *par-dessus* **le mur** NOTE: see note to **3.4.4.2 OVER** for discussion on the distinction between **AU–DESSUS** and **PAR–DESSUS**	he looked *over* the wall
figurative usage	*par-dessus* **le marché**	*into* the bargain
PENDANT expressing time	*pendant* **la journée** **il a travaillé** *pendant* **dix minutes**	*during* the day he worked *for* ten minutes
expressing space	**il était triste** *pendant* **bien des kilomètres**	he was sad *for* many kilometres
POUR expressing time	**elle sera à Poitiers** *pour* **quinze jours** **elles sont ici** *pour* **3 jours** **j'en ai assez** *pour* **une semaine**	she will be in Poitiers *for* 2 weeks they are here *for* 3 days I've got enough *for* one week
figurative usage	**il est bon/gentil** *pour* **moi** **je suis inquiet** *pour* **lui** (cf DE) **échanger une chose** *pour* **une autre** (cf CONTRE)	he is well-disposed *towards* me I'm worried *about* him to exchange one thing *for* another
PRES expressing position	*près de* **l'église** **les villages** *près du* **fleuve** **le village le plus** *près* (R1)	*near* the church the villages *near* the river the nearest village
SOUS expressing position	*sous* **l'équateur** (cf A) *sous* **les Tropiques** (cf A) **il est passé** *sous* **le balcon** *sous* **une tente** (cf DANS) **le chien est** *sous* **la table** *sous* **la pluie/neige** **avoir qch** *sous* **les yeux**	*at/on* the equator *in* the Tropics he walked *beneath* the balcony *in* a tent the dog is *under* the table *in* the rain/snow to have sth *before* one's eyes
expressing time figurative usage	*sous* **le règne de** *sous* **peu** *sous* **une forme littéraire** (cf DANS) *sous* **un jour favorable** *sous* **tous les rapports**	*during* the reign of presently/shortly *in* a literary form *in* a favourable light *in* all respects

sous peine d'amende	*on* pain of a fine
avoir qch *sous* la main	to have sth *at* hand
sous l'emprise/l'empire/ influence/le coup (R1) de	*under* the influence of
sous antibiotique/hypnose/ morphine/perfusion/ traitement/ventilation	*on* antibiotics/*under* hypnosis/ *on* morphine/*on* a drip/ *under* treatment/*on* oxygen
sous l'égide de (R3)/ les auspices de	*under* the auspices of
avoir la situation *sous* contrôle	to have the situation *under* control
la compagnie/l'étudiant/l'équipe était *sous* pression	. . . *under* pressure
la réunion s'est déroulée *sous* la présidence de M . . .	. . . *with* M . . . in the chair

SUR expressing position	*sur* la lune (cf DANS)	*on* the moon
	aller *sur* la lune (cf DANS)	to go *to* the moon
	sur une orbite basse (cf EN)	*in* a low orbit
	mettre qch *sur* orbite	to put sth *in* orbit
	sur le parking (cf DANS)	*in* the carpark (in the open air)
	sur la mer (cf EN) (see note to **3.4.4.2** AT)	*at* sea
	sur l'aéroport (R1) (cf DANS)	*at* the airport (on the runway/ tarmac)
	sur le chantier	*in* the workyard
	sur les docks	*at* the docks
	sur l'hippodrome (R3)/le champ de course	*at* the racecourse
	sur la place (but *dans* le square)	*in* the square (market square)
	sur le stade	*in* the stadium (of competition)
	sur le ring	*in* the (boxing) ring
	les spectateurs s'étalaient *sur* bien des kilomètres	. . . *over* a good many kilometres
	sur l'avenue/le boulevard (cf DANS)	*in* the avenue/boulevard
	NOTE: *sur* indicates greater width than *dans*	
	sur la chaussée	*in* the road (ie the middle)/ *on* the roadway
	marcher *sur* la route (cf DANS)	to walk *on* the road
	donner *sur* la rue	to look *on* to the street (of building)
	sur le trottoir	*on* the pavement
	sur (la) scène	*on* the stage
	sur le tableau noir (cf A)	*on* the blackboard

	la clef est *sur* la porte	the key is *in* the door
	être assis *sur* un canapé/ divan/sofa	to sit *on* a couch/settee
	grimper *sur* le toit	to climb *onto* the roof
	être *sur* mon/un vélo (cf A and EN)	to be *on* my/a bike
	sur la selle	*in* the saddle (of a bicycle)
	un chat est assis *sur* le mur	a cat is sitting *on* the wall
	sur un carnet (cf DANS)	*in* a note-book
	sur le journal (R1) (cf DANS)	*in* a newspaper
	revenir *sur* ses pas	retrace one's steps
expressing time	ça peut durer *sur* plusieurs jours	that could last several days
	sur le tard	late
	elle a dit *sur* le tard que . . .	she said a bit late that . . .
figurative usage	un livre *sur* la mode	a book *about* fashion
	je suis inquiet *sur* son sort	I'm worried *about* his fate/what becomes of him
	naviguer/surfer *sur* le Net	to surf the Net
	sur Internet	*on* the Internet
	sur la toile	*on* the web
	être *sur* la sellette	to be *in* the hot seat
	je le crois *sur* parole	I believe his word
	elle va *sur* ses dix ans	she'll soon be ten years old
	vous recevrez le cadeau *sur* simple demande	you'll receive the present simply by applying
	sur un ton heureux/triste (cf DE)	*in* a happy/sad tone
	huit *sur* dix	eight *out of* ten
VERS expressing position	aller *vers* la ville	to go *towards* town
figurative usage	je viendrai *vers* midi	I'll come *about* midday

The following prepositions have a specific and restricted value: examples illustrating their usage may be found under the appropriate English prepositions in **3.4.4.2**.

à cause de	= because of	au travers de	= across
à force de	= by	avant	= before
à même	= from	avec	= with
à propos de	= about	concernant	= about
à travers	= across	d'après	= according to
au dehors de	= outside	devant	= before
au moyen de	= by	durant	= during
au sujet de	= about	en dehors de	= outside

en raison de	= because of
en travers de	= across
envers	= to
environ	= about
moyennant	= by
parmi	= among(st)

NOTE: although **parmi** is usually used with pl nouns, it may also accompany a sg collective noun:

eg **parmi la foule**

près de	= near
quant à	= as for
sans	= without

NOTE: **sans** + infinitive = present participle:

eg **elle l'a fait sans parler**
she did it without speaking

selon	= according to
suivant	= according

3.4.4.2 *English prepositions*

ABOUT expressing 'concerning'	a book *about* fashion	un livre *sur/au sujet de/à propos de/concernant* la mode
	he doesn't understand anything *about* the problem	il ne comprend rien *au* problème
	I'm worried *about* him	je suis inquiet *de* (R3)/*pour* lui
	I'm anxious *about* his fate/ what becomes of him	je suis inquiet *sur* son sort
expressing 'approxi-mately'	*about* 60 people were present	*environ* 60 personnes/60 personnes *environ* étaient présentes
	I'll come *about* midday	je viendrai *vers* midi
ABOVE expressing position	the church stands *above* the village	l'église est située *au-dessus* du village
	there was a sign *above* our heads	il y avait une enseigne *au-dessus de* nos têtes
figurative usage	to marry *above* one's station	épouser *au-dessus de* soi
ACCORDING TO	*according to* what he says	*d'après/selon/suivant* ce qu'il dit
ACROSS expressing position (**3.6.6**)	he ran *across* the meadow	il traversa le pré en courant
	she swam *across* the river	elle traversa la rivière à la nage
	she walked *across* the road	elle traversa la rue
	they walked *across* the bridge	ils franchirent le pont

NOTE: verbs of motion cannot normally be used with *à travers* when the space crossed is narrow, or limited like a road, a river, a stream, a yard, a field. However, one can say
elle a couru/marché *à travers* les champs, les prés, le bois, la forêt, etc
where distance is implied.

| | his journeys *across* the world | **ses voyages** *à travers* **le monde**
here the idea is concrete |

NOTE: however in
il étudia le communisme *au travers des*
écrits de Marx
he studied communism through . . . *à travers* is
also possible. Although they are largely
synonymous, in their abstract meaning *au*
travers de is of a higher register than *à travers*.

| | the tree fell *across* the road | **l'arbre tomba** *en travers de*
la route |

NOTE: neither *à travers* nor *au travers de* is
possible here

AMONG(ST) expressing position	*amongst* the French there is a custom *amongst* the débris	*chez* **les Français il y a une** **coutume** *parmi* **les débris**
AS expressing position	*as far as* the village	*jusqu'au* **village**
figurative usage	*as* for him to disguise oneself *as* a priest	*quant à* **lui** **se déguiser** *en* **prêtre**
AT expressing position	*at* the equator *at* the north pole *at* sea	*à/sous* **l'équateur** *au* **pôle nord** *sur* **la**/*en* **mer**

NOTE: *en* is more general,
eg il y a un accident *en* **mer**
there is an accident *at* sea, but standing on the
shore, one would more readily say:
il est là, *sur/dans* **la mer**
there he is, *in* the sea

	at home	**à la maison** (cf *in* the house)/*chez* **nous/lui, etc**
	at the doctor's *at* the hotel	*chez* **le docteur** **à l'hôtel**, but *dans* **l'hôtel** = inside the hotel
	at the airport	*dans/sur* (R1) **l'aéroport**

NOTE: *sur* refers to the runway or tarmac; *dans*
to the buildings. Of course *à l'aéroport* may be
used.

| | *at* the docks
at the racecourse | *aux/sur* **les docks**
au/sur **le champ de course** |
| expressing
time | *at* the present time
at the same time | **à l'heure actuelle**
dans **le** (R3)/*en* **même temps** |

	at the beginning of the afternoon	*en* début d'/*au* début de l'après-midi
	at the end of the meeting	*à* la fin de la/*en* fin de séance
	at half-time	*à* la mi-temps

NOTE: *en* première/deuxième mi-temps
in the first/second half

figurative usage	*at* a speed of 50 miles an hour	*à* une vitesse de 80 kms *à* l'heure
	he reads *at* a rate of 10 pages an hour	il lit *à* raison de 10 pages *à* l'heure
	to have sth *at* hand	avoir qch *sous* la main
	at any rate	*de* toutes façons/*en* tout cas
	at stake	*en* jeu

BECAUSE OF	*because of* his age	*à* cause de/*en* raison de son âge
BEFORE expressing position	he stood *before* the house	il se tint *devant* la maison
	to have sth *before* one's eyes	avoir qch *sous* les yeux
expressing time	he'll come *before* 11 o'clock	il viendra *avant* 11 heures
BENEATH expressing position	*beneath* us	*au-dessous de* (R3)/*en dessous de* nous
	to disappear *beneath* the waves	sombrer *sous* les vagues
figurative usage	*beneath* contempt	méprisable
BETWEEN expressing position	*between* the houses	*entre* les maisons
expressing time	a girl *between* 15 and 16 years old	une jeune fille *de* 15 *à* 16 ans
BY expressing position	to travel *by* train	voyager *par* le/*en* train (not *par* train)
	to travel *by* rail	voyager *en* chemin de fer (not *par*)
	to travel *by* plane	voyager *par*/*en* avion
	to travel *by* bicycle	rouler *à* bicyclette/*à* vélo/*en* vélo (R1)

NOTE: when *bicyclette* and *vélo* are qualified in
any way, *sur* is used:
eg **il est *sur* la bicyclette de son frère**

	to travel *by* car	voyager *en* voiture/auto

NOTE: when *voiture* and *auto* are qualified in any
way, *dans* is used:
eg **il est *dans* la voiture de son père**

	to travel *by* motorbike	**aller *à/en*** (R1) **moto** (*en* is more common)
	to travel *by* boat	**voyager *par/en* bateau**
figurative usage	*by* means of	***par/moyennant/au moyen de/à force de/à l'aide de***
	by means of (a person)	***par* l'intermédiaire/ entremise de**
	by a third party	***par* une tierce personne**
	to recognise sb *by* his voice	**reconnaître qn *à* sa voix**
	to know sb *by* sight	**connaître qn *de* vue**
	to read *by* the light of a lamp	**lire *à* la lumière d'une lampe**
	one *by* one	**un *à* un**
	side *by* side	**côte *à* côte**
	step *by* step	**pas *à* pas**
	word *by* word	**mot *à* mot**
expressing measurement	to beat sb *by* 10 metres	**battre qn *de* 10 mètres**
	to increase *by* 10 francs	**augmenter/majorer *de* 10 francs**
	to reduce *by* 10 francs	**réduire *de* 10 francs**
	to bring forward *by* 10 days	**avancer *de* 10 jours**
	to sell *by* the litre/metre	**vendre *au* litre/mètre**
	to hire *by* the hour	**louer *à* l'heure**
	he is more intelligent *by* far	**il est plus intelligent *de* beaucoup**
expressing agent in passive voice	to be bitten *by* a dog (active agent)	**être mordu *par* un chien**
	to be followed *by* a dog (passive agent)	**être suivi *d'*un chien**
DURING expressing time	*during* the day, etc	***durant/pendant* toute la journée/toute la journée *durant*** (R3), **etc**
	during the week	***dans* la/*en* semaine**
	during the reign of	***sous* le règne de** (*pendant* is also possible)
FOR (3.6.1.5) expressing time	I have been living in Paris *for* 10 years	**j'habite Paris *depuis* 10 ans/ *il y a/voilà*/10 ans que j'habite Paris**
	she will be in Poitiers *for* 2 weeks	**elle sera à Poitiers *pour* quinze jours**
	they are here *for* 3 days	**elles sont ici *pour* 3 jours**
	I had been living in Paris *for* 10 years	**j'habitais Paris *depuis* 10 ans**
	he was there *for* 10 years	**il y est resté 10 ans**
	she was *there* for three weeks	**elle était là *pour* trois semaines** (suggests intention of staying for three weeks)

		elle a été là *pendant* **trois semaines**
		(suggests she actually stayed for three weeks) (imperfect tense not possible here)
	to postpone *for* 10 days	**différer/remettre/reporter** *de* **10 jours**
	I've got enough *for* one week	**j'en ai assez** *pour* **une semaine**
expressing 'on behalf of'	to work *for* the Post Office	**travailler** *dans* **les/***aux* **PTT**
	to work *for* the railway	**travailler** *dans* **les/***aux* **chemins de fer**
figurative usage	to be in mourning *for* one's mother	**être en deuil** *de* **sa mère**
	to exchange one thing *for* another	**échanger une chose** *contre/pour* **une autre**
FROM expressing position	the train *from* Paris	**le train** *de* **Paris** (cf TO)
	the road *from* the station	**le chemin** *de* **la gare** (cf TO)
	from the balcony/ramparts (suggesting height)	*du haut* **du balcon/des remparts**
	from town *to* town	*de* **ville** *en* **ville**
	from London *to* Paris	*de* **Londres** *à* **Paris/***depuis* **Londres** *jusqu'à* **Paris** (more precise)
	from door *to* door	*de* **porte** *en* **porte**
	to drink *from* a glass	**boire** *dans* **un verre**
expressing time	*from* time *to* time	*de* **temps** *en* **temps**
	from hour/year *to* hour/year	*d'***heure/année** *en* **heure/année**
	from 10 o'clock *to* midday	*de* **10 heures** *à* **midi**
	from dawn/6 o'clock/the beginning	*dès* **l'aube/6 heures/le début**
	from 1960	*à partir de* **1960**
	from now on	*dès* **maintenant**
figurative usage	*from* what I can see	*d'après* **ce que je vois**
	from what I've heard	*à/d'après* **ce que j'ai entendu**
	from what I know	*à* **ce que je sache**
	from my point of view	*à* **mon point de vue**
	from that point of view	*à* **ce point de vue-là**

NOTE: *au point de vue littéraire* and *du point de vue littéraire* have the same meaning

	from this idea	*à partir de* **cette idée**
	to drink straight *from* a bottle	**boire** *à même* **la bouteille**

IN(TO) expressing position	*in* the Tropics	*aux/sous* (more common) **les** **Tropiques**
	in our country	*chez* **nous**
	in the Alps, etc	*dans* **les Alpes, etc**
	in Paris	*à* **Paris**, but *dans* **Paris** = right in Paris
	in the 19th district (of Paris)	*dans* **le 19ᵉ arrondissement**
	in the Paris area	*dans* **la**/*en* (R3/2) **région** **parisienne**
	in the capital (Paris)	*en* **métropole**/*dans* **la** **capitale**

NOTE: one says **arriver** *dans* **la capitale**

	in the suburbs	*en* **banlieue**

NOTE: *dans* **la banlieue de Paris**, although one
hears increasingly *en* **banlieue parisienne**

	in the street	*dans* **la rue**
	a street *in* Marseilles	**une rue** *de* **Marseille**
	he lives *in* the rue Vanneau	**il habite rue Vanneau**
	in the road (ie the middle)	*sur* **la chaussée**
	in the avenue/boulevard see note for **3.4.4.1** SUR	*dans/sur* **l'avenue/le** **boulevard**
	in the square (market square)	*sur* **la place**
	in the square (small public square with garden)	*dans* **le square**
	in the direction of the station	*du* **côté de la gare**
	in the roads (of a harbour)	*en* **rade**
	in the mountains	*à* **la**/*en* **montagne**/*dans* **les** **montagnes**
	in paradise	*au* **paradis**
	to go *into* paradise	**entrer** *au* **paradis**
	to fall *in* the water	**tomber** *à*/*dans* **l'eau**
	in contact with the water	*au* **contact de l'eau**
	in the air	*dans/en* **l'air**/*dans* **les airs** (R3) (**3.2.2**)
	in space (of astronaut)	*dans* **l'espace**
	to put sth *into* orbit	**mettre qch** *sur* **orbite**
	in a low orbit	*sur* **une**/*en* **orbite basse**
	in a tent	*dans/sous* **une tente**
	in (as contrasted with outside) the house	*dans* **la maison**
	in the stadium (of spectator)	*dans* **le stade**
	in the stadium (of competitor)	*sur* **le stade**
	in the (boxing) ring	*sur* **le ring**
	in the workyard	*sur* **le chantier**
	in places	*par* **endroits**

in the car park	*dans* **le parking** (suggests an enclosed car park)
	sur **le parking** (suggests an open car park)
in solitary confinement	*au* **secret**
in the trees	*aux* **arbres** (with **grimper, monter**) but **se cacher** *dans* **les arbres**
the key is *in* the door	**la clef est** *sur* **la porte**
in a note-book	*dans/sur* **un carnet**
in the paper	*dans/sur* (R1) **le journal**
in the saddle (of a horse)	*en* **selle**
in the saddle (of a bicycle)	*sur* **la selle**
to sit *in* an armchair	**être assis** *dans* **un fauteuil**
in a balloon	*en* **ballon**
in a car/plane/train	*à bord d'***une voiture/un avion/ un train**
to get *into* a plane	**monter** *dans* **un avion**
to go up *in* a plane	**monter** *en* **avion**
wounded *in* the arm, etc	**blessé** *au* **bras, etc**
to fall *into* sb's hands	**tomber** *aux/entre* **les mains de qn**
to have a pipe *in* one's mouth	**avoir la pipe** *à* **la bouche**
to have a book *in* one's hand	**tenir un livre** *à* **la main**
in the sun	*au* **soleil**
to be reflected *in* the sunlight	**se refléter** *dans* **le soleil** (not *au*)
in the rain	*sous* **la pluie**

NOTE: *dans* would indicate that the rain is very heavy

in the snow	*sous* **la neige** (when snow is falling)/*dans* **la neige** (when snow is on the ground)
in the shade	*à* (more common)/*dans* **l'ombre**
in place of	*à la place de/au lieu de*
in his father's shadow	*dans* **l'ombre de son père**
to work *in* the shade	**travailler** *dans* **l'ombre** (lit and fig)
in the bedroom	*dans* **la chambre**

In the following six sets of examples DANS is more specific than A:

to work *in* a mine	travailler *à/dans* **la mine**

NOTE: *à* is general (in the mines), *dans* implies in a particular mine

in the country	*à/dans* **la campagne**
in the fields	*aux/dans* **les champs**

in the garden	*au/dans* le jardin
in the drawing room	*au/dans* le salon
in the kitchen	*à/dans* la cuisine

expressing time

In the following three examples the use of DANS implies 'in the course of':

in the morning	le matin/*dans* la matinée (cf 2.3)
in the afternoon	l'après-midi/*dans* l'après-midi
in the evening	le soir/*dans* la soirée (cf 2.3)
in the early afternoon	*en* début d'après-midi/*au* début de l'après-midi

NOTE: the latter is slightly more literary

in April	*en* avril
in mid-April	*à* la mi-avril
in the spring	*au* printemps
in summer/winter	*en* été/hiver
in the autumn	*à l'/en* automne
in 1950	*en* 1950/*en* l'an 1950 (R3)
in the 21st century	*au* 21ᵉ siècle
in our time	*à* notre époque/*de* notre temps/*de* nos jours
in the time of the Pharaohs	*au/du* temps des Pharaons
I will do it *in* ten days (in ten days' time)	je le ferai *dans* dix jours
I did it *in* ten days (within a period of ten days)	je l'ai fait *en* dix jours
in the space of three weeks	*en* l'espace de trois semaines (not *dans*)
in such weather	*par* un temps pareil
in advance	*à l'/d'/par* avance

figurative usage

in a literary form	*dans/sous* une forme littéraire
in writing	*par* écrit (eg confirmez-le par écrit = confirm it in writing)
to write *in* ink/pencil	écrire *à* l'encre/*au* crayon
in a happy/sad voice	*d'*une voix heureuse/triste
in a happy/sad tone	*d'/sur* un ton heureux/triste
in a strange way	*d'*une façon/manière étrange (hence: la façon/manière dont on fait qch)
in his way	*à* sa manière/*à* sa guise/*à* son gré
in a favourable light	*sous* un jour favorable
in secret/private	*dans* le/*en* secret/privé
in his opinion	*à* son avis
in John's opinion	*de* l'avis de Jean
in his case	*chez* lui
to be *in* danger	être *en* danger
to sleep *in* peace	dormir *en* paix

to sit *in* silence	**rester assis** *en* **silence**
to be *in* mourning	**être** *en* **deuil**
the government *in* power	**le gouvernement** *au* **pouvoir**
in a state of war/siege/ crisis, etc	*en* **état de guerre/siège/ crise**, etc
in the final(s) (of a sport)	*en* **finale**
in the present situation	*dans/en* (R3) **la situation actuelle**
in all respects	*sous* **tous les rapports**
in parenthesis	*par* **parenthèse** (R3)/*entre* **parenthèses**

ON
expressing
position

on the plains	*dans* **la plaine**
on the farm	*à/dans* **la ferme**

NOTE: **sur la ferme** = on top of the farmhouse

to work *on* a ranch	**travailler** *à/dans* **un ranch**
on the ground	*à* (R3)/*par* **terre**
on the ceiling	*au* **plafond**
on the telephone	*au* **téléphone**
pictures hanging *on* the wall	**des peintures pendues** *au* **mur**
a cat is sitting *on* the wall	**un chat est assis** *sur* **le mur**
on the stairs	*dans* **l'escalier**
on the blackboard	*au/sur* **le tableau noir**
to sit *on* a couch/settee	**être assis** *sur* **un canapé/divan/ sofa**
on the stage	*sur* (la)/*en* **scène**
on the path	*dans* **l'allée**
on the pavement	*sur* **le trottoir**
on the roadway	*sur* **la chaussée**
to walk *on* the road	**marcher** *sur* **la route**/*dans* **la rue**
to look *on* to the street (of building)	**donner** *sur* **la rue**
on the Champs-Elysées	*sur* **les Champs-Elysées**
to be *on* a bicycle	**être** *à* **bicyclette**/*à/en* (R1) **vélo**
to be *on* a/my bike	**être** *sur* **un/mon vélo**
on the train	*dans* **le train**

NOTE: *sur* **le train** = on top of the train

on a raft	*en* (general)/*sur* (precise) **un radeau**
on the first page	*à* **la**/*en* **première page**
to put sth *on* a plate	**mettre qch** *dans* **une assiette** (not *sur*)
to have sth *on* one's feet, etc	**avoir qch** *aux* **pieds**, etc
on this side	*de* **ce côté**
on the other side	*de* **l'autre côté**

expressing
time

on May 25th	**le vingt-cinq mai**
on a cold winter's day	*par* **un jour froid d'hiver**
on my arrival/return	*à* **mon arrivée/retour**

figurative usage	*on* the radio	**à la radio, but** *sur* **Radio France**
	on TV	**à la télé, but** *sur* **la première/ deuxième chaîne** = on the first/second channel
	on the Internet	*sur* **Internet**
	on the web	*sur* **la toile**
	on an enquiry mission	*en* **mission d'enquête/ information**
	to go *on* tour	**partir** *en* **tournée**
	shares quoted *on* the Stock Exchange	**des valeurs cotées** *en* **Bourse**
	on pain of a fine	*sous* **peine d'amende**
	to be *on* leave	**être** *en* **permission**
	on behalf of M. Henri	*de* **la part de M. Henri**
	tell him *on* my behalf	**dites-le-lui** *de* **ma part**
	on the other hand	*d'autre* **part**
	he's *on* my side	**il est** *de* **mon côté**
OUT OF expressing position	*out of* the house, I feel fine	*hors de* **la maison, je me sens bien**
figurative usage	it's *out of* the question	**c'est** *hors* **sujet**
	out of breath	*hors* **d'haleine**
	eight *out of* ten	**huit** *sur* **dix**

The following examples represent a very large group of expressions where *out of* = *par*:

	out of compassion	*par* **compassion**
	out of friendship	*par* **amitié**
	out of ignorance	*par* **ignorance**
	out of love	*par* **amour**
OUTSIDE expressing position	the dog is *outside* the house	**le chien est** *au dehors de* (R3)/*en dehors de* **la maison**
	outside the town	*en dehors de* **la ville**
figurative usage	that's *outside* my competence	**cela dépasse ma compétence**
OVER	he looked *over* the wall	**il regarda** *par-dessus* **le mur**
	the bird flew *over* the wall (ie to the other side)	**l'oiseau vola** *par-dessus* **le mur**
	the bird flew *over* the wall (ie along/above the wall)	**l'oiseau vola** *au-dessus du* **mur**

NOTE: *par-dessus* implies a more rapid movement across to the other side, while *au-dessus de* implies either high above or along. *Au-dessus de* can involve a static idea, eg **le ballon est/vole** *au-dessus de* **la ville** (not *par-dessus*)

TO(WARDS) expressing position	to go *to* the moon	aller *dans/sur* la lune (not *à*)
	to go *to* Mars	aller *sur* Mars
	to go *towards* town	aller *vers* la ville
	to go *to* town	aller *en* ville
	to go *to* school	aller *en* classe
	the road *to* the station	le chemin *de la* gare (cf FROM)
	the train *to* Paris	le train *de* Paris (cf FROM)
	to fall *to* the ground (from a height, suggesting a gap between feet and ground)	tomber *à* terre (R3)
	NOTE: *à* is being replaced by *par* in this case; see next example	
	to fall *to* the ground (from a standing/sitting position)	tomber *par* terre
	to go *to* paradise	aller *au/en* (R3) paradis
	to go *to* hell/purgatory	aller *en* enfer/purgatoire
figurative usage	to have good feelings *towards* sb	avoir de bons sentiments *envers* qn
	NOTE: never *vers* with people in this figurative sense	
	he is well-disposed *towards* me	il est bon/gentil *pour* moi
UNDER expressing position	the dog is *under* the table	le chien est *sous* la table
	he threw the ball *under* the table	il jeta la balle *au-dessous de* (R3)/*en dessous de* la table
figurative usage	*under* the influence of	*sous* l'emprise/empire/influence/le coup (R1) de
UNTIL expressing time	I waited *until* seven o'clock	j'ai attendu *jusqu'à* sept heures
	he won't know *until* Saturday	il ne le saura que samedi/il ne le saura pas *avant* samedi
WITH figurative usage	come *with* me	venez *avec* moi
	to be angry *with* sb	être fâché *avec* (more common)/*contre* qn (cf **3.4.3** se fâcher)
	with a trembling hand	*d'*une main tremblante
	with all my heart	*de* tout mon cœur
	with all my strength	*de* toutes mes forces
	with giant strides	*à* pas de géant

3.4.5 Different constructions in French and English

It occasionally happens that where English or French use a verb + preposition + noun or pronoun construction, the other language uses a verb + direct object construction. Such differences between the two languages need to be noted and observed.

271

3.4.5.1   French verb + direct object = English verb + preposition + ^{noun} pronoun

affectionner	= to be fond of
eg **elle affectionne cet endroit/ cette activité**	
approuver qch	= to approve of sth
attendre qn	= to wait for sb
commenter qch	= to comment upon sth
compenser qch	= to compensate for sth
concurrencer qn	= to compete with sb
demander	= to ask for
désapprouver qch	= to disapprove of sth
domicilier	= to pay by banker's order
eg **toutes nos factures sont domiciliées**	
écouter qch	= to listen to sth
expérimenter qch	= to experiment with sth
incendier	= to set fire to
officialiser	= to make official
eg **le maire a officialisé la création d'un centre nautique**	
opérer qn	= to operate upon sb
eg **se faire opérer de l'appendicite**	
payer qch	= to pay for sth
plébisciter	= to vote overwhelmingly in favour of
pleurer qn	= to weep for sb
postuler	= to apply for (a post)
eg **il ne faut pas manquer de postuler l'emploi**	
prêcher qn	= to preach to sb
présider une réunion	= to preside over a meeting
prier Dieu/la Vierge Marie	= to pray to God/Virgin Mary
privilégier	= to give preference to
raisonner qn	= to make sb see reason
(re)chercher qch	= to look for sth
regarder qch	= to look at sth
responsabiliser	= to make responsible
eg **comment responsabiliser les élèves?**	
sécuriser	= to give a sense of security to
eg **il faut sécuriser les citoyens**	
squatter	= to squat in, to take over
eg **les marginalisés n'ont pas le droit de squatter un logement**	

survoler	= to fly over, to overfly
eg **l'avion a survolé la région**	
veiller qn	= to watch over sb
voler qn (cf **3.4.1.5**)	= to steal from sb
voter qch	= to vote for sth

NOTE: **voter pour qn** = to vote for sb

3.4.5.2 *French verb + preposition +* $\frac{noun}{pronoun}$ *= English verb + direct object*

hériter de qch	= to inherit sth
hériter (de) qch de qn	= to inherit sth from sb
influer sur qch	= to influence sth
(but **influencer** + direct object)	
se marier avec	= to marry
téléphoner à	= to telephone

3.5   Negation

3.5.1   Negative words and expressions:

The following negative words and expressions will be examined:

not used with			
ne	non		
used with *ne*	pas	que	rien
	plus	ni . . . ni	aucun
	jamais	personne	

3.5.1.1   *Non*

Non has the following uses:

use	examples
as a negative reply to questions	est–elle là? – Non
	– Je crois que non
	– Tu peux être sûr que non
	tu le feras ? – Peut-être que non
to negate any part of speech except a verb	
noun	c'est sa cousine, non sa sœur
past participle/adjective	une chambre non meublée
prepositional phrase	il entra non sans hésitation
	il habite non loin de Paris

non pas

Non may be combined with other negative words:
more forceful than *non* alone; also negates parts of speech like *non*:

eg **il a des flatteurs, non pas des amis**

j'ai essayé, non pas de le convaincre, mais de lui expliquer mon point de vue

non pas que

see **3.7.2.6**

non plus

meaning 'neither':

eg **je ne le savais pas non plus**

je ne le savais pas. – Ni moi non plus

NOTE: *si* is always used to contradict a negative question or suggestion:

eg **tu ne le feras pas? – Si, je le ferai**

oui may be used like *non* after *que*:

eg **je crois que oui**

peut-être que oui

3.5.1.2 *Pas*

The following usages of *pas* should be noted:

In indirect questions introduced by *si*, *ne . . . pas* is sometimes used to emphasise the doubt in the speaker's mind:

compare **je lui ai demandé s'il ne voulait pas venir**
je lui ai demandé s'il voulait venir

compare **elle se demande s'il n'y a pas de solution**
elle se demande s'il y a une solution

In the following example, unlike the equivalent English sentence, *ne . . . (pas)* directs the listener's attention to the period of time which has elapsed since the last sighting of the person in question:

eg **voilà/il y a deux jours que je ne l'ai pas vu** (R1 + R2)
voilà/il y a deux jours que je ne l'ai vu (R3) } = it's two days since I saw him

In a similar way the French use a negative in the following example, where in English a positive means of expression would be used:

quelle n'a pas été ma surprise/ma stupéfaction quand elle est rentrée? = imagine my surprise when . . .

NOTE: for the word order of adverbs with *ne . . . pas* see **3.3.2**

There are a few alternatives to **ne . . . pas**:

point

point is little used nowadays and has no more emphasis than *pas*

mot

used only with verbs of speaking in R3 usage:

eg **il ne dit mot** = he remained completely silent

goutte

used only with *voir* in R1 speech:

eg **je n'y vois goutte** = I can't see a thing

que dalle

a slang term, used only in R1 speech:

eg **je ne pige que dalle** = I don't understand a thing

pas de	is used with nouns in a negative sentence:
	eg **il n'a pas de livres**
	   il n'a pas d'argent
	   il n'y a pas de solution

pas un	is stronger than *pas de*, and is equivalent to 'not a single one':
	eg **il n'a pas un livre**
	   je ne vois pas une maison
	   pas un des garçons n'a répondu

pas without **ne**	is used in very similar circumstances to **non**, but in a less formal register:

use	examples

to negate any part of speech except a verb:
   noun
   past participle/adjective
   prepositional phrase
	j'ai vu son frère mais pas sa sœur
	elle est jolie, pas belle
	il habite pas loin de Paris
	j'ai assez de pommes, mais pas assez de poires

in informal, often elliptical speech situations	Tu viens ce soir? – Pourquoi pas! Elle vient de mettre au monde des triplés. – Pas possible, je ne savais pas qu'elle était enceinte!

3.5.1.3   *Plus*

ne . . . plus	refers both to time and quantity:
	eg **je suis retourné chercher mon parapluie; il n'y était plus**
	   il n'y travaille plus
	   je ne veux plus de cerises

plus	alone may have a negative value and refers only to quantity: eg **plus de chansons** = no more songs

3.5.1.4   *Jamais*

In more formal R3 speech and writing *jamais* may introduce a sentence (unlike English this does not cause inversion of the subject and verb), but normally it follows the verb:

eg **jamais il n'est venu me voir**
   il ne vient jamais

Jamais used without *ne* sometimes has a negative value by itself:

eg **tu es déjà allé au zoo? – Jamais**

but it is also quite frequently used without *ne*, meaning 'ever':

eg **l'avez-vous jamais fait?**
   sans jamais comprendre
   si jamais il téléphone

3.5.1.5 *Que*

Que must be placed immediately before the element of a sentence which is being qualified (not as in English, where 'only' may be at some distance from the relevant element), with the result that sometimes *que* is a long way from negative *ne*:

eg **il n'est revenu qu'hier soir**
   ce n'était que ce matin que j'ai entendu la nouvelle
   **je ne voudrais lui parler aujourd'hui ou demain qu'en
        présence de son père**
   **je ne viendrai te voir dimanche ou lundi au plus tard que si
        j'ai une réponse**
   cela ne fait que rendre le choix plus difficile

rien que   = merely:

eg **rien qu'à le lire** = merely by reading it
   When *ne . . . que* is combined with *pas* it means 'not only':
eg **il n'y a pas que des tables** = there are not only tables
   In speech *que* may occasionally stand by itself:
eg **ça ne m'a coûté que vingt francs. – Que vingt francs?**

3.5.1.6 *Ni . . . ni*

When *ni . . . ni* is used with two singular subjects the verb may be either singular or plural:

eg **ni l'un ni l'autre ne l'a/ont fait**
   ni le chauffage ni la lumière n'a/ont fonctionné
   Ni . . . ni may be combined with any part of speech except finite verbs, when only one *ni* is required:
eg **il n'a vu ni elle ni moi**
   ce livre n'est ni bon ni utile
   je ne peux ni ne veux y aller
   Ni . . . ni is used in infinitival phrases introduced by *sans*:
eg **sans parler ni à sa mere ni à sa sœur, il partit** (**ni** = either)
   R1 speakers generally avoid *ni . . . ni*, preferring instead a construction with *non plus* (cf **3.5.1.1**):
eg **j'aime pas le prof, l'école non plus**

3.5.1.7 *Personne, rien, aucun*

Personne, rien and *aucun* have negative value themselves when used without a verb.

personne   **je n'ai vu personne**
         qui a frappé à la porte? – Personne
rien   **je n'ai rien fait**
         qu'est-ce que tu as fait? – Rien
aucun   **je n'ai aucun désir de le faire**
         combien de pommes vous reste-t-il? – Aucune

3.5.1.8 *Combinations of negative words*

When combined, negative words are ordered in the following way:

1	2	3	examples
jamais	**plus**	**personne**	je n'y comprends plus rien
		rien	il ne m'a jamais rien donné
		que	il n'y a plus personne
		ni . . . ni	il n'a jamais ni stylo ni crayon
			je ne pourrais jamais plus le faire

3.5.2 The negation of infinitives

The various elements are ordered in the following way:

		examples	
ne pas		il me recommande de ne pas y aller	
ne rien		il m'a demandé de ne rien acheter	
ne jamais	+ **infinitive**		
ne plus		il s'est engagé à ne plus jamais revenir	je vous conseille de ne rien dire à personne
ne / **sans**	+ **infinitive** +	**personne** / **nulle** / **part**	sans voir personne il m'a demandé de n'aller nulle part sans lui

The following illustrates how the position of the negation and the number of negations influence the meaning of the sentence:

je ne peux pas le faire = I can't do it
je peux ne pas le faire = I can not (can refuse to) do it
je ne peux pas ne pas le faire = I can't not do it

The following table shows how more complex constructions involving the negation of infinitives work and are influenced by considerations of register:

	order		examples
R2	**ne pas**	+ **être**/ *auxiliary of past infinitive*	je lui reproche de ne pas être honnête/de ne pas avoir été honnête

	order			examples
R2+R3	**ne**	**+être/** *auxiliary of past infinitive*	**+jamais/ rien/plus**	il me reproche de ne l'avoir jamais compris il me reproche de n'avoir rien fait il me reproche de n'avoir plus rien fait
R3	**ne**	**+être/** *auxiliary of past infinitive*	**+pas**	je lui reproche de n'être pas honnête/de n'avoir pas été honnête
	ne jamais/ rien/plus	**+être** *auxiliary of past infinitive*		il me reproche de ne jamais l'avoir compris il me reproche de ne rien avoir fait

3.5.3 Negation and register

The impact of register considerations upon negation causes the following adjustments to the normal *ne . . . pas* pattern: R1 users and to a lesser extent R2 users tend to prefer *pas* without *ne*, whereas R3 users, and very occasionally R2 users, prefer *ne* without *pas* with certain verbs:

feature	register	examples
no *ne*	R1 sometimes R2	(*je*) *crois pas* *c'est pas juste/vrai* *Henri Laporte? – Connais pas* *ça fait rien*
no *pas*	R3	with *cesser, oser, pouvoir, savoir:* *il ne cesse de pleuvoir* *je n'ose le faire* *je ne sais le prononcer* *je ne saurais le faire*
		in rhetorical questions introduced by *qui* or *que:* *qui ne l'aurait compris?* *qui ne viendrait dans de telles circonstances?* *que ne ferait-elle pour vous plaire?*

feature	register	examples
		in certain set expressions:
		qu'à Dieu ne plaise
		qu'à cela ne tienne = certainly
		je n'ai que faire de vos excuses
		n'ayez crainte
	R3, sometimes R2	in certain conditional clauses:
		si je ne me trompe
		si je ne m'abuse
		s'il n'était venu à mon secours, je me noyais
		si ce n'est
		n'importe

3.5.4   Superfluous ne

In certain types of subordinate clauses a superfluous *ne*, usually known as expletive *ne*, occurs in R3 usage, occasionally in R2, but never in R1.

circumstance	examples
with verbs and expressions of fearing	*avoir crainte/peur, craindre, de crainte/peur* *je crains que vous ne tombiez*
with verbs expressing avoiding and preventing	*empêcher, éviter, prendre garde* *il faut empêcher qu'il ne parte*
with *s'en falloir de peu*	*il s'en faut de très peu qu'il ne comprenne* *peu s'en est fallu qu'il ne tombe*
with expressions of doubt in negative (= probably)	*ne pas douter, ne pas nier, nul doute* *je ne doute pas qu'il n'ait raison* *nul doute qu'il n'ait raison*
with *à moins que* and *avant que*	*à moins qu'il ne revienne le premier* (R2) *avant qu'elle ne puisse sortir, il faut qu'elle prenne son dîner*
in comparisons	*il est plus/moins intelligent que je ne le pensais* *elle l'a accompli mieux que je ne le croyais* NOTE: it is preferable to use *ne le* rather than simple *ne* in these cases

279

3.6 Verbs

It is impossible, given the scope of this book, to present a systematic survey of the types, forms and functions of French verbs. Instead significant differences between French and English usages will be concentrated upon and illustrated.

3.6.1 Tenses

There are many occasions where the usage of tenses in French corresponds closely to the usage of tenses in English. However, it is also the case that there are many other occasions where the usages of tenses in the two languages do not correspond. Taking the present tenses of the two languages as an example, it can be shown that an English present tense will frequently be used in exactly the same way as a French present tense, whereas at other times the French present tense will refer to future or past time in ways that are not possible in English. The same remark also applies to the other tenses. In the following discussion the three principal time-perspectives (present, future and past) will each be examined in detail, indicating the various factors which influence tense-selection in French. Such factors will include register, the attitude of the speaker towards the event, and the precise setting of the event on the time scale. At the end of the three sections on time-perspective, comments about special uses of individual tenses will be found.

3.6.1.1 Present time

From the point of view of tense usage this is the most straightforward of the three time-perspectives mentioned above, in that only the present tense is used.

aspect of present time	conveyed by	examples
present time proper	present tense	*je chante en ce moment*
habitual time		*je mange à six heures tous les jours*
universal time		*deux et deux font quatre*

Continuous tense in present time: in order to convey the English continuous present *I am doing something* (which implies, despite its name, that an activity in progress at the present time is going to stop sooner or later), French has recourse to the following constructions:

construction	register	examples
être en train de + infinitive	R1–R3	*je suis en train de prendre mon déjeuner* *elle est en train de coudre*

construction	register	examples
aller + (*en*) + present participle	R3	*l'industrie va croissant* *les couleurs vont en se dégradant*

Special points concerning the present tense: the present tense may also be used to refer to future time (**3.6.1.2**) and past time (**3.6.1.3**).

3.6.1.2   Future time

The idea of futurity may be conveyed in the following ways:

tense	comments	examples
future	normal usage	*je viendrai demain*
present	the present tense is slowly eroding the future tense; it can be used to describe an event occurring in the near future	*je descends au prochain arrêt* *je viens demain*
	to describe an event in the distant future	*on part la semaine prochaine* *mes parents partent pour la Guadeloupe l'année prochaine*
conditional	normal usage to refer to future in the past	*elle savait qu'il comprendrait*
	also used to express doubt	*avez-vous entendu dire qu'il n'y aurait pas de cours demain?*
	and probability	*il pourrait arriver à temps*
aller + infinitive	to express fulfilling of intention/imminent fulfilment	*tu vas voir* *je vais te l'expliquer* *il va pleuvoir* *attention, tu vas te faire mal!*

NOTE: when the present tense is used instead of the future to refer to future time, it tends to suggest a passive idea, whereas the future suggests a much more active idea, a strong desire even: eg *je viendrai ce soir* is a stronger statement than *je viens ce soir*

A continuous tense in future time may be conveyed in the following ways:

construction	register	examples
être en train de + infinitive	R1–R3	*je serai en train de faire mes devoirs quand tu arriveras à la maison ce soir*

construction	register	examples
aller + (*en*) + present participle	R3	*il est à espérer que la production des voitures ira croissant pendant le restant de cette année*

On occasions French specifies explicitly future time when English leaves time-orientation vague:

eg **faites ce que vous voudrez**

(It is also possible to say in the same circumstances:

faites ce que vous voulez)

Special points concerning the future and conditional tenses:

The future tense is sometimes used instead of an imperative to tone down an order or a request:

eg **tu le feras cet après-midi**

The future perfect and conditional tenses are sometimes used to imply conjecture or allegation:

eg **elle aura manqué le car** (R2) = she's probably missed the coach

il aura su le résultat (R3) = he probably knew the result

il y a eu un accident: il y aurait trente blessés (newspaper language) = there has been a road accident: it is reported (but is not certain) that thirty people have been injured

selon certains rapports il y aurait d'autres projets = according to certain reports other projects exist

The following typical uses of the conditional in French should be noted:

on dirait un fou = he seems mad

on aurait dit un fou = he seemed mad/you would have thought he was mad

(In R3 usage an pluperfect subjunctive might be used:

on eût dit un fou)

3.6.1.3 Past time

Past time may be envisaged in several ways, as the following table demonstrates:

past time envisaged	past	present	tense generally used
as a point of time with no link with or repercussion upon the present	*elle regarda/a regardé par la fenêtre* • point in time		past historic perfect

past time envisaged	past	present	tense generally used
as a point of time which relates to the present	*elle est arrivée tout à l'heure* •————————————→ point in time		perfect
as a period of time	*ils s'amusaient à écouter des disques* ———————— period of time		imperfect
as a period of time interrupted by an event	*elle lisait le magazine quand sa sœur entra/est entrée* ↓ ———————— time		past historic or perfect interrupting imperfect
as a repetition of an action/event, or an habitual action/event	*il prenait son repas à la même heure tous les jours* • • • repeated action/event		imperfect
from the standpoint of present time beyond a significant event in the past to another single event further back in the past	*elle m'a dit que sa mère était repartie* • • ←——— point in time time		pluperfect
from the standpoint of present time beyond a significant event in the past to an event of long duration further back in the past	*il est clair qu'avant de monter le film, il avait passé de longues heures à ramasser du matériel* ————• ←——— period of time		pluperfect

However, usage is not always quite as clear-cut as the table suggests: the past tenses sometimes overlap in usage. The past historic and perfect are sometimes used to record past events and repetitions of events of any duration (normally the prerogative of the imperfect tense) considered from an historical perspective as single events:

eg **il vécut soixante-dix ans**
    la guerre dura trente ans

Conversely the imperfect tense is occasionally used, particularly in journalism, to refer to a single event in the past (normally the prerogative of the perfect or past historic tenses); in this way attention is drawn to the event evoked and a dramatic dimension is added:

eg **il y a cent ans naissait Staline**

dans son discours il évoquait la crise énergétique

hier soir M. Dupont définissait sa théorie sur l'industrialisation

Past time may also be conveyed by the present tense, which denotes an event which has occurred in the recent past:

eg **je quitte à l'instant mon ami**

une lettre me parvient à l'instant

c'est la première fois que je le fais

(**je l'ai fait** is not possible here)

The imperfect tense requires the following sequence of tenses in similar circumstances:

c'était la première fois que je le faisais (**je l'avais fait** is not possible)

There also exists in French an historic present which invests the events recounted with a particularly lively, dramatic quality, as if they were happening in the present:

eg **Après son arrivée, les choses se précipitèrent. Le voilà qui donne des ordres, qui fait des caprices. Tout le monde accourt à son appel. Il distribue des tracts et ils repartent tout de suite.**

As is the case for present and future time and formed in the same way, there exists for past time a continuous tense:

construction	register	examples
être en train de +infinitive	R1–R3	*j'étais/avais été en train de regarder un film à la télévision*
aller + (*en*) +present participle	R3	*la tension entre les états allait augmentant pendant les années 90*

Related to this construction is the following, meaning 'to be about to', which can be used with all tenses:

être sur le point de/près de/en passe de (R3)

eg **le comité était sur le point de/près de/en passe d'accepter le projet**

The following table helps distinguish between circumstances in which the past historic and perfect tenses are used. It should be noted that the perfect tense is the normal tense used in all registers when referring to a past event while the past historic is restricted to R3 usage.

past tense	circumstances of usage
perfect	principally in speech, but also in writing
examples	*j'ai déjà fait cinq années de français.*
	Le premier ministre a annoncé son intention de diminuer les impôts: il a reçu une véritable ovation dans la Chambre des Députés.

past tense	circumstances of usage
past historic	in writing, especially novels, students' essays, fairy stories, etc.; sometimes in newspapers; talks on radio and television dealing with historical topics; formal speeches, lectures; it invests the style with a higher, literary tone; French children learn it early on since they hear it used to recount fairy stories; correct use of the past historic distinguishes the cultured person.
examples	*Il partit, revint et finalement repartit.* *Au bout de quelque temps elle vit la maison.* speech given by General de Gaulle, Edinburgh, 23 June 1942: *Dans chacun des combats où, pendant cinq siècles le destin de la France fut en jeu, il y eut toujours des hommes d'Ecosse pour combattre côte à côte avec les hommes de France. Ce que les Français pensent de vous, c'est que jamais un peuple ne s'est montré, plus que le vôtre, généreux de son amitié.* (C. de Gaulle, *Mémoires de Guerre*, I, Paris, 1954)

Special points concerning past tenses:

The past historic of *vouloir* implies 'tried':

eg **il voulut sortir mais il n'y réussit pas**

Similarly, the past historic of *pouvoir* implies 'managed to', and that of *savoir* 'learned':

eg **au bout d'une semaine difficile il put le terminer**
après trois jours d'attente il sut le résultat

The French pluperfect is occasionally equivalent to an English simple past tense or perfect tense:

eg **je vous l'avais bien dit** = I told you so
nous vous avions parlé du = we've already told you about
 problème   the problem

The past anterior is purely a written tense and is used only in the following situations:

tense of main/ introductory clause	subordinate clause introduced by	tense of subordinate clause
past historic	*après que* *aussitôt que* *dès que* *lorsque* *quand*	past anterior
examples	*dès que j'eus compris, il voulut partir* *quand il eut commandé son dîner, son ami arriva*	

tense of main/ introductory clause	subordinate clause introduced by	tense of subordinate clause
past anterior	*à peine*	past historic
example	*à peine eut-il fermé la porte que sa femme éclata de rire*	

Since the past historic is not used in ordinary speech, the past anterior, being closely allied to it, does not occur there either. Its place is taken either by the pluperfect or, increasingly, by the double compound past tense (in French *le passé surcomposé*):

eg **aussitôt que nous eûmes fini, elle alla se promener**
aussitôt que nous avions fini, elle est allée se promener
aussitôt que nous avons eu fini, elle est allée se promener

Much uncertainty exists over the use of the past anterior with **après que**. This is due to contamination from the use of the present subjunctive (cf **3.7.2.6**) and results in such examples as the following, even in the most highbrow publications, where the pluperfect subjunctive is used instead of the past anterior:

eg **quinze ans après que l'association eût commencé à . . .**

3.6.1.4 Sequence of tenses

The main difference between English and French usages concerns the sequence of tenses in sentences containing a subordinate clause of time or a clause introduced by *quand même*, as the following table illustrates:

tense in main/ introductory clause	tense in subordinate clause	French example	English equivalent
future	future	**je le ferai quand/ lorsque j'aurai le temps**	I'll do it when I've got the time
		je t'aimerai tant que je vivrai	I'll love you for as long as I live
		quand il sera parti, je pourrai allumer la télévision	when he's gone, I can put the television on
past	conditional	**elle me demanda d'écrire la lettre dès que je serais de retour**	she asked me to write the letter as soon as I got back
conditional	conditional perfect	**je lui ai dit que je le ferais quand il m'aurait donné de l'argent**	I told her I'd do it when he had given me some money

Usage with *même si*, *quand même* and their variants is determined by considerations of register:

register	French example	English equivalent
R1	**même si elle me l'avait dit, je n'aurais pas pu le faire**	even if she'd told me, I couldn't have done it
R2	**même si elle était venue, je ne l'aurais pas fait**	even if she had come, I would not have done it
R3	**quand même vous le feriez, je ne viendrais pas** **quand (bien) même le feriez-vous que je ne viendrais pas** **y aurais-je consenti que tout le monde me condamnerait**	even if you did it, I wouldn't come were you to do it, I should not come had I agreed, everyone would have condemned me

The sequence of tenses in sentences containing a hypothetical clause introduced by *si* is as follows:

tense in *si*-clause	tense in main clause	examples
present	present	*si tu as faim il faut manger quelque chose*
	future	*si je la vois, je te téléphonerai*
	future perfect	*si tu continues à manger comme ça, tu auras fini trop tard*
	imperative	*si tu veux du chocolat, va au magasin d'à-côté*
perfect	present	*si vous avez conduit 200 kilomètres vous devez être fatigué*
	future	*si vous avez conduit une telle distance, vous aurez besoin de sommeil*
	imperfect	*si on vous a dit ça, c'était un mauvais tour*
	perfect	*si le professeur est déjà arrivé, il a dû courir vite*
	future perfect	*s'il a lu cent pages ce matin, il aura terminé le livre ce soir*
	imperative	*si tu as fini, porte ton assiette à la cuisine*
imperfect	conditional	*si je la voyais, je te téléphonerais*
	conditional perfect	*si tu m'aimais, tu n'aurais pas dit ça*
pluperfect	conditional	*si tu avais gardé tes gants, tu n'aurais pas froid*
	conditional perfect	*si je l'avais vue, je t'aurais téléphoné*

(For *si* + hypothetical clause + *que* + hypothetical clause, see **3.7.2.6** NOTE B.)

The above sequences of tenses do not apply when *si* is used to introduce an indirect question; future and conditional tenses may be used in the *si*-clause:

eg **je me demande si elle viendra**
   je me demandais si elle viendrait

Usage with *c'est*: unlike the equivalent English phrase *it is/it was*, French *c'est* tends not to vary in tense and may be used to refer to past time:

eg **c'est lui qui m'a demandé d'y aller**

In the following situation involving *fois*, *c'était* is used with reference to past time, and the sequences of tenses in English and French are quite different:

c'est la première fois que je te vois ici	= it's the first time I've seen you here
c'était la première fois qu'elle le faisait	= it was the first time she had done it

3.6.1.5 *Other differences between French and English tense usages*

depuis	**je suis ici depuis dix ans**	= I've been here for ten years
	(but **je n'ai pas été ici depuis dix ans**	= I haven't been here for ten years)
	depuis quand/combien de temps étudiez-vous le français?	= how long have you been studying French?
	j'étais là depuis un an	= I had been there for a year
	je n'étais pas là depuis un an	= I hadn't been there for a year
	depuis quand/combien de temps habitait-il Paris?	= how long had he lived in Paris?
	mille exemplaires ont été publiés depuis 1970	= a thousand copies have been published since 1970
il y a . . . que/voilà . . . que, etc	**il y a dix ans que je suis ici**	= I've been here for ten years
	voilà plus de trois jours que je t'attends	= I've been waiting for you for more than three days
	ça/cela fait dix jours qu'il est là	= he's been there for ten days now
	il y a belle lurette qu'elle a vendu sa maison	= it's ages since she sold her house
	il y avait belle lurette qu'elle avait vendu sa maison	= it was ages since she sold her house
venir de	**il vient d'arriver**	= he's just arrived
	il venait de se baisser quand la voiture l'a heurté	= he had just bent down when the car ran into him

NOTE: a French speaker would not use *venir de* + *venir* but would probably use *arriver*, as in *elle arrive/est arrivée à l'instant*

3.6.2   The infinitive

In French the infinitive may be used in certain circumstances where English would use a finite verb or a participle:

circumstance	examples	
in questions	*que faire?* *pour quoi faire?* *moi partir maintenant?*	*pourquoi le dire?* *comment y aller?* *à quoi bon envoyer une* *lettre?*
as an order	*s'adresser à la direction* *rayer la mention inutile* *ne pas se pencher au dehors*	
in instructions on merchandise	*faire chauffer à petit feu* *remuer la solution* *bien nettoyer la surface à peindre avant de . . .*	
as a narrative infinitive introduced by *et* in R3 speech or writing	*et lui de dire qu'elle avait raison* *et ma sœur de partir tout de suite*	
as a subject	*tromper, c'est mentir* *voir, c'est croire* *se tenir en équilibre sur une jambe n'est pas facile*	
with verbs relating to the senses	*je l'ai vu sortir* *il m'a entendu entrer* *elle sentit son cœur s'arrêter de battre*	

In the following example French, unlike English, does not require a direct object:

j'entendais marcher dans le = I heard someone walking along
    couloir   the corridor

A choice between the infinitive and a *que*-clause is affected by considerations of register when both parts of the sentence have the same subject: use of *que* is considered stylistically clumsy.

structure	R1	R2	R2/R3
present infinitive **versus *que*-clause**		je pense que je peux vous aider	je pense pouvoir vous aider
past infinitive **versus *que*-clause**	je croyais que je l'avais vu	je croyais l'avoir vu il dit qu'il l'a pris elle dit qu'elle ne l'a pas fait	il prétend/nie l'avoir pris/dit elle déclare ne pas l'avoir fait elle reconnaît avoir vu son père la semaine dernière

structure	R1	R2	R2/R3
			elle assure n'avoir pas pris la décision avant de le consulter . . .
			elle nie être sa mère

NOTE: for a discussion of the position of *ne pas* in relation to a past infinitive, see **Negation 3.5.2**

3.6.3   Participles

3.6.3.1   *Present participles*

The following table illustrates the various ways in which present participles are used in French:

adjectival usage	**agreement between participle and noun qualified**
	elle semblait très belle ce matin-là avec ses yeux brillants et ses dents éclatantes
	nous avons des histoires effrayantes à raconter
verbal usage	**no agreement**
	a present participle alone is equivalent to a relative or causal clause
	les automobilistes venant de Cannes ont trouvé des embouteillages affreux
	ne sachant que faire, elle a commencé à lire un roman
	en + **present participle acts as an adverbial phrase of time or manner**
	vous ne réussirez pas en agissant ainsi
	je l'ai vu en passant
	tout en + **present participle expresses simultaneous actions**
	j'ai continué de travailler tout en prenant mon déjeuner

3.6.3.2   *Past participles*

When past participles are used as adjectives they agree with the nouns they qualify:

eg **arrivée au coin de la rue, elle a jeté un coup d'œil en arrière**

   surprise par le mauvais temps, elle a couru s'abriter sous un arbre

   des bruits venus de je ne sais où m'ont beaucoup effrayé

   Certain past participles and *étant donné* function as prepositions. Normally they precede the noun and are invariable; however, a few may also follow the noun and agree in number and gender with it.

	examples
past participle as preposition preceding the noun	vu les conséquences de ses actions, elle a décidé de quitter sa maison étant donné la situation actuelle, la guerre semble inévitable y compris ma tante nous serons cinq excepté une petite minorité, tous les spectateurs se sont bien conduits au match vous trouverez ci-joint quittance passé cinq heures, les bureaux ferment
past participle as preposition following the noun	une petite minorité exceptée, tous les spectateurs se sont bien conduits au match j'ai vendu toutes mes affaires, ma voiture comprise (NOTE: *no* y) les pièces ci-jointes

3.6.3.3   *A difference between French and English usages*

Many past participles in French associated with posture or position correspond to present participles in English:

accoudé	appuyé	juché
accroupi	assis	penché
adossé	blotti	pendu
agenouillé	couché	perché
allongé	incliné	tapi

eg **je l'ai trouvé agenouillé devant le corps de son fils**
   elle restait assise pendant longtemps
   la lampe était pendue au plafond

3.6.4   Formation of compound tenses

3.6.4.1   *Use of 'avoir' and 'être' to form compound tenses*

Most verbs form their compound tenses by combining the auxiliary *avoir* with the past participle. A much smaller number use *être* to form their compound tenses. This group includes all reflexive verbs and certain intransitive verbs:

aller	**naître**	**retomber**
arriver	**partir**	**retourner**
décéder	**parvenir**	**revenir**
demeurer	**rentrer**	**sortir**
devenir	**repartir**	**survenir**
entrer	**ressortir** (2.2.4)	**tomber**
mourir	**rester**	**venir**

When *monter* and *descendre* are used literally they are conjugated with *être*:

eg **elle est descendue**

When they are used figuratively, they are conjugated with *avoir*:

eg **les prix ont monté**

However, when *descendre, monter, rentrer, retourner, sortir* are used transitively, they form their compound tenses with *avoir*:

eg **le porteur a déjà monté vos bagages, monsieur**
il a sorti son revolver

Convenir may be used with either *avoir* or *être* depending upon the meaning intended. When it means 'to suit', *avoir* is the correct form – ie it is used in R2 and R3

eg **l'hôtel m'a convenu**

When it means 'to agree', *être* is the correct form and is used in R3. However, in the latter case *avoir* is more and more widely used and accepted as appropriate for R2:

eg **nous avons convenu de son départ** = we agreed about his/her departure

Certain other verbs use either *avoir* or *être* when no distinction of transitivity or meaning is involved: in such cases it appears that when *avoir* is used an action is implied, and when *être* is used a state is implied:

eg **ce livre a paru avant hier**
ce livre est paru depuis longtemps
also: *accourir, apparaître, disparaître*

With *passer* both *avoir* and *être* may be used without distinction, but it is clear that here and in the previous cases, *être is* being used with increasing frequency:

eg **il est passé ce matin** is more acceptable than
il a passé ce matin

3.6.4.2 Agreement of past participles in compound tenses

Agreement of *être* + past participle: the following table illustrates usage:

non–reflexive verbs as in 3.6.4.1 verbs in passive mood	agreement is always with the subject
examples	**elle est arrivée ce matin** **nous sommes entrés dans la salle de conférence** **elle a été obligée de quitter le magasin** **nous avons été payés d'avance**

reflexive verbs	agreement is with the reflexive pronoun provided it is a direct object
examples	**elle s'est assise à côté de son ami** **hier nous nous sommes couchés à neuf heures**

The following examples illustrate the contrast between those reflexive verbs whose reflexive pronoun is a direct object and those whose pronoun is an indirect object:

pronoun as direct object	pronoun as indirect object
mes deux fils se sont giflés	**mes deux fils se sont donné des giflés**
elle s'est lavée à l'eau chaude	**elle s'est lavé les mains avec de l'eau chaude**

Agreement of *avoir* + past participle with preceding direct object.

Agreement occurs between the past participle conjugated with *avoir* and the preceding direct object:

eg **la voiture que j'ai achetée**
ces filles? je les ai vues tout à l'heure
les bruits qu'elle a entendus

Difficulty arises when the past participle is followed by an infinitive: agreement occurs when the direct object relates to the past participle, but not when it relates to the infinitive:

eg *les personnes* **que j'ai entendu***es* **parler**
    object of past participle
les vers **que j'ai entendu** *réciter*
    object of infinitive
la maison **que j'ai fait** *construire*
    object of infinitive

However, there is a tendency not to make the agreement in any circumstances.

3.6.5 Reflexive versus non-reflexive forms of the same verb

A number of verbs have both a reflexive and non-reflexive form (eg *approcher – s'approcher*). In a small number of cases the two forms may be used interchangeably, but on other occasions there is an important distinction between the values of the two forms, as is illustrated in the following tables:

verbs with no distinction between the values of reflexive and non-reflexive forms	examples
(se) reculer	il s'est/a reculé de dix mètres
(se) terminer	les cours (se) terminent à cinq heures
	le livre (se) termine par un meurtre
(s')imaginer: *the non-reflexive form is more common*	je (m')imagine qu'il a fini le livre

verbs with a distinction between the values of the two forms		examples
unintentional	approcher	il approche la quarantaine
		l'heure approche
deliberate	s'approcher	l'ennemi s'approche de la ville
habitual	fermer	les portes du magasin ferment tous les jours à six heures
specific	se fermer	la porte se ferme lentement
	also (s')ouvrir	
state	coucher	je couche à l'hôtel/sous la tente
action	se coucher	je me couche à six heures
state	arrêter	il a arrêté de fumer = *for good*
action	s'arrêter	il s'est arrêté de fumer = *for the moment, but also **for** good*
		NOTE: *in the imperative, the non-reflexive* arrête! *is used; but* arrête-toi (R1)
state	loger	je loge en ville
action	se loger	il est arrivé en ville et s'est logé à l'hôtel
abstract	incliner	j'incline à penser que tout ira bien
concrete	s'incliner	il s'incline devant l'autel
	also (se) figurer	
less strong	attaquer	il a attaqué le gouvernement
more strong	s'attaquer	il s'est attaqué au gouvernement
	also décider de/se décider à refuser de/se refuser à résoudre de/se résoudre à	
lit	passer	sa sœur est passée ce matin
fig	se passer	qu'est-ce qui s'est passé?
lit	se pencher	elle s'est penchée sur l'eau
fig	pencher	je penche pour la seconde hypothèse
lit	se reposer	je vais me reposer un instant, je suis fatigué
fig	reposer	sa philosophie repose sur trois principes; son corps repose au cimetière (*euphemism!*)
lit	sortir	elle est sortie ce matin
fig	s'en sortir	j'arrive pas à m'en sortir/me sortir de cette pagaille = *I can't really deal with it/sort it out*

3.6.6 Verbs of movement in French and English

An important difference between the French and English verbal systems concerns the way in which expressions of movement are analysed and treated in the two languages. In French the direction of movement is often indicated by the verb itself and the manner of movement by a phrase, either *en* + present participle or an adverbial expression, whereas in English the verb conveys the manner of the movement and an adverb or prepositional expression the direction.

French: *direction indicated by verb*	**English:** *direction indicated by adverb / prepositional expression*
manner indicated by phrase	*manner indicated by verb*
elle a monté l'escalier en courant	she ran up the stairs
il gagna en rampant le mur de la prison	he crawled towards the prison wall
elle revint en boitant de la cuisine	she hobbled back from the kitchen
il entra en coup de vent	he burst in
elle a traversé la rivière à la nage	she swam across the river
elle a descendu l'escalier sur la pointe des pieds	she tiptoed downstairs
elle est revenue à vélo	she cycled back
ils sont montés en masse dans la voiture	they piled into the car
ils sont partis en masse	they piled out/they flooded out/ they flooded away

However, with certain compound prepositions, French follows the English pattern:

French *direction indicated by prepositional expression / adverb*	**English** *direction indicated by adverb / prepositional expression*
manner indicated by verb	*manner indicated by verb*
elle est passée par-dessus le mur	she climbed over the wall
ils se sont promenés le long de la rivière	they walked alongside the river
ils ont marché à travers (les) champs	they walked across the fields
NOTE: **traverser** would be used with **champ** in the singular (**3.4.4.2** ACROSS)	
il a bondi par-dessus	he jumped over

295

Often where the manner of movement is specified in English, it is left vague or is ignored completely in French: a general verb is used in French where English uses an explicit verb, although English may also use a general verb like French:

> eg **il a traversé la rue** = he walked across the road/he crossed the road

Implicit within *traverser*, for example, is the idea of walking; if the person had run across the road, the phrase *en courant* would have been added.

3.7   Subjunctive mood

Whereas the subjunctive is extremely rare in English and is by and large restricted to R3 usage, verging in fact on the positively archaic, in French the subjunctive is still a mood to be reckoned with. What is often disconcerting to the student about the French subjunctive is that in some cases its use seems to conform to clearly defined rules, whereas in others it seems to be a matter of choice. In the following discussion the term 'black and white' subjunctive will be applied to those circumstances where the use of the subjunctive is obligatory, and the term 'grey' subjunctive to those where a degree of choice is permissible. It should be noted with respect to the 'grey' subjunctive that its use is often determined by instinct, particularly on the part of someone who is very conscious of the way he/she uses language. The expression of doubt is often associated with the subjunctive – in other words, if an idea is not clearly substantiated or validated, the subjunctive may be used. Consequently, the subjunctive appears more frequently and regularly in R3 usage than in R1 usage. Although an R2 user will attempt to use the 'grey' subjunctive in accordance with traditional prescriptions, the 'grey' subjunctive and even the 'black and white' subjunctive may disappear in speech through inadvertence and because of the frequent breaks in continuity of structure which are characteristic in particular of R1 speech, but also of R2 speech. It is considered a sign of ignorance when a person omits the subjunctive incorrectly – and this is not uncommon. It is vital for learners to be aware of this. It should also be noted that in some areas of France, particularly rural ones, the subjunctive is hardly used. (It is comforting to realise that the French themselves experience difficulty with certain forms of the subjunctive, using for example *veuillons* for the correct *voulions*, and *aie* for *ait*.) It is interesting to speculate that the decline of the subjunctive in French is parallel to, but lags a long way behind, that of the subjunctive in English.

3.7.1   Sequence of tenses with subjunctive in subordinate clause

As far as the sequence of tenses with the subjunctive in a subordinate clause is concerned, it is important to understand that R3 practice often differs from that of the other two register divisions. In broad terms the practices may be characterised as follows:

	R3, R2 + R1		R3	R2 + R1
il faut	qu'il vienne	il fallait	qu'il vînt	. . . qu'il vienne
il faudra	qu'il vienne	il fallut	qu'il vînt	. . . (qu'il vienne)
il a fallu	qu'il vienne	il faudrait	qu'il vînt	. . . qu'il vienne

	R3	R2 + R1
je dois m'en aller	avant qu'il (n') arrive	. . . avant qu'il arrive
je suis allé me coucher	avant qu'il (ne) soit arrivé	. . . avant qu'il arrive
le policier était parti	avant qu'il (n') arrivât	. . . avant qu'il soit arrivé
nous avions décidé de partir	avant qu'il (ne) fût arrivé	. . . avant qu'il soit arrivé

From this it appears that the imperfect subjunctive is to all intents and purposes unknown in R1 and R2 speech – if it does occur it is usually for jocular purposes or as a parody of more elevated usage. It survives in refined R3 usage, in speeches and stories, but even in these cases it is the third person singular which is generally met; the other forms are avoided and are replaced by the present subjunctive and occasionally the perfect subjunctive. It is, in fact, in prose writing that the imperfect subjunctive most frequently occurs. It is quite legitimate therefore for foreign language learners of French not to use the imperfect subjunctive in speech, although they should be aware of its appropriateness in formal writing. It may be that there is a tendency for the subjunctive to be particularly preserved with those common verbs where the indicative and subjunctive tenses are widely divergent in form:

eg   *aller:*   va   –   aille
     être: est   –   soit
     faire: fait   –   fasse

3.7.2   'Black and white' subjunctive

The subjunctive occurs regularly in the following circumstances:

3.7.2.1   in certain archaic set expressions:

advienne que pourra
vive le roi
puissé-je trouver le bonheur!
n'ayez crainte
sachez que (R3/R2)

3.7.2.2   at the beginning of a sentence to indicate surprise, an order or a desire:

que j'aille trouver le garçon? Certainement pas!
qu'il le fasse maintenant
que Monsieur nous écrive à ce sujet

3.7.2.3 *to mark hypothesis/conditional value:*

> **qu'il reste ou qu'il parte, cela m'est égal**
> **ne fût-ce que pour . . .**
> eg **ne fût-ce (que) pour quelques jours** = were it only for a few days

3.7.2.4 *when a noun clause introduced by que precedes the main clause: this usage is limited to R3 speech:*

> **qu'il fasse beau demain est certain**
> **qu'il y eût beaucoup de spectateurs tout le monde en est convenu**

3.7.2.5 *to express 'whoever', 'whatever', 'wherever', etc:*

whoever	**qui que vous soyez**
whatever	**quoi qui arrive**
(pronoun)	**quoi qu'il fasse**
wherever	**où que vous alliez**
whatever	**quel que soit votre problème**
(adj)	**à quelque distance que cela paraisse**
however	**quelque difficile que cela paraisse**
	si grand soit-il/qu'il soit
	pour grand qu'il soit
	aussi longtemps que vous travailliez

> NOTE: the use of *si* for however + adjective is more common than that of *quelque/pour* + adjective

3.7.2.6 *after the following conjunctive expressions:*

conjunctive expression	comments
à condition que	
afin que	R2 and R3
à moins que	in R3 usage *ne* is often inserted before the verb (**3.5.4**): eg *à moins qu'il ne vienne aujourd'hui*
après que	logic and tradition require an indicative tense after *après que* when referring to a past event. However, prevailing usage (R1 and R2) prefers the subjunctive when *après que* refers to the past, but not to the future: eg *après qu'il soit arrivé, je lui ai dit . . .* there is often confusion between the past anterior and the imperfect subjunctive after *après que* in written French: eg *après qu'il eût accepté* instead of *après qu'il eut accepté* (cf **2.6.1.3**)
à supposer que	
avant que	in R3 usage *ne* is often inserted before the verb (*à moins que* above)

conjunctive expression	comments
bien que	
de crainte que	in R3 usage *ne* is often inserted before the verb (*à moins que* above)
de façon que/à ce que	it is only when *de façon que/à ce que* expresses intention that it is followed by the subjunctive mood: *il faut revenir de façon qu'il te voie* when it expresses result an indicative tense is required: eg *il est revenu de façon que je l'ai vu* the newer form *de façon à ce que* is superseding the older expression *de façon que*
de manière que/à ce que	see comments for *de façon que/à ce que*
de peur que	in R3 usage *ne* is often inserted before the verb (*à moins que* above)
de sorte que	see first two comments for *de façon que/à ce que*
en attendant que	
encore que	R3
jusqu'à ce que	
malgré que	
non (pas) que	R3
(pour) autant que	R3
pour peu que	R3
pour que	
pourvu que	
quoique	
sans que	
soit que ... soit que	R2/R3
sous réserve que	R3

NOTE A: when the following conjunctive expressions refer to a future or conditional idea, a future or conditional indicative is used:

eg **bien que   malgré que**
    encore que   quoique
eg **bien que je ne pourrai pas venir, ma sœur le fera**

NOTE B: the subjunctive is used in R3 usage in the second of a set of coordinated conditional clauses when *que* is used instead of *si*:

eg **si la pluie cesse et qu'il fasse beau demain, nous sortirons**
but not when it is introduced by *si*:
eg **si la pluie cesse et s'il fait beau demain, nous sortirons**

3.7.2.7   *in clauses dependent upon verbs and expressions indicating desiring, wishing, begging, ordering, forbidding, preventing*

(this list and those in subsequent sections are not exhaustive, but include the most frequently encountered verbs and expressions):

verbs and expressions of desiring, wishing, etc	comments
aimer mieux	
attendre	
s'attendre	+ *à ce que*
commander	R3
consentir	R3
décréter	R3
défendre	
demander	R3
désespérer	R3
désirer	
dire	R3
empêcher	with *empêcher, ne* is sometimes inserted before the verb in the subjunctive in R3 usage (**3.5.4**)
entendre	R3
éviter	with *éviter, ne* is sometimes inserted before the verb in the subjunctive in R3 usage (**3.5.4**)
exiger	
faire attention	+ *à ce que*
implorer	R3
insister	+ *pour que*
interdire	
s'opposer	+ *à ce que*
ordonner	
préférer	
prier	R3
proposer	
souhaiter	
supplier	R3
tenir	+ *à ce que*
veiller	+ *à ce que*
vouloir	

3.7.2.8   *in clauses dependent upon verbs and expressions indicating a feeling (eg joy, fear, regret):*

verbs and expressions of feeling	
avoir hâte	= to be anxious eg *j'ai hâte que mon petit ami revienne de ses vacances* = I can't wait for my boyfriend to come back from his holidays

verbs and expressions of feeling	
avoir peur	in R3 usage *ne* is sometimes inserted before the verb in the subjunctive (**3.5.4**)
craindre	in R3 usage *ne* is sometimes inserted before the verb in the subjunctive (**3.5.4**)
s'étonner **se féliciter** **s'indigner** **se plaindre**	
redouter	R2/R3; in R3 usage *ne* is sometimes inserted before the verb in the subjunctive (**3.5.4**)
refuser **regretter**	

verbs and expressions of feeling		
être	**choqué**	**honteux**
	content	**mécontent**
	désolé	**ravi**
	étonné	**satisfait**
	fâché	**surpris**
	heureux	**triste**
il est	**agaçant**	**embêtant**

3.7.2.9 *in clauses dependent upon verbs and expressions indicating denial, doubt, evaluation, impossibility, necessity, possibility:*

verbs and expressions of denial, doubt, etc		
il y a avantage + *à ce que*		
il y a intérêt/avoir intérêt + *à ce que*		
il y a opportunité + *à ce que*		
avoir besoin R1		
démentir R3	**il est**	**bon**
douter		**contradictoire**
nier		**curieux**
il/c'est dommage		**douteux**
il faut		**essentiel**
il importe R3		**exclu**
peu importe		**impératif**
il s'en faut de peu		**important**
ce n'est pas la peine		**impossible**
il semble/il semblerait		**improbable**

---

verbs and expressions of denial, doubt, etc

NOTE: *il me/lui semble que* (ie *sembler* + indirect object) is always followed by the indicative. However, in such expressions as *il me semble important que* and *il ne me semble pas que* the subjunctive is used.	**il est inadmissible** **inévitable** **juste** **légitime** R3 **naturel** **nécessaire** **normal**
supporter NOTE: often used in the negative or with a negative connotation: eg *je supporte difficilement que . . .*	**opportun** R3 **paradoxal** **peu probable** NOTE: *il est probable que* is followed by the indicative (but cf **3.7.3.3**) **possible** **préférable** **rare** **temps**

3.7.2.10   *in clauses dependent upon a superlative formed with 'plus' or 'moins' (but cf 3.7.3.1):*

eg   **c'est le livre le plus comique que j'aie jamais lu**
      c'est le garçon le plus amusant que je connaisse
      c'est le moins que je puisse dire

3.7.2.11   *in clauses dependent upon verbs and expressions indicating chance:*

verbs and expressions of chance	comments
risquer	
il arrive que	
il est fréquent que	
il n'y a aucune chance que/pour que	*que* is preferred to *pour que* nowadays
il y a de grandes chances que/pour que	*que* is preferred to *pour que* nowadays
il y a le danger que	
le hasard a voulu que	
c'est un hasard que	

3.7.3   **'Grey' subjunctive**

As stated earlier (**3.7**), use of the subjunctive frequently corresponds to a high register of language. R3 users may introduce subtle shades of meaning into their French by a discreet balancing and contrasting of indicatives and subjunctives, the latter being used to imply a subjective attitude to what is being said, the former to convey a concrete fact:

eg **c'est la dernière partie de football que j'ai vue**
c'est la dernière pièce de Molière que j'aie à étudier

It is often what precedes the verb followed by the subordinate clause that determines the use of the subjunctive. In the following cases an element of doubt is present which triggers the subjunctive for R3 users:

eg **je ne puis m'imaginer qu'elle ait tenu sa promesse**
je suis loin d'espérer qu'elle revienne
je n'ai pas l'impression qu'il soit convaincu
je refuse de croire qu'il soit coupable
j'ai du mal à croire qu'elle soit Anglaise

Such distinctions are systematically ignored by R1 users and frequently, but not always, ignored by R2 users.

The grey subjunctive occurs in the following circumstances:

3.7.3.1 *in clauses dependent upon a superlative (but not formed with plus, 3.7.2.10) and similar expressions (such as 'dernier', 'premier', 'seul', 'ne . . . que'):*

meilleur, pire, dernier, etc

R1+R2	R2+R3
c'est le meilleur/pire élève que je connais	que je connaisse
il n'y a que le professeur qui le fait	qui le fasse
c'est le seul de mes collègues avec qui je me suis vraiment lié d'amitié	je me sois vraiment lié d'amitié

NOTE: after expressions involving *fois*, such as *la dernière/seule fois que*, the indicative mood is always used.

3.7.3.2 *in clauses dependent upon a negative or indefinite antecedent:*

negative or indefinite antecedent

il n'y a personne qui	il faut quelqu'un qui
il n'y a rien qui	je préfère/préférais quelque chose qui
il n'y a pas de sujet qui	j'ai besoin d'un homme qui
ce ne sont pas des gens qui	indiquez-moi un médecin qui
il n'y a aucun pays qui	je désire une situation qui

3.7.3.3 *in clauses dependent upon expressions denying and questioning*
certainty, probability:

expressions denying and questioning certainty and probability

il n'est pas/est-il	certain
	clair
	probable
	sûr
	vraisemblable

Under this heading are included certain expressions associated with
doubt which were excluded from **3.7.2.9**: verbs and expressions
indicating denial, doubt, etc:
il n'y a pas de doute
il ne fait pas de doute
il n'est pas douteux

3.7.3.4 *in clauses dependent upon verbs of thinking and declaring in the*
interrogative and/or negative:

verbs of thinking and declaring in interrogative and/or negative		examples
accepter	dire	croyez-vous qu'il vienne?
admettre	envisager	je ne dis pas qu'il ait raison
comprendre	expliquer	comment expliquez-vous qu'ils ne
concevoir	penser	soient pas revenus?
croire		j'envisageais que tout le monde
		soit présent

In R3 usage the verbs in the first column may also be followed by the
subjunctive when they are used declaratively:
eg **j'admets qu'il ait raison**

3.7.3.5 *in clauses dependent upon expressions of the following type:*

	example
le but/dessein/l'intention est que	le fait qu'un étudiant soit (R3)/
le fait que	est (R2) plus intelligent n'est
	pas surprenant
il se fait que/ce qui fait que	elle est arrivée ce matin, ce qui
	fait que je suis resté à la
	maison (R2)
il se trouve que (R2)	l'auteur a publié plusieurs
sachez que (R2 and R3)	ouvrages sur l'art, ce qui fait
espérer	qu'il soit invité à assister à
prévoir	. . . (R3)

NOTE: uncertainty exists over usage with *espérer*. Traditionally, the verb is associated with the indicative, but in R1 speech it is possible to hear the subjunctive (the practice should not be imitated):

j'espère qu'il vienne

In R3 speech the subjunctive is also acceptable in such cases as

il est à espérer que les statistiques soient correctes

j'aurais espéré que mon frère ait les billets

je n'espère pas que mon frère me fasse confiance

NOTE: when *prévoir* = to foresee, the indicative is used; when = to intend, to mean, the subjunctive:

eg *j'ai prévu qu'elle reviendrait, et effectivement, elle est revenue*

j'ai prévu qu'elle écrive la lettre

3.7.4   Avoiding the subjunctive

Because of uncertainty over correct forms and grey areas of usage, it is often advisable to avoid using the subjunctive. This may easily be done in certain circumstances:

3.7.4.1   *when the main and dependent clauses have the same subject, it is possible to use a preposition + infinitive rather than the subjunctive:*

prepositions	to replace
à condition de	à condition que
afin de	afin que
à moins de	à moins que
avant de	avant que
de crainte de	craindre que/de crainte que
de façon à	de façon que/à ce que, de sorte que
de manière à	de manière que/à ce que, de sorte que
de peur de	avoir peur que/de peur que
sans	sans que

3.7.4.2   *certain prepositional phrases are available to replace clauses with a subjunctive:*

prepositional phrases	to replace
avant mon départ	avant que je (ne) parte
à mon insu	sans que je le sache
à ma connaissance	autant que je sache

3.8 Pronouns

The following section contains a selection of problems concerning personal pronouns.

3.8.1 Second person pronouns

The following table shows broadly the situation in which *tu (toi, te, ton, ta, tes)* and *vous (votre, vos)* are used as modes of address in the singular:

mode of address in singular

TU	VOUS
used when speaking to: young children parents near relatives domestic animals	*used when speaking to:*
	all others
used between: friends workmates soldiers in the same unit children in the same school	

However, actual usage is far more complicated than this table would suggest, and is affected by a large number of factors, such as age, personal attitudes, social circumstances, relationships within a hierarchy, etc.

For obvious sociological reasons, the general movement has been away from *vous* to *tu*. Whereas once, probably all teachers used *vous* when addressing older pupils (from the age of 15 upwards), a good number no longer observe this practice; similarly with the priest. However, *tu is* strictly forbidden across the grades/ranks in the armed services. The appropriateness of *tu* or *vous* can often be obscured if, for instance, a child's age is not known. Indeed genuine awkwardness may ensue if a child's age is not known, and the situation might arise where an older person would find it necessary to ask a younger person's permission to *tutoyer* her/him if their age is unclear. The age of 14 or 15 upwards would, initially at any rate, require the respectful *vous*.

Catholics now follow the well-established Protestant example of using *tu* to address God in their prayers. At the same time in certain aristocratic families, parents use *tu* to their children, while the latter use *vous* to their parents. This *Vous-Régence* is particularly applicable to the highest echelons of government. It is often parodied in French

films and plays: use of inappropriate pronouns in certain contexts –
switching from distance (use of *vous*) to intimacy or humiliation (use
of *tu*) – can produce comic or odd effects. In play, children sometimes
mimic members of high society by using the *vous*-form. *Tu* is used
with pets.

The point to be remembered is that the use of both *tu* and *vous*
contains subtleties capable of expressing strong feelings, likes and
dislikes, a sense of distance, superiority, indifference and so on. Thus,
a driver, on observing poor driving by an unknown motorist, could
easily say: '*T'as eu ton permis de conduire dans une pochette-surprise?*' (= a
child's present with a surprise item). The intimate form puts the guilty
driver in his place. Since English no longer possesses two second
person pronouns, the subtleties, social tactics and jokes possible in
French cannot be effectively conveyed in translation from French into
English. When François Mitterrand, leader of the Socialist party,
became President of France and heard left-wing colleagues say: '*Allez!
on se dit tu*', he is alleged to have replied icily: '*Comme vous voudrez!*' In
a similar way movement up or down the social hierarchy can create
problems: if two people have been on close terms and have been in
the habit of addressing each other as *tu*, and if their contact is broken
because one of them rises up the social/professional/academic ladder,
on a subsequent meeting there may be a problem as to which pronoun
to use – as a convenient solution the third person indefinite pronoun
on might be resorted to. Another problem arises when one meets for
the first time the partner of a friend with whom one is naturally on *tu*
terms; this is all the more acute if partners are present: does one use
the respectful *vous* because one does not know the partner, or *tu*
because of one's association with the friend? *Tu* and *vous* can even be
used between two people at different times of the day! Two colleagues
who run a hairdressing business in Paris use *vous* on the premises and
tu when they are away from work. The pronoun *tu* would not suit
their formal approach to their profession. A well-known example of
the sexual exploitation of the different values of the two pronouns
occurs in a song by Juliette Greco, where it is said: '"*Déshabillez-moi*"
est bien plus érotique que "déshabille-moi"': use of *vous* rather than *tu* adds
a connotation of exciting suggestiveness (distance in intimacy) to the
liaison!

The most awkward moment occurs in the actual transition from
vous to *tu*, that is in passing from the stage of respect to that of
friendliness, etc. This is felt especially acutely between the sexes and if
a speaker inadvertently addresses a stranger as *tu*, an apology is
required (on the other hand, if it were done deliberately . . .).

Finally, if *A* is addressed in the *tu* form by *B*, he/she should not
automatically use the *tu* form in return. Again a safe solution is to use
on as a provisional expedient. Considerations of age dictate the use of
the pronoun here.

3.8.2   Third person pronouns

3.8.2.1   'il' or 'ce'?

In French constructions equivalent to English 'it's nice to meet you', it is sometimes difficult to decide whether to use *il est* or *c'est*, or *à* or *de*. The following table illustrating the possible usages shows that it is a matter of what the pronoun refers to, and at times a matter of register as well:

introducing a new idea or statement		examples
R2 + R3	*il est* + **adjective** + *de* + **infinitive**	il est difficile de lire le livre
R1	*c'est* + **adjective** + *de* + **infinitive**	c'est difficile de lire le livre

with reference to a preceding idea or statement		example
R1, R2 + R3	*c'est* + **adjective** + *à* + **infinitive**	il a couru le cent mètres en dix secondes – c'est difficile à faire

3.8.2.2   *le*

In addition to its normal function of referring to persons, *le* is sometimes used to effect a link between what is being said and what has just been said, occasionally in situations where no equivalent exists in English:

eg **il voulait être grand et il l'est** = he wanted to be big, and he is

pauvre, il risque de l'être = he's in danger of being poor

grand, il veut l'être = he wants to be important

dites-le-moi = tell me

il est plus/moins grand que je ne le pensais = he's bigger/smaller than I thought

cela va mieux que je ne le pensais = that's better than I thought

mademoiselle, êtes-vous infirmière? – Je le suis = I am

The pronoun *le* forms an integral part of certain verbal expressions, such as:

l'échapper belle = to have a narrow escape

l'emporter sur qn = to get the better of sb

le prendre de haut = to act arrogantly

se le tenir pour dit = to take it as said

On the other hand, the following examples are equivalent to English expressions with *it*:

$$je \begin{cases} considère \\ estime \\ juge \\ trouve \end{cases} \begin{cases} difficile \\ impossible \\ inutile \\ nécessaire \\ prudent \end{cases} de = I \dots it \dots to$$

3.8.2.3 on

On is usually treated as a masculine singular subject pronoun:

eg **quand on n'a rien à faire, on trouve le temps long**

However, it may also be used with reference to feminine or plural subjects and the appropriate agreements of adjectives and past participles (but not finite verbs) are made:

eg **quand on est mère, on est fière de ses enfants**

on a beau être citoyens, on n'est pas toujours égaux

on a été sages aujourd'hui? (parent speaking to children)

on est venus aussi vite que possible (two or more people speaking)

On functions only as a subject; when it is required to express a direct object or other complement other forms are used:

complements of *on*		examples
reflexive	se	on se lève, on se lave
	soi (*R3 only*)	on doit aider les plus infortunés que soi
		de temps en temps on doit prendre une décision soi-même
non-reflexive	nous (*including speaker*)	on voit bien ses cheveux gris
	vous (*excluding speaker*)	quand elle est près de nous/vous

In R1 speech it is not uncommon for *nous* to be used in apposition to *on:*

eg **nous autres Anglais, on le fait d'une autre façon**

The possessive adjective associated with *on* is the *son, sa* series:

eg **on entre, on enlève son chapeau et ses gants**

Often in R3 usage, for the sake of euphony, the form *l'on* is preferred. It should scarcely be necessary to point out that *on* is used much more frequently in French than *one* is in English (which is more or less restricted to R3 usage in that language). In the past, in R3 writing, *on* was frowned upon as too loose and informal a pronoun, and *nous* is often still preferred to it in such circumstances. In fact *nous* can also replace *je* in the same way, functioning as a singular pronoun, with reference to a male in the first example and to a female in the second (and therefore requiring agreement of the past participle):

eg **nous sommes tenté de suggérer que . . .**

puis nous nous sommes efforcée de décrire . . .

3.8.2.4 soi

Soi, the strong form of the reflexive pronoun, is used only with certain indefinite words and expressions such as *on*, *chacun* and impersonal *il*:

eg **il faut/on doit le faire soi-même**
chacun pour soi

NOTE: the strong form used with reflexive verbs is *lui* (*-même*) and not *soi*:

eg **l'enfant a réussi à se laver lui-même**

3.8.3 en

En functions in two ways:

adverb of place	pronoun:
	with partitive value
	used with verbs, past participles, adjectives, nouns, numerals + *de*

en as adverb:

eg **il sort de la ville: il en sort**
il vient de Paris: il en vient

en as pronoun:

As a pronoun *en* seems to have a number of different values, ranging from reference to specific objects to an extremely indeterminate use, merely providing a weak link with what has been said previously. This use often has no equivalent in English: consequently corresponding English versions are given below where appropriate. Some of the following examples, graded according to the degree of explicitness of reference of *en*, contain fixed expressions.

eg **voici une fourchette – Servez-vous-en**
quel est son prénom? je ne m'en souviens pas
voici un cadeau pour votre fille – Je vous en remercie
est-ce que tu as fini tes devoirs? – J'en ai fait les deux tiers
j'ai congédié le premier; il s'en est présenté un deuxième
est-ce que tu as cueilli toutes les pommes? – Non, il en
reste les trois quarts
l'histoire de Matthieu et de Sylvie est fascinante – on
devrait en faire un livre
je suis enfin arrivé! – J'en suis content/heureux/fâché/ravi/
désolé
il ne peut que s'en prendre à lui-même = he's only got himself to blame
nous devons nous en rapporter à l'arbitrage du juge = we have to accept the judge's decision
elle s'en est remise à la discrétion de son petit ami = she put her trust in her boyfriend's discretion
je lui en veux de ses actions = I've got a grudge against him/her because of what he/she did

j'en passe, et des meilleurs (after listing things)

elle en a vu de toutes les couleurs = she's seen the lot (ie had
   all sorts of experiences)

il faut les/l'en empêcher = you'll have to stop them/him/her

je vous en prie = don't mention (it)

il ne veut pas en démordre = he won't give up

il risque d'en découdre avec son frère = he's in danger of
   having a fight with his brother

on en a bavé = we had a hard time

j'en appelle au juge/à votre bon sens/à votre générosité = I
   appeal to . . .

comment en est-il arrivé là? = how did he get into that state?

je n'en reviens pas = I can't get over it

le sort en est jeté = the die is cast

il en est des collèges comme dans certains lycées = it's the
   same with some 'collèges' as with . . .

les discussions n'en sont qu'à leur début = discussions are just
   beginning

j'en ai fini avec des vacances en janvier = I've had enough of
   holidays in January

elle n'en est pas à sa première défaite = this isn't her first
   defeat

ce genre d'erreur en dit long sur l'éducation de nos jours =
   this type of mistake says a lot about education nowadays

NOTE: no agreement is made between *en* and the past participle in
compound tenses conjugated with *avoir*, since *en* is not a direct object:

eg **elle a des robes comme j'en ai eu**

   c'est le type de jeune fille comme j'en ai connu par le passé

Strictly speaking *en* is not used with reference to people: compare
the two examples:

   on devrait en faire un livre where *en* refers to either an
      indeterminate or non-human antecedent and

   **ses tournées font de lui l'artiste le mieux payé des Etats-
      Unis**

However, such examples as the following are normal despite the
censure of the purists:

eg **est-ce qu'il y a des médecins? – Oui, il y en a**

   il en a fait son premier ministre

In a comparative expression involving quantity *en*, as well as an
expletive *ne*, is required in the subordinate clause in R3 speech:

eg **il ne faut pas donner a l'événement plus d'importance
      qu'il n'en a**

In R1 and R2 speech, when highlighting of an object indicating
quantity occurs by moving it to the head or end of the clause, *en* is
required before the verb:

eg **du papier, j'en ai trouvé**

   il y en a, des livres

3.8.4 y

Like *en*, *y* functions both as an adverb and as a pronoun:

adverb of place	pronoun:
	used with verbs, past participles, adjectives, nouns, numerals + *à*

y as adverb

eg **je vais au collège: j'y vais**
   êtes-vous arrivé? – Oui, j'y suis arrivé

y as pronoun

y does not have the range of values of *en*:

eg **je pense à ce que vous avez dit: j'y pense**
   est-il décidé à le faire? – Oui, il y est décidé
   elle l'y a encouragé = she encouraged him to do it
   elle l'y a poussé = she pushed him into doing it
   je n'y réussirai pas
   je n'y vois pas clair

As with *le* and *en*, *y* forms part of a verbal expression:

il y va de ma vie

3.9 Usage with names of countries

The following table illustrates the usage of prepositions with respect to names of countries:

	M names beginning with cons	M names beginning with vowel	F names
position in	au	en	en
examples	il est au Portugal	il est en Iran	il est en France
movement towards	au	en	en
examples	il va au Portugal	il va en Irak	il va en France
movement away from	du	d'	de★
examples	elle vient du Danemark	elle vient d'Iran	elle vient de Belgique

★*de la* is no longer used in this context, except in:
il vient de l'Inde

When the country is qualified by an adjective the following usage is observed:

dans la France contemporaine
dans le Canada d'aujourd'hui
dans le Japon moderne
When referring to the north or south of a country, one usually says:
il est dans le nord/sud de la France
Less common is:
il est dans la France du nord
NOTE: both **elle est en Italie du Nord/du Sud** and **elle est dans le nord/le sud de l'Italie** are common.
Note also the different uses of capital letters here. Only **dans le nord/sud de l'Angleterre/de la France** (ie not **en**) is possible.

For usage with names of islands, see the individual islands listed below. For names of towns with distinctive French forms, see **2.7.2**.

3.9.1   France

	gender	il est/va	examples	exceptions
Regions	F (the majority)	en	en Bourgogne en Bretagne en Normandie en Provence en Lorraine du Sud = in the southern part of Lorraine	none
	M	dans le	dans le Poitou	en Anjou en Limousin
Departments	M	dans le	dans le Finistère dans le Gard dans le Gers dans le Jura dans le Loir et Cher dans le Lot dans le Var	
	F	dans la/en	dans la/en Charente dans la/en Gironde en is more common than **dans la**	
		en	en Corse (du Sud) en Côte d'Or en Saône et Loire en Vendée	
	Fpl	dans les	dans les Alpes Maritimes dans les Bouches du Rhône dans les Landes dans les Yvelines	

Mountainous areas:	**il est/va + dans**:

eg **dans les Alpes (du Nord/du Sud)**
      dans les Pyrénées
      dans les Vosges

Names of towns beginning with a definite article: the article combines with *à* and *de* as in normal circumstances:

eg **il est au Creusot, au Havre, au Mans, à la Rochelle**
   il vient du Creusot, du Havre, du Mans, de la Rochelle

Movement away from regions, departments and mountainous areas

gender	preposition	examples
M	du	**il vient du Jura**
Fsg	de	**il vient de Normandie, de Vendée**
Fpl	des	**il vient des Alpes Maritimes**

Contrary to English, names of inhabitants of regions and towns are very common in French:

eg **Auvergne**   **Auvergnat**
   Bretagne   **Breton**
   Franche-Comté   **Franc-comtois**
   Normandie   **Normand**
   Poitou   **Poitevin**

Apart from the usual *Parisien, Marseillais, Lyonnais, Toulousain, Nantais* and *Strasbourgeois*, here is a small selection from a vast number of less easily recognisable ones:

Besançon	**Bisontin**
Evreux	**Ebroïcien**
Ile de France	**Francilien**
Lisieux	**Lexovien**
Pont-Saint-Esprit	**Spiripontain**
St Etienne	**Stéphanois**

All these nouns may also be used adjectivally.

NOTE:

La Côte d'Azur = the French Riviera
La Riviéra   = the Italian Riviera

Although *Comté* is masculine, je one says *La Franche Comté*; the adjective is *franc-comtois*.

Below is indicated how the name of each country is used. The classification is by continents except in the case of France, which has been treated separately.

NOTE: with nationality a capital letter is used, while with a pure adjective a small letter is used

eg **elle est Française**
   c'est une Française
   une ville française

With names of languages a small letter is used:
eg **elle parle très bien le français**

3.9.2   Europe

il est/va	elle vient	adjective
en Albanie	d'Albanie	albanais
en Allemagne	d'Allemagne	allemand
en Andorre	d'Andorre	
NOTE: à Andorre =		
Andorra the capital		
en Angleterre	d'Angleterre	anglais
en Autriche	d'Autriche	autrichien
aux Baléares, à	des Baléares, de	majorquin, espagnol
Majorque	Majorque	
en Belgique	de Belgique	belge
en Biélorussie	de Biélorussie	biélorusse
en Bosnie	de Bosnie	bosniaque
en Bulgarie	de Bulgarie	bulgare
à Chypre	de Chypre	cypriote, chypriote
en Corse	de Corse	corse, français
en Crète	de Crète	crétois
en Croatie	de Croatie	croate
au Danemark	du Danemark	danois
en Ecosse	d'Ecosse	écossais
en Eire, en République	d'Eire, de la République	irlandais
d'Irlande	d'Irlande	
en Espagne	d'Espagne	espagnol
NOTE: au/en pays	du pays basque	basque (une Basquaise)
basque		
en Andalousie	d'Andalousie	andalou/andalouse
en Estonie	d'Estonie	estonien
en Finlande	de Finlande	finlandais/finnois (**2.3**)
au Pays de Galles	du Pays de Galles	gallois
en Flandre/dans les	de Flandre/des	flamand
Flandres	Flandres	
en Grande-Bretagne	de Grande-Bretagne	britannique

NOTE A: dans les Iles britanniques

NOTE B: Counties: dans le Kent, etc *except* en Cornouailles

NOTE C: *the noun/adjective* anglo-saxon *is commonly used for the English but this includes the North Americans, Australians etc (ie all the 'white' countries where English is spoken).*

NOTE D: *few French people see any difference between* les Anglais *and* les Britanniques *or between* l'Angleterre, la Grande-Bretagne *and* le Royaume-Uni.

en Grèce	de Grèce	grec (F grecque)
au Grœnland	du Grœnland	danois

il est/va	elle vient	adjective
en Hollande, aux Pays Bas	de Hollande, des Pays Bas	hollandais, néerlandais
en Hongrie	de Hongrie	hongrois
en Irlande du Nord/ en Ulster	d'Irlande du Nord	britannique, irlandais
en Irlande du Sud	d'Irlande du Sud	irlandais
en Italie	d'Italie	italien
NOTE: au Vatican à San Marino/ Saint-Marin		
en Lettonie	de Lettonie	lette/letton
en Lithuanie	de Lithuanie	lithuanien
au Luxembourg	du Luxembourg	luxembourgeois
NOTE: à Luxembourg = *Luxemburg town*		
à Malte	de Malte	maltais
à Monténégro	de Monténégro	monténégrin
en Norvège	de Norvège	norvégien
en Pologne	de Pologne	polonais
au Portugal	du Portugal	portugais
en Roumanie	de Roumanie	roumain
au Royaume-Uni	du Royaume-Uni	britannique
en Russie, dans l'ex-URSS (Union des Républiques socialistes soviétiques)	de Russie, dans l'ex-URSS (Union des Républiques socialistes soviétiques)	russe
NOTE: en Prusse	de Prusse	prussien
en Sardaigne	de Sardaigne	sarde, italien
en Serbie, en Grande Serbie	de Serbie	serbe
en Sicile	de Sicile	sicilien, italien
en Slovaquie	de Slovaquie	slovaque
en Slovénie	de Slovénie	slovène
en Suède	de Suède	suédois
en Suisse	de Suisse	suisse (une Suissesse)
NOTE: le lac Léman/ le Lac de Genève = *Lake Geneva*		
en République Tchèque/en Tchéquie	de la République Tchèque	tchèque
en Turquie	de Turquie	turc (F turque)
en Ukraine	d'Ukraine	ukrainien
en Yougoslavie	de Yougoslavie	yougoslave

NOTE *the following compound adjectives:*

anglo-français	hispano-français
franco-anglais	germano-russe
franco-britannique	russo-allemand
franco-espagnol	

franco-espagnol

NOTE ALSO: dans les pays baltes *but* les régions baltiques

3.9.3   Afrique

il est/va	elle vient	adjective
en Afrique du Sud	d'Afrique du Sud	sud-africain
en Algérie	d'Algérie	algérien
en Angola	d'Angola	angolais
au Bénin	du Bénin	béninois
au Botswana	du Botswana	botswanais
au Burkina Faso/ Bourkina Faso (*form-erly* la Haute Volta)	du Burkina Faso/ Bourkina Faso (*form-erly* la Haute Volta)	burkinabé/burkinais (*formerly* voltaïque)
au Burundi	du Burundi	burundais
au Cameroun	du Cameroun	camerounais
en Côte d'Ivoire	de la Côte d'Ivoire	ivoirien
en Egypte	d'Egypte	égyptien
en Ethiopie	d'Ethiopie	éthiopien
au Gabon	du Gabon	gabonais
au Ghana	du Ghana	ghanéen
en Guinée	de Guinée	guinéen
au Kenya	du Kenya	kenyen/kenyien
au Libéria	du Libéria	libérien
en Libye	de Libye	libyen
à Madagascar	de Madagascar	malgache
au Malawi	du Malawi	malawi
au Mali	du Mali	malien
au Maroc	du Maroc	marocain
à (l'île) Maurice (*but often, although mistakenly*, aux îles Maurice)	de l'île Maurice	mauricien
en Mauritanie	de Mauritanie	mauritanien
au Mozambique	du Mozambique	mozambiquais
en Namibie	de Namibie	namibien
au Niger	du Niger	nigérien
au Nigéria	du Nigéria	nigérian
en Ouganda	d'Ouganda	ougandais
en République Centrafricaine	de la République Centrafricaine	centrafricain
en République Congolaise	de la République Congolaise	congolais

il est/va	elle vient	adjective
à la Réunion	de la Réunion	réunionnais
au Ruanda	du Ruanda	ruandais
au Sénégal	du Sénégal	sénégalais
en Sierra Leone	de Sierra Leone	sierra-leonien
en Somalie	de Somalie	somalien
au Soudan	du Soudan	soudanais
en Tanzanie	de Tanzanie	tanzanien
au Tchad	du Tchad	tchadien
au Togo	du Togo	togolais
en Tunisie	de Tunisie	tunisien
en Zambie	de Zambie	zambien
au Zimbabwe	du Zimbabwe	zimbabwéen

NOTE: l'Afrique du Nord *refers mainly to* le Maghreb, ie le Maroc, l'Algérie, la Tunisie. *Its southern equivalent is* l'Afrique Australe (*Southern Africa*), *not to be confused with* l'Afrique du Sud (*South Africa*). NOTE *the following compound adjectives:*
afro–asiatique   égypto–israélien   israélo–égyptien

3.9.4   Asie et Australasie

il est/va	elle vient	adjective
en Afghanistan	d'Afghanistan	afghan
en Australie	d'Australie	australien
au Bangladesh	du Bangladesh	bengladais
en Birmanie	de Birmanie	birman
au Cambodge	du Cambodge	cambodgien
au Kampuchéa	du Kampuchéa	
en Chine	de Chine	chinois
NOTE: sino- *in compound adjectives: eg* sino-vietnamien		
en Corée du Nord, du Sud	de Corée du Nord, du Sud	nord-coréen, sud-coréen
en Inde	de l'Inde	hindou, indien; *the latter is the more correct term*
NOTE: aux Indes *is outmoded as a political expression, but is still used*		
en Indonésie	d'Indonésie	indonésien
au Japon	du Japon	japonais
au Laos	du Laos	laotien
en Malaisie	de Malaisie	malaisien
au Népal	du Népal	népalais
en Nouvelle-Calédonie	de Nouvelle-Calédonie	néo-calédonien

il est/va	elle vient	adjective
en Nouvelle Zélande	de Nouvelle Zélande	neo–zélandais
au Pakistan	du Pakistan	pakistanais
aux Philippines	des Philippines	philippin
à Singapour	de Singapour	singapourien
à Sri Lanka	de Sri Lanka	sri lankais
en Tasmanie	de Tasmanie	tasmanien
en Thaïlande	de Thaïlande	thaïlandais
au Tibet	du Tibet	tibetain
au Vietnam	du Vietnam	vietnamien

NOTE: il est/va en Extrême-Orient, il est/va en Asie du Sud-Est, les pays du pourtour pacifique = *the countries of the Pacific rim.*

3.9.5   Moyen-Orient

il est/va	elle vient	adjective

en Arabie Séoudite
    NOTE: Saoudite *is*
    more common, but is
    refuted by purists
	d'Arabie Séoudite	séoudien

dans la Bande de Gaza		
en Cisjordanie (*West Bank (of Jordan)*)	de Cisjordanie	cisjordanien
en Egypte	d'Egypte	égyptien
en Irak	d'Irak	irakien
en Iran	d'Iran	iranien
en Israël	d'Israël	israélien

NOTE: Israël *is not*
    preceded by a definite
    article: eg le
    premier ministre
    d'Israël; Israël est
    un petit pays		

en Jordanie	de Jordanie	jordanien
au Liban, au Liban- Sud	du Liban	libanais
en Syrie	de Syrie	syrien
au Yémen, au Yémen du Sud	du Yémen	yéménite

NOTE: il est au Proche-Orient, au Moyen-Orient

3.9.6 Amérique du Nord

il est/va	elle vient	adjective
au Canada	du Canada	canadien
au Québec	du Québec	québécois
aux Etats-Unis	des Etats-Unis	américain
NOTE: *in speech often* aux USA		

NOTE: For individual States, the usage is:
dans l' before vowel or mute **h**
au before M beginning with cons
en before F beginning with cons
eg **dans l'Ohio, dans l'Utah**
  au Nevada, au Texas, au Yukon (in Canada)
  en Californie, en Caroline du Nord, du Sud, en Alaska
Other states with distinctive French forms:
  Dakota du Nord, du Sud, Floride, Georgie, Louisiane, Nouveau Mexique, Pennsylvanie, Virginie Occidentale
NOTE: **un Peau Rouge, un Indien** = a Red Indian/Native American

3.9.7 Amérique Centrale

il est/va	elle vient	adjective
aux Antilles (= *West Indies*)	des Antilles	antillais
aux Bahamas	des Bahamas	bahamien
à la Barbade	de la Barbade	barbadien
aux Bermudes	des Bermudes	bermudien
aux Camaïans	des Camaïans	
aux Caraïbes	des Caraïbes	caraïbe
NOTE: les Caraïbes = *either the Caribbean sea or the islands*		
au Costa Rica	du Costa Rica	costaricain
à Cuba	de Cuba	cubain
à la Dominique	de la Dominique	dominicais
à la/en Guadeloupe	de la Guadeloupe	guadeloupéen
à/en Haïti	de Haïti	haïtien
à la/en Martinique	de la Martinique	martiniquais
NOTE: in these three cases en *is more common than* à (la)		
au Guatémala	du Guatémala	guatémaltèque
au Honduras	du Honduras	hondurien

il est/va	elle vient	adjective
à la Jamaïque	de la Jamaïque	jamaïquain
au Mexique	du Mexique	mexicain
au Nicaragua	du Nicaragua	nicaraguayen
au Panama	du Panama	panaméen
NOTE: à Panama = *in Panama City, the capital* (*not to be confused mith* Paname, *a popular term for Paris*)		
à Porto Rico	de Porto Rico	portoriquain
en République Dominicaine	de la République Dominicaine	dominicain
au Salvador	du Salvador	salvadorien
NOTE: à San–Salvador = *in San-Salvador, the capital.*		

3.9.8   Amérique du Sud

il est/va	elle vient	adjective
en Argentine	d'Argentine	argentin
en Bolivie	de Bolivie	bolivien
au Brésil	du Brésil	brésilien
au Chili	du Chili	chilien
en Colombie	de Colombie	colombien
en Equateur (= *Ecuador*)	d'Equateur	equatorien
en Guyane	de Guyane	guyanais
aux Malouines (= *the Falklands*)	des Malouines	malouin
au Paraguay	du Paraguay	paraguayen
au Pérou	du Pérou	péruvien
en Uruguay	d'Uruguay	uruguayen
au Vénézuéla	du Vénézuéla	vénézuélien

NOTE: il est en Amérique du Nord, du Sud, en Amérique Centrale
NOTE ALSO *the compound adjective:* latino–américain

3.9.9 Seas, Oceans and Mountains

	preposition	examples and comments
seas	dans la/en	dans la/en Mer du Nord, dans la/en Mer Noire, dans la/en Mer Caspienne, dans la/en Mer de Chine, dans la/en Mer du Japon, dans la/en Manche, en Méditerranée is preferred to dans la Méditerranée NOTE: the use of **outre** = across, on the other side eg **outre-Atlantique**, **outre-Manche**, **outre-Rhin** R3/2
oceans	dans le	dans l'(Océan) Atlantique dans l'(Océan) Pacifique
	dans le/en	only with **Océan Indien**
mountains	dans le	dans le Caucase dans l'Himalaya dans l'Oural
	dans la dans les	dans la Cordillère des Andes dans les Alpes (fpl) dans les Andes (fpl) dans les Pyrénées (fpl) dans les Montagnes Rocheuses/les Rocheuses (fpl) NOTE: **outre-Pyrénées**

Useful geographical phrases:	sous les/aux Tropiques sous la ligne du Cancer/du Capricorne	à l'équateur au pôle nord, au pôle sud

3.10 Changes of word class

It happens quite regularly in modern French that words change their word class. This especially affects adjectives, which are used widely as adverbs or nouns and is exploited in the main to achieve economy of effort. What occurs is that a potentially long expression is reduced to its basic and most significant component(s) (eg **travailler d'une manière dure** is reduced to **travailler dur**; **la science/industrie aéronautique** is reduced to **l'aéronautique**). This phenomenon is known as ellipsis.

The following examples illustrate the most common tendencies:

adjective as adverb

In these circumstances the adjective, now an adverb, remains invariable.

bon – sentir bon

cher – coûter cher, vendre cher

eg **cette voiture coûte cher; je vends cher ma liberté**

clair – voir clair

court – s'arrêter court, tourner court

eg **l'expérience a tourné court**

doux – filer doux (R1) = to keep a low profile

dur – travailler dur

faux – chanter faux

ferme – travailler ferme, tenir ferme

fort – frapper fort, pousser fort, serrer fort

eg **frappe/pousse/serre plus fort!**

grand – ouvrir grand

eg **ouvrez grand les portes; ouvre grand ta bouche**

haut – haut placé

eg **un fonctionnaire haut placé**

juste – deviner juste, raisonner juste, tomber juste, viser juste

lourd – peser lourd (lit and fig)

eg **ce panier pèse lourd; la responsabilité du travail lui pesait lourd**

mauvais – sentir mauvais

net – s'arrêter net

sec – se briser sec

eg **la branche s'est brisée sec**

adjective as noun

There are many examples; here is a selection:

l'aéronautique, l'agroalimentaire, l'audio-visuel, l'économique, l'électroménager, la générale (= dress rehearsal (in theatre)), **le marginal** (= drop-out), **la maternelle** (= nursery school), **le mobile** (telephone), **la nationale** (= the main road, eg **la nationale six** which runs south from Paris), **le politique, le portable** (radio), **la première** (= première of a film etc), **le primaire** (= primary education), **le/la responsable** (= official), **la terminale** (= final year at school eg **être en terminale**), **le textile, un/une universitaire** (= university teacher/academic).

The names of elections are nearly always reduced to the significant term:

eg **les législatives, les municipales, les prud'homales** (= for an industrial tribunal), **les régionales**

past participle as noun

Some of these are well established in the language:

eg **blessé, délégué, handicapé**

There is not always a direct English equivalent, especially when they are used in the singular; consequently translating some of them is difficult out of context. Often an expression involving 'someone who is . . .; a . . . person' will have to be resorted to. However, these words are very often used in the plural, and in such cases an English equivalent is easier to find, but not always:

eg **les appelés** = military conscripts, **les laissés pour compte** = outcasts, those rejected by society, **les marginalisés** = marginalised, **les oubliés** = the forgotten ones, **les privilégiés** = inititiated/privileged, **les salariés** = wage earners, **les sinistrés** = disaster victims

Here is a list of other common past participles used to indicate various types of person:

abruti, **accidenté**, **administré** (usu in pl), **bien/mal aimé**, **appelé**, **banni**, **blessé**, **brûlé** (also **grand brûlé** = someone suffering from third degree burns), **condamné (à mort)**, **décédé**, **déporté**, **détenu**, **disparu**, **divorcé**, **doué**, **drogué**, **élu**, **enragé**, **envoyé**, **exclu**, **exilé**, **gradé** (= non-commissioned officer), **habitué**, **handicapé**, **initié**, **insurgé**, **intéressé**, **intoxiqué** (= person who has been (food) poisoned), **licencié**, **miraculé** (= someone who has been saved miraculously), **mort**, **névrosé**, **obsédé**, **passionné**, **proscrit**, **rescapé** (= survivor), **retraité**, **révolté**, **sondé** (usu in the pl, = those polled/those who take part in a survey), **surdoué**, **taré**, **tourmenté**

eg **il roule comme un abruti** = he drives like a moron

on a transporté les accidentés/les blessés/les brûlés/les intoxiqués à l'hôpital de la ville la plus proche

il se croyait miraculé = he thought a miracle had been worked on him (eg after an operation)

les retraités/les salariés ont droit à une majoration de trois pour cent

l'écrivain est l'un des grands tourmentés de notre siècle

les sondés ont répondu unanimement que . . .

blindé = armoured vehicle is a rare case where a person is not involved.

noun as adjective
This concerns colour words:
eg **des étoffes marron, des yeux noisette, des cheveux châtain**

Vocabulary list

Words and expressions contained in Sections 2.1 to 2.4

abaisser 52
abattre 56
abonné 127
aborder 82
abords 85
absorber 52
abstraction, faire 93
abuser 49
accomplir 31
accomplir un devoir 36
accomplissement 31, 49
accord 31
accord tomber d' 81
accorder 97
s'accorder 80
accord, être d' 80
accroissement 52
s'accroître 52, 84
achèvement 31
achever 31, 52
acteur 45
actuel 31
addition 102
adjoint 33
affaiblir 33
s'affaiblir 52
affronter 52
âgé 128
agenda 31
agent de conservation 36
agent de police 117
agglomération urbaine 128
agonie 31
agoniser 31
agrandir 53, 84
agréer 31, 80
agrément 31
agresser 86
agressif 37
agriculteur 103
aide 38, 39
aide venir en 81
aider 81
aigle 39

aimé/aimée, bien 81
aine 34
air 42
aire 42
aise, bien à l' 50
alcool à brûler 92
alentours 85
alité 50
alléchant 83
allée 31
allocution 96
allumer 45
alpestre 53
alpin 53
s'altérer 31
amant 81
amende 34
amener 53
amie petite 81
ami petit 81
amoureux 81
amusant 45
amuser 33
an 53
analyser 102
ancien 128
angoisse 31
année 53
annonce 31
annuel, congé 127
anoblir 53
anse 116
antique 128
s'apercevoir 53
aplanir 53
aplatir 53
apogée 123
apparaître 72
apparition 53, 81
appeler 82
appétissant 83
application 49
apporter 54
apposer 54
appréhender 46
apprendre 101
s'approcher 54, 82

âpre 120
apurer 54
aquarelle 115
arc 54
arche 54
argent 35, 83
argenté 54
argentin 54
argument 55
argumentation 55
arôme 113
arrêt, maison d' 118
arrêter 46
arrivage 55
arrivée 55
artère 90
aspirine 39
assassinat 46
assembler 55, 95
asservir 55
assistance 38, 49
assister 46, 81
assortiment 123
astucieux 121
atelier 37
attacher 55
attendrissant 51
attentat 95
attentif 55
attentionné 55
atténuer 34
attirant 83
attractif 55, 83
attrayant 55, 83
attribuer 97
audience 49
augmenter 84
auprès 55
auto 32
automobiliste 35
autoroute 90
avance 55
avancée 55
avancement 55
s'avancer 82, 83
avantage 33
avertissement 31
avide 106

avilir 33
axe 31
axe routier 91
bagne 118
bahut 98
bâillon 34
baiser 56
baisser 52, 56
bal 42, 49
balance 56
balancer 31, 46, 108
balancier 56
balançoire 56
balle 42, 44, 49, 56, 84, 85
ballon 56, 84, 92, 118
ballot 56
bananier 86
banc 56, 90
bandit 46
banlieue 85
banque 50
banquette 56, 90
bans 56
bar 42, 50
barbouze 117
baril 56
barillet 56
barque 85
barrage 32
barre 42, 50, 56
barreau 56
barrière 117
barrique 56
bascule 56
bassin 108
bateau 56
bâtiment 46, 85, 86
bâtisse 86
batterie 123
se battre 56, 87
bazarder 108
bergère 90
besogne 125
beugler 57
bibliothécaire 35
bibliothèque 35

2456152R00185

Printed in Great Britain
by Amazon.co.uk, Ltd.,
Marston Gate.